# I LOVE THE SEASIDE

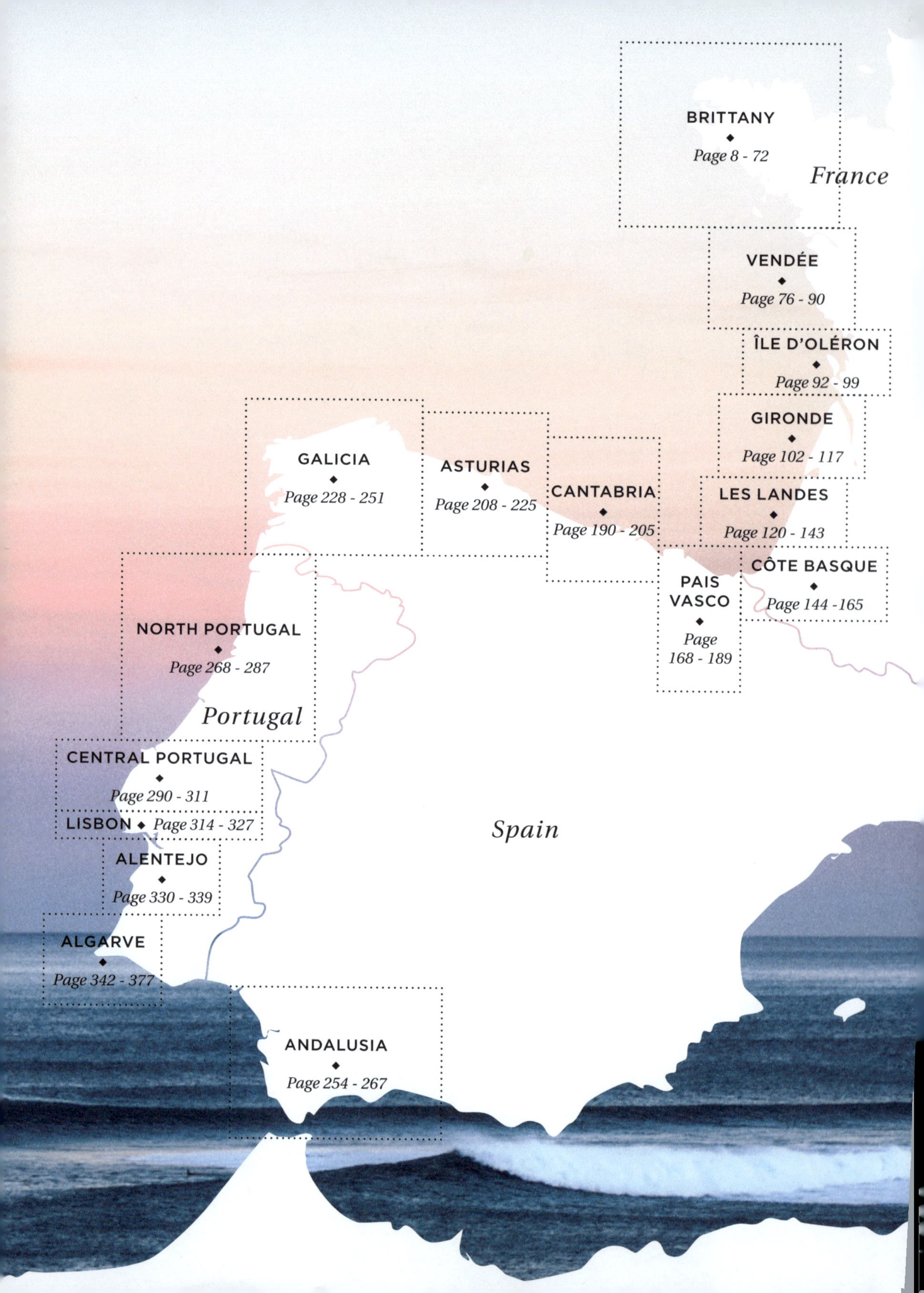
BRITTANY
Page 8 - 72
France
VENDÉE
Page 76 - 90
ÎLE D'OLÉRON
Page 92 - 99
GIRONDE
Page 102 - 117
LES LANDES
Page 120 - 143
CÔTE BASQUE
Page 144 -165
PAIS VASCO
Page 168 - 189
CANTABRIA
Page 190 - 205
ASTURIAS
Page 208 - 225
GALICIA
Page 228 - 251
NORTH PORTUGAL
Page 268 - 287
Portugal
CENTRAL PORTUGAL
Page 290 - 311
LISBON
Page 314 - 327
ALENTEJO
Page 330 - 339
ALGARVE
Page 342 - 377
Spain
ANDALUSIA
Page 254 - 267

# CONTENTS

Photo: Melchior van Nigtevecht

# A WORD FROM US

Travelling the shores of southwest Europe for many years, we discovered amazing places and wonderful spots: areas of natural beauty, cities and historic sites - all the way from the magical shores of Brittany in France to the Moorish influences in Andalusia. Everywhere we went, we met inspiring seaside people, from surfers and entrepreneurs, to travellers and artists.

Needless to say, this book is about the seaside. It's about every aspect of it, because that's what we love. It's about travelling, about surfing, about people.
And we hope you love it too, and enjoy the first edition of the I Love the Seaside guide as much as we've enjoyed creating it.

We want you to get into the feeling of a trip before you're even going. We want you to remember that awesome adventure. We want you to have a lovely tool in hand and use it over and over again.

*We're here to inspire, so you can go and explore.*

# HOW TO USE THIS GUIDE

◆

This guide takes you from Finistère, in Brittany, down the west coast of France and along the coast of northern Spain, around the seaside of Portugal, then all the way to the southern shores of Andalusia. You don't have to follow the same route; just hop on and off anywhere you like, using a chapter, skip-hopping to your next destination, or sitting at home in your armchair, leafing through the guide and dreaming of your future adventure!

We move from one area to the next, using a central location from which you can go and explore, but it's essentially the surfbreaks, the beaches, and the ocean of course, that take the place of your compass. All the things we recommend for you to discover are within a day's reach of the seaside.

# PRICES

◆

Due to seasonal price changes, especially for hotels and campsites, we've chosen to use symbols which give you an indication of price ranges.

◆

•€• *Cheap as chips*
•€€• *Pretty reasonable*
•€€€• *Affordable treat*
•€€€€• *Luxurious extravagance*

◆

## SURF SCHOOLS AND SHOPS

Big thing in this guide, of course. The schools and shops mentioned within are either approved and loved by us, or recommended by trusted partners. Those that we don't mention: it doesn't mean they're inferior, malfunctioning or what-not. Certainly not. In some surfing areas there are so many, with so little difference between them, that in those areas we were very picky and chose those we feel offer special character or atmosphere, that add a twist to the definition of surf shop. In the areas where schools and shops are scarce, we mention any in the area, because they can be useful if in need of wax, leash, repair, etc.

## SURF SPOTS

On our travels along the coast of southwest Europe we met so many friendly locals, surfers and saltwater addicts. Most of them were happy to share waves and even take us out to their favourite local - but sometimes secret - surf spot. We respect that, and them, and therefore try to avoid misusing those warm and welcoming gestures. None of the surf spots mentioned in our guide are secret, they're known to many surfing nomads. That doesn't mean there aren't many more spots out there. So, since we're huge fans of exploring and meeting new people to learn, share, and make friends, we encourage you to do a little exploring yourself, with that same respect in mind. We sincerely hope you understand our choice.

*Not all who wander are lost.*

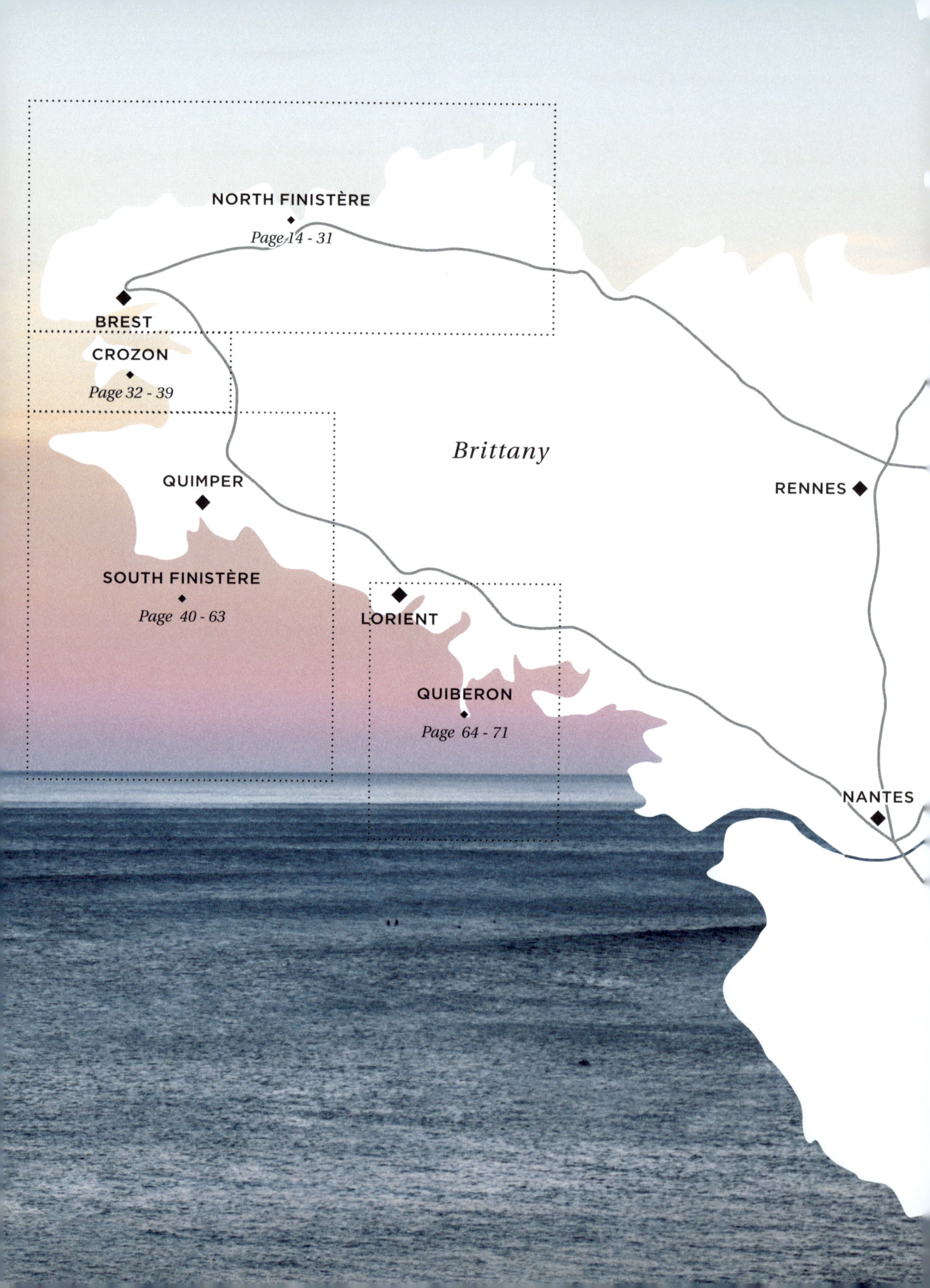
NORTH FINISTÈRE
Page 14 - 31
BREST
CROZON
Page 32 - 39
Brittany
QUIMPER
RENNES
SOUTH FINISTÈRE
Page 40 - 63
LORIENT
QUIBERON
Page 64 - 71
NANTES

# BRITTANY

◆

Where most places feel depressing in a rainstorm, northwest Brittany exposes its true nature on the roughest days. Of course the Breton landscape is very attractive on windless sunny days, when the ocean appears deceptively tropical. But stormy weather, howling winds, a shaft of sunlight sharply contrasting a dark grey sky will merely emphasise the uncultivated beauty of its granite cliffs, abers (inlets), reefs and rocky bays. Menhirs and dolmens, still standing around, are silent witnesses of a prehistoric Celtic culture. To this day the Breton have their own language with Celtic roots, spoken by a minority, mostly in the western part. Surfing-wise you will need to learn the exact science of tidal coefficient. But then, professor, this is Europe's most rewarding surf playground. Exposed to Atlantic swells from N, W and S direction, you can bet on surf somehow somewhere along Brittany's 1500 plus km jagged coastline. Although 'Breizh' breaks are getting more popular every season, the unpredictable weather and cold water will probably never attract the crowds. There's a saying about Breton weather, whenever a stranger complains about the rain: "En Bretagne, il ne pleut que sur les cons", what it comes down to: In Brittany, it only rains on fools. But still, expect four seasons in one day. And, really, it's très cool to wear your raincoat.

## TRAVEL INFO

◆

Travelling by campervan? Some free camping is tolerated off-season, but campsites are cheap and charming. If you choose to free camp, please make use of the many services to empty chemical toilet and waste water.

### BY BOAT

◆

From **Plymouth**, England (year round)
**w.** brittanyferries.com
From **Cork**, Ireland (April - Nov)
**w.** brittanyferries.com
From **Rosslare**, Ireland (May - Sep)
**w.** irishferries.com

### BY AIR

◆

**Brest Bretagne Aeroport**, 10 km northeast of Brest. Some direct flights from UK, Spain and Italy, most flights however via Paris (1h15). Shuttle between airport and Brest centre.)
**w.** brest.aeroport.fr

**Rennes- Saint-Jacques Aeroport**, just a few km southwest of Rennes town centre. Direct flights from (amongst others) Holland, UK, Germany, Spain, Belgium, Austria. Bus 57 takes you to the city centre of Rennes.
**w.** rennes.aeroport.fr

# HIGH HAT?

*Bigoudène coiffe*

The extraordinary towering Bigoudène coiffe you see on stickers, ads and key chains but rarely on Breton ladies themselves, is a traditional headdress worn in the old days up until after the second world war, when it became less fashionable. But really, what ended it – it's said – is when transporting oneself in a car became popular, a low roof simply wouldn't fit a 30 cm tall hat. There are still a few ladies who do wear the Bigoudène coiffe, one of them is a bit of a celebrity and appears on posters and ads for Breizh Cola.

# SURFER-TRAVELLER TYPE BRITTANY

*You love room to roam, long hikes, great views, making a study of tides, swell and wind direction, buckwheat crêpes and cider, cold water, reefs, and beachbreaks with boulders and stones, public parties and folk festivals, friendly faces, patron saints, stone farmhouses, Celtic vibes, getting lost in translation and mixing up Plouescat, Plougoulm, Plouxané or Plouhinec.*

# DON'T MISS

◆

*Fest-Noz*

Every Breton town, village and community, celebrates their culture and identity in traditional style, at a Fest-Noz (night party). Themes to celebrate are plenty, it can be sardines, clams, and seafood in general, mills, saints and harvests. In summer you can party somewhere almost every night.

There's just no better way to meet the local community than to join the dancing in circles and figures, accompanied by hypnotic bagpipe, harp, accordion or clarinet music. Every generation is represented, and some villages have adapted their Fest-Noz to modern times with reggae, jazz and rock. Usually the celebrations are free and there's plenty of local food for a few euros, like 'moules et frites', crêpes, fresh seafood, soup, cider and beer. Since 2012, Fest-Noz has been on the UNESCO list of Intangible Cultural Heritage of Humanity. It's hard to miss a Fest-Noz because you'll see signs, posters and flags everywhere announcing when and where to party.

# USEFUL WORDS

◆

*Horaires des mares = tide tables.* Given the extreme tidal differences it's a necessity to keep these at hand. Not just to plan your surf sessions wisely, they may come in handy to visit small offshore islands by foot.

*Marée basse* = Low tide
*Marée haute* = High tide
*Yec'hed mad!* = Cheers! (Pronounce yeahmat)
*Chañs vat!* = Good luck!

Photo: Marinus Joris

Photo: Alexandra Gossink

# BRETON FOOD FACTS

## KOUIGN-AMAN

Pronounced something like queen-ah-mahn, meaning 'butter cake'. If you want to keep your cholesterol low and your dental enamel intact, don't eat. But if you yearn for instant happiness, do eat! It's about half butter, half croissant dough, dusted with caramelised sugar and salt. Oh boy, it's GOOD. A speciality from Douarnenez, but today most bakeries in the Finistère area make their own version.

## FAR BRETON

Custard cake with prunes (preferably soaked in Armagnac).

## CRÊPES AND GALETTES

Crêperies in Brittany are not just a place you go to for a sweet snack; au contraire, you'll have a full hearty dinner and sweet dessert if you take your orders right. Start with a savoury galette, which is made from buckwheat flour and stuffed with everything from meat, cheese, or seafood, to eggs and vegetables. You can always order a salad on the side if it's not leafy enough for your taste. Then finish with a sweet crêpe, made from wheat flour, sprinkled with sugar and brandy or filled with ice-cream, jam, fruits or chocolate. Even if the pancakes themselves are thin, the fillings are usually not.

PERROS GUIREC (I)
TRESTRAOU (II)
4,5,23
13,14
3
LE DOSSEN (IV)
ROSCOFF
MAUVAISE GRÈVE (V)
1,2,8,9,10,11
PORS AR VILLEC (III)
SANTEC
7,20
6,26
12,19,21
CLÉDER
D10
27
16
LOCQUIREC
24,25
D786
Pays de Léon
North Finistère
18
22
D58
D786
15,17
MORLAIX

# IN AND AROUND ROSCOFF

The northern part of Brittany, Pays de Léon, is called the Golden Belt because of the cultivation of many vegetables, like tomatoes, potatoes, chicory, cauliflowers and artichokes - the latter being the favourite of all French chefs. The fertile soil, you will notice passing the fields, is often enriched by seaweed. In this part, and especially Île de Batz, just off Roscoff's coast, organic agriculture has become something of a speciality.

Located at the entrance of Morlaix Bay, Roscoff – Rosko in Breton – has a history of marine trade in linen, salt and wood that goes back as far as the Middle Ages. Then there's the Roscoff onion, a distinctive pink veggie. Writer Alexandre Dumas, who spent some time in the petit town, highlighted the Roscoff onion in his Great Dictionary of Cuisine in the late 19th century and added to the fame of the vegetable. Soon the first grower and trader found a profitable market and sailed to England to sell onions door-to-door, followed by more farmers and labourers selling onions, using bicycles as transport, carrying up to 150 kg of onions. They got nicknamed Onion Johnnies, or ar Johnniged in Breton. Very eye-catching of course, so you'll still see a lot of onion-decorated bikes around town. A two day Fête de l'Onion is celebrated every summer.

**Tourist office** on Quai de la République.
**Train:** Connection to Roscoff by regional train or bus from Morlaix station (25 mins)

## TO DO

Learn about the extreme tides, seaweed and diverse wildlife at the **Station Biologique** (**1**) Roscoff, also known as the 'Labo'.

**a.** Place Georges Teissier, 29680 Roscoff
**t.** 2 98 292 323
**w.** sb-roscoff.fr

Let the algae and seaweed do wonders for your skin in the **Hotel Thalasstonic** (**2**). Thermal baths, spa, massage and an outdoor swimming pool with sea view, from 1 to 6 day courses.

**a.** 16, Rue Victor, Roscoff
**t.** 2 98 292 020
**w.** hotel-roscoff.com

Hike and picnic on the **Île de Batz** (**3**), preferably on windless days - there's not much protection from howling winds on the island, but the absence of cars, the pearly white sand of Grève Blanche beach and the microclimate (palm trees!) are a real treat. Crossing by boat takes 15 minutes, regular services; bicycles may be taken on the boat. There's a waterfront campsite, a hostel and two B&B's if you want to stay the night.

Explore the **exotic botanic garden Jardin Georges Delaselle** with a unique collection from the five continents and over 2500 species, including a fine collection of palms. Open every day from April to October, guided tours available. 15 min walk from the pier to the garden gate.

**t.** 2 98 617 565
**w.** jardin-georgesdelaselle.fr

A short drive to the east brings you to **Perros-Guirec (4)**. Although not within the Finistère borders, it's certainly worth checking. If not for surfing, it's certainly worth paying a visit to Côte de Granit Rose, the 300 million year old pink granite stone formations in Ploumanac'h, between the beaches of Trestraou and Saint-Guirec.

Single girl? Make sure to visit the chapel at Ploumanac'h, dedicated to the saint Kireg. Unmarried women are known to push a needle into the saint's nose (its statue, that is). Legend has it that if the needle sticks, they will be married within a year.

A great way to explore this area is taking the 2 hour **SUP tour** (**5**) along the pink granite coast with former surf and SUP champ Alexis Deniel, usually starting at the beach of Trestraou. Ponant Surf School.

**a.** 2 Rue Maréchal Joffre,
22700 Perros-Guirec
**t.** 2 96 231 838
**m.** 6 17 182 055
**w.** ponantsurfschool.fr

**Le Dossen** (**6**): This 1,5 km stretch of beach west of Roscoff is often too blown out for surfing, so to make the best of a bad situation, visit the **Sliding and Gliding Centre**, **Rêves de Mer**. They'll take you sand yachting (char à voile): sailing on sand in a little kart.

**a.** Centre de Glisse de Santec Plage
du Dossen, 29250 Santec
**t.** 2 98 694 078
**w.** revesdemer.com

Le Dossen is a beautiful natural site and very inviting for long hikes or MTB. Less speedy, but good exercise, is to wait until the tide drops and **hike to Île de Sieck**, the island in front of le Dossen - just make sure you return max two hours after low tide.

Explore the underwater world near le Dossen and go diving with (fully qualified) **scuba diving centre Aquacamp (7)**. They offer exploration diving, training and try-out sessions in a friendly, small-scale business. Open all year round according to schedule, information and reservations only, by phone or contact through website, Port Neuf, Sibiril.

**t.** 6 84 931 574
**w.** aquacamp-plongeesibiril.overblog.com

## EAT/DRINK/HANGOUT

◆

**Café Ty Pierre** (**8**), watch a day in Roscoff go by from the terrace facing the harbour, laid-back atmosphere, the brasserie serves breakfast (open at 07:00!), snacks, food and drinks. Open year round. •€•

**a.** 1 Rue Gambetta, 29680 Roscoff
**t.** 2 98 697 275
**w.** cafetypierre.fr

**Creperie les Amours Jaunes** (**9**), serves galettes and crepes from organic flour, organic cider, salads and veggie pancakes. Open 7/7 days. •€•

**a.** 18 Rue Amiral Reveillere (historic centre), 29680 Roscoff
**t.** 2 98 611 904

**La Moussaillonne** (**10**), funky decorated brasserie with sea view in the historic centre, serves fresh and homemade crepes, pizzas, moules frites, burgers. Closed on Monday, open 7/7 days in July and August. •€€•

**a.** 38 Rue Amiral Reveillere, 29680 Roscoff
**t.** 2 98 697 050
**w.** lamoussaillonne.com

**Hôtel Restaurant 'Chez Janie'** (**11**), near the old harbour, friendly atmosphere, views over the old port, at the heart of the historic town, restaurant offers local produce, speciality is stuffed artichokes. •€€•

**a.** le Port, 5 Rue Gambetta, 29680 Roscoff
**t.** 2 98 612 425
**w.** chezjanie.fr

# IN AND AROUND CLÉDER

◆

A short drive to the southwest of Roscoff you'll find this small town with great surroundings. In August and September you can pick blackberries for breakfast and see fields full of artichokes. The ocean appears extremely turquoise at Plage des Amiets because of its fine white sand. Dividing the beach in two are big boulders and rocks in which the eye of the beholder can discover pieces of art, or... boulders and rocks. Two guardhouses at either side of the beach were placed in the 17th century to see one another, as part of a control and protection system. The GR34 (part of the Grand Route) passes here, once used by les douaniers (customs officers) to guard the coast from smugglers, now a hiking trail along the coast of Brittany.

## TO DO

◆

In summer, guided horse or pony rides in the countryside or along the coast, duration: 1hr or 2 hrs. From beginner to advanced level (from 8 years), groups, adapted to level. For children (3 to 9 years), pony rental by the hour or half hour, under the responsibility of parents (without instructor.) **Horse Riding In Cléder (12)**.

**a.** Rue Ar Balusen- Roguennic, 29233 Cléder
**t.** 6 68 520 595

**Planetarium de Bretagne (13)**: One of Europe's largest planetariums, offering astronomical and scientific shows, nocturnal planet watching and exhibitions. Open all year.

**a.** Parc du Radôme, 22560 Pleumeur-Bodou
**t.** 2 96 158 030
**w.** planetarium-bretagne.fr

**Le Village Gaulois (14)** was recommended to us by many locals with kids. A low-key, outdoor theme park, fully sponsored and run by volunteers, with games to play, history to learn and pleasure to be had by doing a lot of fun stuff. Open from April to September.

**t.** 2 96 918 395
**w.** levillagegaulois.org

**Eco Park Adventures Penzé (15)**, 5 levels of adventure tracks, through the woods and tops of trees, also a kids' mini park. Open from March to September, (in summer every day from 10:00 hrs).

**a.** RN D769 Penzé-Taulé
**t.** 2 98 790 321
**w.** ecopark-adventures.com

## EAT/DRINK/HANGOUT

◆

Don't miss the weekly **Bio Market**, every Thursday from 17.00 – 19.00, all year round.

**a.** Kerantosfal, Ferme Bio de Kerantosfal, 29233 Cléder

In the small centre, **La Rose des Vents (16)** serves seafood, couscous, paella, cassoulet. Family (and dog!) friendly place, open 7 days a week for lunch and dinner. •€• •€€•

**a.** 8 Place Charles de Gaulle, 29233 Cléder
**t.** 2 98 694 241
**w.** la-rose-des-vents-restaurant.fr

## SHOP

◆

Whenever you see the essential oils **Bonnes Herbes de Kerlaoudet (17)**, you know they're from Finistère. A farm in Guiclan (near Kermat) grows and produces medical and aromatic plants, pesto, oil and herbal tea. It's sold in shops and bio-markets in North Finistère. You can visit the farm in Guiclan (between Croas ar Born and Kermat) every Friday from 17:00 to 19:00 hrs. Open all year.

**a.** Kerlaoudet Vraz, 29410 Guiclan
**t.** 2 98 210 717

## SLEEP

◆

Here's a treat: sleep in a cabane hanging in the woodland at 6 – 12 m high, or choose a lodge hidden in the forest, a tree-hut, Bubble, Sahara or glamping tent, in the middle of 38-hectares of nature surrounding the family chateau, **Les Cabanes de Kermenguy (18)**. Open 01 Apr – 15 Nov. •€• •€€•

**a.** Chateau de Kermenguy, 29233 Cléder (it's not easy to find, on the webpage is a full description, or, adding to your adventure: you'll receive the full address and coordinates after making your booking)
**t.** 6 62 139 137
**e.** contact@kermenguy.org
**w.** kermenguy.org

Villas Ouest rents out several houses and apartments. **La Villa de la Plage (6)** is a 6-person, bright (lots of large windows), white house with garden, facing le Dossen beach, bicycles and a canoe at your disposal. Open all year. •€€• •€€€•

**a.** Rue de Beg ar Rest, 29250 Mogueriec
**t.** 2 98 683 307
**e.** j.berrou@wanadoo.fr
**w.** villas-ouest.com

**Camping Roguennic (19)**, big campsite, main attraction is that it's right at the beach, 42 acres in the middle of the dunes with pitches for tents, caravans and campervans. Rental of mobile homes and bungalows, small indoor heated pool. Open from March to October.

**a.** between Plage de Kerfissien and Rue de Tévenn Kerbrat, Roguennic, 29233 Cléder
**t.** 2 98 696 388
**e.** contact@campingvillageroguennic.com
**w.** campingvillageroguennic.com

**Le Theven**, is situated in a botanical garden with a view over Pors Misclic beach (surf spot Mauvaise Grève), 5 wooden lodges with grand comfort and a top deck. In the same grounds are a restaurant and a cocktail lounge bar, open air if the weather allows it. Open all year. •€€•

**a.** Plage de Pors Misclic, Mogueriec Sibiril
**t.** 2 98 613 874
**w.** letheven.com

**Combi Joli** rents out Combi VW vintage campervans. You can rent a board or inflatable SUP, a bike and bbq to take with you on your road trip as well. Combi Joli is based in Brest, contact for reservation. •€•

**t.** 6 61 798 789 (Olivier Lintanf)
**e.** Olivier@combijoli.fr
**w.** combijoli.fr

**Prat Bian (21)** 'the small field' consists of 3 gîtes (2-5 persons) and 2 chambres d'hotes in authentic local architecture, close to Amiets beach (Cléder), amidst artichoke and cauliflower fields. The totally renovated house used to belong to co-owner Jacqueline's parents. Open all year. •€•

**a.** 29430 Plouescat (exact directions on website)
**t.** 2 98 619 727
**m.** 6 30 368 160
**e.** jacqueline.marical@gmail.com
**w.** pratbian.com.

**Ti Tulipe (22)** lies on a large plot of grassland in the countryside, hemmed in by bushes and trees. Dutch couple Wilco and Sandra Berkel created their dream; their own house, two cottages and 3500m2 campsite with space for 6 pitches (there could be loads more, but they prefer to give their guests peace and room to roam). You can bring your own tent, camper or caravan or rent a spacious tent. At the terrain for all to use is a communal dining room/hangout and wifi, and for the kids, a trampoline, swing and tennis/volleyball net. Sandra and Wilco are sweet and energetic hosts, and willing to share their knowledge of and love for the area. Wilco, who is also an avid surfer, is your best local guide for breaks unknown to most. He's one of these guys that knows the exact science of tidal coefficients as mentioned earlier, you see. Open year round (cottages), camping open from April to October. •€•

**a.** Keroignant, 29420 Plouvorn
**t.** 2 98 610 812
**m.** 6 99 711 959
**e.** info@titulipe.com
**w.** titulipe.com

# SURF

**Perros-Guirec (I)** has two spots. And although we'd like to begin our guide in Finistère, we do mention these because of the beautiful pink granite rock formations just west of Perros-Guirec. The smaller bay, **Pors Nevez**, in the east corner of town, is a beachbreak with some rocks and boulders, works from small to medium n-nw swell.

Just west of Pors-Nevez is Plage de **Trestraou (II)**, a little more northeast facing beachbreak, therefore protected in west winds, works from medium n-nw swell. Both beaches can be crowded in summer. All levels. Shower/toilet/restaurant/surf shop/school/easy parking.

**Pors ar Villec (III)** in the small town Locquirec is a sand-covered reef that can be perfect for longboards in small clean nw swells, and fast and hollow on bigger days. Following the road (D64) a little to the west you'll find a beachbreak in a small bay, **Le Moulin de la Rive**. All levels. Surf school at both beaches/easy parking/toilet.

**Le Dossen (IV)** is the perfect beach for learning to surf, or easy surfing on clean, windless days. The long stretch of beach east of the river mouth is extremely exposed to wind so easily blown out. Longboarders or SUPs better head towards the west side of the beach between the two river inlets (Plage Enez Glaz, park at Rue du Theven) at low tide for easy, long rides on clean days. Works on small to medium n-nw swells. All levels.

**Mauvaise Grève (V)** at Plage du Théven, reefbreak in beautiful small bay, narrow take-off zone near rock in the middle, dedicated locals. This is one of those typical North Finistère breaks that needs a little study of the tidal coefficients, we've seen it work at all tides, but it really depends on how extreme the tidal differences are (which can build up to 8m). Low tide exposes the reef completely. Small parking area/shower/toilet/surf school.

# SCHOOL RENTAL REPAIR

**Ponant Surf School and Shop (23)**

**a.** 2 Rue Maréchal Joffre,
22700 Perros-Guirec
**t.** 2 96 231 838
**m.** 6 17 182 055
**w.** ponantsurfschool.fr

**Surf School Surfplaya (24)**, Surf, SUP and bodyboard, rental and lessons, opened in 2015 at Pors ar Villec. Open all year.

**a.** 14 Rue de Porz ar Villec,
29241 Locquirec
**t.** 6 26 604 502
**w.** surfplaya.com

**Surf School Surfing Locquirec (25)**, surf, SUP and bodyboard, rental and lessons. Open all year.

**a.** la Plage du Moulin de la Rive,
29241 Locquirec
**t.** 6 27 064 887
**w.** surfing-locquirec.com

**Reves de Mer (26)**, surf, SUP and bodyboard, rental and lessons. Open all year, by reservation.

**a.** Centre de Glisse de Santec,
Plage du Dossen, 29250 Santec
**t.** 2 98 694 078
**w.** revesdemer.com

**Ecole de Surf de Leon (27)**, surf, SUP & kayak, rental, lessons and tours. Open all year, operates at different beaches, like La Mauvaise Grève and Plage du Théven.

**a.** 170 Beg Tanguy, 29250 Sibiril
**t.** 6 66 463 049 (Jean Baptiste Bodenes)
**w.** ecole-surf-leon.com

BOUTROUILLES
(I)
20
D10
9
PLOUGUERNEAU
D10
1
ST PABU
(II)
D125
LA CHAPELLE
(III)
2
5
LANNILIS
LESNEVEN
ST-PABU
6,7,21
4
3
PLOUDALMÉZEAU
PENFOUL
(IV)
22
8
10
Pays des Abers
North Finistère
D68
D788
N12
D13
LAMPAUL-PLOUARZEL
E50
12
BREST
19
N165
E60
BLANC
SABLONS
(V)
PORSMILIN
LE CONQUET
15,18
D789
14
11,16,17,23
13
PORSMILIN
(VI)
LE PETIT
MINOU
(VII)

# IN AND AROUND ABERS

◆

Following the coastal route further up towards Brest, make a little detour towards the Phare de l'île Vierge. The area around the lighthouse is stunning. There are dozens of small islands, bays and inlets that give shelter to birds and boats and restless minds. Camping is easy and there are lots of houses for rent. If you want to write that book or thesis, or just want to contemplate life, this is the place. You can walk the cobbled streets of tiny towns or lose your sense of direction hiking along the winding and twisting coastal paths. The abers (inlets) l'Aber Wrac'h, l'Aber Benoît and l'Aber Ildut are best explored on a SUP, in a kayak, or whatever floats and sails.

## TO DO

◆

**Surfing des Abers (1)** offers SUP river-tours on all three rivers, from April till December.

**t.** 6 63 879 173
**w.** surfing-abers.com

**Centre de Voile de l'Aber Wrac'h (2)** also offers SUP tours and rental of SUPs, kayaks or catamarans to explore the l'Aber Wrac'h and l'Aber Benoît. Open all year.

**a.** 4 Le Port, 29870 Landéda
**t.** 2 98 049 064
**w.** cvl-aberwrach.fr

**Coeur Ocean (3)**, ah yes, ocean heart, it's all good really what's on offer: kayak to l'Île Vierge, along l'Aber Benoît or in the Baie de Tréompan. Or SUP to l'Île Carn. There are 3 kinds of yoga-classes on offer, in nature, in a yurt or on a SUP.

**a.** 25 Kervao, 29830 Ploudalmézeau
**t.** 6 51 031 075
**w.** coeurocean.fr

**Kayak tour (4)** around l''île d'Yoch just in front of Port d'Argenton, Landunvez, a bit further south down the coast. You start opposite the lighthouse, Phare du Four, and paddle through the channel towards l'île d'Yoch, which is a protected natural reserve. On the island you learn about the fauna and flora, néolithic findings and more. The guide, Eric, speaks English too. Open in July and August, the tour takes about 2 hours, start time depending on the tide, meeting point Nautisme en Pays d'Iroise.

**a.** Ancre An Eor, Portsall,
29830 Ploudalmézeau
**t.** 2 98 487 623
**e.** npi.ploudalmezeau@ccpi.fr
**w.** nautisme-pays-iroise.com

## EAT/DRINK/HANGOUT

◆

Get into the Celtic mood in **L'Auberge du Pont (5)**, set in an old mill with a terrace on the river l'Aber Wrac'h. Live music (again, think Celtic). On the menu: Fruit de Mer, coquilles, clams and some meat. Open all year, every day for lunch and dinner. •€€•

**a.** along the D113, just after crossing the river to the south, 29870 Paluden
**t.** 2 98 041 669
**w.** aubergedupont.com

In this typical tiny Breton town between the Aber Wrac'h and Aber Benoît you'll find **Bô'm (6)**, nomadic cuisine in a 'house kitchen' for either take-away or sur place. You'll recognise the restaurant since it's in a modern wooden building. Chocolat chauds, tea, coffee and cakes, sandwiches, pasta boxes, wraps, pies, veggie dinners. On sale: local algae herbs, chocolate, honey, olive oil and wine. Le Good-Food indeed. Open Monday till Friday 10.00 - 17.30. •€•

**a.** ZA Kerlouis, Rue Alsace Lorraine,
29870 Lannilis
**t.** 2 98 025 017
**w.** resto-bo-m.fr

Get your oysters, coquilles and crustaceans from **Les Viviers de Prat Ar Coum (7)**, a family of oyster farmers since 1898, their restaurant, right at the river l' Aber Benoît, is open July and August. •€€•

**a.** Prat Ar Coum, Lannilis
**t.** 2 98 040 012
**w.** prat-ar-coum.fr

Following the rocky coastal road further up towards Brest you'd easily skip the small Port d'Argenton (Landunvez, right after surf break Penfoul). Why stop here? Maybe because you'll get the same feeling we did: very nostalgic. Sip a tea and eat a cake in **Fleur des Thes (8)**, feeling like a shipper who's just harboured after a long haul sailing. It's an old fishing boat transformed into a tearoom, and there's no denying it still smells of boat, ropes and harbour. Some local products and souvenirs on sale as well. Open all year, low season from 14:30 to 19:30, high season from 10:30.

**a.** Route de la Cale, 29840 Landunvez
**t.** 2 98 899 764

Photo: Marinus Joris

## SHOP

◆

The **Hoalen Ocean Store** (**9**) is located right in front of the lighthouse in what used to be a shipyard. It's nowhere near a popular surf spot or a hip town, (actually, it's not near a town at all), but it's got a killer view of the impressive Phare de l'île Vierge.

Hoalen's got the ocean in its DNA, the very name meaning 'sea salt' in the old Breton language and the logo a 6-fingered seaweed. Its ambassadors are surfers, sailors, sea-people. There are a few more Hoalen shops in Brittany and one in Paris, but this is where it all started. The old boathouse has been made into a very cool shop with clothes, accessories, swimsuits, wetsuits and a well stocked (surf and ocean-related) library. The garden has wooden benches and a wooden shack where they sell drinks and snacks.

The staff, besides being very friendly, are helpful with giving information on the area, heating up your baby's milk-bottle and fixing you a coffee at the same time. Check out the times and possibilities for fitness and yoga classes in the garden, or SUP tours around the Phare. (No, Hoalen didn't pay us to put in the kind words, they stand out on their own, and we like it!) Open all year (closed on Monday).

**a.** Lieu-dit Kelerdut, Lilia, 29880 Plouguerneau
**t.** 2 98 047 365
**w.** hoalen.com

## SLEEP

◆

Sleeping in a yurt, the Mongolian way, is a special feeling. **Coeur Ocean** (**3**) rents out 3 yurts, situated at camping Municipal de Lampaul Ploudalmézeau, with direct access to the beach. Open from June to September. ◆€◆

**a.** 25 Kervao, 29830 Ploudalmézeau
**t.** 6 51 031 075
**w.** coeurocean.fr

**Surfing des Abers** (**10**) have two surf houses facing the ocean in Porspoder, open all year. ◆€◆

**a.** 9 Rue du Port à Porspoder
**t.** 6 63 879 173
**w.** surfing-abers.com

# IN AND AROUND LE CONQUET

This port town sits at the western tip of north Finistère, from here ferries leave to the island Ouessant. Le Conquet and Ouessant are part of the marine nature reserve Iroise, a protected refuge for fish, sea birds, whales, dolphins and seals.

## TO DO

**Plage des Blancs Sablons (11)**, and the dunes right behind it provide perfect hiking, biking and picnic space. From the beach you can walk towards the Pointe de Kermorvan, at the tip of the peninsula, which gives you a view over Le Conquet and all the little boats floating or lying around, depending on the tide.

The island **Ouessant (12)** is the north-westernmost part of France, but, you know, whatever, there are better reasons to visit the island: like witnessing the great sense of community – the island's got 200 inhabitants, plus some 400 'part-time', who live, work and share together a history of fighting, surviving, and giving in to ocean fury. Everybody on the island has had at least one family member taken by the sea. The island's coastline is too rough and rocky to surf, but hiking or renting a bike is a great way to get to know the island. And who knows, you might bump into Yann Tiersen, the composer of the melancholy music for the movies Goodbye Lenin and Amélie, who loves the isolated island and owns a house there. The main centre is Lampoul, the few pubs and restaurants prepare everything with love, they have to - everybody knows everybody here!
A 75 min trip with the ferry from Conquet's harbour takes you past the Iroise islands to Ouessant, daily from April to November, no cars allowed.

**w.** ouessant-voyages.com

Despite all modern techniques used by ships, lighthouses still play an important role in Brittany, with its many islands, rocks and treacherous currents. The lighthouse of **Saint-Mathieu (13)** indicates the route into the narrows of Brest harbour. You can visit the lighthouse (163 steps) and the abbey at its foot. Open all year.

**a.** la Pointe Saint-Mathieu, 29217 Plougonvelin
**t.** 2 98 890 017

From surf spot **Plage de Portez (14)**, in Porsmilin (Locmaria-Plouzané), you can follow the coastal path GR34 to the west end, passing Plage de Porsmilin and an old gunnery, and enjoy the views towards the sheltered bay of Plougonvelin.

## EAT/DRINK/HANGOUT

Along the beaches of Porsmilin, on Boulevard de L'Océan, there are a few restaurants, a good option is the old **'Crêperie' (15)**; not hard to miss - look for a place where it seems that time stopped somewhere in the fifties of the past century. Cute, very cute!

**Le Relais du Vieux Port**'s (**16**) restaurant downstairs from the hotel, is usually chockfull of tourists and locals alike. It feels like a Sailor's inn, with good food. Open all year. •€•

**a.** 1 Quai du Drellach, 29217 Le Conquet
**w.** lerelaisduvieuxport.com

## SLEEP

◆

**Le Relais du Vieux Port**'s (**16**) decoration gets you in the mood for a boat trip, so a good option if you want to catch an early ferry to Ouessant. Hotel rooms are on the first floor with a good view of the river and harbour.
Open all year. •€•

**a.** 1 Quai du Drellach, 29217 Le Conquet
**e.** hotel@lerelaisduvieuxport.com
**w.** lerelaisduvieuxport.com

On Ouessant the **Hotel Ti Jan Ar C'hafe** (**12**) is like having a sleepover at your slightly eccentric hippie-chic aunt's while she's out. Big and comfortable rooms, each with their own theme, sunny garden and terrace. Open all year. •€€•

**a.** Kernigou, 29242 Ouessant
**t.** 2 98 488 264 or 6 70 892 923
**m.** contact@tijan.fr
**w.** tijan.fr

**Camping Plage des Blancs Sablons** (**17**), just behind the dunes close to the beach, also rents out mobile homes and chalets. Open June to September.
•€• •€€•

**a.** Route de la Presqu'île Kermorvan, 29217 Le Conquet
**t.** 2 98 360 791
**e.** info@les-blancs-sablons.com
**w.** les-blancs-sablons.com

**Camping Municipal de Portez** (**18**) is just behind the Plage de Portez, rents out mobile homes as well, ocean view. Open from 18 April to 19 September. •€•

**a.** Rue de Portez, 29280 Locmaria-Plouzané
**t.** 2 98 484 985
**e.** camping-portez@locmaria-plouzane.fr
**w.** locmaria-plouzane.fr

**Campervans** (**18**): just before the entrance of the Camping Municipal de Portez is a parking area with free water and the possibility to empty your toilet and water, 5 euro to stay overnight (open all year).

**a.** Rue de Portez, 29280 Locmaria-Plouzané

# IN AND AROUND BREST

Rade de Brest, the natural harbour of Brest, has been a perfectly sheltered base for naval activities since the Roman days, and home to the French navy since the 17th century. The reason Brest looks like it does nowadays is exactly because of that harbour; 90% of the city was bombed during World War II by the Allies to prevent the Germans from using the harbour as their submarine base.

From an aesthetic perspective, the city is rather unprepossessing and too windswept to put up lots of trees. Even in the heart of the city you'll feel like you're on the outskirts. Post-war flats, chequerboard model streets. But its link to the sea is omnipresent, in attractions like the Océanopolis Ocean Discovery Park and the impressive 'Les Tonnerres de Brest', an international boat, sea and sailors festival held every four years. And also in less obvious institutions, like the Naval Academy and one of the largest research institutes focused on the sea, Ifremer. So, Brest may not be the city to stroll through rustic streets and admire ancient buildings but it is a university town, so you will find shops, restaurants and bars that are just like in every other student city: creative and lively.

## TO DO

Two festivals not be missed when you're around are **Astropolis**, usually held in August, France's oldest and biggest 4-day electro festival, (w. astropolis.org), and **Les Jeudis du Port**, free live music and street theatre in the harbour on Thursdays throughout summer (mid July to mid August).

If you want to know what's going on in the ocean, **Océanopolis (19)** houses more than a thousand species of aquatic animals. Open all year, except from January 4 to January 25.

**a.** Port de Plaisance du Moulin Blanc, 29210 Brest
**w.** oceanopolis.com

**Château de Brest (19)** is still in use in its original role as a military fortress. How on earth did it survive the bombings when all else in Brest was falling apart! It also houses the Museé National de la Marine and follows the history of the city. Open all year.

**a.** Boulevard de la Marine, 29200 Brest
**w.** musee-marine.fr

Usually the best places to hang out are the student quarters, in Brest that would be **Quartier Saint-Martin**, with Place Guérin as its centrepiece.

## SLEEP

A good option to stay overnight in Brest is **Hotel Saint Louis (19)**, urban vibe, right in the centre, near the station, comfy and clean. There's a family room available that sleeps 4. The hotel even understands that the Breton weather can make you feel grumpy and want to stay indoors, so they provide for a dinner in your room, or an umbrella. Open all year. •€•

**a.** 6 Rue Algésiras, 29200 Brest
**t.** 2 98 442 391
**e.** info@brest-hotel.com
**w.** brest-hotel.com

Photo: Marinus Joris

# SURF

**Boutrouilles (I)** at Kerlouan is a pretty, white sand beach embraced by granite rocks. Sand over reef, works at all tides, exposed so doesn't need much swell and is easily blown out. Very friendly atmosphere, popular beach in summer. All levels. Easy parking/surf school.

**Saint Pabu (II)**: This usually hollow beachbreak needs a big nw swell to work, because it's blocked by offshore oyster farms and little islands. All levels. Easy parking.

Heading west from **Saint Pabu**, you'll find oyster farms and reefs along the shore. Best option would be reefbreak **La Chapelle (III)** (near the chapel), not a beginners break, works low to mid tide.

A bit further down is **Penfoul (IV)**, at a river mouth. It's a very small break, works at all tides but best around high tide. Picks up more swell than you would expect, excellent for beginners, lots of people learning how to use a SUP in waves. No beach facility but there's a campsite and a surf school (Sweet Spot). Parking on the east side overlooks the break but requires walking over stones to the line-up. At the west bank, near the campsite, you can paddle out from a beach. Needs n-nw swell, all levels. Easy parking/surf school/campsite.

Beginners better try the **Plage des Blancs Sablons (V)**, the big bay north of **Le Conquet**, lots of space with a backdrop of dunes and green hills. Parking and hiking trails galore. No beach facilities. A hike from here towards the point of the peninsula gives you a view over Le Conquet and all the little boats floating or lying around, depending on the tide. All levels. Easy parking/campsite/surf school/restaurants.

Around Pointe Saint -Mathieu there are two very small bays just south of **Plougonvelin** with a lot of potential in me-

dium to bigger w-nw swell, and good protection from north winds. **Plage de Portez** is a beachbreak with rocks and the small **Plage de Porsmilin (VI)** has a left-hand reefbreak which, when on, doesn't leave much space for many surfers. Beautiful setting - a small bay surrounded by green hills, little parking space. More parking options at Plage de Portez and then walk the coastal trail (5 mins). Both bays have no facilities, but Plage de Portez has a beach bar, l'Albatros, and some restaurants further down the road.

Near Brest: **Le Petit Minou (VII)**, a beauty of a bay, surrounded by cliffs and a lighthouse watching over it. Because of its proximity to the city, it can be crowded and competitive (city attitude doesn't rub off easy, even in the water). Hollow beachbreak with rocks, works in small to medium s-w or medium to big n-w swell, best at low tide. All levels, but beware of rips and rocks. If it's all too crowded for your taste, exploring along the cliffs can sometimes be rewarding. Easy parking/surf school.

# SCHOOL RENTAL REPAIR

**Surfing Abers**, lessons and rental, surfboards, SUPs and bodyboards, in Plouguerneau (Plage Grève Blanche), Saint Pabu and Lanildut. Open all year.

**t.** 6 63 879 173
**w.** surfing-abers.com

**Pagan Surf School (20)**, dedicated surf, SUP, bodyboard lessons. Open all summer season, but it pays to enquire out of season, it's a mobile surf school.

**a.** Plage de Boutrouilles, Kerlouan,
**t.** 6 66 028 449 (Anthony Demon)

**Surf and Skate (21)** fabrication and repair

**a.** Rue St. J. Baptiste de la Salle, 29870 Lannilis
**t.** 6 95 939 567 (Jezekael Lagadec)

**Sweet Spot surf school**'s **(22)** been around a while, (since 2006) offering surf and SUP lessons at Penfoul and Le Petit Minou (surf only). Open from March to December.

**a.** Plage de Penfoul, 24 Lanhallès, 29840 Landunvez
**t.** 6 86 14 18 69
**w.** sweetspotsurf.com

**Surfing Iroise surf school (23)**, surf, bodyboard and SUP, rental and lessons, located at the Camping des Blancs Sablons. Open from April to December.

**a.** Camping des Blancs Sablons, 29217 Le Conquet
**t.** 6 15 330 698 (Yannick Allançon)
**w.** surfing-iroise.com

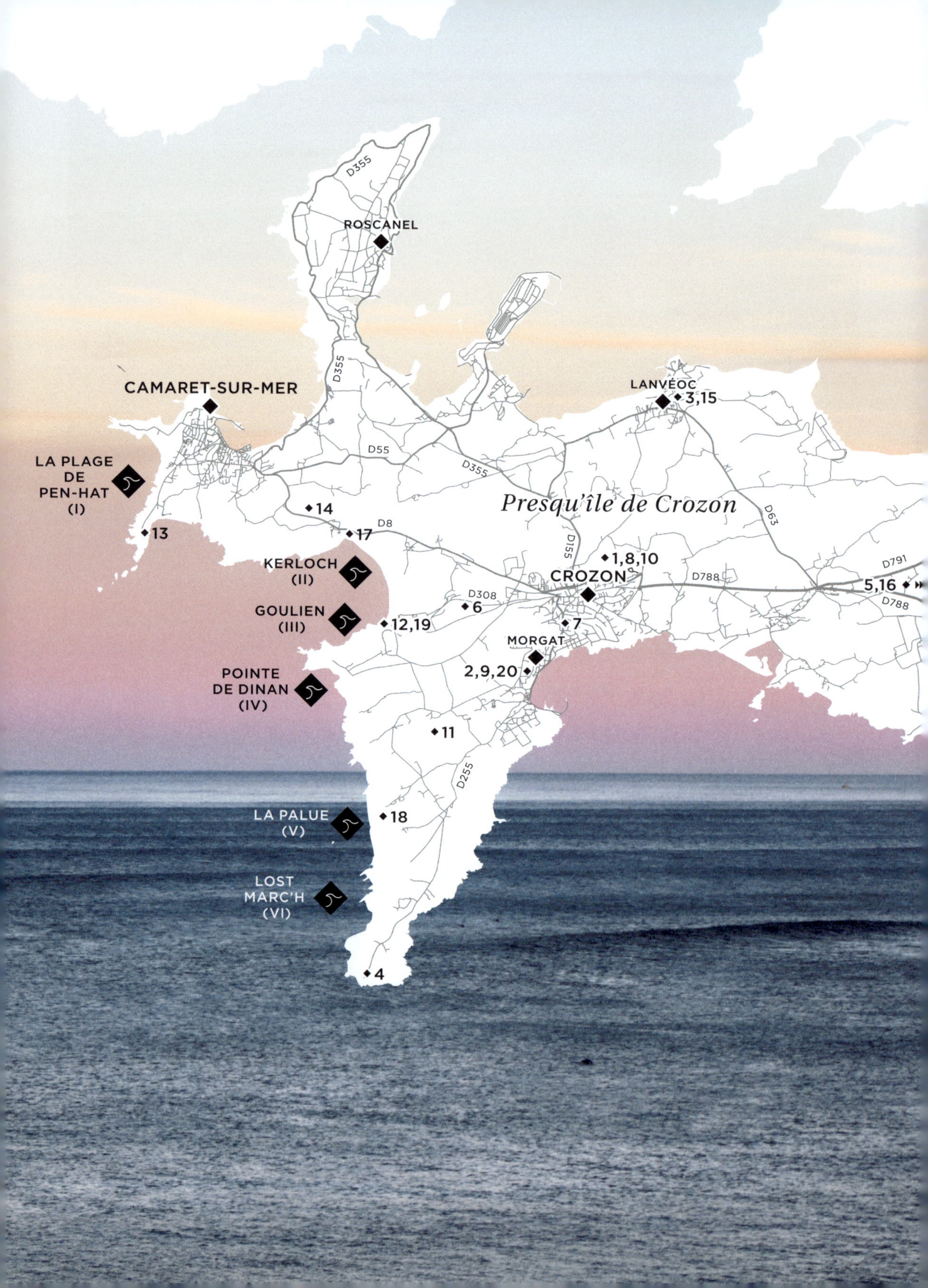
D355
ROSCANEL
D355
CAMARET-SUR-MER
LANVÉOC
3,15
LA PLAGE DE PEN-HAT (I)
D55
D355
Presqu'île de Crozon
D63
14
13
17
D8
D155
1,8,10
KERLOCH (II)
CROZON
D788
D791
5,16
D308
6
D788
GOULIEN (III)
12,19
7
MORGAT
2,9,20
POINTE DE DINAN (IV)
11
D255
LA PALUE (V)
18
LOST MARC'H (VI)
4

# IN AND AROUND CROZON AND MORGAT

The Crozon peninsula is probably one of the most popular tourist areas of Brittany. And for very good reason: as part of the Armorique Regional Nature Park it's an outdoor heaven with its green hills and fields, bays, reefs, cliffs, and seaside resorts. For most of us culturally-challenged surfers, it's also a great (and easy) introduction into customs and history, because it's hard to avoid the medieval churches, fine cuisine, local markets, fishing ports and folk festivities, and their deeply rooted Celtic heritage. Garbage bins are a rarity in the Crozon area for some reason, yet they manage to keep it fairly clean. So, keep your garbage with you until you find that rare garbage-bin, making it a trashure hunt. They're out there, we can assure you!

Crozon is the main town of the peninsula and almost attached to it is seaside resort Morgat. Morgat was once a fishing port that grew on sardine sales, but nowadays it's mainly a touristic summer resort. But it's touristic on a relative scale, as it's still a very low-key, outdoorsy sort of tourism with a mix of sailing, surfing and family holidaymakers. Along the boulevard that embraces a big bay, all the way up to the harbour, you'll find bars, restaurants, ice-cream parlours and terraces. The beach itself is so protected that it's a safe and perfect playground for small kids.

**Tourist office** in Place d'Ys, 29160 Crozon.
**Bus** to and from Quimper (1h10)

## TO DO

◆

**Festival du Bout du Monde** (**1**), a big and entertaining 3-day long festival with world music, reggae, funk, in an extremely good atmosphere, usually at the beginning of August. Lots of families or groups of friends attend this festival, it's definitely a social and fun outing, at the heart of Parc Naturel Régional d'Armorique, Crozon.

**t.** 2 98 270 032
**w.** festivalduboutdumonde.com

**Mountain biking**: there are over 10 different well marked bike-trails for different levels, easily explored on your own, or get free itineraries at any tourist office.

**SUP, kayak or sail** (**2**): from the quiet bay of Morgat with Centre Nautique. Either on a 10 metre sail yacht with your family learning sailing manoeuvres, or discover places like caves and creeks, reachable by kayak or SUP only. Open July and August.

**a.** Centre Nautique de Crozon Morgat, Port de Plaisance, 29160 Crozon-Morgat (opposite the beach)
**t.** 2 98 160 000
**m.** info@cncm.fr
**w.** cncm.fr

**Hiking same here as for cycling** ; easily explored on your own, as long as you have some sense of direction. There are several routes you can follow, maps for free at all tourist offices. And of course, taking a small portion of the 1800 km GR34 is always an option; maybe you fancy the 10km (3,5 hr) hike from Cap du Chèvre to Pointe du Dinan. We don't need to mention the stunning views, do we? It's a relatively easy trail, maybe not in flip-flops, but any comfortable shoes will do.

Exploring the coastline of Crozon with a **pack-donkey** as your companion, now there's something else. The donkeys of **Océ'âne** (**3**) (âne is donkey in French) are well taken care of and adorable animals. You can take (family) hikes for anything from a few hours up to 5 days.

**a.** Kéraël, 29160 Lanvéoc
**t.** 6 32 248 619
**w.** oceane-crozon.net

**Maison des Minéraux** (**4**) organise a lot of active and interactive ways to discover the history and facts about the environment of the peninsula; like why, where and how the rocks have been formed the way they are, how metals are made, what flora and fauna can be found. **Balades Sonores**, for example, is an interesting way to get to know le Cap de Chèvre by walking and listening to stories, songs and sounds. A lot is in French only, but the permanent exhibition about the rocks and minerals of the peninsula can be followed in English and German.

**a.** Maison des Minéraux, Saint-Hernot, Route du Cap du Chèvre
**t.** 2 98 271 973
**w.** maison-des-mineraux.org

**Cider tasting** (**5**) at Maison du Cidre de Bretagne: in July and August there's a guided visit, juice and cider tasting every day at 15:00 hrs. In June, September: on Wednesday at 15:00 hrs. Shop and Crêperie is open from June to September. If you really want to find out what it's all about you can participate in the 'initiation à l'oenologie du cidre', by reservation.

**a.** Ferme de Kermarzin, Route de Crozon (D791), 29560 Argol
**t.** 2 98 172 167
**w.** maisonducidredebretagne.fr

Get lost in **Le Labyrinthe** (**6**), a big maze made out of wood. If you follow the tales and riddles in the correct order you might find the way out, but miss a clue or lose your intuition, you might get lost. On the way you'll find out about the mysterious history of labyrinths and ancient rituals (also in English). Kids will love this one. Open all year (but restricted in low season), D308, 2 km from Crozon towards Pointe de Dinan, just after Camping Les Pins. Contact Michel Tréguier.

**t.** 6 64 664 556
**w.** peninsulabyrinthe.com

## EAT/DRINK/HANGOUT

◆

Coming from Crozon, right at the entrance of Morgat, don't miss **Thé à L'ouest** (**7**). It's a teashop, it's a boutique, a lunchroom, épicerie and what-not. It's a cosy feelgood place with cute things to buy and see and a cool place to hang out and read a magazine, or have a tea and a chat and some fine pastry to go with that. In summer they've got live music on Saturdays and there are art exhibitions. Run by warm and welcoming French Aleth and her British husband, it's not hard to see where this un-French salon de thé got its charm from. Open all year, (times change in season).

**a.** 96 Boulevard de la France Libre, 29160 Crozon-Morgat
**t.** 2 98 269 783

## SHOP

◆

**Daily fresh market** with local produce in the centre of **Crozon** town, in front of the church Saint-Pierre. Some stalls have biological fruits and vegetables, dairy, meat and bread. Open every day except Monday, all year, only in the morning.

The 'meilleur' **bakery** in Brittany, maybe in France we dare say, is right here, next to the supermarket Lidl. **Le Fourn' île** (**8**) has been up and running just over 10 years. In charge, a passionate young couple, whose mission in life must be pleasing other people with friendliness and delicious stuff. Their (biological) bread, pastries and cookies are handmade and baked right in plain sight in a big wood oven. The hardest part here is choosing between all the options: brioches, baguettes, bread with nuts, sesame, raisins, whole-grain, traditional, with olives or chocolate. No wonder people line up here to get their kicks. Le Fourn'île, Boulangerie Artisanale is open daily (except Sunday and Thursday.

**a.** Zac du Bourg, (at the parking of the supermarket Lidl) 29160 Crozon

In the same square, in a wooden building opposite the entrance of Lidl, the **biological store**, **Bio Presqu'île** (**8**), seems a bit unorganised at first sight, but it's well stocked with organic, local, biological food and non-food. Open daily (except Sunday).

**a.** Zac du Bourg, Rue Yves le Gallo, 29160 Crozon
**t.** 2 98 261 171

**Absolute Surf** (**9**), one of not so many surf shops on the peninsula, the usual surf shop gear and surf necessities like wax, suits, boards and some locally crafted accessories, very friendly and well-informed staff. Surf school since 1989 (ESB - Ecole de Surf de Bretagne, a guarantee label for surf schools), rental of suits, surfboards and SUPs. Open all year, (surf school open from April to October).

**a.** 4 Rue Kreisker, 29160 Crozon-Morgat
**t.** 2 98 170 196
(board repair: 6 12 902 881)
**w.** absolutesurf.com

**Hoalen Ocean Store**, same concept as the stores in Brest and Pays des Abers; cool clothes, wetsuits and coffees. Open every day (except Monday and Tuesday in winter).

**a.** 20 Quai Kador, 29160 Crozon-Morgat
**t.** 2 98 270 438
**w.** hoalen.com

## SLEEP

◆

**Camping de la Presqu'île** (**10**), one of the many campsites on the peninsula, but situated near town (Morgat) and ocean, surf-family friendly and open all year. Besides campsite for your tent or campervan, they rent out different types of mobile homes and chalets. New is the 'Coco Sweet', a mix between mobile home and luxury tent. Camping also has rental bikes, SUPs and surfboards. Open all year. •€•

**a.** Boulevard Pralognan la Vanoise, 29160 Crozon-Morgat
**t.** 2 98 271 236 / 6 83 368 415
**e.** info@camping-presquile-de-crozon.fr
**w.** camping-presquile-de-crozon.fr

**Kastell Dinn** (**11**) (not a castle) gives you the choice of staying in either a renovated boat, a regular house, or a roulotte (wooden cabin). To get there leave Morgat, direction Kerlouantac and Lostmarc'h, after 2 km at the start of the village you'll find the house. Open all year. •€•

**a.** Hameau de Kerlouantec, 29160 Crozon
**t.** 6 62 529 661
**e.** menezpat@gmail.com
**w.** sejour-insolitebretagne.com

**Camping la Plage de Goulien** (**12**), just 100 m from the beach (and surf spot), but protected from the wind. Campsite in a green setting, also châlets and mobile homes available. •€•

**a.** Kernavéno, 29160 Crozon-Morgat
**t.** 6 08 434 932
**w.** camping-crozon-laplagedegouline.com

# IN AND AROUND CAMARET-SUR-MER

◆

Port town with all the port town charms, and for reasons of light, views and atmosphere it attracts artists, so there are lots of little galleries and ateliers. From here you can drive all the way up to Spanish Point (and almost touch Brest, it's so close) and check various small bays along the way. Even better and certainly more impressive are the views from the 70m tall cliffs of Pointe de Pen-Hir. Some parts here are bird sanctuaries. Please take care not to disturb the birds if you're clambering around, especially during nesting/breeding season.

## TO DO

◆

**Climbing Pointe de Pen-Hir (13)**; if you're up for a bit more challenge than just enjoying the views from the cliffs, **Ya'Ka** offers introductory courses as well as trails for advanced climbers. Open from April to September.

**e.** yakalela29@gmail.com
**t.** 6 73 417 875

## EAT/DRINK/HANGOUT

◆

Bar restaurant **Ti-Son (14)**, you'll pass this coming from Kerloch beach towards Camaret-sur-Mer on your right-hand side. Although we do acknowledge the charm of most of Brittany's 'rustic' bars and restaurants, Ti-Son's nice décor with driftwood ornaments, solid wooden tables and a sunny garden, is a welcome breath of fresh air. On the menu: big portions of home-made French fries, clams, duck, salads, all for a very reasonable price. Open all year. •€•

**a.** on the D8, Keranguyader, 29570 Camaret-sur-Mer
**t.** 2 98 815 423

## SLEEP

◆

**Ty Natur (15)**, situated in a natural park (Parc Naturel Régional d'Armorique) and near the beach of Rade de Brest (don't expect surf here, but it's only a short drive to Kerloch and La Palue), are the 4 to 5 person 'roulottes', wooden cabins. There are two roulottes, 'Camelia' and 'Hortensia', 100% ecologically constructed, with southwest-facing terraces. On demand you can order breakfast, a sauna, massage, or join in a vegetarian dinner. Open all year. •€€•

**a.** 9 Rue Fuenteun ar Ménez, 29160 Lanvéoc
**t.** 2 98 275 517 (Roswitha and Jean-Michel Zimmer)
**m.** contact@ty-natur.fr
**w.** ty-natur.fr

**Ty Anna (16)** is a hideaway in a protected nature park (they were the first and only ones to build in the park). Not in the immediate proximity of the surf coast, but far too nice not to mention. Their wooden 3-bedroom house is set on the banks of the River Aulne, at the entrance to the Crozon Peninsula. Open all year, reservation on website. •€€• •€€€•

**a.** Kergadalen, 29590 Rosnoën
**w.** ty-anna.com

Photo: Alexandra Gossink

# SURF

**La Plage de Pen-Hat (I)** is the most consistent spot near **Camaret-sur-Mer**, beachbreak with strong rips at either side of the bay. Needs small to medium w swell, but picks up a little less than La Palue to the south, best at low to mid tide. When it's really big you can try the beautiful bay of **Veriac'h**, a bit further down, following the D8 towards Pointe-de-Pen-Hir. The best known spot, and the place to check in medium and bigger w-nw swells is beachbreak **Kerloch (II)**. Although it's well known, it's a very large crescent shaped bay, so crowds do spread out. The northern part is visible from the road (D8) and protected from w winds. At low tide you can walk down the beach all the way to the southern end, **Goulien (III)**. From the D8 you can reach the beach from the northern and the southern part. Some wild camping in the dunes behind the beach as long as you keep it quiet and clean. All levels. Easy parking/restaurant/surf school.

From **Pointe de Dinan (IV)** you can see the reefbreak down the cliffs, a right 'power wave' that needs a medium sized w-nw swell and is protected from n winds. Uneven reef and rocks. Can be crowded, advanced level. Parking on top of the cliff.

**La Palue (V)** is the most popular summer spot on the Crozon peninsula, maybe even in Brittany. Because it's so exposed, even the slightest w-nw swell brings rideable waves to its shores. Expect crowds, but then again, it's a big bay, wide beach and room to paddle a bit. It's a very friendly atmosphere and scenic surrounding, but be aware, especially with kids: people drown here regularly because of strong undercurrents. You can check this beach all the way to **Lost Marc'h (VI)** at the northern end of the bay. Some wild camping is done, even in summer, but forest rangers will not appreciate you putting all your camping gear out. All levels. Easy parking/surf school.

# SCHOOL RENTAL REPAIR

**Surf School Moby Dick (17)**, operates at **Plage de Pen-Hat** and **Kerloch**, small-scale surf school run by two brothers. Open from April to November, contact Nicolas and Philippe.

**t.** 6 28 351 692 / 6 68 853 119
**w.** mobydick.fr

**Absolute Surf (18)**, ESB surf school, since 1989, lessons and rental of suits, surfboards and SUPs, operating mainly at the beach of **La Palue**. Shop open all year, school open from April to October.

**a.** 4 Rue Kreisker, 29160 Crozon-Morgat
**t.** 2 98 170 196
(board repair: 6 12 902 881)
**w.** absolutesurf.com

**Surf Oxygene (19)**, surf school in the protected bay of Plage de Goulien, small groups only (up to 8 persons).

**a.** Plage de Goulien, 29160 Goulien
**t.** 6 64 118 714
**w.** surfoxygene.com

**Ocean Pirogue (20)**: SUP lessons and rental, canoe tours and Hawaiian outrigger challenges. Operating from Plage de Goulien (next to the campsite) and Plage de Morgat (2 Place d'Ys).

**t.** 6 61 926 435
**w.** oceanpirogue.com

LE RIS (I)
1
DOUARNENEZ
8,10,11
14
BEUZEC-CAP-SIZUN
D7
BAIE DE
TRÉPASSÉS
(II)
D7
D765
CLÉDEN-CAP-SIZUN
D765
2
PLOGOFF
17
D43
D43
3
4,5,6,15,16
D784
ESQUIBIEN
AUDIERNE
D2
20
Cap Sizun
South Finistère
7,9,12,13
18,22
23
D784
ST TUGEN
(III)
D784
PLOZÉVET
19
D2

# IN AND AROUND DOUARNENEZ

In contrast to the green and hilly Crozon peninsula, Cap Sizun is open and rugged. In summer, the hundreds of round straw bales make you want to run into the fields and climb them (ah, why don't ya!). Driving through the small streets of medieval villages requires some skilled manoeuvring, careful not to hurt those white, purple and pink hydrangeas adorning the stone walls. The seaside villages and landscape reveal what to expect from the weather and the ocean. In the old days, when central heating and insulation were yet to be invented, houses were built in a valley, with the windows and doors facing southwest to protect them from the relentless northwest winds.

Douarnenez is the first seaport town you enter coming from the Crozon peninsula. Not the grand sardine and conservatives port it used to be; it's a tranquil town where a lot of French have their second house. But there's still some sardine and other fish business going on, try some fresh seafood at the Nouveau Port and Port du Rosmeur. There are some calm family beaches at both sides of the Pouldavid rivermouth.

**Tourist Office** at 1 Rue du Dr Mevel, Douarnenez.

## TO DO

◆

Voted one of the most beautiful villages in France, and very much on the tourist-trail but nevertheless uber-cute, is **Locronan (1)**, half an hour south-east from Douarnenez. The small town is covered within an hour by foot, but it's here you can take in how things used to be in the 16th century. Thanks to movie-director Jean-Pierre Jeunet (Delicatessen, Amélie), all electrical wires and fixings reminding of modern times were removed from the village in preparation for his 2004 movie, 'A Very Long Engagement', making Locronan an even more highly sought-after location for filming. Every Tuesday morning there's a market with farmer produce at the Place de la Marie.

From **Douarnenez towards Pointe du Raz** there are numerous bays, inlets and coves to discover, not many surfable, but definitely worth the hike and checking the force of the Atlantic. Most plants and flowers are strong and can cope with the storms and wind, but extreme bad weather can do harm, too much salt and wind burns the plants. Many of the inlets down the cliff - now used by fishermen - were used in the Second World War as hideaways from German enemies.

**Baie des Trépassés (2)**, a well-known surf spot, its very name, 'Bay of the Dead', sounds threatening enough to scare some folks off, but it's all based on a misunderstanding in translation really. The old Breton name was avon, meaning 'river', since a waterway leads to the bay. When the bay's name was translated to French it was mistaken for anaon, which means 'the dead'. Still, the beautiful bay and its location, between Pointe du Raz and Pointe du Van, have plenty of myths attached to them.

**Hiking around Pointe du Van and Pointe du Raz (3)**. Raz is the old word for current, it's exactly at Pointe du Raz where two currents meet. So the ocean is always moving here (and attracting bass; they eat the little fish, that can't escape anywhere in the strong current at low tide but into the mouth of the bass). A good way to learn about the Pointe du Raz area is going on a hike with a local guide. It's very easy to do this by yourself, just following the GR34, but it does pay off in getting to know some of the legends and traditions of the area. One we can definitely recommend is local girl Marie l'Aod; she'll tell you everything from information about plants, birds and history, tales of lighthouse keepers and their families, to myths and local gossip. On top, she'll carry a delicious picnic lunch with local products like cheese, strawberries, eel and beer. From April to October, or on request for groups, contact through CRT (Comité Régional Tourisme).

**t.** 2 98 749 506

*A little quest for you: guess which composer the sculptor of the statue overlooking Pointe du Raz, 'Our Lady of Shipwrecked Persons', was a huge fan of... (look real close!)*

**Pony and Horse Riding (4)** around Pointe du Raz: Centre Equestre de Feunteun Aod. Open all year.

**a.** 5 Route de Kerledec, 29770 Plogoff
**t.** 2 98 706 740
**w.** cheval-capsizun.com

## EAT/DRINK/HANGOUT

◆

One of our old time favourites is **Crêperie Le Raz de Sein (5)** - between our also favoured surf spots Baie des Trépassés and Saint Tugen. Very friendly, family-run place, charming with its unaffected manner. On the menu? Crêpes and galettes of course, salads, some seafood and cider. Open all year. •€•

**a.** 58 Route de la Pointe du Raz (D784), Plogoff (on route from the Baie to Saint Tugen, opposite the Biscuiterie)
**t.** 2 98 706 785

**Hotel-Restaurant Kermoor Spa (6)**, which you'll see from the coastal road toward Plogoff, may not look very attractive from the outside, but their kitchen is great: seafood with the use of local and seasonal products and nicely set plates. The spa has a Hammam, Jacuzzi, swimming pool with current, and massages available; Swedish, Thai and Hawaiian Lomi-Lomi, and reflexology. Open all year. •€€•

**a.** 18 Rue de la Plage, 29770 Plogoff
**t.** 2 98 706 206
**w.** restaurant-kermoor.com

For a pizza at the seaside, check **La Casa Bana (7)**, with a terrace overlooking the ocean. Open every day in summer until the end of September for pizzas, mussels, club sandwiches and drinks. Find La Casa Bana opposite Plage Le Pouldu. •€•

**a.** Impasse Le Pouldu, 29770 Esquibien
**t.** 2 98 702 015

## SHOP

◆

**Breizh Rider Surf and Skate Shop (8)**, boards, accessories, decorations, clothes, and rental of surfboards, SUPs, wetsuits and skates. Open all year.

**a.** 21 Rue Voltaire, 29100 Douarnenez
**t.** 2 98 110 882
**w.** breizh-rider.fr

**Atelier du Pain (9)** is your address here for delicious bread, pain and patisserie, and devilishly good Kouign Amann. Their speciality? 'Le Royal Chocolat' and 'Tout Chocolat'. Oh la la. Open all year, 7:00 to 19:15 hrs.

**a.** on the corner of Route de la Pointe du Raz (D784) and Impasse de la Croix Rouge, 29770 Esquibien

## SLEEP

◆

One way to explore Brittany is by campervan. If you don't own your own van, these must be by far the coolest vehicles to travel along the rugged coast of Brittany, **Vintage Camper** rents out VW vans from the sixties. Family or solo traveller, there should be a suitable type for you. Campers are equipped with the basics, and other necessities like a toilet or barbecue can be rented. Rennes is two hours by train from Paris, or you can leave your own car at Vintage Camper. Available all year. •€• •€€•

**a.** 22 Rue de la Donelière, 35000 Rennes
**t** 6 38 731 125
**w.** vintage-camper.com

**Hotel Ty Mad in Douarnenez (10)** is a treat, all rooms decorated in a slightly different style, and you can feel it's done with love, using old Indian ornaments, antiques, design, and flea-market in the best possible mix. Ty means house, Mad means good, or nice. And it is a Nice House: a Hammam-style spa, garden, and very inventive cuisine. Ty Mad is a boutique-style hotel, but it's got that French charm of squeaking doors and windows. If you don't stay here, we recommend you try the restaurant. Open all year. •€€• •€€€•

**a.** Plage Saint-Jean,
29100 Douarnenez Tréboul
**t.** 2 98 740 053
**e.** info@hoteltymad.com
**w.** hoteltymad.com

**Camping Indigo Douarnenez (11)**, located at a woodland site within walking distance from the Douarnenez bay, this family-friendly camping also rents out fully equipped luxury tents (some even with a cosy woodstove) and wooden mobile homes. Open from May to September. •€• •€€•

**a.** 69 Avenue du Bois d'Isis,
29100 Douarnenez
**t.** 2 98 740 567
**e.** info@camping-indigo.com
**w.** camping-indigo.com

**Chambre d'hôtes Chez Tante Phine (12)**, with a name like that you must feel at home. Traditional house decorated in a warm, personal style, tranquil garden, use of bicycles, dinners are served on reservation. The owners run a 'brocante-antiquité' store with the same name. Open all year. •€€•

**a.** 2 Place de l'église, 29770 Esquibien
**t.** 2 98 701 388
**e.** cheztantephine@gmail.com
**w.** chez-tante-phine.com

**Chambre d'hotes Ty Ana (13)**, in an old authentic house with blue woodwork, at the entrance of Esquibien, decorated with old family furniture giving it all a genuine Cap Sizun feel, 4 rooms, 9 persons. Open all year. • € • • €€ •

**a.** 43 Rue Surcouf , 29770 Esquibien
**t.** 2 98 702 058 / 6 60 795 500 (Anne)
**e.** anne.cigan@orange.fr
**w.** locations29.com/hebergements/lacroixrouge

Photo: Mannus Jons

**Camping Pors Peron** (**14**), 12 km west of Douarnenez, in a quiet and rural area on the Cap Sizun peninsula, campsite and well-equipped canvas lodge tents and mobile homes for rent. Open from April to September. •€•

**a.** RN 165, 29790 Beuzec-Cap-Sizun
**t.** 2 98 704 024
**e.** info@campingporsperon.com
**w.** campingporsperon.com

**Chambre d'hôtes and Table d'hôtes "Gîte An Tiez Bihan"** (**15**) is located near Pointe du Raz and Baie des Trépassés. Chambre d'hôtes has five rooms. Gîtes for 2 to 5 persons, and a communal rural-style kitchen. Non-guests can also make a reservation for the Table d'hôtes. Open all year. •€• •€€•

**a.** 16 Kerhuret, 29770 Plogoff
**t.** 2 98 703 485
**e.** fumoir.29@wanadoo.fr

**Camping Kerguidy-Izella** (**16**) is a small-scale campsite built around an old farmhouse, like many campsites in this area. There are also spacious rooms for rent in the former farmhouse. The proprietors strive for a reduction of $CO_2$ and encourage guests to use public transport. If anyone can help you in how to establish this, it's Annick and Jean-Noël, the owners. Open all year. •€•

**a.** Ferme de Kerguidy Izella, 29770 Plogoff
**t.** 2 98 703 560 / 6 31 780 902
**e.** fermelebars@orange.fr

**Camping Keringard** (**17**), hosts Anne Briand and Yves Keringard run this small-scale campsite (25 places), also built around an old farm, and rent out two gîtes in the same area, near Cléden-Cap-Sizun. They also rent out a mobile home, at walking distance from Baie des Trépassés, near Pointe du Raz. Camping open from April on (until the last guests leave?), gîtes and mobile home available all year. •€•

**a.** Keringard, 29770 Cleden-Cap-Sizun
**t.** 6 49 228 737 / 2 98 706 678
**e.** yvanne29@outlook.fr
**w.** keringard.free.fr

# IN AND AROUND AUDIERNE

Life seems to take place around the harbour area in Audierne, on the estuary of the river Goyen: in the 17th and 18th century merchant houses that line the river, you'll find lots of restaurants, art galleries, bars, an ice-cream parlour and a few shops. So, park your car and take a stroll, it's not that big. The bay of Audierne continues all the way to Penmarc'h, no more cliffs, just beach, as far as the eye can see, ridged by pebbles, dunes and ponds.

**Tourist Office** at 8 Rue Victor Hugo.

## TO DO

Of the many galleries to visit in Audierne, we like to recommend **Galery A l'Ancre de Chine (18)** from artist Yves Dussin. Step into his world, clearly inspired by the ocean, islands and boats. Open all year.

**a.** 1 Rue Marcellin Berthelot, 29770 Audierne
**t.** 2 98 750 821

**Pors Poulhan (19)**, small harbour worth a stop on your way from Audierne towards la Torche via the coastal route. Usually some fishermen are working on their boats or waiting for high tide to sail away. Opposite the harbour you can park your car and start long hikes, towards Pointe du Raz or inland. Check out the newly renovated mills in la Vallée de Tréouzien.

A path, starting from the parking lot, leads through the green valley to **Les Moulins de Tréouzien (20)**: completely renovated in 2015 from old ruins to working water and windmills, one producing buckwheat flour and the other electricity. The best thing is: you can see exactly how everything works and buy freshly baked bread at the weekend - how close to its production can you get! They also sell locally produced honey (the beekeeper's workshop is just a stroll away from the mill, in a yurt), confiture and, of course, buckwheat flour.

Tasting cider at least once is essential, Brittany's ciders are less sweet, more fresh and don't be surprised; they're served in a bole à cidre, a teacup really. **Cidrerie de Tromelin (21)**, has a French guided tour of cider-making, followed by a free cider tasting. Just buying home-made cider, apple juice and other local products is also possible on weekdays from 10:00 to 18:30 hrs and Saturday morning.

**a.** 29790 Mahalon
**t.** 2 98 745 508

One of the most established cider houses is Kerné. You can have a taste of it at **Cidrerie Kerné (22)**. Besides 4 kinds of cider and apple juice, they sell home-made jams, local honey, chocolat and conserves. Open all year, Mesmeur (signs along the road).

**a.** 29710 Pouldreuzic
**w.** cidre-kerne.fr

**Debbie Seidman (18)**, energetic **massages** and traditional Chinese massages, on reservation.

**a.** 2 bis Rue Ernest Renan, 29770 Audierne
**t.** 6 62 678 805
**w.** etre-bien-etre.fr

## EAT/DRINK/HANGOUT

◆

Home-made **ice-cream** with fresh fruits, created by local waterman Renaud Noyelle, in **Cap Délices Glacier (18)**. Open every day in summer.

**a.** 2 Quai Anatole France, 29770 Audierne
**t.** 6 80 555 925

**Crêperie An Teuzar (18)** is loved by locals and tourists alike, can be very busy. Open all year (closed on Sunday). •€•

**a.** 6 Quai Camille Pelletan
29770 Audierne
**t.** 2 98 700 046

**L'Escale (18)**, tea shop in the daytime, pub from whatever hour you want it to be a pub. Open all year, every day from 11:00 hrs.

**a.** 2 Rue Lesné, 29770 Audierne
**t.** 2 98 701 754

## SHOP

◆

Weekly **farmers market** in Audierne, on Saturday: 8-12 Quai Jean Jaurès.

When you're in need of a **launderette**: The Laverie du Port is open every day from 08:00 to 20:00 hrs.

**a.** 2 Place de Republique, 29770 Audierne

**Surf Shops (18)** are, strangely enough, not generously provided in Brittany, but the few you can find are generally well stocked, staffed with friendly people and done up above average, with local brands or boards, some art or classy clothes. Audierne's got **Adrénaline**, a two-storey surf and lifestyle shop to check out. They also rent out bicycles! Open all year.

**a.** 3 bis Quai Anatole France,
29770 Audierne
**t.** 2 98 700 798
**w.** esb-audierne.com

**Bio store La Tisanière du Pont (18)**, sells organic cosmetics, tea, essential oils and food supplements. Open all year.

**a.** 6 Rue Laennec,
29770 Audierne

## SLEEP

◆

**Loqueran (23)** is a small, family-friendly campsite and hotel, and rents out gîtes as well, in a green setting near Audierne. You'll find lots of hikers here, and the owners are keen to advise you on holidaying and activities without using your car. Open all year. •€•

**a.** Pied à Terre à Loquéran, BP 55.
29770 Audierne
**t.** 2 98 749 506
**e.** loqueran@free.fr
**w.** loqueran.com

**Charcuterie Surf House (24)**, although the name suggests otherwise, is definitely more than just a surf house, and no, it's not a butcher. The surf house started out in a previous location, an old butcher's house, some years ago. When they found their current location in a neighbouring village, they kept the name, but moved for good reasons - more space, big garden, out of town, but within walking distance from the beach and Audierne's lively harbour hub. All rooms have a view over the big garden, with hammocks and easy deckchairs. Inside; a cosy woodstove, couch and big kitchen provide all you need to feel at home. Hosts Janneke and Alex insist you do just that, and, with Alex being a local boy, he can provide you with a lot of tips for the area. Couples, families, single travellers (20+) all fit in fine. Open all year. •€•

**a.** 26 Rue des Lavandieres, 29780 Plouhinec
**t.** 6 22 240 082
**e.** info@surfhouse.fr
**w.** surfhouse.fr

# SEASIDE LOCAL: LAURENT GUEGUEN

Plume d'Avion is Laurent Gueguen, a local shaper whose creativity and sheer life-loving attitude are infused into the shapes, colours and designs of his boards. He shapes fish, mini-logs, single-fins and noseriders, in all volumes, shapes and lengths, using classic design and new innovations, with a slight reservation about following fashion. Alternative boards he likes to call them. We met him the first time in a parking lot in Portugal, where he was on a trip, testing some of his boards, with a couple of friends. Of course, we stopped by his shaping bay some months later in Brittany; we'd seen his boards and were curious - or hungry - for more. He lives with his family in the country, on a plot of land where he built his own wooden house and has his shaping bay/atelier on the same piece of land. Laurent is a warm and welcoming guy, softly spoken but never quite able to hide his enthusiasm when taking one of his boards off the rack, talking and explaining about the shape or design.

Officially just a few years into shaping boards with Plume d'Avion (since 2013), he started as far back as 1997, shortly after he learned to surf and was curious to shape a board for himself. He now shapes 2 to 3 boards a month. "I like a board to work for you, so I don't shape 'performance' boards per se", he says. Custom-made, resin-tinted, spray painted, or the use of batik cloth bought in Sri Lanka and Indonesia, all his boards have a very graphic touch. "I don't like white boards too much", he laughs, "I like drawing, painting, I like photographs and graphic design, it's where I get my inspiration from". A creative soul he certainly is; he loves making art, for fun, he loves making music, for fun. And he loves seeing a person with a smile on his face after surfing one of his boards.

*I like drawing, painting, I like photographs and graphic design, it's where I get my inspiration from.*

You can find his boards online, or visit the shaping bay when you're in the area, preferably on reservation.
**a.** Menez Queldrec, 29710 Plozévet (between Plozévet and Pouldreuzic) **t.** 6 82 345 474
**e.** plumedavion@gmail.com **w.** plumedavion.com

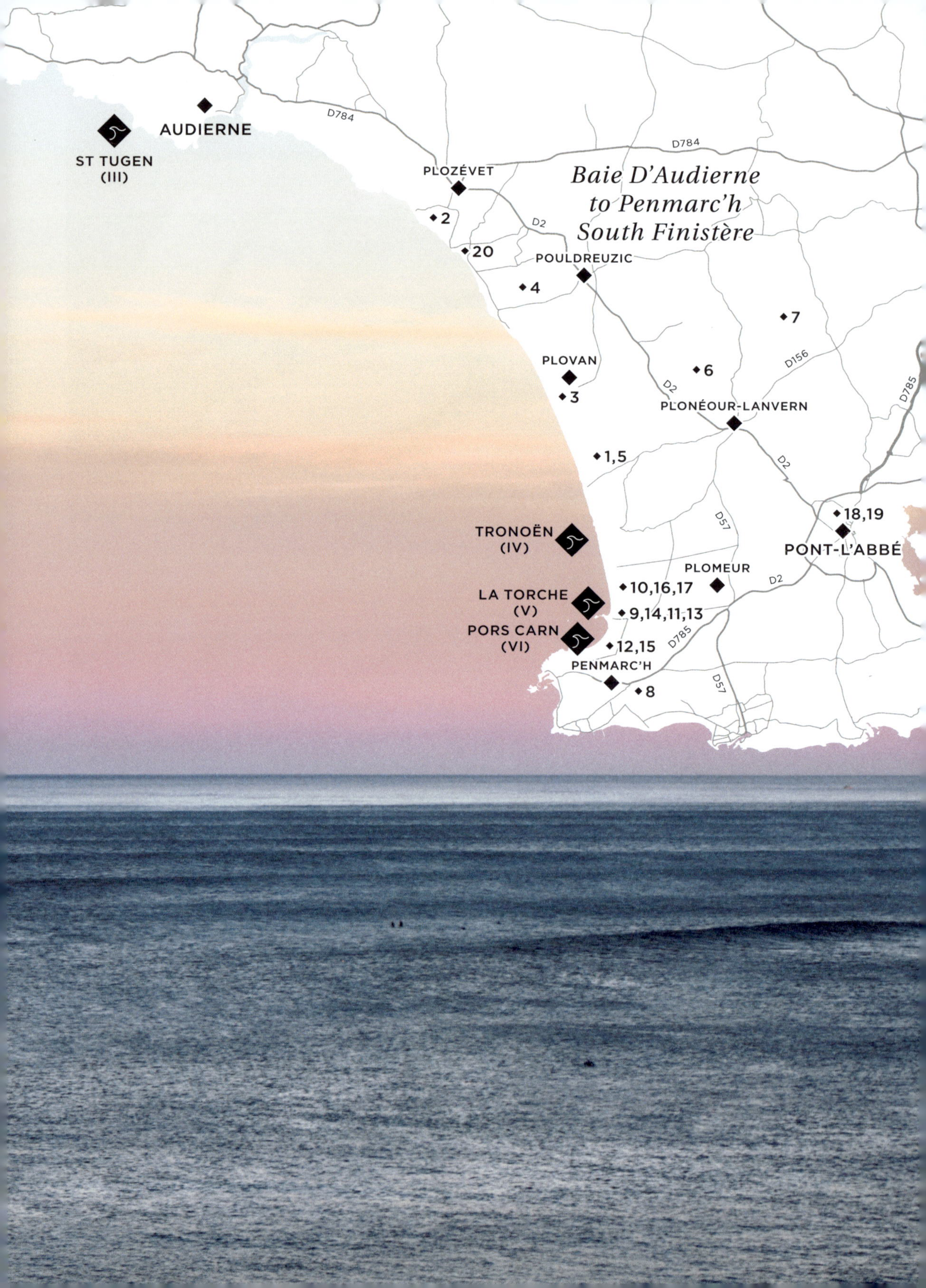
Baie D'Audierne
to Penmarc'h
South Finistère
AUDIERNE
ST TUGEN
(III)
D784
D784
PLOZÉVET
2
D2
20
POULDREUZIC
4
7
PLOVAN
6
D156
D2
D785
3
PLONÉOUR-LANVERN
1,5
D2
D57
18,19
PONT-L'ABBÉ
TRONOËN
(IV)
PLOMEUR
10,16,17
D2
LA TORCHE
(V)
9,14,11,13
PORS CARN
(VI)
12,15
D785
PENMARC'H
8
D57

# IN AND AROUND PENHORS

**Going further south along the coast from Plozévet there are surf breaks 'aplenty'. It's finding the right tide and swell, of course, but because of its position – from south-west to west facing – it can differ completely from one beach to another, even with only a few kilometres in between them.**

Checking several beaches along the Baie D'Audierne is not an ordeal whatsoever. Tune your radio to MFM (non-stop French music) and enjoy the ride from the port of Pors Poulhan, passing the beaches of Plouhinec to Plovan, stop for a drink or small snack at Penhors, then follow the road going a bit inland behind the dunes, wetlands and nature reserve of Tréguennec - haven to hundreds of bird species - ending up at the most well-known and popular surf break of Brittany: Pointe de la Torche.

Photo: Marinus Joris

## TO DO

◆

**Horse riding**, following several trails, for instance the path round the Baie D'Audierne to La Torche, find out more about trails and availability through Comité Départemental de Tourisme Equestre du Finistère.

**w.** cdte29.fr

Trails and tours on the beaches of Tronoën, La Torche and surroundings: **Centre Équestre de La Torche**. Open all year.

**a.** Kermeil , 29120 Plomeur
**t.** 2 98 586 951 / 6 50 791 796
**w.** centre-equestre-latorche.fr

**Mountain biking** can be done throughout Finistère, trails are flagged up with 2 circles and a triangle – red for national routes, yellow for local routes, and brown for routes in protected natural parks. Each circuit has its own number, noted on the signpost, and a colour for difficulty. Green and Blue = Easy, Black = Difficult. Between Douarnenez and Quimper and between Quimper and Pont-l'Abbé, former railway tracks have been turned into greenways for biking and hiking.

Visit the farm to buy fresh goat cheese and mozzarella from **Chèvrerie de la Baie** (**1**), and get up close and personal with the goats, sheep, horses and buffalo. Open on Sundays and holidays, in July and August every day.

**a.** Kergaradec, 29720 Treguennec (from Ploneur, take the D156 towards the ocean)
**w.** chevrerie-delabaie.com

## EAT/DRINK/HANGOUT

◆

A brilliant phenomenon in summer, and especially in this part of Brittany, is the **pop-up crêperie**. They're here and there and everywhere. At Plage du Menhirs, between Plozévet and Penhors, you can find the mobile **Ty Rozell** (**2**), which means 'House of Rozell' - Rozell being the utensil used to role and flatten the crêpe on the hot plate. •€•

**t.** 6 82 345 474

**Penn Ar Bed** (**3**), bar, pizzeria and crêperie at Plage de Penhors, eat, drink, and enjoy, with a view of the ocean, some days with live music. Open all year, every day. •€• •€€•

**a.** 2 Route de Penhors, 29720 Plovan
**t.** 2 98 543 675

## SLEEP

◆

**Les Bulles Bleues** (**4**), bed and breakfast with a stylish twist, 3 rooms and a family suite (each room with its own theme), breakfast with home-made goodies and local produce from the garden. Dinner can be booked, simple but inventive cuisine, with products and

vegetables from the very same garden. Open all year. •€• •€€•

**a.** 7 Rue de Ty Corn, Lababan, 29710 Pouldreuzic
**t.** 2 56 105 872 / 6 12 555 360
**w.** lesbullesbleues.com

Near the wetlands and nature reserve of **Tréguennec**, Monsieur et Madame Texier-Pauton have 3 traditional stone gîtes for rent, **La Chaumière Pont Nevez** (**5**). A few steps from the endless bay of Audierne, surrounded by nature, all houses are decorated with seaside ornaments, in a well-cared for, homely manner. Very family/kids friendly with toys to play in the garden. Open all year. •€€•

**a.** Pont Nevez, 29720 Tréguennec
**t.** 2 98 820 261 / 6 80 157 274
**w.** pont-nevez.com

**Camping de Lestréguéoc** (**6**), now here's a campsite we can recommend. Situated amidst an apple orchard, cosy and spacious at the same time, because owner Claudia likes to keep it that way. 25 pitches with enough room for every happy camper to feel comfortable, yet enough feelgood activity to get in contact with your neighbours; like crêpe-nights and pizza-parties where everybody brings their own ingredients and kids can create their favourite pizza. There's a big farm shed for music nights, sitting at shared tables. There are horses, donkeys and goats. You can either place your own tent, caravan or campervan in one of the shady places, or rent a roulette de charme (feeling like a gypsy but with all the comfort you could wish for), a lodge-tent or a wooden chalet. Showers and toilets are simple but clean. Open all year for the roulettes and chalets, camping in season. •€•

**a.** 29720 Ploneur-Lanvern (look for the signs driving on the D2 from Plozévet towards Pointe de la Torche)
**t.** 2 98 876 914 / 6 73 099 297 (Claudia Durand)
**e.** durand.claudia@wanadoo.fr
**w.** campingdelestregueoc.pagespro-orange.fr

From the same owner as Camping Lestréguec, Claudia, another wonderful, 4-person gîte de charme: **Brin D'Ouest** (**7**), with a big garden, fireplace and nicely decorated rooms. Open all year. •€€•

**a.** Kerhua, 29720 Plonéour-Lanvern
**t.** 2 98 876 914 / 6 73 099 297
**e.** durand.claudia@wanadoo.fr
**w.** gitebrindouest.com

# IN AND AROUND POINTE DE LA TORCHE

At the southern end of Baie d'Audierne is a rocky headland, from where you can see the 40 km long stretch of sand all the way north to Audierne. From here you can check the surf of Pors Carn to the south and La Torche to the north. Further down from La Torche, you'll see an old bunker on the beach, a souvenir from the Germans. This part is Plage de Tronoën. Inland from here, behind the dunes and fields, is a gothic chapel with one of the oldest calvaries of Brittany: stone carvings depicting Christ's life. Although in an isolated area, busloads of tourists mark the spot. It is an impressive site after all... or is it the naked-breasted Virgin, giving birth to Jesus that's attracting the hordes? In season, coloured carpets of flowers brighten up the fields. The sandy soils around Tronoën prove excellent conditions for growing daffodils, hyacinths or tulips (count the number of Dutch names at the flower farms).

## TO DO

**Market at Penmarc'h**, local produce on offer. Open all year, every Friday morning at Saint-Guénolé port. In summer, every Monday evening between 16:30 and 19:30 hrs at the lighthouse Saint Pierre.

**Saint-Guénolé (8)**, the harbour quarter of Penmarc'h, is an important tuna and sardine port for France. As many parts on the western coast of Europe, the area around the west-facing harbour and the beaches around Pointe de la Torche, like Pors Carn, are nicknamed 'Côte Sauvage' – wild coast. There are not many hills to protect the land from strong wind, so it's flat as a dab, but this, and the fact that a big part of the area used to be wetlands, creates magical lights, especially at sunrise and sunset. In summer you won't be alone, but you can climb the 227 steps of **Phare d'Eckmühl**, a still active lighthouse, at 65m it's one of the tallest in the world (open to public from April to September).

At the **fishmarket**, **Océane Alimentaire (8)** (the large grey stone building in the main street, Rue du Port Saint-Guénolé), the fresh catch is auctioned daily, also free entry to the public. Try the **pain au figue** at **Boulangerie Patisserie du Port** in the same street, and definitely (really, definitely) try the **take-away crêpes** of '**Les Bigoudènes de Saint-Gué**', in the same grey stone building next to the fishmarket.

## EAT/DRINK/HANGOUT

There are a few restaurants, bars and crêperies before entering the parking area of Pointe de la Torche. **Le Crayon Vert (9)** holds a good balance between price and quality; live music in summer on Wednesday and Saturday. Good ambience, locals and tourists alike. Open all year except January.

**Crepeatao (10)** is set just behind Tronoën beach. The name Crepeatao refers to the Breton nationalistic saying Breizh Atao, which means as much as 'Brittany forever'. On the menu - besides crêpes and galettes - salads and local beers. Open from May (weekends) to end of August, located at the side of the road to Plage de Tronoën, Saint-Jean Trolimon.

**Rise UP café and surf art (11)**: In 2014, Sebastian, owner of Rise UP, until then a mobile surf school, created a sleek place with a warm ambience; art exhibited on the walls, friendly staff and a garden to hang out. Next-door neighbour, shaper Josselin, of Zeppelin boards, built a skate ramp in the very same garden. There's even a room attached to the bar where you can jam with Sebastian and his musical friends. (For surf school see Surf section.) Open all year.

**a.** Pointe de la Torche – Roz an Tremen, 29120 Plomeur
**t.** 2 98 982 155
**w.** rise-up-surfschool.com

**Le P'tit Camion (12)** is certainly more than just a pop-up crêperie, it's a hangout, music venue, restaurant and coffee shop all in one. Meet the lovely Flo and Ben strutting their cuisine-stuff in a cool vintage VW van at Plage de Pors Carn. And vegetarians, don't worry, a great veggie-quinoa-burger is on the menu too! Friday nights are reserved for live music. Find them at the site of Dezert Point Surf School.

**a.** 171 Rue du Musée Préhistorique, 29760 Penmarc'h
**t.** 6 82 255 272

## SHOP

◆

The little **shop and atelier** of Amélie Fish, **Poissonnerie Deglinguee (13)** is kinda funky. In summer she has a pop-up shop next to Atlantic Surf Shop at **Pointe de la Torche**. She'll paint your surfboard or teach you to paint. If you don't find her there, contact Amélie.

**t.** 6 64 278 952
**w.** ameliefish.blogspot.fr

## SLEEP

◆

**Campervans**: Off season, some wild camping is allowed, as long as you keep a low profile and make use of the official **campersites** to empty your water tank and chemical toilet. There are enough of them around, well flag-posted, and every year the number is growing. Spending a day or two on a campsite won't dent your budget too much, since campsites in Brittany come cheap.

**Point de la Torche (14)** has a big parking area where wild camping is not allowed, but campervans can park in a little field just 50 metres away from the parking. Toilets (not too clean, to say the least) at the parking near the beach.

Behind the dunes of Plage de Pors Carn and Tronoën there are several **villas for rent**, like the 5-person Villa Surf with 3 bedrooms and shared bathroom, or Villa Clipper for 10 persons with 6 bedrooms and 2 bathrooms. The villas are traditional stone houses decorated in an easy, clean, down-to-earth style with subtle ocean details, like a driftwood coffee table or paddles used as coat rack. **Les Villas Heol (15)**, open all year (pets welcome, except in summer). ◆€◆ ◆€€◆

**a.** 133 Rue des Cables Sous Marins, 29760 St-Guénolé-Penmarc'h
**t.** 2 98 940 027 or 6 82 228 613
**e.** roselyne.ligot@wanadoo.fr
**w.** latorche.fr

**Gîtes de Tronoën (16)** used to be an old farm; now renovated into 4 cottages, it's situated between the medieval Tronoën chapel and the beach of Tronoën, right in the middle of the dunes. In spring you'll see the tulip fields in full bloom. The gîtes' (from 4 to 6 persons) interiors are simple and each has a private entrance, garden and terrace. It's the location that's just stunning. Open all year. ◆€◆

**a.** Pen Ar Vouez, 29120 Saint-Jean Trolimon, contact for reservation
**t.** 2 98 821 104 / 6 22 146 666
**e.** contact@lesgitesdetronoen.fr

Within walking distance from the beach and Pointe de la Torche is a little concentration of **refurbished traditional fishermen's houses (17)**. You can either rent one or both - pretend you have your own village, why not. Extremely nice setting, especially for those who love to hike, bike, surf and be surrounded by nature. Gîte de Kerdu, 5 to 7 persons, and Gîte Kerheol, 7 persons, both have storage for boards or bikes, a fireplace, and pets are welcome. Open all year, contact for reservations. ◆€◆ ◆€€◆

**t.** 2 98 511596 / 6 08 026 014 (Ronan Pensec)
**m.** ronanpensec@yahoo.fr
**w.** kerdu.fr

The wooden lodges of **Atlantic Location (13)**, right next to the Atlantic Surf Shop are located conveniently close to the breaks around Pointe de la Torche (500 m). Fully equipped, sleeps up to 6 persons. Open all year. ◆€◆

**a.** Route de la Torche, 29120 Plomeur
**t.** 6 08 630 571
**e.** yannicklecoz@orange.fr
**w.** atlantic-location.fr

# SURF

**Le Ris** (**I**) is the first beach you'll see, coming from Brest, just before driving into **Douarnenez**. Except from north-east, it's well protected from strong winds in any other direction and needs a big w-nw swell to work. You'll have to have a bit of volume for this beach-break though, the wave it produces is long, easy and weak. So, party on longboarders and SUPs. Safe beach for kids to learn. Works best at upcoming to high tide. Most of the beach disappears at high tide. All levels. Small parking/toilets.

**Baie de Trépassés** (**II**), the big bay between Pointe du Raz and Pointe du Van, is one of the reasons you want to surf in Brittany. It has the coldest water (well, maybe that's not a good reason), it's clean, has a backdrop of rocky cliffs and a green valley, and several peaks to choose from. Beachbreak with some boulders, fun when it's small, powerful when bigger. The bay's exposed to wind, but you can find a little shelter in the utmost corners. Works at all tides, but better at low tide (although depending on sandbanks and rocks that shift through the seasons). All levels. Easy parking/toilets/restaurant/surf school.

When you see **Saint-Tugen** (**III**) in pictures, you'd swear it's somewhere tropical and warm. The water is crystal clear, fine white sand making it even bluer. What gives it away that you're actually in Brittany - the big lumps of seaweed. It's a fun drive through the small streets of medieval town Saint-Tugen to get to the beach. Beachbreak with rocks and boulders, powerful waves, and a thumping shorebreak with high tide. Works on small sw swells and medium w-nw swells. All levels except beginner (unless under guidance of surf school). Easy parking/toilet (near lifeguards).

Photo: Geert-Jan Middelkoop

Between Audierne and **Pointe de la Torche** (**V**) there are several breaks to be found, due to its position and length. It's just a hop on and off from the coastal road to check for, usually, uncrowded surf.

The long stretch of beach north of **Pointe de la Torche** is one of the most well-known spots in Brittany, for good reason: under the right conditions, waves break at the Pointe – a rocky headland – and roll in orderly lines along the rocks towards the beach. It can handle a bit of size, especially round the Pointe. You can make use, but also be very aware, of the current alongside the rocks, to take you out to the line-up. They call it 'l'ascenseur', the elevator, for a reason. La Torche, of course, gets busy: easy access, protection from the Pointe, consistent, home to surf, SUP and windsurf contests, and the further north you go, towards **Tronoën** (**IV**), or even further up, the less surfers in the line-up. Works with small to medium w, nw, and sw swell, best mid to high tide. In summer: no surfing between the blue flags, that's swimming area.

When La Torche is too big, or too crowded, try **Pors Carn** (**VI**), at the south end of Pointe de la Torche, towards Penmarc'h. Also, it's safer for beginners and kids to surf Pors Carn than La Torche. Easy parking/toilets/ surf school.

# SCHOOL RENTAL REPAIR

Confused by which surf school to choose? Any **ESB** (Ecole de Surf de Bretagne) labelled surf school should provide a guarantee of safe classes with experienced teachers.

You'll find one in **Penhors, Baie des Trépassés** and **Pointe de la Torche**. The surf school at La Torche is also the first established surf school in Brittany.

**w.** ecole-surf-bretagne.fr

Looking for a new or second-hand surfboard, or any surf-related item, or maybe want to sell or swap your own board? **Pichavant Surfing**'s (**18**) got 350m2 dedicated to everything surf-related. Open all year (closed on Sunday).

**a.** Zone Artisanale Kermaria,
29120 Pont l'Abbé
**t.** 2 98 873 939
**w.** pichavantsurfing.com

**S.A.W. Surfboards** (**19**), shapers workshop initiated by Loïc Bourdon. Get your repair done, a custom board shaped or choose (or drool over) one of his resin-tinted logs. Any type of board is possible but Loïc's style is especially inspired by a combination of classic longboards, fish and simmons. Open all year, but phone to make sure.

**a.** Rue des Pins, Z.A. du Guiric,
29120 Pont-l'Abbé
**t.** 6 52 276 575
**w.** saw-surfboards.fr

With a passion for surfing and teaching, Julien Jallet makes a fine surf instructor. Hard to miss his mobile surf school **Soul Surfing Skol** (**20**), since he's driving around in a very red firemen's truck. Make your reservation by phone and meet Julien at the beaches of **Plouhinec** or **Plovan**, depending on tides and circumstances. Lessons are taught in French and/or English, with a personal approach, classes limited to 8 persons. Open April to October.

**t.** 6 98 162 829
**w.** soulsurfingskol.com

Photo: Marinus Joris

Cool school **Rise Up (11)**, on the road to **Pointe de la Torche**, has a coffee shop, a place to hang out and a skate ramp in the garden. The school offers lessons, courses and board rental, small groups and passionate teachers. Open all year.

**a.** Pointe de la Torche – Roz an Tremen, 29120 Plomeur
**t.** 2 98 982 155
**w.** rise-up-surfschool.com

**Zeppelin surfboards (11)**, next door to Rise Up, is a longtime Breton shaper who loves shaping vintage, 70s boards, single fins, and longboards, but also shapes performance shortboards for the hot local groms, or on demand. And very handy to know: he does repairs too. Open all year.

**a.** Pointe de la Torche – Roz an Tremen, 29120 Plomeur
**t.** 6 63 616 905
**w.** zeppelinisbeautiful.blogspot.com

**Atlantic Surf Shop (13)** at Pointe de la Torche offers lessons, boards for rent and has a well stocked shop for all your surfing necessities, from leashes, wax, clothes and skateboards, to flip-flops. Open all year except mid January to mid February.

**a.** Route de la Torche, 29120 Plomeur
**t.** 2 98 587 487
**w.** atlanticsurfshop.com

**Surf School Dezert Point (12)** is situated at the beach of Pors Carn, at the south side of Pointe de la Torche. Offers surf lessons, SUP and surf rental, friendly staff and live music venues in summer. Open all year.

**a.** Plage de Pors Carn, 171 Rue du Musée de la Préhistoire, 29760 Penmarc'h
**t.** 2 98 521 390
**w.** dezert-point.com

Quimper Area
South Finistère
QUIMPER
1,6,7,9
E60
N165
D784
D34
D785
FOUESNANT
3
8
5
PONT-L'ABBÉ
CONCARNEAU
N165
PONT-AVEN
2
4

# IN AND AROUND QUIMPER

◆

**The coast from Penmarc'h to Lorient finds little in the way of waves, due to its south orientation; but just passing through, either inland or along the coast, without at least checking some sites or cities would be a pity.**

Quimper is the oldest city in Brittany. The medieval quarter, with its half-timbered houses, is built around the junction of the two rivers, the Steir and the Odet, with Place Saint-Corentin and the Gothic cathedral as its centre. Easily covered on foot in an hour at most, although there are enough terraces, shops and restaurants to slow you down. The many small bridges along the Odet are decorated with flowers and plants. To have a view over the city you can climb the tree-covered 87m high Mont Frugy - which is like a vertical walk in a park – to the south of the river Odet.

**Tourist Office** in Place de la Resistance.

## TO DO

◆

**The Festival de Cornouaille (1)**, the week-long festival, usually held in July in Quimper, began as far back as 1923 and is still one big celebration of Breton culture. Concerts, bagpipe players, a parade, dancers, and dressing up in traditional costume; it's all one Big Up to their Celtic roots. And it will be just you and some quarter of a million other locals, tourists, artists and musicians.

Post-Impressionist painter Paul Gauguin loved **Pont-Aven (2)** so much he settled for a while in the late 19th century. And it's still known as the **artist** town of Brittany; you'll find many art galleries and artist's studios. You can follow a trail called 'In the steps of Gauguin' that takes you along the harbour and the banks of the Aven river. The Musée des Beaux-Arts de Pont-Aven reopened in 2016 after a renovation, in the same square as the tourist office, Place de L'Hôtel de Ville.

The **archipelago Les Glénan (3)** resembles the Caribbean so much, you forget you're in France (as long as you don't try to swim, you'll end up with brain-freeze). Really; white sand, transparent water, no surfing, just hiking, enjoying nature, sailing, SUP or kayak. It's a protected nature reserve and if you're in any way into birds, it's not just a to-do, it's a must-do. Waiting for the boat to cross to Les Glénan from Fouesnant, you can establish that Fouesnant is indeed a fishing port, come early and see the fishermen sell their catch of the day directly to the local community. Book your trip through the tourist office.

**a.** 4 Espace Kerneveleck,
29170 Fouesnant
**t.** 2 98 511 888
**w.** tourisme-fouesnant.fr

**Animal Park Quinquis (4)** is a concept of animals in the wild, in direct contact with the public. Several varieties of animals roam in freedom, co-existing with the visitors in a preserved Botanical Park. There are rest areas and you're allowed to have a picnic among the animals (think rabbits, deer, geese, horses, pigs, tortoises – it's not as if there's a tiger lurking). Great stuff for kids. Open April to October.

**a.** 29360 Clohars-Carnoët (between Quimper and Lorient, 5 minutes from the beach of Pouldu-Clohars)
**t.** 2 98 399 413
**w.** parcanimalierduquinquis.com

**Adrenature (5)** is an outdoor adventure park with several circuits and levels (also night circuits), accessible from age 4. Open April to November.

**a.** Lieu dit Moulin du Cosquer,
29140 Melgven (between Quimper and Quimperlé)
**t.** 6 82 787 910
**w.** adrenature.fr

## EAT/DRINK/HANGOUT

◆

**Les Halles de Quimper (6)**, 70 stalls with local produce, from patisserie, seafood and cheese, to wine and liqueurs in a large **indoor market**. Open all year, every day (Sunday only in the mornings).

**a.** Les Halles Saint-François,
16 Quai du Steir, 29000 Quimper

**Galerie Artem (7)**: modern local artists, creative activities for kids, different exhibitions. Open all year.

**a.** 16 Rue Sainte-Catherine,
29000 Quimper
**t.** 6 95 210 476

If you're missing out on the good food in the regular supermarkets, the organically grown veggies and other biological items, check the big Coop Bio, Brin d'Avoine. Open all year (closed on Sunday).

**a.** 5 Allée de Kernénez,
Creac'h Gwen, 29000 Quimper

**Le Café Local (8)**, a popular local hangout, café, restaurant, music venue, cocktail and tapas bar. Lively, in summer regular live music and DJ sets. Open all year, from Wednesday to Sunday.

**a.** Kerhor, 29120 Combrit (along the D144, between Penmarc'h and Quimper)
**t.** 2 98 535 676

## SHOP

◆

**Dezert Point (9)** Surf School has two shops in Quimper, a **surf shop** and a skate shop. The surf shop offering a wide range of surf wear and technical equipment, the **skate shop** has absolutely everything related to skate. Both shops are staffed with enthusiastic specialist surfers and skaters. Open Tuesday to Saturday.

**a.** Surf Shop, 5 Place de Locronan,
Skate Shop, 3 Rue de la Providence,
29000 Quimper

Photo: Alexandra Gossink

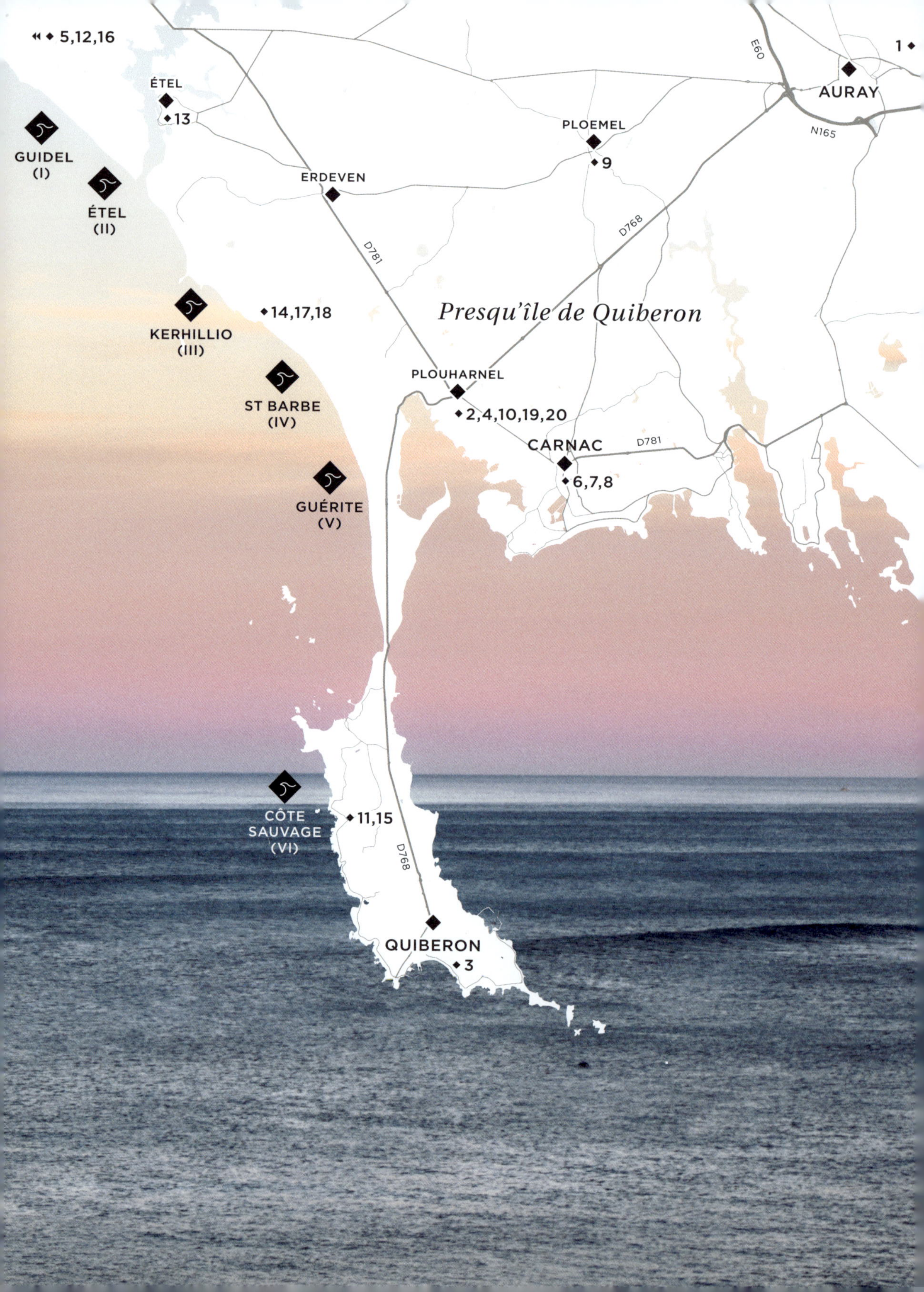
5,12,16
1
AURAY
E60
N165
ÉTEL
13
GUIDEL (I)
ÉTEL (II)
PLOEMEL
9
ERDEVEN
D781
D768
Presqu'île de Quiberon
KERHILLIO (III)
14,17,18
ST BARBE (IV)
PLOUHARNEL
2,4,10,19,20
CARNAC
D781
6,7,8
GUÉRITE (V)
CÔTE SAUVAGE (VI)
11,15
D768
QUIBERON
3

# IN AND AROUND QUIBERON PENINSULA

◆

**If you want a taste of Brittany, but don't feel like travelling all the way up to Cap Sizun or northern Finistère, the Quiberon peninsula, reaching out into the Atlantic for 14 kms, is a good option. The ocean is a little warmer, they've got great oysters, the cities of Lorient, Rennes, Nantes and Vannes are close by.**

In August, it's a bit of an ordeal to get to the north of the peninsula. At the narrowest point, which is just 22 m wide, the road (D768) bottlenecks and it can take hours to go forth, or back. Hiking here is as great as it is everywhere along the coast in Brittany, maybe even better, since the landscape varies from rocks to dune and heathland, protecting the western side of Quiberon against the roaring ocean. The calm bay at the eastern side, from the peninsula to Trinité Sur Mer, serves as a perfect area for oyster cultivation - the oysters feast on the rich marine nutrient base of these waters. Carnac is France's own Stonehenge: megaliths galore, fields full, laid out like a Neolithic flower carpet, the flowers being menhirs and dolmens.

## TO DO

◆

Festival **Au Pont du Rock** (**1**), the oldest summer music festival of Brittany (over 25 years), well known for booking new and yet to be discovered talent - rock, world and indie music, for two days, usually end of July.

**a.** l'espace Maurice Melois, 56140 Malestroit
**w.** aupontdurock.com

Don't skip the little village of **Plouharnel** (**2**) just because it's only a passage to Quiberon. Stop here, and even better, stay for a bit. From here you're close to the surf (Les Crevettes, La Guérite, Sainte-Barbe), the good food (Les Clefs de Presqu'île), the surf shop and hangout (ATS Surf Shop).

**a.** Tourist office: Rond-Point de l'Océan

**Quiberon** (**3**), the main town on the peninsula, is a pretty seaside town, touristy of course, with lots of seafood restaurants, crêperies, hotels, and Breton souvenirs like striped shirts and conserves. Nothing too hip and happening, but nothing too loud either. If you want to avoid the bottleneck situation in summer, hop on the Tire-Bouchon, a train that takes you from Plouharnel to Quiberon and back for less than 6 euros. Runs several times a day in July and August. You're allowed to take your bicycle for free. Tire-Bouchon means… yes indeed, corkscrew.

Explore the underwater world, **dive** around the shores of the peninsula with either **Centre Haliotis Plongée** in Port de Portivy.

**w.** haliotisplongee.com

Or **Quiberon Plongée** in Quiberon.

**w.** quiberon-plongee.com

**Cycle** your way around: there are several cycle routes in the area, one of them is a tour around the Quiberon peninsula, taking about 2,5 hrs. Many places in Quiberon (town) rent out bicycles, **Les Vélos de la Baie** is on the route from Plouharnel to Quiberon. Open from April to September.

**a.** Bois du Bego, 56340 Plouharnel
**t.** 7 82 063 238/6 80 783 721
**w.** lesvelosdelabaie.com

How about this: a 3-day surf course, where you start your day checking the surf, on a horse. **Club Hippique de la Plage** (**4**), near Plage Sainte-Barbe, offers tours, courses, and this combi with surfing in cooperation with the ESB surf school. French and English spoken.

**a.** Kersily-Sainte Barbe, 56340 Plouharnel
**t.** 6 26 252 821
**w.** clubhippiquedelaplage.tumblr.com

**Kayak tours** (**5**) on the river D'Étel, either by yourself in a rental kayak or guided tours. You'll get a detailed map of the waterways with different routes to choose from. Open from April to September.

**a.** 73 Rue du Passage d'Étel, Port du Magouër, 56680 Plouhinec
**t.** 7 70 742 723
**w.** ty-kayak.fr

**Massages, reflexology and well-being** (**6**): treatments by Michelle Gentils, reservations.

**a.** 44 Route de Kerlann, 56340 Carnac
**t.** 6 08 852 236
**e.** michelle.gentils@orange.fr

Not enough ocean therapy from surfing? **The Carnac Thalasso and Spa** (**6**) is the first 100% bio Thalasso Spa in France. All sorts of treatments, like Ayurvedic Thalasso, massages, or just visit the hammam and sauna.

**a.** Avenue de l'Atlantique, 56340 Carnac
**w.** thalasso-carnac.com

Within a 4 km area, the megalithic sites Le Ménec, Kerlescan and Kermario at Carnac, consist of almost **4000 menhirs** (**7**). Fields full, row after row, of massive stones is rather impressive. Add to that the fact that no one really knows how they ended up there, and why in that order. Carnac's alignments aren't as famous as the magical Stonehenge family in the UK, which is a bit of a mystery in itself, since it's the largest alignment of its sort in the world. It's well accepted that the standing stones had a sacred function, but not knowing whether they're temples, sacred burial grounds or, who knows, a big calendar telling what day full moon is, adds to your magical mystery tour.

Magic, though, is a bit far-fetched when you visit the sites in summer; not only are they fenced in order to protect the surrounding vegetation, the hordes of tourists make it hard to imagine any shamanistic rites.

There are **guided tours** though, which allow you to enter the fields and, of course, get better informed about the mysterious biggies. If you have the chance, visit between October and April, when you can roam the fields freely.

**a.** Lleu-dit le Ménec, 56340 Carnac (from Auray: secondary roads D768 and D781 towards Carnac)

**Sarah Hebert (8)**, one seaside local you sure want to meet: ocean girl, water woman, windsurf champ, kitesurfer, stand-up paddle boarder. She spent her youngest years on a boat with her parents, sailing across the world, rocked by the waves. She continues to travel the world as a competing windsurfer, and when she's not, you can still meet her, in, or near the ocean. Her motto 'with heart, everything is possible', is quite literal: after being diagnosed with a heart rhythm disorder in 2006, doctors advised the installation of a defibrillator. Within a few months of the operation she was right back on the highest sport level track, winning the European Championships in windsurfing. What she really wants to teach with this motto: all dreams are possible, despite difficulties in life. Join Sarah in SUP fitness/yoga classes, beach yoga, SUP tours or even a 2-hour SUP Gastronomique tour where you discover all the gastronomic goodies the Carnac area has to offer. Contact for reservations.

**t.** 6 75 625 732
**e.** sarahhebert@hotmail.com
**w.** windsurf-transatlantic.com

Get lost in the **Popcorn Labyrinthe (9)**, 5 hectares of giant maize. The cornfield is transformed into a **labyrinth** every summer with different routes. Open from 4th of July to 4th of September.

**a.** D768 Route de Quiberon, (Pontreval), 56400 Ploemel

## EAT/DRINK/HANGOUT

◆

**Crêperie La Clef de la Presqu'île (2)** is one of those places where you like to hang out just a bit longer than the time it really requires to finish your crêpe or coffee. Its homely atmosphere and tempting menu, surfboards on the ceiling, a shop attached with products like locally brewed beer, canned salted caramel bonbons, conserves of sardines in artistic cans and friendly staff is why. Yves, owner of Crêperie La Cléf de la Presqu'île, decided some years ago to run his crêperie the way it's run now, and, he says: "I've loved my work from day one, I used to work in restaurants where I had to wear suits and tie. Now I work in my t-shirt and flip-flops, and it feels like I have friends round the house, sharing ciders, coffee and good food." You can enter the shop from 2 sides. •€•

**a.** 15 Avenue de l'océan and 4 Rue de la Poste, 56340 Plouharnel
**t.** 2 97 523 550
**w.** laclefdelapresquile.com

**Bar Brasserie Le Massena (2)** is an easy-going local and tourist hangout with friendly staff. A good place to use the internet, go for a beer on the terrace, a simple but excellent moules et frites, or goats cheese salad.

**a.** 1 Place du Général de Gaulle, 56340 Plouharnel

In summer you can order a pizza-to-go at **Surfin Pizza (2)** (those fine thin crust pizzas). Open in July and August from 18:00 hrs. •€•

**a.** 11 Place du Général De Gaulle, 56340 Plouharnel
**t.** 6 68 942 014

**Restaurant L'Hippocampe (10)**, located near the oyster beds of Pô, between Carnac and Plouharnel, with a view of the bay, serves creative and original, fresh seafood-based menus (how about finishing your plate of langoustines, oysters and prawns with a dessert of Breton buckwheat slices, boiled bananas, caramel and hazelnuts). Reservation recommended. • €€• •€€€•

**a.** Route de Carnac, Kerhuéno, 56340 Plouharnel (direction of Pô)
**t.** 2 97 291 017
**w.** restaurant-lhippocampe.com

**Restaurant Le Bateau Ivre (11)**, great location in the harbour of Portivy, popular with local folks and usually quite busy, especially around lunch and sunset. •€• •€€•

**a.** 9 Quai Saint-Ivy, 56510 Saint-Pierre-Quiberon
**t.** 2 97 309 919

Of the many restaurants, cafés and tea shops in the town of Quiberon, on Quiberon peninsula, **Meli Melo (3)** stands out in looks, vibe and menu. The interior is like an English poem, read out loud with a French accent (try to imagine that…). Petit-déjeuner (breakfast), sandwiches-to-go, coffees and teas, freshly baked bread and cakes.

**a.** 33 Rue de Port Maria,
56170 Quiberon

Opposite Meli Melo is Bar-Restaurant **Un Petit Goût De (3)**, with an original, fresh décor, like seats from wooden pallets, you can either sit inside or on the terrace at the back. Popular with locals, on the menu tapas and the usual French suspects like canard, seafood and veal, but prepared with an Asian twist. Great cocktails and live music. •€€•

**a.** 33 Rue de Port Maria, 56170 Quiberon
**t.** 6 85 198 204

**Café de la Barre (12)**, hangout for local surfers and skaters, regular (live) music and dance venue, from reggae to drum'n'bass, friendly staff.

**a.** 73 Rue Passage d'Étel (Magouër),
56680 Plouhinec

It's a good idea to get lost in the maze of towns, villages and hamlets surrounding the peninsula. Étel, at the rivermouth of Rivière D'Étel, is one of those small villages to get your pain or charcuterie and practise doing next to nothing on a terrace. Check the easy-going, colourful fish-restaurant, oyster bar and hangout **Ché Luz (13)** overlooking the river. •€• •€€•

**a.** 1 Cours des Quais, 56410 Étel
**t.** 6 10 777 053

**Le Coota (14)** is the one of the best places to go out in this area. Live music, jam sessions, good vibes. Sam, the owner, is a musician, surfer, kiter. Since this place is close to a popular wind and kitesurf beach you will find quite a few of those around. Check the ceiling of Le Coota: on the white parts, all paid musicians who ever played here leave their signature, remark or drawing; on the black parts all the jam-musicians leave theirs. In summer there are jam sessions every Thursday and Saturday. Open every day from 17:00 hrs, in winter from Thursday to Sunday.

**a.** Kerhillio, 56410 Erdeven (on Boulevard D'Atlantique, near the entrance and parking of Kerhillio beach)

Taste or get your oysters-to-go from the Jenot family at **Tibidy Huitres (6)**, oyster cultivators since 1937.

**a.** 171 Rue du Pô, 56340 Carnac
**t.** 2 97 520 815
**w.** tibidy-huitres.com

At cocktail bar **La Baignoire Joséphine (6)** you'll find local surfers, sailors, singles and families alike. Lots of colours and wood, green plants, cosy in winter, shaded (terrace) in summer, you'll get that tropical vibe the moment your mojito is served. Situated right next to the tourist office.

**a.** 16 Allée des Alignements,
56340 Carnac

## SHOP

◆

**Markets**: every Friday morning in Plouharnel, small but excellent, mostly local products, free-range chicken, homemade kouign amann, oysters and seafood, at Place Général de Gaulle (the main square). Bio market: every Thursday afternoon in Auray, from 17:00 to 20:00 hrs on Place Notre Dame.

**ATS Surf Store (6)**: there are 3 surf stores under the Board Kulture umbrella, initiated by one of the first-generation surfers in Brittany. There are 2 in Plouharnel (see Surf section). The flagship store in Carnac is a lifestyle store and the place to check out clothes, accessories and brands like Patagonia, Rhythm, Lightning Bolt, Loreak Mendian, Breton-based Feal Mor (= 'true to the ocean' in Breton) and the very cool and creative stuff (clothes, art, cards, mugs) from local label Mersea People.

**a.** 40 Avenue des Druides, 56340 Carnac
**w.** board-kulture.com

## SLEEP

◆

**Campervans (15)**: Small camper parking, free, with facilities to empty your water/toilet, pay for water and electricity. Rue du Stade, in front of the Salle du Sports at Saint Pierre Quiberon.

Local seaside photographer **Laurent Vidal (2)** runs a light, spacious, and homely **Bed & Breakfast**, with terrace/garden and inspiring photos. Located conveniently near several beaches, surf spots, and within walking distance of shops and restaurants. •€•

**a.** 12 Rue de la Baie, 56340 Plouharnel
**t.** 6 80 623 270
**e.** photomer@laurentvidal.com
**w.** photomer.com

At **Le Petit Poisson Vert (16)**, between Lorient and Quiberon peninsula, you can either rent a cute and ecological house, a vintage caravan or T3 campervan. The house (2 to 4 persons) has an enclosed garden, and is decorated with lots of wood. The vintage camper is decorated in style, has an awning and outside kitchen, and sleeps up to 4 persons. The owners provide 3-course meals on reservation, made with love, and local and seasonal produce (also vegetarian). Open all year. •€• •€€•

**a.** 8 Kermaric, 56680 Plouhinec
**t.** 2 97 367 950
**e.** lepetitpoissonvert@gmail.com
**w.** lepetitpoissonvert.fr

**Camping Municipal de Kerhillio (17)** is a plain, simple, no fuss campsite right at the beach, in the middle of the dunes. Kerhillio is a popular kite and windsurf beach. Next to the campsite is a (paid) campervan parking. Open from June to September. •€•

**a.** Boulevard D'Atlantique, 56410 Erdeven
**t.** 2 97 556 923

**Les Ormeaux (18)** is a campsite at Kerhillio beach, but also rents out some Breton-style stone houses near the beach in Erdeven. From a 2 person studio to a 10 person renovated 'maison de caractère'. •€• •€€•

**t.** 2 97 556 757 / 6 07 196 878
**e.** ormeaux.lofficial@wanadoo.fr
**w.** lesormeaux.fr

**Camping à la Ferme (19)** is exactly what its name suggests: a campsite at a farm. There are 10 places for a caravan or campervan, in an enclosed green area, a hot shower and electricity, tout simple and extremely cheap in price, within walking distance of the centre of Plouharnel. Perfect option if you don't need any frou-frou, fuss or services, but like an intimate setting at the farm. Open from April to September.

**a.** Saint Guénahel (Voie Communale Saint Guenhaël), 56340 Plouharnel
**t.** 2 97 523 380 (Raymond)

**Camping de la Lande (20)**, in the same area, at the entrance to the peninsula, has place for 88 pitches and rents out mobile homes (4 persons). Open June to September (mobile homes from May). •€• •€€•

**a.** 3 Rue du Brahen, 56340 Plouharnel
**t.** 2 97 523 148
**w.** campingdelalande.com

# SURF

This area, even more so than the rest of France, loves to enforce height restrictions, so, prepare to walk a bit to your surf breaks and beaches if you're travelling in a bigger van.

**Guidel Plage** (**I**) (near Lorient) is a fairly consistent beachbreak that works best with w-sw swell. On your way from Finistère to Quiberon it's your best bet to find waves. All levels. Easy parking (also a small parking area for campervans, allowed to stay one night)/surf school/surf shop.

**Barre D'Étel** (**II**) is a beachbreak at the estuary of the Étel river, best at nw swell and low tide, has strong rips and currents and powerful left-breaking waves, not a spot for beginners. Enter from Étel. Intermediate and advanced level. Easy parking/shower.

**Kerhillio** (**III**), mostly known for its kite and windsurfing conditions, exposed, not a quality beachbreak, but a great backdrop of dunes, a cheap campsite right at the spot and close to Bar Coota. Best with small n-ne swell, at mid tide. All levels. Easy parking/campsite/restaurant/bar.

You can find surf spots all along the arc of the 10 km beach at Plouharnel, so if it feels too crowded for your taste, walk a bit further or park your car at the next spot. We name a few, from the north to the south, but really, it's a huge stretch of beach to explore all by yourself.

**Sainte Barbe** (**IV**), consistent, exposed beachbreak, usually you'll find a lot of longboards, fish or SUPs here, but don't mistake the big boards for beginner level, it's a favourite break for many excellent surfing locals. So, needless to say: respect is called for. Works best on small to medium w-sw swell at mid to high tide. All levels. Easy parking.

**La Guérite** (**V**), also known as 'tata beach'- you'll figure out what the tata stands for. Average west-facing beachbreak, consistent but exposed, best with small to medium nw-w-sw swell, works at all tides. All levels. Easy parking/surf school.

Photo: Marinus Joris

# SCHOOL RENTAL REPAIR

◆

**Côte Sauvage (VI)**: Along the coastal route to the town of Quiberon lies a 2 km stretch of cliffs, hiking paths, bays and inlets. It's one of the most well-known areas for surfing in south Brittany. Some spots and beaches will disappear completely at high tide, some will be surprisingly large at low tide, like the beach at Port Bara. The latter being easily accessible, therefore very popular. But especially at low tide the crowds spread out. Nice backdrop, pretty beach and short hollow rides galore. Works on small to medium w-sw swell, best at low to mid tide. Easy parking near breaks, although most limited (in summer) to 2m height. Vans can park at the side of the road.

Surf shop, shaper and school **ATS** (**2**) has 2 surf shops and an ESB surf school in Plouharnel (and one shop in Carnac, see Shop section). They offer board rental, surf lessons and surf camp. The shop on Avenue de L'Ocean has a 'secret' bar upstairs. It's a hangout for local surfers, a cool shop with friendly staff, that – besides the surf necessities – sells surf-related books, boards and some clothes (shirts and sweaters) from their own brand. Even if there's high demand, the shaper of Atao (which means Forever in the Breizh language) works on the boards just by himself, the brand wants to stay small like that and keep the soul, even if it means they can only provide about 120 boards a year.

**a.** 6 Avenue de L'Océan,
56340 Plouharnel
**w.** ecole-surf.com
**w.** board-kulture.com

# BRETON LOCAL RECIPE

### LA SUCRÉE/SALÉE

Chef and owner Yves, from La Clef de la Presqu'île, shared with us the recipe of his favourite galette: "La Sucrée/Salée". This makes for a great feast any time of the day... pre-surf breakfast, anyone?

### RECIPE FOR +/- 10 GALETTES

You can buy your galettes ready-made in a good Breton crêperie, or do-it-yourself.

### INGREDIENTS LA GALETTES

*200 grams Buckwheat Flour*
*0.5 litre of Water*
*Salt*

### INGREDIENTS LE FILLING

*Goats' cheese*
*(about 100 grams per person)*
*Bacon (2 slices per person)*
*Apple pieces cooked with butter and sugar*
*Just a little Honey*

### LES DIRECTIONS

- Mix the ingredients for the galette and let the mixture stand overnight
- After standing, add a little more water to the mix if necessary
- Cook the bacon and set aside
- Pour galette mixture to cover thinly a hot oiled pan, cook till golden on both sides
- Add the goats' cheese on top of the galette and let it melt
- Then add the bacon and apple pieces
- Finish with a drizzle of honey

*Fold just the sides of the galette over so the centre is open (it should look like a very pretty parcel), then eat up and enjoy!*

#ONLYTHECOMMITTED

Photo: Marinus Joris

# 1. BALANCE: TREE POSE

◆

*Vrksasana*

***Who doesn't want to have immense mental focus and a deep sense of calm throughout the day?***

*With balance poses you can create just that; as we try to balance, we naturally drop extraneous thoughts to focus on the task at hand. That's why this pose can instill a deep sense of calm through its requirement for intense, unwavering alertness. It's also an amazing pose to improve your surfing, which above any other skill, requires balance. As your board glides along moving ocean currents, you need to stay upright and centred in order to do the same!*

### *Benefits:*

*Mental & physical balance. Improves pelvic stability. Tones the muscles of the standing leg. Heightens focus, concentration, and sense of calm.*

### *How:*

*Stand with your feet together. Raise the right leg, and bend it at the knee. Put the foot as high on the inner thigh as possible and press it against the inner thigh - the foot and heel should press hard against the inner thigh. See if you can keep both hips level and move the inner top of bent leg back. Raise and straighten the arms above your head, hold the pose for a while. Then lower the leg and change sides.*

### *Note:*

*Protect your knee. Don't press your raised foot into the knee of the standing leg. If unable to lift it to your thigh, press it into your calf.*

ÎLE-DE-NOIRMOUTIER
2
D758
A83
CHALLANS
D753
Vendée
D948
8
A87
D38
D6
SAINT-GILLES-CROIX-DE-VIE
1,5,7
GRAND PLAGE (I)
3
LA ROCHE-SUR-YON
LA SAUZAIE (II)
D38
9
BRETIGNOLLES
6,10,24
A87
D160
LES DUNES (III)
BREM
4,13,14
SAUVETERRE (IV)
OLONNE-SUR-MER
20,26,27,28,39,40
LES SABLES-D'OLONNE
11,12,15,19,21,22,23,25
16
D949
BAIE DES SABLES (V)
29
17
LUÇO
JARD-SUR-MER
34,41
D105
LONGEVILLE (VI)
30,35
D746
TRANCHE-SUR-MER
31,32,36,37,42
18
D46
LA PHARE L'EMBARCADÈRE (VII)
ÎLE DE RÉ
LA ROCHE
33,38

# VENDÉE

Small villages with white or honey coloured stone houses are scattered along the Vendée seaside. As if it's a written law, all woodwork is ocean blue and green (in fact, woodwork from fishermen's houses used to be painted with the remainders of boat paints, which were blue and green). Vineyards and fields of maize and sunflowers divide clusters of houses and farms.

Vendée is miraculously overlooked by the surf hordes - although summer crowds tell you otherwise. It's not unknown to the surf world: international surf events are held at La Sauzaie. The beach and reef of Sauveterre are never deserted and the bay of Les Sables d'Olonne is well protected from north winds, and therefore a much sought-after spot. Summer is crazy, of course it is; Vendée being the second sunniest department of France, and holidaying families' paradise with adventure parks and zoos. But from the end of summer until the beginning of the next July, it's all still there, without the crowds. Vendée may be not as stylish as the French Basque coast, surfy-cool as Les Landes, or wild as Brittany, but it is as sweet and kind and beautiful as your imaginary French girlfriend.

# TRAVEL INFO

Infrequent bus services are run between some of the towns by sovetours.fr, regular services are run within the towns. From Nantes train station there are trains to Les Sables D'Olonne and Saint-Gilles-Croix-de-Vie.

## BY AIR

**Aéroport Nantes Atlantique**
located just outside the city's peripheral motorway ring road. Direct flights to most European destinations like UK, Ireland, Holland, Belgium, Germany, Spain and Portugal. The Navette Tan Air shuttles between airport and the train station of Nantes.

**w.** nantes.aeroport.fr

## BY TRAIN

**TGV Paris Montparnasse - Nantes**
(2 hrs)

**w.** voyages-sncf.com

# SURFER-TRAVELLER TYPE VENDÉE

*You're a pine forest wanderer, love long stretches of beach, and want to absorb as much sun as possible, are not afraid of crowds in summer, or are looking for a perfect uncrowded off season get-away, you're a canned Sardine adept, and like swallowing oysters with a tasty local wine.*

# VENDÉE FOOD FACTS

## SARDINES MILLÉSIMÉES

The Sardines Millésimées from Saint-Gilles-Croix-de-Vie are like a special vintage wine. They're caught in spring, selected for their colour and texture, cleaned and pickled. After they're dried the sardines are briefly baked in oil and dried again. The next day, head and tail are cut off and the fish bedded in a fruity olive oil, finding their new temporary homes in specially designed tins. Only after 6 months of ripening are they sold. Just like a good wine, the tins should be turned from time to time over the years. You can keep these sardines up to 10 years, and apparently, their taste only gets better and better. Since most of their tins have such artful design it almost feels like a waste to open them.

## LA SABLAISE

La Sablaise is a well-established family-run conserverie, situated near the port of Sables d'Olonne. It all started with a fish soup, prepared in the winter by chef and restaurant owner Gilles Martineau, it grew increasingly popular by demand, and was therefore preserved to be served in summer as well.

Apparently so delicious that he enlisted the help of his sons, who joined the business of selling the family recipe.

The Conserverie La Sablaise started its company with the soup in 1990 and now produce a range of seafood specialities, such as soups, rillettes, marinades and sauces. La Sablaise is known for traditionally working with fish from sustainable and regional fisheries and never adding colouring, thickeners, flavourings or preservatives. (That's why you'll also find La Sablaise products in the Biocoop, a biological supermarket chain in France).

# IN AND AROUND SAINT-GILLES-CROIX-DE-VIE

Originally two towns on either side of the river Vie, Saint-Gilles-sur-Vie (south) and Croix-de-Vie (north) joined in 1967 to form Saint-Gilles-Croix-de-Vie. The two are now connected at the Pont de la Concorde. Like many seaport towns, it owes its very existence to the ocean. In the Middle Ages, Saint-Gilles-sur-Vie became a hustling and bustling port, accommodating big ships. The Belle Époque villas in the area are a silent reminder of the wealthy owners and traders. The settlement of Croix-de-Vie on the other side of the estuary started around 1600, when fishermen were given plots of land and started building their homes. It expanded in the 19th century with the start of the fish canning process, and Croix-de-Vie became the first sardine harbour in France. The development of railways from the 1880s made it possible for holidaymakers from Nantes and Paris to reach the seaside town, and it really never stopped from there; making Saint-Gilles-Croix-de-Vie the popular seaside resort it is today.

**Tourist office** at Place de la Gare.

## TO DO

Check the surf on a morning stroll along the boulevard embracing **Grand Plage** (**1**) in Saint-Gilles-Croix-de-Vie, there're lots of restaurants, cafés and terraces to grab a bite. A large section of beach disappears with the rising tide, keep that in mind before you lay out your towel, work on your tan and fall asleep. Or walk further north around the dunes toward the fishing harbour and Comptoir de la Mer, at Place de la Gare (near the train station) to stock up on conserves.

Visiting **Île de Noirmoutier** (**2**) just north of Saint-Gilles-Croix-de-Vie makes for a great non-surfing day out. It has a very old-fashioned holiday-in-France feel to it, so make sure you drive a 2CV and bring your picnic basket.

It's connected with a bridge from the mainland, but, the key thing to get into the mood is by crossing to the island via Le Passage du Gois; in use since the 16th century, the causeway is just over 4 kms and is covered by up to 4 m of ocean at high tide. So, wait until low tide, or go within the 2 hours before or after. You can join the hordes of shellfish collectors, either digging up their own meal or selling their harvest to restaurants. There are rules

Photo: Mannus Joris

and quotas for this, so if you decide to join in, ask the local tourist office first. You'll notice what happens when people are too slow and don't make it to the end in time – their cars stranded on the causeway as the tide comes up. From the Chateau de Noirmoutier you'll have a view over the island's salt pans, low-lying fields and marshes, or granite cliffs to the north. But save the best for sunset: Plage des Dames. A wooden jetty, beach huts and a lighthouse; if there were waves here it would come pretty close to the perfect seaside escape.

**Le Grand Défi, Forest Adventure (3)** is what its name implies, an adventure park in the forest and a great way to treat energetic kids to some climbing, zip-lining and treetop trailing. There are 20 courses, from toddler safe to extremely difficult. Open all year.

**a.** 40 Rue de l'Étoile,
85150 Saint Julien des Landes
**t.** 2 51 987 902
**w.** grand-defi.com

Wine tasting, get a small tour of the process or buy your wines directly from the vineyard of **Laurent Pajot (4)**. In 1953 his great granddad, Jean Pajot, created this family-run vineyard, with white and rosé wines on offer. Open all year, closed on Tuesday and Friday mornings between June and September (you'll find Laurent with his wines on those days at the market in Brem-sur-Mer).

**a.** 68 Rue Croix Pénard,
85470 Brem-sur-Mer
**t.** 6 17 702 793
**w.** laurentpajot.free.fr

## EAT/DRINK/HANGOUT

◆

Some places stand out in a crowd, especially a crowd of 'pretty much the same', as is the case with bars and restaurants on the boulevard of Grand Plage. **Bar Theo Spot (5)** offers drinks and tapas in the cool décor of wooden tables, vintage furniture and a terrace with seaview. Open all year from 15:30 hrs, closed on Monday and Tuesday. •€•

**a.** 6 bis Place Rochebonne,
85800 Saint-Gilles-Croix-de-Vie
(in a side street at the north end of the boulevard)

**Le Spot (6)**, one of the nicest hangouts around, and with the same owner as Theo Spot in Saint-Gilles-Croix-de-Vie, has a killer view of the ocean and sunset. Big terrace with chairs and benches made from scrap wood and comfy pillows. They serve freshly prepared cocktails, some snacks, and in summer there's live music, with an ocean-minded vibe all around. Open from April to September. •€•

**a.** 1 Avenue de l'Océan,
Plage de la Parée,
85470 Bretignolles-Sur-Mer

## SHOP

◆

**Markets in Saint-Gilles-Croix-de-Vie**: Throughout the year, fresh local produce on offer, every Tuesday, Thursday and Sunday morning, in Place du Vieux Port. Every Wednesday and Saturday morning, in Place Guy Kergoustain (on the Croix-de-Vie side of the river). Evening markets are held in July and August.

For your healthy variation on the daily French breakfast of coffee and cigarettes, get your wholesome food at Biological supermarket **Bio Monde** (**7**).

**a.** 77 Boulevard de L'Egalité,
85800 Saint-Gilles-Croix-de-Vie
(at the Port La Vie)

## SLEEP

◆

A few of Vendée's many castles have been rebuilt as hotels. You can pretend to be chatelaine at **Château des Bretonnières sur Vie** (**8**), a castle from the 19th century, in a calm environment with 4 very different, classic but characteristic suites. Open May till mid-September. •€€• •€€€•

**a.** Route de Coëx, Hameau de Vie,
85220 Commequiers
**t.** 2 51 392 936 / 6 62 175 801
**e.** chateaudevie@wanadoo.fr
**w.** chateaudevie.wix.com/chateaudevie

Indulge in the manor manner at **Manoir de l'Eolière** (**9**). This 1885 country house is situated in the forests behind Brétignolles-sur-Mer, has 3 beautifully decorated comfortable rooms, each with their own terrace. Dutch, French and English are spoken. Open April to October. •€€€•

**a.** 85220 Landevieille
**t.** 2 51 336 983 / 6 32 316 685
**w.** manoir-eoliere.fr

Combining traditional architecture with up-to-date knowledge of eco-construction, the owners of **La Ferme du Marais Girard** (**10**) created wooden villa-pontoons and apartments in an old farm, using as many sustainable materials as possible. They also have organic veggies and fruit for sale, and run La Comptoir, an épicerie with a spacious teashop attached, offering home-made biological products, drinks, food and cakes, decorated with straw bales, and a sunny terrace outside. Open all year, (Le Comptoir opens only in July and August). •€€• •€€€•

**a.** 116 Rue du Marais Girard,
85470 Bretignolles-sur-Mer
**t.** 2 51 330 870 / 6 11 733 99
**e.** contact@lafermedumaraisgirard.fr
**w.** lafermedumaraisgirard.fr

# IN AND AROUND LES SABLES D'OLONNES

Like so many popular coastal towns, Les Sables d'Olonnes seems locked in fierce battle between old grandeur versus fast (tourist) money. Dull apartment buildings are squashed between characteristic and colourful houses. Its attraction as a seaside resort for the well-to-do from Nantes and Paris grew with the arrival in 1880 of the same train that dropped tourists at Saint-Gilles-Croix-de-Vie. The more you move away from the boulevard, by the way, the prettier the town gets.

## TO DO

**Festival Yoga du Monde (11)** is a yearly 3-day yoga festival, usually held on the final weekend of August, you can join in different styles of yoga classes, meditation, conferences, enjoy music and food – veggie of course.

**a.** Centre de Congrès Les Atlantes, 1 Promenade M. Joffre, 85100 Les Sables d'Olonne
**t.** 2 51 953 771
**w.** yogadumonde-festival.com

**The Spa at the Atlantic Hotel (12)** has a jacuzzi, hammam, infra-red sauna, ice fountain to seriously cool down, a sensory shower and a tearoom. The spa is accessible for both hotel guests and visitors, but it's advisable to book in advance. Open all year.

**a.** 5 Promenade Godet, 85100 Les Sables d'Olonne
**t.** 2 51 953 771

In the midst of the Marais (wetlands), **La Cabane (13)** found the most perfect setting for an oyster and wine bar. In a renovated shed, with a large wooden terrace on a waterway, overlooking even more waterways and low-lying fields, they've done an excellent job in creating a place you want to hang out, relax, watch the sun set with a locally brewed La Cabaude beer in hand, or sip an oyster and swallow your wine in one go. Or the other way around, doesn't matter, it's all cool. Some afternoons there's live music. But, before you start getting too comfy on the cushions in the sun, join one of the SUP tours through the wetlands and to the sea, rent a kayak, or catch your own fish from a canoe, from Octosup, stationed at La Cabane. Open during holiday season.

**a.** Chemin de la Ch'noue, (it's signposted from the main road) 85470 La Chabossière à Brem Sur Mer
**t.** 6 76 700 460
**w.** lacabane-brem.fr

Contact for **Octosup**:

**t.** 6 62 812 724
**w.** ecoledestanduppaddle.fr

**Horse and pony riding (14)** through the wetlands, the forest, or along the beaches with Ecurie du Bois de la Touche. Open all year, preferably by reservation.

**a.** La Rigordière, 85470 Brem-sur-Mer
**t.** 7 70 108 885
**e.** ecurieduboisdelatouche@live.fr

**Les Salines (15)**: Discover the Marais d'Olonne by kayak, SUP, or by boat tour, with a history course about the process of salt mining, and the option to make your own sea-salt (or more conveniently, buy it from the boutique). Open from April to October.

**a.** 120 Route de l'Aubraie,
85100 Les Sables D'Olonne
**t.** 2 51 210 119
**w.** lessalines.fr

**La Folie de Finfarine (16)**, house of the bee and honey. Learn about how the bees live and how honey is made. There's a museum, bee garden, shop, exhibitions, and possibility to observe the bees. Open from April to October.

**a.** Chemin des Écoliers, 85440 Poiroux
**t.** 2 51 962 250
**w.** finfarine.fr

**Château des Aventuriers (17)** is a fantasy park for kids, with interactive and educational games (translated into English, German and Dutch) with themes like dinosaurs and pre-history, pirates or secrets of the castle. Open April to September.

**a.** Route des Sables d'Olonnes,
85440 Avrillé
**t.** 2 51 223 306
**w.** chateau-aventuriers.com

On a flat, or surfed-out day, you can treat your body and mind to some 'bien-être' at **Zen Au Marais (18)**. At the same secluded nature area as eco-lodge Dormir Ben'aise, you'll find a beauty of a **Hammam** and all kind of massages and treatments to choose from: Traditional, Ayurvedic, Thai, and Kobido (Japanese facial).

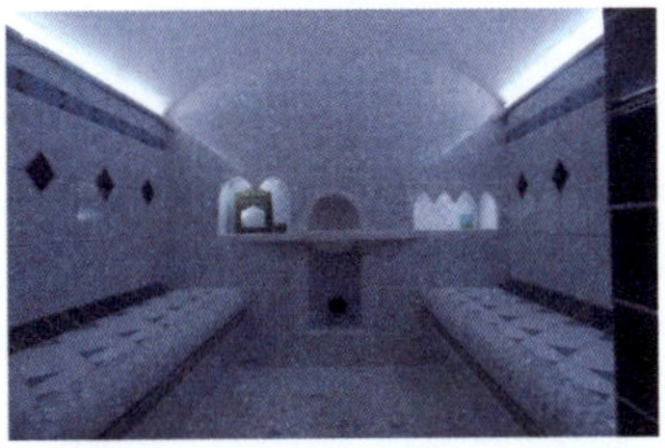

Massages are done with biological essential oils. Top it off with a tea, or champagne, whatever the mood dictates. Open all year, preferably by reservation.

**a.** La Polterie, 85420 Maillezais
**t.** 2 51 872 642 / 6 43 884 829
**e.** contact@zenaumarais.fr
**w.** zenaumarais.fr

## EAT/DRINK/HANGOUT

◆

**Sombras Café (19)** is right at the boulevard, looking out over the ocean. On the menu are coffees, smoothies, bagels, muffins, to go or enjoy on the terrace. Their cool décor stands out from among the other cafés along the boulevard. Open all year, closed on Monday, (at the time of updating this guide, Sombras Café was negotiating a new location on or near the boulevard, so the following address may change). •€• •€€•

**a.** 21 Promenades Georges
Clemenceau,
85100 Les Sables d'Olonne
**w.** sombras.fr

Between Sables d'Olonne and Brem-sur-Mer, a bit inland, spread over 32 hectares, bordering the salt marshes of Pays des Olonnes, you'll find the family-run vineyard **Organic Cave Michon (20)**. Don't you just love your wine being all natural; Cave Michon uses only vegetable, animal and mineral-based mixtures for their vines and wines. Open all year, Monday to Friday.

**a.** La Croix Bégaud,
85340 L' Île d'Olonne
**t.** 2 51 331 304
**w.** domainesaintnicolas.com

## SHOP

◆

Daily fresh **market** at Marché des Halles Centrales, Rue des Halles, 85100 **Les Sables d'Olonne**.

Make your own creations or buy handmade colourful jewellery and small decorations at **Atelier-Boutique Espeleta (21)**. "We make creations of our fantasy and colourful jewellery, decorations and unique raku poterie. But you can also learn how to do it yourself in one of our workshops, or place a personalised order," says Sandra Tiberghien of Espeleta. Open all year from Wednesday to Saturday, July and August open every day.

**a.** 29 Rue des Halles,
85100 Les Sables d'Olonne
**t.** 2 53 819 240
**w.** espeleta.fr

**ElMar (32)**, seaside-stylish shop with a lot of urban and surf-related brands; like Rhythm, Poler, Amuse and Deus. You'll find clothes, accessories and funny items, like deer-shaped candles for Christmas. Open all year, closed on Tuesday.

**a.** 48 Promenade Georges Clemencau, 85100 Les Sables d'Olonne
**w.** elmar-shop.com

**Le Lab Sablais (33)**, designs inspired by the very seaport town in which they are created, like the lights above sea, the fishermen's boats and the lighthouse. Mostly known for its barcode-striped shirts with the longitudes of French (seaside) towns on it, the shop offers a constantly changing supply of creative items. Open all year.

**a.** 38 Boulevard de Castelnau, 85100 Les Sables d'Olonne

**Les Trois Fillettes (34)** is the work of a local textile creator of home-made colourful aprons, bags, table decorations, pen cases, book covers, plaids. She has a shop at home, opening times can vary, depending on the season (or open by reservation).

**a.** 7 Rue Montée de la Pierre, 85470 Brétignolles-sur-Mer
**t.** 6 10 104 285
**w.** lestroisfillettes.com

## SLEEP

◆

Bed and Breakfast **Maison L'Épicurienne (35)**, offers 5 rooms with distinctively different décor, in a renovated 1920s villa in a small side street off the main boulevard. Seems everything is designed and done to please the guests: a generous breakfast buffet, room for your surfboards and bicycles, or use of bicycles, DVDs. The only thing you have to do, and it can be a bit of a mission, is choose between the stylish rooms. Open all year. •€€•

**a.** 9 Rue Villebois Mareuil, 85100 Les Sables d'Olonne
**t.** 6 71 848 937
**e.** contact@maisonlepicurienne.fr
**w.** maisonlepicurienne.fr

**Oasis Residence Sauveterre (36)** rents out 3 houses (1 for 4-6 persons / 1 for 6-8 persons / 1 for 8-10 persons). Available all year. •€€•

**a.** 21 Route de la Mer, 85340 Olonne-sur-Mer
**t.** 2 51 201 313
**e.** contact@oasis-sauveterre.com
**w.** oasis-sauveterre.com

The lodges of **Octopus House (37)** are set in a big garden, with lots of wood and surfy interiors. Close to Plage des Granges. There's Makaha for 6 persons, perfect for families; Nahoon for 2 persons; and the lodge for 2 persons. Available all year. •€• •€€•

**a.** Route des Amis de la Nature, La Citadelle, 85340 Olonne-Sur-Mer
**t.** 6 62 812 724
**w.** octopusglisse.com

**Domaine Les Rousselières (38)** has a small campsite, 5 gîtes (2 to 10 persons), 3 mobile homes, and a 2-person chambre d'hôtes. All have access to a small heated swimming pool, a pony called Pilou, and if you should happen to bring your horse along... he's welcome too! Gîtes are available all year, campsite, pool and chambre d'hôtes are open from May 15 to September 15. •€•

**a.** 85340 Olonne-sur-Mer
**t.** 2 51 953 308 / 6 44 306 240 (Véronique et Dominique Mandret)
**e.** dv.mandret@wanadoo.fr
**w.** lesrousselieres.com

**Chambre d'Hotes Dormir Ben 'Aise (18)**, is an eco-responsible escape in the middle of the countryside and marshland. From breakfast to toilet, it's all within an ecological nature-friendly system. •€•

**a.** La Polterie, 85420 Maillezais
**t.** 2 51 872 642 / 6 43 884 829 (Cécile Viennot)
**e.** contact@dormirbenaise.fr
**w.** dormirbenaise.fr

# IN AND AROUND TRANCHE-SUR-MER

Tranche-sur-Mer is a busy summer town, the centre not quite as charming as the outskirts or the beach, but if you look closely you'll find a few nice places to hang out, shop or eat. First check out the **Tourist Office** on Place de la Liberté, it's big, very well stocked and friendly, they even have a bowl of water for your dog.

## TO DO

Of the many **hiking** opportunities in the area, we liked the path that starts from the parking at Plage de la Mine at Saint-Nicolas. It leads you through the forest, along fields of sunflowers, towards Pointe du Payré at the estuary of Le Payré. You can check the surf from here, and if there is any, either choose to walk all the way back and forth with your board or drive all the way round to Plage du Veillon. This is the huge beach at the other side you'll see from the point.

**Plage du Veillon** (**39**) is a popular beach in summer with lots of parking space, a shaded picnic area, a crêperie, playground for kids, surf school, beach bar, mini golf, and a beach library with books and newspapers. Some people prefer to swim or cool off in the estuary rather than the ocean, you can walk towards the banks of the estuary from the beach.

If it's a windy day, you can go sand-sailing at low tide at the Plage de la Terriere, contact **Aerobeach** (**20**).

**t.** 6 71 310 885
**w.** aerobeach-charavoile.com

Bicycle rentals from **Bien Eric** (**40**).

**a.** 23 Rue des Sables,
85360 La Tranche-sur-Mer
**t.** 6 50 124 752

## EAT/DRINK/HANGOUT

A great place to do your shopping is **Jard-sur-Mer**, and especially on Monday, market day. The centre of town is exactly what you expect of a traditional French town. You can skip the supermarkets on your way down, take out your bags and fill them with pastries from the boulangerie, fresh legumes and seasonal fruits at the market, poultry or meat from the charcuterie. Just about everybody knows everybody in town, so do take your time shopping, and polish up your French while listening in on all the conversations about weather, local politics, newborn babies and health enquiries about family members.

On the main square in the centre of **La Tranche-sur-Mer (41)** you'll find a few wooden shacks with terraces, one housing a Sushi Bar, another offering oysters, and Le Spoon, where there are cocktails on the menu; open from April to September.

**a.** 1 Place de la Liberté,
85360 La Tranche-sur-Mer

At restaurant **La Cantine (41)** you can enjoy good quality burgers, tapas, curry, and moules et frites for a fair price, in a non-pretentious setting.

**a.** 3 Rue Aristide Briand,
85360 La Tranche sur Mer

Opposite restaurant La Cantine is a bar, simply called **Bar (21)**, a laid-back hangout for locals and tourists alike.

Another place for drinks or chill-out in big leather couches and watch a game on one of the big screens is **Starfish & Coffee (41)** (yes, like that Prince song), friendly staff, live music, late night beers.

**a.** 34 Avenue Maurice Samson,
85360 La Tranche-sur-Mer

A good place for easy but delicious bites, just opposite the Starfish & Coffee bar, is **restaurant Stefiouz (41)**. •€•

**a.** 41 bis Avenue Maurice Samson,
85360 La Tranche-sur-Mer
**t.** 6 76 827 899

**Le Blue Mob (41)**, 'sympà' tapas bar and restaurant with terrace, friendly staff and some live music. Open from February to October. •€• •€€•

**a.** 26 bis Avenue Maurice Samson,
85360 La Tranche-sur-Mer
**t.** 9 81 191 819

**Le Panier de Mr Auguste (41)** is a small, popular oyster bar and seafood restaurant, go here for some delicious grilled sardines, fruits de mer or moules à la plancha. Open from April to September. •€• •€€•

**a.** 2 Rue du Maupas,
85360 La Tranche-sur-Mer
**t.** 7 70 653 913

At sunset, if you move down to Plage du Corps de Garde, you'll find winebar **La Case d'Elo (42)**, where you can plant your feet in the sand and enjoy a menu of oysters, local Vendée dishes, some live music, and dance until far beyond sundown. Open in summer from 10:30 till midnight.

**a.** Plage du Corps de Garde,
Quartier du Phare,
85360 La Tranche sur Mer
**t.** 6 61 012 647

## SHOP

**Gaia Natura (41)** sells beautifully wrapped, French fifties-style biological and natural cosmetics.

**a.** 22 Avenue de la Plage,
85360 La Tranche-sur-Mer

On your way down south, from Vendée to Les Landes, give yourself a treat and stop for a look – or to pick up your pre-ordered board – at **UWL Surfboards Surf Shop (43)**. With an area of 700m2 it's one of the biggest European surfboard manufacturer's. They've got stock or custom surfboards, and collaborations with international influential and creative guest shapers at the UWL workshop. Open Monday to Saturday.

**a.** ZAC des Fourneaux,
3 Rue Albert Denis,
17690 Angoulins-Sur-Mer,
Poitou-Charentes
**t.** 5 46 270 027
**w.** uwl-surfboards.com

## SLEEP

**Jard Vacances (44)** has 4 apartments, 1 studio, 2 gîtes, a camper parking area and swimming pool. Open all year. •€€•

**a.** 2 Chemin des Combes,
85520 Jard sur Mer
**t.** 2 51 203 519 / 6 20 104 525
(Eric and Laure Lemesle)
**e.** info@jardvacances.com
**w.** jardvacances.com

Photo: Marinus Jons

Between the many, many **campsites** in Vendée with dizzying entertainment, endless slides and large pools and what-nots, tranquil and traditional campsites are a breath of fresh air. The following campsites have just that on offer:

**Camping les Ramiers (45)**. Open from April to September. •€• •€€•

**a.** 10 Chemin des Pins,
Les Conches, 85560 Longeville Sur Mer
**t.** 2 51 333 221 / 6 09 862 204
**e.** accueil@campinglesramiers.com
**w.** campinglesramiers.com

**Camping le Pacific (46)** is a calm, shady campsite with 20 pitches, 6 mobile homes and 2 caravans to rent. Open April 01 to October 15. •€• •€€•

**a.** 3 Chemin de la Pacifique,
la Terrière, 85360 La Tranche-sur-Mer
**t.** 2 51 300 738
**w.** campingpacific.com

**Camping La Grande Vallée (47)** is a tranquil campsite despite its 61 pitches and 9 mobile homes for rent. Located just 700 m from the beach, with family-friendly entertainment, like petanque competitions. The free transport 'Fun Bus' stops here frequently to drop you off into town or at other beaches. Open April to September. •€• •€€•

**a.** Plage la Griére, 145 Boulevard du Marechal de Lattre de Tassigny,
85360 La Tranche-sur-Mer
**t.** 2 51 301 282
**e.** c.lagrandevallee@orange.fr
**w.** campinglagrandevallee.com

**Camping Le Verger (48)** is a good option if you're coming from, or on your way down south towards Les Landes. It's a small campsite in an idyllic nature setting, run by the very friendly and welcoming couple Catherine and Sylvain. As they say themselves, in that sweet French accent, "Here every people says good morning, enquires each other of what they have done, and we spend a lot of time to help them to discover the area. That is nice job for us, we are not business men, we have people visiting us in our garden, that's all." There are 25 pitches, 2 fully furnished gypsy caravans and 1 safari tent in an orchard where you can pick your seasonal fruit. You can rent bicycles and there's a small grocery store. Open from the end of June to the beginning of September. •€•

**a.** 27, Jean Pierre Pigot,
17139 Dompierre sur Mer
**t.** 5 46 349 100
**e.** contact@campingleverger17.com
**w.** campingleverger17.com

Photo: Geert-Jan Middelkoop

# SURF

From crowded beachbreaks, to fast hollow reefs, to secret spots, **Vendée** has surf potential aplenty. The secrets we leave to your own exploring.

The beachbreak at **Grand Plage, Saint-Gilles-Croix-de-Vie** (**I**), can have fun and fast waves, in summer you'll have plenty onlookers from the boulevard and beach. Not the best break around and can be crowded, but then again, it's a big bay and if you go further south, urbanisation and crowds thin out. More consistent than most beaches around, so a good place to check when everywhere else is either closing out or flat. Works in small to medium nw-w-sw swell, holds bigger swells, but the paddle out is a bit of a nightmare. Works in all tides. Big part of the beach disappears at high tide, descending can be tricky. All levels. Parking (a bit of a hassle in summer)/ restaurants/bars/surf school.

**La Sauzaie** (**II**) in Bretignolles-sur-Mer is a powerful, hollow pointbreak reef with tubular sections, which used to be a WQS contest site, and is still a contest site for National and International surf contests. So, fair to say it's not a beginner break - the level of surfing at this break is high and competitive. Due to its location, along the coastal road that runs through Bretignolles-sur-Mer, it's perfect to watch or photograph the surf, sitting on the rocks, looking down on the break. Starts working in swells from 1 m to bigger, nw-w-sw swells, all tides except low. Advanced level. Easy parking / restaurants / bars.

**Les Dunes** (**III**), beachbreak near the summer resort Brem-sur-Mer. It's a large stretch of beach, with some seaweed covered stones and reef at low tide, where people sometimes collect shellfish. Easily accessible, also easily blown out, but a good option for learning or trying to advance. Works at all tides, but tends to close out at high tide or when it's too big, small to medium w-sw swell. Easy parking/surf school/ restaurants/campsites.

**Sauveterre** (**IV**) is one of the most beautiful spots in the area. Surrounded by the Olonne woods, backed by dunes and an endless stretch of beach. The further you move away from the big parking area, the quieter it gets. Easily blown out, works in all tides, small to medium nw-w-sw swell, the reef can handle some size. Beachbreak: all levels. Reef: intermediate and advanced level. Easy parking/bar/toilet/surf school in summer/campsites.

**Baie des Sables (V)**, the city bay of Les Sables d'Olonnes, is a beachbreak that serves as a refuge in strong northern winds or big swells, because of its protected location. As with most of Vendée's well-known spots, it's crowded in summer, but the rest of the season is fine. Works with (and is protected from) big n swells and in small to medium sw swell, all tides. All levels. Parking can be a bit of a hassle/bars/restaurants/surf school.

The beachbreaks at **Longeville-sur-Mer (VI)**, Les Conches, Bud-Bud and La Terrière, are well known to locals and travelling surfers alike, some wild camping is done off-season in the woods just behind Bud-Bud. This is also the perfect break if you like a short hollow and fast wave, of course depending on the sandbanks. The long stretch of beach, backed by dunes, is inviting for hikes, and the rewards are less crowds and quiet beaches. Depending on sandbanks, works in all tides, from small to medium nw-w-sw swell. All levels. Easy parking/toilets in summer/surf school/campsites.

**Le Phare du Grouin du Cou (VII)** and **L'Embarcadère** (that's the name of the pier) are the main surf breaks of La Tranche sur Mer. The pier is a popular and usually crowded spot when it's working. The wave's fast but is long and stays open, so it's a good spot to work on your manoeuvres; that is, if you get the chance to catch a wave - the take-off zone is très, très small. You can either paddle or walk back towards the take-off zone at the pier. All tides except high. The lighthouse, a bit to the north, works in a similar way, with long rides. Both spots need a big w-sw swell to work properly. The lighthouse has a rocky bottom, all tides except low. Intermediate level. Easy parking/surf school.

# SCHOOL RENTAL REPAIR

◆

**Octopus Glisse** (**49**), surf, SUP, wave-ski, knee-board, bodyboard, lessons and rental.

**a.** Plage de Granges, La Cachere, 85340 Olonne-sur-Mer
**t.** 6 62 812 724
**w.** octopusglisse.com

**Ohana Surf School** (**50**), surf, bodyboard, school and rental. Open from April to October.

**a.** Plage de Sauveterre, 85340 Olonne-sur-Mer
**t.** 6 87 449 531
**w.** ohanasurf.net

**Duke Surf and SUP** (**51**), surf, SUP, bodyboard, lessons and rental, only small groups, up to 8. Open in season.

**a.** Plage du Grand Boisvinet, entrée n°16, 85520 Jard-Sur-Mer
**t.** 6 51 436 379
**w.** dukesurfschool.com

**Koa Surf School** (**52**), surf, SUP, bodyboard, lessons and rental.

**a.** Plage de la Terrière, La Tranche-sur-Mer
**t.** 6 12 572 951
**w.** koasurfschool.com

Photo: Melchior van Nigtevecht

CHASSIRON
(I)
2,17
SAINT-DENIS D'OLÉRON
LA BRÉE-LES-BAINS
6
LES
BOULASSIERS
(II)
LES HUTTES
(III)
24,25
D734
SAINT-GEORGES D'OLÉRON
D126
5
11,12,20,21,22
D734
D274
SAINT-PIERRE D'OLÉRON
1,7,14,16,28
D126
D274
D734
23
Île d'Oléron
DOLUS D'OLÉRON
3,9,15,18
LE CHÂTEAU D'OLÉRON
13
D26
VERT BOIS
(IV)
LES ALLASSINS
(IV)
LE-GRAND-VILLAGE-PLAGE
4,27
D26
D126
SAINT-TROJAN-LES-BAINS
8,10,14,19,26

# ÎLE D'OLÉRON

Most of the 22 thousand inhabitants of the island of Oléron are fishermen, oyster farmers, wine-makers, or entertain tourists in one way or another. Connected with the mainland by a 3 km+ toll-free bridge, the island's population obviously increases during holidays, especially in summer, as it's a popular summer destination for many French and other European tourists.

## SURFER-TRAVELLER TYPE ÎLE D'OLÉRON

*You like coloured huts, fish, oysters, and quiet country roads, or don't mind getting stuck in tourist traffic, love family-focused to-dos and go-tos, and patiently waiting for a big winter swell to hit the coast of France so you can surf those protected spots of the island.*

## TRAVEL INFO

Bring your bicycle! You can avoid being annoyed and getting stuck in summer traffic.

### BY AIR

The **nearest airport** is La Rochelle-Île de Ré, 2,5 km northwest of La Rochelle. Direct flights to and from UK, Belgium, Germany, Portugal, Italy and Ireland. Regular bus service to Rochelle centre.

**a.** Rue du Jura, 17000 La Rochelle
**w.** larochelle.aeroport.fr

### BY TRAIN & BUS

From Paris Montparnasse there's a **train** to La Rochelle (3 hrs). From here you can catch the **bus** to the island, usually just two a day. The buses stop in Le Chateau and Saint-Pierre.

**Timetables for the train:**
**w.** voyages-sncf.com

**Timetables for the bus:**
**w.** lesmouettes-transports.com

### BY FERRY

There's a small, fast **ferry** running between La Rochelle and Boyardville on Île d'Oléron (50 mins).

**Info:**
**w.** oleron-larochelle.com

# IN AND AROUND ÎLE D'OLÉRON

◆

More of a family-vacation-station than a surfers hotspot, but Île d'Oléron does have a few beaches and reefs attracting the growing tribe of wave riders. You'll never be more than a half hour (car) drive away from anything on the 20 km long island, so you can explore a few spots quickly before deciding where to go in.

## TO DO

◆

With over 170 kms of bike paths, biking seems like an excellent option to discover the island. **Velos 17 (1)** rents out bicycles from 6 locations throughout the island. Delivery at your address is possible with a 7-day booking. Open all year.

**a.** 111 Avenue de Bel Air, 17310 Saint-Pierre-D'Oléron (main address)
**t.** 5 46 471 405
**w.** velo17loisirs.com

From the top of **Chassiron Lighthouse (2)** at the extreme north of the island you'll have a view over the island, the Atlantic Ocean, Île de Ré, Île d'Aix and the city on the mainland, La Rochelle. The lighthouse stretches 46 metres into the sky, and you can walk the 224 steps all the way up. From the lighthouse there are hiking trails leading west and south along the rocky coastline. You'll see les écluses, stone wall fishing traps from the 14th century, amongst the reefs.

**Yoga et Bien-être à l'Île d'Oléron (3)** offers (English spoken) yoga classes & workshops; on a SUP, in a Mongolian yurt (in Dolus), or Element Yoga on the beach (in Gatseau, l'Écuissière, Boyardville and l'Ileau). For all classes, locations and updates it's best to check their Facebook page (Yoga-à-la-Plage-à-l'île-dOléron). Open from June to September.

**a.** 39 Route du Stade, 17550 Dolus-d'Oléron
**t.** 7 86 295 208
**w.** yogaoleron.com

With **Oléron SUP (4)** you'll explore the marais (marshland), channels, baie de Gatseau, fortifications of Vauban and Citadelle du Château d'Oléron. You can either join a calm water tour or learn to ride waves on a SUP.

**a.** 33 Rue des Aires, 17370 Le Grand-Village-Plage
**t.** 6 19 694 349
**w.** oleron-sup.fr

SUP, kayak or canoe (2-3 persons or 2 persons and 2 kids), through the marais and past oyster farms on a 3 to 5 hr tour with **Aloha Canoe Oléron (5)**. By reservation, leaving 1 to 1,30 hrs before high tide, moving with the tides. Open from April to October.

**a.** Chenal de la Perotine, La Saurine (entre Boyardville et Sauzelle) D126, 17190 Saint-Georges-d'Oléron
**t.** 6 61 697 578
**w.** aloha-canoe-oleron.com

## EAT/DRINK/HANGOUT

◆

Crêperie by day, bar in the evening, club at night, **Les Ecluses** (**6**) has drinks, pancakes, free outdoor concerts and DJ sets on the menu.

**a.** Forêt du Douhet,
17840 La Brée-les-Bains
**t.** 5 46 765 637

**Vignoble Favre et Fils** (**7**) is a family-run vineyard, dedicated to organic wine cultivation. Not only wines, also Cognac, Pineau des Charentes (local aperitif) and liqueurs on offer. Open all year. Guided tours of the cellar; every Thursday at 10:30 during high season.

**a.** Village La Fromagerie,
17310 Saint-Pierre-d'Oléron
**t.** 5 46 470 543

Seafood restaurant **Le Bout au Vent** (**8**) sits at the end of the harbour in an old cabana, with a view of the bridge, open waters and oyster farms. Open all year. •€•

**a.** Quai Antony Dubois,
17370 Saint-Trojan-les-Bains
**t.** 5 46 760 543

Restaurant **Maha Prana** (**9**) serves biological, Indian and other food, according to season, garden grown and, très important, their (good) mood. •€• •€€•

**a.** 20 Route du Large, Vert Bois,
17550 Dolus-d'Oléron
**t.** 5 46 753 837

**La Villa Marthe** (**10**) is an artisanal charcuterie and 'traiteur' since 1958, located in a characteristic 1911 house near the Port de la Côtinière. You can either buy their products or enjoy them in the garden behind the house, served on wooden boards and accompanied by locally produced lemonade, wine and bread. •€€•

**a.** 35 Rue du Port, La Cotinière,
17310 Saint-Pierre-d'Oléron
**t.** 9 50 231 644

Small wooden **Snack "A l'Ouest"** (**11**) sits right on the beach, often there's live music on offer. Home-made snacks from local produce.
Open April to September. •€•

**a.** Grande Plage de Domino,
17190 Saint-Georges-d'Oléron
**t.** 6 22 200 300

**Restaurant le Grain de Sable** (**12**) is part of Hotel la Petite Plage. The (very child-friendly) restaurant uses local, organic and seasonal products.•€• •€€•

**a.** 839 Rue de l'Océan, Domino,
17190 Saint-Georges-d'Oléron
**t.** 5 46 765 228

## SHOP

◆

At **Couleurs Cabanes** (**13**), over 30 creative craftsmen and artists blend in perfectly amongst the oyster farmers at the oyster port. They're situated in colourful, wooden ateliers. Walk around, admire, or better yet, purchase some of their work, fresh from their creative hands. Expositions and music events are held regularly.

**a.** Avenue du Port, Le Château-d'Oléron
**t.** 6 89 712 569
**w.** couleurs-cabanes.fr

**Ateliers Retour de Plage** (**14**) is a local manufacturer of beach and seaside inspired jewellery. The two ateliers are situated in former oyster cabanas at different addresses.

**a.** Le Port, 1 Quai Raoul Coulon, 17370
Saint-Trojan-les-Bains and
2 Rue du Général de Gaulle,
17310 Saint-Pierre-d'Oléron
**t.** 5 46 764 293 / 5 46 763 317
**w.** retourdeplage.fr

**Tamarindo Surf & Coffee Shop (15)**: Boards, second-hand and new, rental of boards, skate and surf wear, also rents out bicycles and serves as a friendly hangout with a coffee corner. Open all year.

**a.** Bois de Bussac, RD 734,
17550 Dolus-d'Oléron
**t.** 5 46 751 068

**Cocoa Gliss & Co (16)** has clothes, skate and surf wear and boards. Open all year.

**a.** Avenue du Général LeClerc,
17310 Saint-Pierre-d'Oleron
**t.** 5 46 761 981
**w.** cocoagliss.com

## SLEEP

◆

**Camping Le Chassiron (17)** is a small family-friendly campsite at the foot of the Phare de Chassiron, 300 metres from the sea, quiet and peaceful setting. Some exotic places to spend your nights in: besides 5 Roulottes (circus caravans) for 2 to 8 persons, there's a yacht (yes, really, anchored on a piece of land) and a vintage silver Airstream caravan. Open from February to December. •€•

**a.** 17 Rue des Pérots,
17650 Saint-Denis-d'Oléron
**t.** 5 46 768 056
**e.** lechassiron@gmail.com
**w.** campinglechassiron.blogspot.fr

Surrounded by nature, **Camping Indigo Les Chenes Verts (18)** is a calm and quiet campsite, 50 m from the Ecuissière beach. 100 pitches and 50 fully equipped wood and canvas tents. Open May to mid September. •€• •€€•

**a.** 9 Passé de l'Ecussière,
17550 Dolus-d'Oléron
**t.** 5 46 753 288
**e.** Chenes-verts@camping-indigo.com
**w.** camping-indigo.com/en/oleron-les-chenes-verts-indigo-campsite-france

**Camping Indigo Oléron les Pins (19)** sits in the heart of a majestic pine forest in Saint-Trojan-les-Bains. 150 pitches and 65 fully equipped wood and canvas tents (their tents even include a sink, toilet and shower). Open May to mid September. •€• •€€•

**a.** 11 Avenue des Bris,
17370 Saint-Trojan-les-Bains
**t.** 5 46 760 239
**e.** oleron@camping-indigo.com
**w.** camping-indigo.com/en/oleron-les-pins-indigo-campsite-france

**Les Chambres d'Hotes d'Ici et de Là (20)** is a bed and breakfast with 3 rooms, a sunny courtyard, close to the beach and bakery (très important!) and in the heart of the old village of Domino. Open April to November. •€• •€€•

**a.** 20 Impasse de Quéreux, Domino,
17190 Saint-Georges-D'Oléron
**t.** 6 22 200 300
**w.** leschambresdoleron.com

**Hôtel de Charme La Petite Plage (21)** has 9 rooms, each with their own private terrace overlooking the beach and ocean. They care a lot about recycling, using biological products and eco-labels. The hotel is combined with **restaurant le Grain de Sable**, which uses local, organic and seasonal products. Open from February to October. •€• •€€•

**a.** 839 Rue de l'Océan, Domino,
17190 Saint-Georges-d'Oléron
**t.** 5 46 765 228
**w.** lapetiteplage.com

**Les Blancs Galets (22)** has 3 tastefully decorated houses (4 to 6 persons), full of comfort – think: jacuzzi, several sun terraces - situated in the dunes close to the beach (Plage de Chaucre) and pine forest. •€€• •€€€•

**a.** 40 D Allée des Epinouses,
17190 Saint-Georges-d'Oléron
**t.** 6 22 086 282
**w.** lesblancsgalets.com

If you're not too picky about decoration and style, **Motel Île de Lumière (23)** is a good choice because of its perfect situation in the dunes, overlooking the sea, and being close to just about everything on the island because of its central location. They've got 45 attached rooms with terrace. Can't find anything to do or to relax on the island itself? (Really?) The motel has a heated pool, sauna, fitness room and tennis-court. Open April to October. •€€•

**a.** Avenue des Pins, la Cotinière,
17310 Saint-Pierre-d'Oléron
**t.** 5 46 471 080
**e.** ile.de.lumiere@wanadoo.fr
**w.** moteldelumiere.com

Photo: Melchior van Nigtevecht

# SURF

The whole set up and location of the island shows potential, but most spots do need a decent swell to work. The atmosphere in the water is very friendly; embrace this friendliness, since the best advice is given by those very locals, especially about the strong currents and rips. Height restrictions make parking bigger vans close to the break quite difficult. Usually you can park at the side of the road.

**Chassiron (I)**, on the northern tip near the Chassiron lighthouse, is one of the most consistent but also the heaviest break of the island, which requires a walk on the reef first (wearing reef booties makes a lot of sense). Best to enter at mid tide to low tide, works only at low tide, in nw-w-sw small to medium swell. Strong currents. Experienced surfers only. Easy parking.

**Les Boulassiers (II)**, just south of La Brée les Bains, only works in swells over 3m that wrap around the island. A long mellow lefthander that works best at high tide in big nw-w swells, but it rarely breaks. All levels. Easy parking.

**Les Huttes (III)**, at Pointe de Trois Pierres, is a powerful beachbreak in an area with lots of campsites. Beware of the heavy shorebreak (or take advantage of it if you're a little ripper). Works at all tides, best in small to medium nw-w-sw swell. The stretch of beach to the south offers more peaks. All levels. Easy parking/surf school.

**Vert Bois** and **Les Allassins (IV)** at Le Grand-Village-Plage are popular spots, easily accessible and consistent beachbreaks, although they need a bit more swell than you'd think. Further south, on the same stretch of beach, is **Saint-Trojan-les-Bains**, usually a bit quieter because you have to walk over the dunes to reach it. Sandbanks change, so peaks shift. Best in medium nw-w-sw swell, works at all tides. All levels. Easy parking/surf school/restaurant.

# SCHOOL RENTAL REPAIR

**Enjoy School Surf (24)**, surf, SUP, bodyboard, lessons and rental, works from Plage des Huttes.

**a.** 4 Rue du Martin Pêcheur, La Cotinière, 17310 Saint-Pierre d'Oléron
**t.** 6 29 373 741
**w.** enjoy-ecole-surf.fr

**Diabolo Fun Watersports School (25)**, Surf, SUP, windsurf, blo-kart, Hobie Cat sailing, lessons and rental, been around since 1988, operating from Plage des Huttes. Open all year.

**a.** Plage des Huttes, (next to snack bar La Biouve) 17650 Saint-Denis-d'Oléron
**t.** 5 46 479 897
**w.** diabolofun.com

**Ecole de Surf Moana (26)**, owner Baptiste Dalmon teaches surfing with the same enthusiasm to 6-year olds as 80-year old surf novices and speaks French, English, Spanish. Open April to October.

**a.** 28 Avenue des Bouillats, 17370 Saint-Trojan-les-Bains
**t.** 6 80 143 657
**w.** moana-surfschool.com

**Kabana Surf (27)**, surf lessons and rental, right at the beach of Grand-Village. Open April to October.

**a.** 17370 Le Grand-Village-Plage
**t.** 6 08 923 456
**w.** kabanasurf.com

**Illegal Surfboards (28)**, local shaper and the place to go for repairs.

**a.** 23 Rue Etchebarne, 17310 Saint-Pierre-d'Oleron
**t.** 6 63 281 705
**e.** rudywoodpecker@gmail.com

Photo: C-Skins

# 2. HIP OPENER: EKA PADA UTKATASANA

◆

*One-Legged Chair Pose*

***If you want to surf well and prevent problem pains, this pose helps keep your hip joints mobile.***

*Many actions in surfing, especially our take-off, need open hips, to allow fast moves to be made with ease. Turns and creating speed down the line also require some pretty intense flexibility and manoeuvrability out of your hips; so keeping your hip joints flexible brings many benefits. Of many hip openers, this pose also improves your balance - one of the most important aspects of surfing!*

***Benefits:***

*Outer hip mobility & balance. Aids mental focus.*

***How:***

*Start by bringing weight onto your left foot, and slowly raising the right foot. Place the flexed right foot above your left knee while simultaneously bending your left leg. You can hold your foot and knee, to help you achieve balance, and give some push to lengthen the torso away from the legs. Once you have found your balance stay in the pose for a bit, to create optimum balance and opening in the hip joint. Then lower the leg and change sides.*

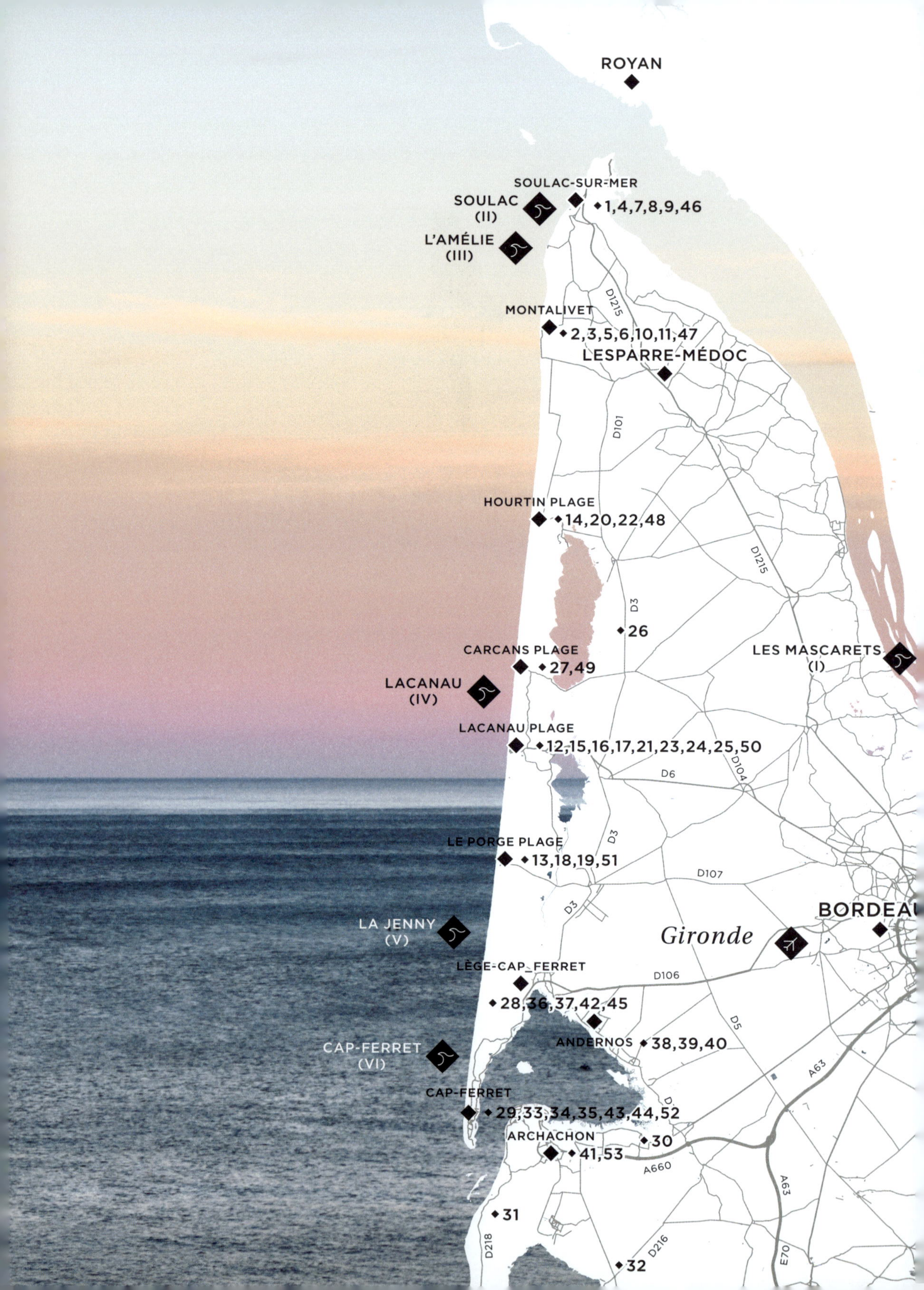
ROYAN
SOULAC-SUR-MER
1,4,7,8,9,46
SOULAC
(II)
L'AMÉLIE
(III)
D1215
MONTALIVET
2,3,5,6,10,11,47
LESPARRE-MÉDOC
D101
HOURTIN PLAGE
14,20,22,48
D1215
D3
26
CARCANS PLAGE
27,49
LES MASCARETS
(I)
LACANAU
(IV)
LACANAU PLAGE
12,15,16,17,21,23,24,25,50
D104
D6
D3
LE PORGE PLAGE
13,18,19,51
D107
D3
LA JENNY
(V)
BORDEAU
Gironde
LÈGE-CAP-FERRET
D106
28,36,37,42,45
D5
ANDERNOS
38,39,40
CAP-FERRET
(VI)
A63
CAP-FERRET
29,33,34,35,43,44,52
ARCHACHON
30
41,53
A660
A63
31
D218
D216
E70
32

# GIRONDE

Just north of Les Landes - France's most well-known surf area - the coastline of the Gironde department has pretty much the same on offer as its popular twin to the south. But it's much quieter, more rural, the smell of pine is omnipresent, the line-ups are emptier, and there's room to roam if it still feels crowded. One of the reasons could be that, driving down from the north, you have to travel to Bordeaux first, and then make your way up again. Unless you take the ferry from from Royan to Le Verdon, but it's costly. Coming from the south is easier, although there's the Bassin d'Arcachon to go around.

The seaside resorts come to life in summer, are still lively in autumn, and seem like ghost towns in winter. Of course there's more to Gironde than surfing beachbreaks. There are bike trails galore and lakes to sail, fish and SUP, wine producing chateaux along the banks of the Gironde estuary in the north and Andernos, at the Bassin d'Archachon to the south, is the centre for oyster fishing.

## SURFER-TRAVELLER TYPE GIRONDE

*You love to camp, sunbathe or walk around naked, explore endless stretches of fine sandy beach, thus surfing beachbreaks, paddle in large lakes, get lost in forests, jump off high dunes, drink Medoc wines, the smell of pine.*

Photo: Melchior van Nigtevecht

# TRAVEL INFO

Public transport is not the most convenient way to travel, a car is recommended. But if you stick to one or two places, you'll be fine without a car.

## BY FERRY

By Ferry: crossing the estuary of Gironde, coming from the north via the coast, can save you a lot of time and petrol. Money-wise it may not be cheaper, but a boat trip eh! Always nice. The Ferry Royan crosses from Royan to Le Verdon in Gironde (and vice versa) every 40 minutes in summer, the rest of the season 6 to 8 times a day. A campervan with 2 persons will cost you a little less than 50 euros, a car with 2 persons around 30 euros.

**Schedules and prices:**
**w.** bernezac.com

## BY TRAIN

Trains from Bordeaux Saint-Jean run daily, north to Le Verdon (2 hrs) and south to Archachon (1 hr).

**Schedules and reservations:**
**w.** horaires.captaintrain.com

## BY AIR

Aéroport de Bordeaux-Mérignac, situated 6 km west of Bordeaux, in Mérignac, is a large airport with direct flights to and from almost all countries in Europe. There's a direct bus to and from Bordeaux Saint-Jean station.

**a.** 33700 Mérignac
**w.** bordeaux.airport.com

# IN AND AROUND SOULAC-SUR-MER

◆

Soulac is surrounded by dunes, beaches and pine forest. 19th century villas stand shoulder-to-shoulder with apartment buildings from more recent build. It's the historical element that sets Soulac apart. At the top of Rue de la Plage stands the Basilique that once was a shelter for pilgrims from England on their way to Santiago de Compostela. It's now a protected monument under UNESCO World Heritage.

**Tourist office** at 68 Rue de la Plage.

## TO DO

◆

All along and between the Gironde estuary and the ocean, the **Médoc peninsula**, you'll find wine houses aplenty. Following the D2 along the estuary from the northern end of the peninsula to Bordeaux, passing Pauillac - the epicentre of Médoc wine making and vineyards - is like taking the Route 66 of wine châteaux.

If you like to indulge in a week of yoga and surfing, **Yoga sur Mer** (**1**) offers just that. In summer you can join meditation and yoga classes on the beach. Open from June to October, email Katja Thomson (German yogini) for the next schedule, as it may change every season. Mostly classes are at the Eco Camping le Royannais (using their yurt) or the beaches of Verdon and Soulac.

**t.** 7 85 258 828
**e.** thomson@yogasurmer.fr
**w.** yogasurmer.fr

It may not be the first thing on your mind to take your kids to while on holiday, but the **Médoc Polo Club** (**2**) is the first-time polo club for all ages. They've got kids' polo, beach polo, paddock and arena polo, polo on foot, bike and wooden horse. French and English are spoken, open all year.

**a.** 96, Route d'Hourtin, 33930 Montalivet
**t.** 5 56 410 595 / 6 77 818 871
**w.** medocpoloclub.com

**Parc de l'Aventure** (**3**) as the name suggests, takes you on a spin of energetic outdoor activities like tree climbing, a trail full of riddles, treasure hunting, pedal carting, sumo combatting, trampoline jumping, donkey rides, archery and mini rock climbing. If it's a bit much for you, you can always just rent a bike, or wait in the restaurant for everyone else to get tired. Open from April to October.

**a.** Lède de Montalivet, 33930 Montalivet
**t.** 5 56 090 788 / 6 80 709 488
**w.** laforet-aventure.com

**Premier Grand Cru Classic**, longboard Pro-Am (pro's and amateurs) with an international field of longboarders, in several classes. Some fine prizes to win: The over 50s Legend Division winner will take home his weight in wine bottles. Usually held at the end of September in Montalivet.

**w.** longboard-proam.com

## EAT/DRINK/HANGOUT

◆

Wine bar **Le Comptoir du Vin** (**4**) has – besides wine of course – a choice of tapas and live music (in summer) on the menu. Open all year. •€• •€€•

**a.** 5 Rue Holagray, 33780 Soulac-sur-Mer
**t.** 5 56 597 334

Café Restaurant **Le Globe Trotter** (**5**) has, as its name implies, an eclectic menu of Asian, European, South American, and for sure some other continent's dishes. So you can choose from fajitas to ceviche, either sitting inside in a bit of an Endless Summer meets Médoc kind of décor, or outside in their garden. Open from May to September. •€• •€€•

**a.** 9, Avenue de la Brède, 33930 Montalivet

Photo: Melchior van Nigtevecht

## SHOP

◆

**Spyder Surf Shop (6)** imports all kinds of classic longboards, logs, retro single fins, and fish, directly from California. Owner Philippe Rodes knows a thing or two about boards and fins and can be of great help in choosing your new retro. Spyder Surf Shop's been around since 1989. You'll also find handplanes from Hawaii, accessories, beach bikes and clothes.

**a.** 11 Avenue de l'Ocean,
33930 Montalivet,
**t.** 5 56 093 471 / 6 08 573 553
**w.** surf-longboard.com

## SLEEP

◆

Environmentally friendly **Camping le Royannais (7)** has 2 to 6 person chalets, mobile homes, cottages and tipi tents on stilts on offer. New, from 2016 on, is the 'sweet coconut', a mix of tent-come-apartment in cylinder form. Also on offer: yoga classes, lectures and environmental films in their new yurt. •€• •€€•

**a.** 88, Route de Soulac,
33123 Le Verdon-sur-Mer
**t.** 5 56 096 112
**e.** camping.le.royannais@wanadoo.fr
**w.** royannais.com

There are campsites galore along the coast, from little naturist ones to large sites with 24-hour entertainment on offer. We picked out a few no-fuss, pretty peaceful, shady campsites close to the beach.

**Camping de l'Ocean (8)**, 300 m from L'Amélie Plage. Open from June to September. •€• •€€•

**a.** 62 Allée de la Négade,
Plage de L'Amélie, 33780 Soulac-sur-Mer
**t.** 5 56 097 610
**e.** camping.ocean@orange.fr
**w.** camping.ocean.pagesperso-orange.fr

**Camping les Sables d'Argent (9)** Mobile homes, pitches and cabins right at the beach (L'Amélie Plage). Open from April to September. •€• •€€•

**a.** 39-43 Boulevard de L'Amélie,
33780 Soulac-sur-Mer
**t.** 5 56 098 287
**e.** contact@sables-d-argent.com
**w.** sables-d-argent.com

**Camping La Chesnays (10)**: Mobile homes, chalets, bungalow tents and lodges, and 60 large pitches in the pine forest, 6 km from the beach, as they state, 'far from stress, close to nature'. Open from May to September. •€• •€€•

**a.** 8 Route de Mayan,
33930 Montalivet
**t.** 5 56 417 274 / 6 02 252 711
**e.** lachesnays@camping-montalivet.com
**w.** camping-montalivet.com

**Hôtel l'Océan 2 (11)** is a cool place, hipster-ish in a good way, directly facing the ocean. The hotel has 10 small but sleekly designed rooms and 2 studios on offer: Studio Village ('skate') and Studio Ocean ('surf'). Bar and terrace are both nice hangouts in themselves. Open all year. •€€•

**a.** 27, Boulevard Front de Mer,
33930 Montalivet-les-Bains
**t.** 5 56 099 098
**e.** reservations@hotellocean.com
**w.** hotellocean.com

# IN AND AROUND LACANAU-OCÉAN

Being the most popular and well-known surf spot for this area, the little seaside part of Lacanau attracts lots of holidaying and travelling surfers and their families. And shops, bars and restaurants all offering somehow surf-related items, drinks and food. But of course, if you visit just off-season, say October, it's a chilled out place. And with that much stretch of beach and forests, and a big lake, it makes a perfect place for an outdoorsy holiday; with the occasional opportunities to go bar hopping, coffee sipping or boulevard lounging. Make sure to do some shopping for fresh local produce at the market every Wednesday.

**Tourist office** in Avenue de L'Europe.

## TO DO

**Cycle**. There are cycle paths going from town to town, leading through forest, along beaches and dunes, and it's by far the best way to explore the area. In every town, at campsites and some hotels, you'll find rental bikes.

SUP on the canals and lakes around Lacanau with **Banana Surf School** (**12**), tours of 2 and 3 hours, the latter complemented with a pause for some local food and wine-tasting. Aurélie Junot, longtime Lacanau local surf girl, accompanies the tours and loves to share her knowledge of the area and the environment.

**a.** 16 Boulevard de la Plage, 33680 Lacanau-Océan
**t.** 6 60 056 280 (Aurélie)
**e.** bananalacanau@gmail.com

**Le Peuple des Cimes** (**13**) offers some acrobatic tree climbing trails, not only in daytime, but also at night. Open from June to September.

**a.** Plage du Gressier, 33680 Le Porge Océan
**t.** 6 99 435 636
**w.** lepeuplesdescimes.fr

## EAT/DRINK/HANGOUT

**Bar Restaurant le Surf** (**14**) is, of course, very near the surf, about 100 m from the beach of Hourtin. Decorated with lots of wood, a big terrace, attracting local surfers and tourists alike, who can enjoy regular concerts, DJ sets, or just a sunset beer. •€• •€€•

**a.** 25 Avenue Jean Laffite, 33990 Hourtin
**t.** 5 56 091 139
**w.** le-surf-restaurant-hourtin.com

**Le Cabanon de Christine** (**15**) is a small garden taverne with tasty wines and seafood like oysters, moules, calamares on the menu. Open all year. •€• •€€•

**a.** 6 Rue Henri Seguin, 33680 Lacanau-Océan
**t.** 6 85 216 456

**La Fiancée du Pirate** (**16**) is a veritable little seafood eatery between the many fast food and 'all-day-happy-hour' bars and restaurants. They serve tasty delicacies like oysters, caviar with vodka, pata negra and biological wines. In their shop you can find local produce and Médoc specialities. And you've got to love their name. •€• •€€•

**a.** 12 Avenue Henri Seguin, 33680 Lacanau-Océan
**t.** 7 87 362 060

**Le Bistrot des Cochons (17)**, the pig's bistro, is filled with bric-à-brac objects, has a laid-back atmosphere and in summer you can cool down on their terrace, which is shaded by wisteria trees. Their cuisine is regional and makes use of fresh and local produce. Open from February to November.
•€€•

**a.** 1 Rue du Docteur Darrigan,
33680 Lacanau Océan
**t.** 5 56 031 561

Decorated like a brocante or collector's museum, **Pizzeria des Bois (18)** looks good inside as well as outside, with creative decorations and arty pictures on the wall. Gentle staff and excellent pizzas, great atmosphere. Open all year. •€• •€€•

**a.** 1, Avenue du Gressier,
33680 Le Porge Océan
**t.** 5 57 709 137

**Restaurant and rum distillery Le Galip (19)** has a hearty Caribbean and gourmet-style cuisine. Good choice when you're hungry, they're quite well known for their large portions. Open all year. •€• •€€•

**a.** 9 Avenue du Gressier,
33680 Le Porge Océan
**t.** 5 56 265 218

## SHOP

◆

**Home Spot (20)** surf shop's got all the essentials you might need and is just a step from the beach. Friendly and knowledgeable staff.

**a.** 21, Avenue Jean Lafitte,
Hourtin Plage, 33990 Hourtin

**L'Atelier de la Vache (21)** from artisanal maestro Arnaud Mantis, produces handmade leather products, 'maroquinerie', bags, belts, hats, and prepares everything leather.

**a.** 13 Avenue Henri Seguin,
33680 Lacanau-Océan
**t.** 5 57 703 215

## SLEEP

◆

If you plan a road trip, but don't have your own wheels, check **Camp in Van**. They rent out campervans from Bordeaux Airport. There are 3 campervans and 2 vintage VW campers available. •€• •€€•

**a.** 205 Allée Isaac Newton,
Zone Boulac Dauphine,
33127 St Jean d'Illac (Bordeaux Airport)
**t.** 7 82 442 956 / 5 56 721 535
**e.** contact@campinvan.com
**w.** campinvan.com

Boutique-style **Atlantic Villa (22)** is a chambre d'hôtes and bed & breakfast, some 800 m from the lake of Hourtin. We love the fact that Atlantic Villa is entirely carbon neutral, generating its own electricity, heat and hot water. They've got a heated saltwater swimming pool, 4 luxury rooms and 1 apartment with mezzanine (2 to 6 persons). •€€•

**a.** 22 Rue Du Pommier, 33990 Hourtin
**t.** 5 56 093 547 / 6 11 677 111
**e.** info@mysite.com
**w.** atlanticvilla.com

Some 200 m from the beach, **Villa Zenith (23)** is a perfect near-the-surf house. It's a traditional stone villa from the beginning of the 20th century, with a spacious garden, an indoor and outdoor kitchen, where you can prepare your dinner in the open air on a summer evening. The owners, a local family, like to call it 'a collective living accommodation', because it's not just another surf camp, but more aimed at adult surfers, maybe travelling alone or with some friends. You can either choose to stay in a room with bunk beds or a twin bedroom, they don't have double beds, so don't get all romantic with your buddy. Open from April to October. •€•

**a.** 16 Avenue Adjudant Guittard,
33680 Lacanau-Océan
**t.** 5 56 263 649 / 6 84 608 808
**e.** contact@lacanau-zenith.com
**w.** lacanau-zenith.com

Chambres d'hôtes **La Pomme de Pin (24)** is situated in a quiet area of Lacanau Océan, amidst pine forest. Nothing too special, but great location, spacious rooms and nice terraces in front of every room looking out onto a garden filled with plants and trees. Open all year. •€€•

**a.** 64 Avenue Plantey,
33680-Lacanau Océan
**t.** 6 62 969 330

**Villa Les Bois Flottés (25)** 'driftwood' is hidden in the Canaulaise forest, just steps from the lake of Moutchic. A very peaceful place due to its location and exotic decorations, brought back by the owners from their travels. You can either stay in one of the 5 bedrooms or one of 3 lodge tents in the garden. There's a teeny-tiny gym, a bbq and a swimming pool. Bikes and surf gear available. The Villa has a close cooperation with Banana surf school, surf shop and surf café. Open from April to September. •€€•

**a.** 1798 Chemin de Ceinture de Talaris,
33680 Lacanau
**t.** 5 56 031 497 / 6 85 878 663
**e.** olivier@villa-lesboisflottes.com
**w.** villa-lesboisflottes.com

Camping **La Prairie Aire Naturelle (26)** is a très laid-back and tranquil campsite with 25 spacious pitches, a mobile home and a gîte (4-5 persons). It's situated 17 km from the ocean and 7 km from the sweet water Hourtin lake, in the midst of pine forest. Close to the vineyards and the Châteaux du Médoc, and cycle paths joining lake and ocean. Being surfers themselves, the owners are happy to provide you with daily updates on conditions and the best places to go to. Open from April to October. •€•

**a.** 225 bis Route St Hélène de l'Etang,
33121 Carcans
**t.** 5 57 175 109
**w.** campinglaprairie-carcans.fr

**Village de l'Océan (27)** is within 5 minutes walking distance from the surfbreaks of Carcans. It's got 25 free-standing wooden cottages for up to 7 persons. Open March to November. •€• •€€•

**a.** 5 Rue de la Forêt, 33121 Carcans
**t.** 5 57 704 839
**e.** villageocean@mairie-carcans.fr
**w.** village-ocean-carcans.com

# IN AND AROUND ANDERNOS AND THE ARCACHON BAY

The south end area of Gironde has a strong California feel to it. Laid-back but in a fancy and orderly manner somehow. You'll fit in perfectly, pedalling your beach cruiser, board under arm, barefoot but wearing a big flappy hat and linen blouse of one of those fine French designers. Andernos, situated at the northeast side of the Bassin D'Arcachon, is a centre for oyster fishing, lined with huts where fresh catch is landed and sold. Most of the huts double as restaurant. The bay itself, depending on high or low tide, covers 150 km² (high) or 40 km² (low). Some parts are natural preservations.

## TO DO

**Graffiti spotting**: The many bunkers, or remains of bunkers, dotted along the beaches of Gironde serve as a canvas for graffiti artists, it's like an outdoor public art gallery. The bunkers are part of the 5000 km long Atlantic Wall, a coastal defence system built in WWII. The ruins of these and other defensive fortifications are found on beaches from Norway to Spain.

Discover the Bassin d'Arcachon with a SUP or kayak at **La Cabane à Gliss (28)**. Visit Île aux Oiseaux, bird island, or the oyster parks and the salted meadows of Lège-Arès. Half and full days paddling, using the tides. Open from May to September.

**a.** Plage Publique de l'Avenue du Port Claouey, 33950 Lège-Cap-Ferret
**t.** 6 66 842 335
**e.** lacabaneagliss@orange.fr
**w.** lacabaneagliss.com

**Yoga sur la Plage (29)** offers Kundalini Yoga on the beach. Open and accessible to all, classes are held in the same manner as they would be held in a classroom, with a focus on the breath and meditation.

**a.** Plage de l'Horizon, 33970 Cap Ferret
**t.** 6 11 328 024 (Nirmalbir Kaur)
**w.** yoga-keala.com

Some serious bird spotting can be done at **Parc Ornithologique du Teich (30)**, a 120 hectare nature reserve around the brackish waters of abandoned salt meadows. Bluethroats, heron, wild duck, storks and swans are amongst the 260 species of migratory birds that can be spotted throughout the year. There's a small parking place for campervans to stay overnight. You know what they say: the early bird catches the worm...

**a.** Rue du Port, 33470 Le Teich

**Dune de Pyla (31)** in the south of the Arcachon bay is the highest dune in Europe, reaching 107 m high. There used to be sandboarding possibilities, but it's a protected UNESCO site now. You can still climb it, enjoy the grand views and simply be amazed by the pile... eh, pyla of sand.

**a.** Route de Biscarrosse, 33260 La Teste-de-Buch

Work a real wooden Hawaiian outrigger with **Yak Ocean (32)**, or discover the Arcachon bay and Cazaux lake (Sanguinet) on a SUP or in a kayak. Also a possibility to SUP and outrigger at Plage de Caton and Plage de Haitza, or kayak at the Port du Teich (nature reserve). Open from April to October.

**a.** Chemin de Sabas, après le Camping les Oréades, 40460 Sanguinet
**t.** 6 11 920 583
**e.** contact@yakocean.com
**w.** yakocean.com

## EAT/DRINK/HANGOUT

Hotel, restaurant and bar **Cocotte's (33)** got a Californian vibe, with a stylish vintage interior, white painted wooden balconies, big easy chairs and a sunny terrace. They serve home-made products. Open from April to October. •€€•

**a.** 62 Avenue de l'Océan, 33970 Cap-Ferret
**t.** 5 57 705 913

Restaurant **So Phare Away (34)** sits, contrary to what their name suggests, actually close to the lighthouse of Cap Ferret, on the avenue leading towards the Phare. If their French cuisine doesn't make you happy, you'll sure cheer up from the décor of brightly coloured wooden panels, chairs and tables, and large wooden terrace. Open all year. •€€•

**a.** 32 Avenue Nord du Phare, 33970 Cap-Ferret
**t.** 5 56 602 287

Surf shop and Sandwicherie **Chez Nounours (35)** is the soul product of surfer Patrick Villigente. Being a longtime experienced waterman, he knows a thing or two about a surfer's cravings. So, make sure you order that typical French delicacy: Pain Américain. Whotzzdah? Your French fries and steak haché served on a panini, with lots of sauce. And there are plenty more pre and post surf snacks on the menu. With a true surf spirit, Chez Nounours makes for a fun hangout as well. Open all year. •€•

**a.** 22 Rue des Goélands, 33970 Cap-Ferret
**t.** 5 56 037 162

Enjoy your oysters, fruit de mer, and other ocean delicacies at **Degustation Le Tatch** (**36**). Situated at the port, with an easy-going feel to it and simple but très cool decorated terrace, you'll have a view over the Arcachon bay. Open all year. •€€•

**a.** Port de Piraillan, Impasse de l'Anse, 33950 Cap-Ferret
**t.** 6 21 798 799

Another great seafood place is **La Cabane 57** (**37**). Set in an original clapperboard shack at the port, you can feel, smell and taste the tradition of oyster and clam culture, your feet almost touching the water while you eat. Great place for watching the sunset from the terrace, or in winter, warming yourself at the heater (it's one of the few places here that's heated during winter). Open all year. •€• •€€•

**a.** Port de Piraillan, 40 Rue du Littoral, 33950 Lége-Cap-Ferret
**t.** 6 13 298 760
**w.** lacabane57.com

## SHOP

◆

Surf shop **Mel x Chris** (**38**) is not just any other surf shop. It's a gallery with surf-related art exhibitions, in store clothes from a selective choice of small brands like Sen no Sen, Loreak Mendian and Alfredo Gonzalez stockings, the occasional home-made jams, and some fine boards (logs, fish, longboards). But you can also just enjoy a coffee or soda and contemplate the growth of the fruits and plants surrounding you, in their garden.

**a.** 136 bis Boulevard de la République, 33510 Andernos
**t.** 6 07 850 195

**Du Sable dans le Maillot** (**39**) is a concept store. Yeah, that may sound a bit vague, but there's really no other way to give a label to this store. You'll find home decorations, jewellery, gifts, bags, nice staff... Go check it out, and undoubtedly you'll find an item that you can't live without.

**a.** 3 Boulevard de la Plage, 33510 Andernos

At **BABA** (**40**), Comptoir Épicurien, you'll find selected wines, champagne and beers, to buy, taste or just look at and drool on. Their taste in spirits is as fine as their décor.

**a.** Place du 14 Juillet, 33510 Andernos

At **Chez Ernest** (**41**) it's all about boards, beards, music and motorcycles. And clothes too. Not because it's the latest craze, but because they're really into that. Cool place, friendly guys, local hangout, just go and check it out, you'll be one of the very few tourists passing by!

**a.** 19 Rue du Maréchal de Lattre de Tassigny, 33120 Arcachon

Photo: Melchior van Nigtevecht

## SLEEP

◆

**Camping le Truc Vert (42)**, as the name suggests, is a green whatchamacallit: a huge campsite, no mobile homes, just pitches, 300 m from the beach but totally surrounded by green. If you're not into dancing, maybe avoid this campsite in July and August, since it has 2 disco nights per week. Open from May to September. •€• •€€•

**a.** Route du Truc-Vert, 33970 Lège-Cap-Ferret
**t.** 5 56 608 955
**e.** info@trucvert.com
**w.** trucvert.com

**The Surf Shack (43)** is a Californian, surfy-style cottage for 2 persons, with private terrace and garden, 2 minutes from Plage d'Horizon. Available all year. •€€•

**a.** 23, Allée des Cigales, 33970 Cap-Ferret
**t.** 6 10 801 221 (Catherine Lataste)
**e.** thesurfshack@hotmail.fr

Whether you're sleeping in the 'Divine' or 'Exotica' guestroom, the Sunset Suite or The Villa, your stay at **Yamina Lodge (44)** will definitely put you in relaxation modus. There's a great garden, a common lounge with fireplace, bikes to use and a spa. Every little detail of the place c'est génial and you can almost feel the love put into it, making the place look beautiful. Available all year. •€€€•

**a.** 169 Avenue de Bordeaux, 33970 Cap-Ferret
**t.** 6 14 693 680
**e.** contact@yamina-lodge.com
**w.** yamina-lodge.com

**Villa Etche Ona (45)** has 5 spacious and comfortable rooms, some with terrace. The garden of the villa looks out over the Arcachon bay. Open all year. •€€• •€€€•

**a.** 92, Route du Cap Ferret, 33950 Lège-Cap-Ferret (next to Port Piraillan)
**t.** 6 64 910 091
**e.** lacaze.mline@orange.fr
**w.** villa-etcheona.com

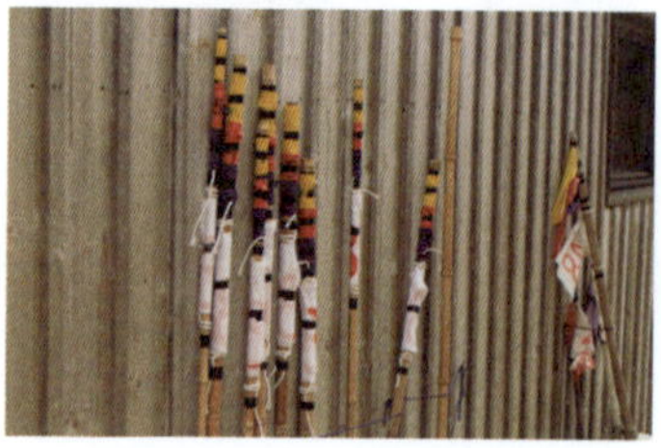

Photo: Melchior van Nigtevecht

# SURF

Almost all surf breaks along the Gironde coast are west-facing beachbreaks that work best with a small to medium nw-w-sw swell and preferably windless days or offshore breezes.

Surf when there's no surf: **Les Mascarets** (**I**), the tidal bore, can be surfed once in a while when a spring tide pushes masses of water down the Gironde. Expect polluted water and a slow party wave that goes on forever. Join the party from north of the village of Saint-Pardon.

**Soulac** (**II**): Being so close to the rivermouth, sand builds up offshore, downsizing bigger swells. So, waves will always be a bit smaller at this beachbreak when everywhere else is big. All levels. Surf school/restaurant/easy parking.

From **L'Amélie** (**III**) to **Lacanau** (**IV**) it's like a wave itself, going from empty, even deserted off-season, slowly building up to packs and crowds towards the south. Of course it's all depending on sandbanks and their shape, but it definitely pays to put on some hiking boots, bring a daypack and explore north of the boardwalk of Lacanau. All levels. Surf school/restaurant/easy parking.

Nudist beaches not only bring that je ne sais quoi feel to your session, they're usually less crowded. Between Lacanau and Cap Ferret you can try Le Petit Crohot, or **La Jenny** (**V**) (named after the naturist Village 'La Jenny') which requires a 20-minute walk from the naturist park. All levels, but be wise; because of its isolation and sometimes strong currents it does take knowledge and experience, so never go solo.

North of **Cap Ferret** (**VI**) there are numerous breaks to be found, beware of eroded jetties and strong currents.

**Nouvelle Vague** (**46**), surf lessons, rental of surfboards and SUPs. Open from April to October.

**a.** Plage de la Negade, Soulac-sur-Mer
**t.** 7 88 554 150
**e.** nouvellevague.surfschool@gmail.com
**w.** soulac-nvsurfschool.com

**Monta Surf School** (**47**) run by former French and international longboard competitor and lifeguard Thomas Bilbao, offers various events, lessons (longboard, SUP, tandem), coaching and rental of boards.

**a.** 15 Rue de Mayne Mounin (south side), 33930 Vendays-Montalivet
**t.** 6 81 944 590
**w.** montasurfschool.com

# SCHOOL RENTAL REPAIR

**Surfing Médoc** (**48**): lessons and rental, organises tidal bore surfing at Les Mascarets (when it's on), they run surf camps in summer, and do SUP tours on Saturday morning on the Hourtin lake (except July and August).

**a.** Résidence Plein Océan, Avenue Jean Laffite, 33990 Hourtin
**t.** 5 56 090 247
**w.** surfing-medoc.com

**Rod's Surf Shop** (**49**) is your go-to place for repairs or a newly shaped board by longtime shaper Rodolphe Scheel (longboards, shortboards, fish). The shop's got all the surf essentials you need and has been around since 1988.

**a.** 1 Avenue de la Plage, 33121 Carcans
**t.** 5 56 034 700
**w.** rods-surf.com

**Banana Surf School** (**50**) offers surf lessons, small groups only. Surf teacher Aurélie Jonot is an avid surfer herself, she's been surfing for 20 years and has over 13 years experience of teaching surf lessons.

**a.** 16 Boulevard de la Plage, 33680 Lacanau-Océan
**t.** 6 60 056 280
**w.** gite-lacanau.com

**Skeepskool** (**51**) offers lessons and rental of all sorts of boards, short, mini-mal, longboards, SUP and boogie boards. They operate from the main beaches of Le Porge and La Jenny. Open from June to September.

**t.** 6 70 608 426
**w.** ecole2surf.com

**Surf Center** (**52**) has over 30 years of experience teaching surfing to novice, intermediate and advanced surfers.

**a.** Plage d'Horizon, 22 Avenue des Goélands, 33950 Cap-Ferret
**t.** 5 56 606 105
**w.** ecole-surf-cap-ferret.com

**Surf Mobile** is a mobile surf school and offers guiding, finding the best conditions and waves in the area, adapted to the level of practice, from beginner to advanced. Based in Cap Ferret, but contact by phone or email.

**t.** 6 62 723 801
**w.** surf-mobile.fr

**Ecole Surf En Buch** (**53**) works from Plage de Petit Nice and Plage des Arbousiers. No surf? Join a tour around Arcachon bay or Bird Island with a Polynesian outrigger or SUP.

**a.** Plage des Arbousiers, 33120 Arcachon
**t.** 6 80 054 695
**w.** ecoledesurf-arcachon.com

# JULIAN VAN VLIET IS UNEEK

Meet Julian Yoshi van Vliet, KEEN ambassador, engineer, shaper, surfer, and foremost: innovator. A one-of-a-kind personality, making unique and inspiring choices. After studying water management and industrial ecology, his love for the ocean led him to where he is now; not only experimenting with natural fibres and bio-based epoxy as a surfboard shaper, but also inspiring the surf and design industry to think differently. Appropriately nicknamed 'The Professor' by his fellow surfers, he uses his inquisitive nature and knowledge to re-invent and develop what already exists.

*"In my heart I know I can make a difference, using new insights and technology to create a surf industry that has less impact on the environment, and think of new ways to design and build boards."*

Like the UNEEK collection by KEEN, where they're ditching traditional machinery and conventional materials for a simple two-cord construction, Julian is stripping down and rethinking technology used to build boards. All board designers and shapers know that surfers have different styles, bodies and abilities, and especially, different wishes. With the help of others, he invented the Boardboxx - a new shaping machine that is designed to make surfboard shaping accessible and possible for everyone. "It's an open source, really, for amateur and professional shaping enthusiasts, open to sharing knowledge." says Julian: "I want to inspire and enable anyone to become a DIY shaper. So surfers will be able to self-craft their boards, not only to their level, but also to meet their wildest imaginations."

Julian chose to make a difference, moving in full force, to keep an open mind to change and development, and be an icon of innovation. That's what makes him UNEEK.

KEEN UNEEK

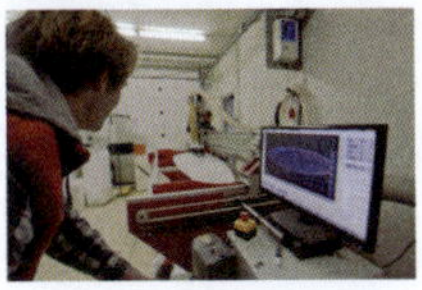

@keenuneek

ARCACHON
A660
D218
D216
7
BISCARROSSE
(I)
BISCARROSSE PLAGE
1,3,4,5,6,8,40,41,42
BISCARROSSE
2,3
PARENTIS-EN-BORN
D43
D652
18
E70
MIMIZAN
(II)
MIMIZAN
9,10,13,14,15,19
D652
D44
A63
12,20
Les Landes
CONTIS
11,17,21
16
D652
D42
A63
SAINT-GIRONS
LÉON
CASTETS
D142
MOLIETS
22,25
34
MESSANGES
26,32,33,43
E5
VIEUX- BOUCAU
(III)
27,28,29,35,36,44
VIEUX-BOUCAU
23,37,38
DAX
24,30,31,39
D79
SOUSTONS
D824
SOORTS-HOSSEGOR
D810

# LES LANDES

Although this is France's, maybe even Europe's, most popular surf area, it's also one of the most heavily forested (watch out for those hunters out there, you don't want to get shot in the butt) and least densely populated areas of Europe. Of all the houses you do stumble upon, a lot are second homes, only inhabited in summer. So, even if it seems like sometimes, at some point and in certain areas, you can't escape the crowds, rest assured: you can. Even in the midst of summer. Just be prepared to hike an extra mile, search beyond the dunes, and in the evening; return to one of the seaside resorts to meet your fellow surfers, find your spot at the bar, or shop for a funky outfit in one of the many surf shops, boutiques and outlets.

## TRAVEL INFO

The most convenient way to travel in Les Landes is to bring your own ride or rent one. Or rent a campervan (see Sleep section)!

### BY AIR

**Aéroport de Bordeaux-Mérignac**, situated 6 km west of Bordeaux, in Mérignac, is a large airport with direct flights to and from almost all countries in Europe.

**w.** bordeaux.airport.fr

Or **Biarritz – Anglet – Bayonne Airport,** located between the towns of Anglet and Biarritz, just off the N10. Several low-cost airlines ensure regular connections from London, Brussels, Dublin and Stockholm.

**w.** biarritz.aeroport.fr

### BY BUS

Not really ideal, but you can get from let's say **Biscarrosse** to **Mimizan** by bus, or to **Bayonne**. Bus lines within Les Landes are handled by RDTL.

**w.** rdtl.fr

### BY TRAIN

Nearest train stations are **Bordeaux**, **Ychoux** or **Arcachon**.

**w.** sncf.com

# SURFER-TRAVELLER TYPE LES LANDES

◆

*You can handle surf all day, party all night, don't mind getting up early to avoid crowds and surf schools, love shopping, love discounts and love to hang out in some pretty cool bars, bike, hike, get lost in the woods looking for empty beachbreaks, run in to a WSL surfer, surf the most famous and photographed surf breaks of France, and don't feel intimidated by boards with sponsor stickers.*

# IN AND AROUND BISCARROSSE

◆

Although not one of the seaside villages from Biscarrosse to Soustons is the same, they pretty much offer 'la même': surf shops and schools, shops with beach necessities, and lots of bars and restaurants, campsites and activities that are only open in summer. So it's a good thing to try to discover the little differences and find some really cool places while you're at it (with a little help from us, of course). Biscarrosse is divided into Biscarrosse-Plage, at the beach, and Biscarrosse-Bourg, at the side of the Biscarrosse lake. With the 'Bisca Bus' service you can travel between the city (Bourg), the lake, and the beach.

**Tourist office** at 55 Place Georges Dufau.

## TO DO

◆

**The Yoga Beach House (1)** is a sanctuary with simple and mindful living and yoga principles at heart. You can either join yoga classes, events and workshops, or a full yoga holiday. Classes are in English and French. The studio has a wood burner for hot yoga classes, and the house has comfortable guest bedrooms. Yoga Beach House is a retreat centre for visiting host teachers and students from around the world. SUP, yoga, surf lessons, bikes and transfers can be arranged. Open all year, retreats are from March to October.

**a.** Rue des Pinsons,
40600 Biscarrosse-Plage
**w.** yogabeachhouse.com

At **Aqua Zen Fish (2)** you can let little friendly fish (Garra Rufa) nibble at your feet and legs, it saves a scrub, is a funny but definitely not unpleasant sensation, and leaves your legs and feet beautifully soft, because the fish eat all the dead skin cells. Bit too tickly for your taste? You can also try an energising reflexology session.

**a.** 82 Impasse de Neuville,
40600 Biscarrosse
**t.** 6 45 417 564
**w.** aqua-zen-fish.com

There are two **skate parks (3)**, one in Biscarrosse-Bourg (town) and one in Biscarrosse-Plage. Both have free entrance.

**a.** Place Dufau 40600, Biscarrosse-Plage
**a.** 236 Avenue Alphonse Daudet,
40600 Biscarrosse

**Cycling** is a perfect way to discover the area and there are 50 kilometres of routes. Several addresses rent out bicycles, from beach cruisers to mountain bikes.

## EAT/DRINK/HANGOUT

◆

**Markets**: Friday (Place du Marché) and Sunday (Avenue George Clémenceau) morning, year round in Biscarrosse-Bourg. Every Saturday morning at Place Dufau in Biscarrosse-Plage.

**Restaurant L'Archipel Bar & Art (4)** has a Hawaiian feel to it, with totems, wood-carvings and flowers. They've got salads, crêpes and fresh fish on the menu, caught by La Patron himself, and some live music evenings. Open all year.

**a.** 511 Avenue de la Plage,
40600 Biscarrosse-Plage
**t.** 5 58 043 476

## SHOP

◆

**Surf Art Galerie La Vigie – Maison du Surf (5)** has some pretty cool Surf Art expositions, but it's also a shop and surf school – it was one of the first in this area actually! Or you can just warm up after a session with a coffee and a sweet snack. Open all year.

**a.** 788 Boulevard Des Sables,
40600 Biscarrosse-Plage
**t.** 5 58 783 779
**w.** la-vigie-biscarrosse.com

There are a lot of surf shops around here, **Natural Surf Shop Café (6)** is one that stands out, especially for its choice of local and smaller brands on sale, like Sen no Sen, Oh Dawn and Soöruz. Open from March to December.

**a.** 526 Boulevard des Sables,
40600 Biscarrosse-Plage
**t.** 6 18 984 041
**w.** naturalsurfshop.bigcartel.com

## SLEEP

◆

**We Dub You Campervans** are based in Bergerac. You can either fly in, pick up the van, make a road trip in southern France, or drive it to Spain and book your return flight from Girona. Rent one of their fun classic VW campervans and choose to go basic, or pimp your ride with options such as ipad, movies and electric bikes. Available all year. •€• •€€•

**e.** funtimes@wedubyou.com
**t.** 4 42 071 939 058
**w.** wedubyou.com

**Camping Le Petit Nice (7)** is not that petit, but it's shaded by pine trees, with direct access to the beach and is located next to Dune de Pyla. They have mobile homes for rent and – very handy – a take-off zone for paragliding. Open April to September. •€€•

**a.** Route de Biscarrosse,
33115 Pyla-sur-Mer
**t.** 5 56 227 403
**e.** petit-nice@franceloc.fr
**w.** petitnice.com

Indulge in a little surf chique at **Côte & Dune Chambres d'Hôtes (8)**, a Californian-style white wooden boutique guest-house, spacious, with comfortable bedrooms. All balconies, windows and terraces open onto a central patio with a pool. Each room has its own individual style, inspired by the ocean and forest, and named after a famous surf spot. There are yoga lessons and Ayurvedic massages available. •€€•

**a.** 675 Avenue Gabriele d'Annunzio,
40600 Biscarrosse-Plage
**t.** 6 08 963 173 / 5 58 081 729
**e.** contact@cotedune.fr
**w.** cotedune.fr

# IN AND AROUND MIMIZAN

Like Biscarrosse, Mimizan is divided into two parts; the sea resort, and a bit inland, the town of Mimizan itself, backed by pine forest and the Aureilhan lake. The north and south of the town are also divided by the river that runs from the lake to the sea. Although a big part of the lake is a protected environment, nautical activity is possible; like SUP, kayak tours and sailing.

**Tourist office** at 38 Avenue Maurice Martin.

## TO DO

**Hiking and biking (9)**: there are many routes that are either marked or just easy to follow. Between Mimizan and Espécier is walking route Sentiers de la Mailloueyre. At the start/finish, in the parking and picnic area, you'll find a forest hut surrounded by trees with signs explaining how 'gemmage' works: the process of tapping a pine tree to collect resin, which was a big industry in the area up until the 1980s. Easy route to follow with kids, it's about 3 km long, with some viewpoints.

**Yoga on the beach (10)**: in summer Jalan Yoga offers outdoor yoga classes; choose between dynamic vinyasa yoga and gentle yoga classes. If you want to join one of the classes, simply make a reservation by phone or mail. For (year round) classes in the studio check the schedule on the site.

**a.** 1500 Route des Quartiers,
40200 Mimizan
**t.** 7 81 786 262
**e.** info@jalanyoga.com
**w.** jalanyoga.com

**Contis Plage (11)**: just like all the others, it's one of those little seaside resorts that only comes to life in summer, but it's all quite nicely done; the few bars, shops, houses and restaurants seem to have had a tad more attention to decoration and atmosphere, with use of wood and colour painting. You can visit the Contis lighthouse (in July and August), strangely enough built in the forest, not right at sea; and it's the only lighthouse in this area, from Cap Ferret to Cap Breton.

For a family day at the beach and forest, **Plage de l'Espécier (12)**, between Contis and Mimizan, serves the purpose pretty well. There's a spacious parking and picnic area (très clean, despite there being no garbage disposals - the signs kindly requesting to take it home seem to work!), a small playground for toddlers and a 'parcours acrobatique' to climb, crawl and swing on ropes (**Bias Aventure**, open in July and August). Because it's a long walk to the beach it's quieter than most beaches. Beach has lifeguards in summer, but always beware of currents. There are no beach facilities, except a surf school in summer.

## EAT/DRINK/HANGOUT

◆

**Markets**: every Friday morning all year round in Mimizan-Bourg (town), seasonal and regional products, Place Felix Poussade. In Mimizan-Plage there's a covered market which is open all year; check out Benico Bio, who sells his biological fruits and vegetables here. From June to September there's an outdoor market every Thursday morning.

Watch the sunset with a cocktail in hand at **A Noste** (**13**), a small bar and tapas restaurant, facing the ocean. Open from May to September.

**a.** 7 Boulevard de la Côte d'Argent, 40200 Mimizan-Plage

Eat, drink, chill, dance or rock at the **Pura Vida Surf Bar** (**14**), and yes, expect lots of holidaying surfers and surfettes here. Closed in winter.

**a.** 8 Rue de la Poste, 40200 Mimizan-Plage

For a night out in an intimate setting, drinks, snacks, concerts and DJs, check **Bar L'Art Other** (**15**).

**a.** 9 Rue de Casino, 40200 Mimizan-Plage

In nearby small town Lit-et-Mixe, Bar Restaurant **L'Art H** (**16**) has tapas, grill platters and French cuisine on offer. Big shaded terrace, with a little jazz and soul on the side. Bar is open all year, restaurant in summer season. •€€•

**a.** 223 Avenue du Marensin, 40170 Lit-et-Mixe
**t.** 5 24 266 516

At Contis-Plage you'll find **Sushi-Be** (**17**) for some delicious freshly made sushi. While waiting for your sushi you can admire some ceramic pottery from local artist Silvie Caule, since the sushi bar is connected to Poterie Ternet. •€€•

**a.** 387 Avenue de l'Ocean, 40170 Contis-Plage
**t.** 7 88 031 019
**w.** sushibe.fr

## SLEEP

◆

The **Aloha Surf Lodge** (**18**) has room for up to 15 people, who can divide themselves between 5 comfortable rooms, warm up in the jacuzzi, make use of the swimming pool, slackline, bikes, skateboards and a tennis table. The concept is the brainchild of pro-riders and watermen Nicolas Capdeville and Vincent Duvignac, who also offer weeks of (high level) intensive surf courses. You can choose from B&B rooms up to complete full-board. Surf course includes video analysis, personal advice and transport to the best surf conditions. Open in season and by reservation. •€€•

**a.** 1287, Route de Labadan, 40200 Sainte-Eulalie-en-Born
**t.** 5 58 097 816 / 6 20 525 740
**e.** alohasurflodge@aol.com
**w.** surflodge.fr

On our quest to find the best places to stay; either nice, likeable, beautiful, homely, family-run, or friendly-near-the-ocean places, we came across a few that actually had it all, like **Pura Vida Lodge** (**19**). Sven and Elles, longtime residents of Mimizan, run the Pura Vida Lodge with love. It shows in the details. Home-made, local and organic breakfasts, a secluded garden with lots of flowers, trees, hammocks, solar shower and a swimming pool. Small driftwood decorations, spacious rooms and lounge, make Pura Vida a comfy lodge for surfers and their family and friends. They offer special 30+ weeks, surf and yoga weeks and surf coach courses. Open from May to October. •€• •€€•

**a.** 50 Avenue Maurice Martin, 40200 Mimizan-Plage
**t.** 5 58 081 742 / 6 10 956 909
**w.** puravidalodge.com

**Camping Le Tatiou** (**20**) is situated in the middle of the pine forest, within walking distance of the quiet Plage de l'Espécier. Bungalows, tents, and mobile homes for rent, or try the 'campétoiles'; a sleeping cabin on poles, 2 metres above the ground with a transparent roof to watch the stars. Open from April to September. •€• •€€•

**a.** 1791 Route de Lespecier, 40170 Bias
**t.** 5 58 090 476
**e.** camping-le-tatiou@bias40.fr
**w.** letatiou.bias40.fr

**Campervans** (**21**) can stay overnight and empty toilets near the Contis lighthouse, 500 m from the beach. Open all year, paid in summer, free from December to February.

**a.** 301 Avenue de Phare, 40170 Contis-Plage

# IN AND AROUND VIEUX-BOUCAU-LES-BAINS

From Moliets, Messanges and Vieux-Boucau to Soustons, there are campsites, surf schools and breaks galore, lots of bars and restaurants to choose from and endless hike and bike opportunities. If you can avoid busy summer months when all the surf camps and schools take over towns and beaches, you'll have the best of both worlds: a lively scène in and around the seaside resorts, and lots of waves to yourself. But even in summer, there's a way to escape it all, it just takes that extra leg to go and explore.

**Tourist office** at 11 Mail André Rigal.

## TO DO

Thai and Ayurvedic massages, reflexology, yoga and zumba, all at a surf school? Brian and Mia, and the team of **Zen 'n Surf School** (**22**) give a whole new meaning to surfing and feeling good. There's the Zen side, where Mia combines her two passions, 'water and well-being', by giving massages and sophrology (relaxation sessions with the help of breath, meditation, yoga and stretching techniques), either indoor or on the beach. Check the schedule on their website or drop by for a chat about all the possibilities (from surf and yoga to Nordic walking) at this friendly and welcoming place. For the surf side, see surf section. Open from April to October.

**a.** 249, Val de Lamartine,
40660 Moliets-et-Maa
**t.** 5 58 971 297 / 6 11 558 132 (Mia)
**w.** zen-n-surf-school.com

**SUP Land** (**23**) offers SUP lessons and tours on the Souston lake, on the connecting river and in the ocean. Also intermediate and perfecting technique classes in the waves. SUP Land is run by former Les Landes SUP champ David Latastère. Info and reservations by phone or mail.

**t.** 6 73 512 649
**w.** supland.fr

Add a bit of cool to your bike tour and rent a beach cruiser at **Free Landers** (**24**).

**a.** Avenue de la Pêtre,
Place des Commerces du Lac Marin,
40140 Soustons
**t.** 5 58 480 981
**w.** location-velos-freelandes.com

## EAT/DRINK/HANGOUT

**Restaurant Ti'Bou** (**25**) is situated in a characteristic old hostel with woodwork from the 19th century. Their cuisine is a fine mixture of using tradition and innovative creativity. A friendly atmosphere and excellent food, using quality products. Open all year. •€€•

**a.** 14 Avenue du Général de Gaulle,
40660 Moliets-et-Maa
**t.** 5 58 431 225
**e.** info@tibou-moliets.fr
**w.** tibou-moliets.fr

**Restaurant La Hitillère** (**26**) offers good food and a good vibe in their warmly decorated restaurant. Practice your French and wise up with their 'quotes' hanging from the wall and on the menu. Home-made french fries, use of seasonal veggies, copious meals: breakfast, lunch, tapas and dinner. Open from March to October. •€€•

**a.** 9 Avenue de l'Océan, 40660 Messanges
**t.** 5 58 421 617

Restaurant Bar **Larroseur (27)** has pizzas and burgers and over 80 brands of beer on the menu. There's art on show and live music events. Open all year. •€•

**a.** 25 Rue du Capitaine Saint Jours, 40480 Vieux-Boucau-les-Bains
**t.** 5 58 574 247

**La Saladerie Grill Tarterie Les Tropiques (28)** for a tasty 'croque monsieur' in a tropical setting. Open all year, except January. •€•

**a.** Place des Tamaris, 40480 Vieux-Boucau-les-Bains
**t.** 5 58 481 125

Get your cocktails, shots and salsa at **Caribbean Bar La Vague (29)**, or chill out in the hammock chairs on the terrace. Tapas and snacks on the menu, and live music in summer. Open from March till October. •€•

**a.** 43 Avenue de la Plage, 40480 Vieux-Boucau-les-Bains
**t.** 6 32 418 760

Take a Breton break and enjoy your sweet crêpes and savoury galettes under the trees with a view of the Soustons lake at **Creperie Chez Suzette (30)**. •€•

**a.** Commerces Du Lac Marin De Port D'Albret, 15 Avenue De La Petre, 40140 Soustons
**t.** 5 24 625 637 / 6 41 040 006

Hard to imagine you'll find a delicious nasi goreng and saté, accompanied by a Bintang beer in the row of small snack restaurants at the entrance to Soustons Plage. But the petit **Balian Café (31)** serves just that (oh, and if you really must: salads and burgers too). Great after-surf dinner in a warung-like eatery, fast and friendly service. •€•

**a.** 2 Montée de la Plage, Soustons Plage
**t.** 5 58 470 160

## SLEEP

◆

**Campervans (32)** can stay overnight at a parking area within walking distance of the beach of Messanges. First night is free, every second night you pay a small fee per person. No services. (Take the D82 to the beach, turn right just before the last parking area).

**a.** Plage La Dune, 40660 Messanges

The concept of **Eco Nature Surf Camp (33)** derived from the Australian backpackers scene, with the aim to welcome travellers – solo, friends or family - in an open and friendly environment. The eco in its name is taken seriously, by conserving energy, water and electricity, but you'll still find the comforts of a swimming pool, jacuzzi in the woods, use of bicycles, pool table, and wifi. There are 4 rooms (max 14 persons) in their big house, that's surrounded by green, and 2 tents in the garden. You'll be in the good hands of brothers Benoît Cail and Pacôme Cail, longtime passionate surfers and skaters. Open from April to October. •€•

**a.** Quartier Moutic-Route d'Azur, 40660 Messanges
**t.** 6 33 479 469
**e.** ecoledesurf@yahoo.fr
**w.** nature-surf-camp.com

**Camping Du Toy (34)** is a bit more inland, but a gem, especially for families with young kids. It has 35 spacious pitches, the site is decorated with sculptures and wooden carvings, and the bathrooms with mosaics which the owner created over the last 30 years. You can also choose to rent a rural gîte, a châlet or a maisonette. Kids can climb ropes and slide and jump on the trampoline; entertainment in an outdoor style. Open from May to September. •€• •€€•

**a.** 1284 Route des Carroués, 40990 Herm
**t.** 5 58 915 516
**e.** mail@camping-du-toy.com
**w.** camping-du-toy.com

German-owned **Atlantic Surf Lodge (35)** has spacious rooms, from 2 to 5 persons, run by friendly staff. The vibe is very relaxed and aimed at 25+ surfers. There's a big garden and lounge where you can chill, read a book, socialise with fellow guests, try your skills on the Indo board or slackline, and you can use bicycles and skateboards. Breakfast and dinner are also suitable for vegetarians. They offer surf lessons for beginners and intermediates and also organise yoga weeks. Open from May to October. •€• •€€•

**a.** 7 Rue du Pignadar,
40480 Vieux-Boucau-les-Bains
**t.** 6 33 385 131 (Jodie and Uli)
**e.** jodie@atlantic-surflodge.com
**w.** atlantic-surflodge.com

**Vieux-Boucau Surflodge Villa Tiki (36)** is just a hop-skip away from the beach. The villa has 3 bedrooms – 1 double and 2 dorms. A hut in the garden accommodates 2 to 3 people. There are hammocks in the garden to chill out, a bbq and boards, yoga courses on offer, and wetsuits and bikes for rent. Open from March to November. •€• •€€•

**a.** 5 Avenue des Dunes,
40480 Vieux-Boucau-les-Bains
**t.** 6 86 523 630 (Ivan Rey)
**e.** contact@vieuxboucau-surflodge.com
**w.** vieuxboucau-surflodge.com

**The Secret Spot B&B (37)** is set in a characteristic old farmhouse, recently renovated in the original style. It has 5 rooms, a spacious lounge area and dining room, 3 sundecks, and a pool. 'Surf-n-Yoga' packages available. Open from May to October. •€• •€€•

**a.** 470 Rue Henri Goalard, 40140 Azur
**t.** 5 58 482 921 / 6 31 497 999
(Troy and Nelly Ferry)
**w.** secretspotlodge.com

**Aire Naturelle Pesson (38)** is a rural camping park in the pine forests, 6 kms from the beach of Messanges. Quiet, but with all the necessary comfort. Open from April to September. •€•

**a.** 921 Route de Messanges,
40140 Azur (Soustons)
**t.** 5 58 483 049
**e.** contact@campingpesson.com
**w.** campingpesson.com

Campervans can stay at **Aire Soustons Plage (39)**, perfectly situated at the lake, forest and close to the beach. Facilities to empty water and toilet. Open all year. •€•

**a.** Avenue de la Petre, Soustons Plage

# SURF

From Gironde to the Basque country the coast stretches in a straight line of west facing sandy beaches, providing countless surfable breaks. As with the seaside resorts themselves, all spots are slightly unique, because of the constant changes of sandbanks that build up in different shapes and sizes. The big draw to this part of France for surfers is the endless possibility, and the shape, size and power of the waves. They're created by 'baïnes'; offshore pools or lagoons. Between the pools, sandbanks build up that give the perfect-for-surf shape to the waves. The downside is the danger of strong currents – people drown every year and you can't see the underwater pools and rips. Then there's the wind: there are no protected spots, so when it's big and onshore winds rule, check out our To Do section.

**Biscarrosse-Plage** (**I**) has all the options you can expect from a beachbreak; lefts, rights, a hollow shorebreak, but doesn't handle too much size or wind. Shifting sandbars determine where to go in, but from the south end all the way up to Mimizan is restricted military zone! Best at mid-tide and nw-w-sw small to medium swell, be aware of strong currents. All levels. Easy parking/toilet/restaurant/surf school/surf shop.

**Mimizan-Plage** (**II**) offers options for surf on either side of the rivermouth. Can be polluted near the estuary. From Mimizan to the south, Lespecier, Contis-Plage to Messanges, there are plenty of possibilities to surf quieter breaks. At **Vieux-Boucau-les-Bains** (**III**) it's getting more crowded, but again, move a bit further away from the main access points to the beach and you'll be fine, even in summer. Best at mid-tide and nw-w-sw small to medium swell, be aware of strong currents. All levels. Easy parking/toilet/restaurant/surf school/surf shop.

# SCHOOL RENTAL REPAIR

◆

**Kiwi Surf School and Beach Club (40)**, surf lessons, rental, kids club, trampoline, and swimming lessons in a pool on the beach. Owners, Clement and Dhélia, are two-time tandem surfing World Champions. Open from April to October.

**a.** 503 Boulevard d'Arcachon, 40600 Biscarrosse-Plage
**t.** 5 58 071 458 / 6 84 359 099
**w.** kiwisurfbiscarrosse.com

**Point Break Surf School (41)**, surf and SUP lessons, and rental.

**a.** 66 Résidence Océan, Place de l'Océan, 40600 Biscarrosse-Plage
**t.** 5 58 097 159
**w.** surfbiscarrosse.com

**So What SurfBoards (42)**, shapes and repairs (from longboard, shortboard, fish to gun).

**a.** 467 Impasse des Pluviers, 40600 Biscarrosse-Plage
**t.** 5 58 783 710
**w.** sowhatsurfboards.free.fr

**Zen 'n' Surf School (22)**, all levels surf school with video analysis, bilingual teachers. Every first Sunday of the month you can help them clean the beaches (and earn a 10-minute massage!). Massages, yoga-classes and more on offer as well (see To Do section). Open from April to October.

**a.** 249, Val de Lamartine, 40660 Moliets-et-Maa
**t.** 5 58 971 297 / 6 11 558 132 (Mia and Brian)
**w.** zen-n-surf-school.com

**Desert Point Surf Shop (43)**, rental, lessons, repair and shop with all essentials. Open from April to October.

**a.** Centre, 40660 Messanges
**t.** 5 58 491 211 / 6 81 415 703
**w.** surf-messanges.com

**Alternative Surf School (44)**, surf coaching with video analysis, lessons for all levels, rental of shortboards and longboards. Open all year for surf coaching.

**a.** Plage de l'Estacade, Résidence de la Plage, Rue des Goëlands, 40480 Vieux-Boucau-les-Bains
**t.** 6 03 060 642 (Vincent Guelfi)
**w.** alternativesurfschool.com

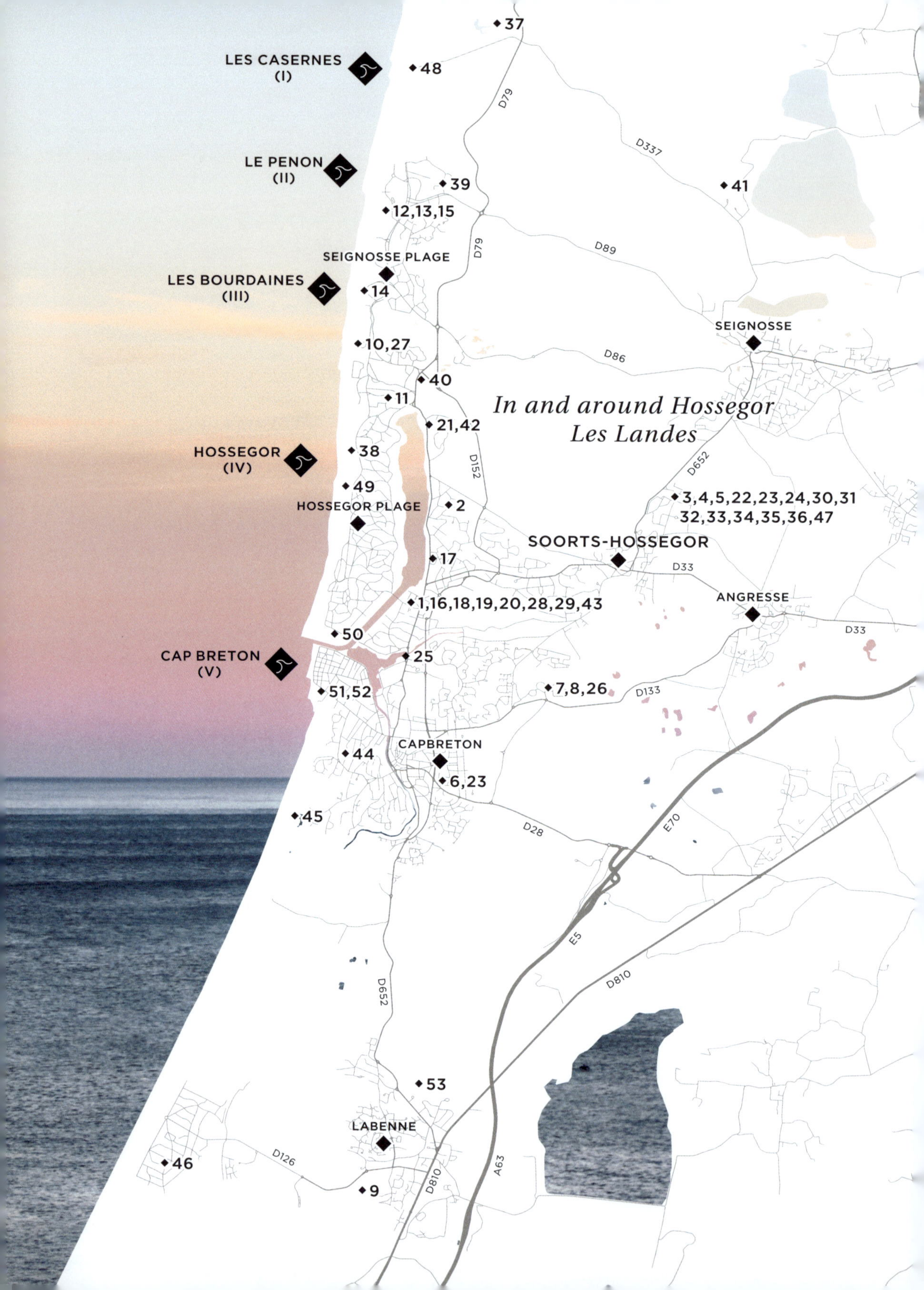
In and around Hossegor
Les Landes
37
LES CASERNES (I)
48
D79
D337
LE PENON (II)
39
41
12,13,15
D79
D89
SEIGNOSSE PLAGE
LES BOURDAINES (III)
14
SEIGNOSSE
10,27
D86
40
11
21,42
HOSSEGOR (IV)
38
D152
D652
49
HOSSEGOR PLAGE
2
3,4,5,22,23,24,30,31
32,33,34,35,36,47
SOORTS-HOSSEGOR
17
D33
ANGRESSE
1,16,18,19,20,28,29,43
D33
50
CAP BRETON (V)
25
51,52
7,8,26
D133
CAPBRETON
44
6,23
45
E70
D28
E5
D810
D652
53
LABENNE
46
D126
9
D810
A63

# IN AND AROUND HOSSEGOR

Vibrant, stylish in a laissez-faire manner, and yes, always busy in summer. That about sums it up for this area. From Seignosse to Labenne, life is saturated with surfing: a yearly site for the WSL Championship Tour, renowned outlet heaven for surf brand aficionados (Soorts-Hossegor) and headquarters of the French Surf Federation.
You will find that, as a tourist, you'll blend in fine with the mix of locals and semi-locals; since a lot of foreigners have adopted this area, drawn by the surf, to set up business or for a temporary change of scene. It doesn't have the 'put out the plastic chairs for summer and be gone in winter' routine that most of the seaside resorts seem to stick to - Hossegor actually continues along with its everyday life in winter, albeit in second gear.

## TO DO

Tune in to **Surf FM** (102.3 FM on your radio from April to October, online all year round), by far the best radio station you've ever listened to. Trust us.

**w.** surf-fm.fr

**Collect driftwood** and get creative. After big, stormy surf, the ocean spits a lot of pieces of wood, and even entire trees onto the beach (alongside trash, so while you're at it, might as well pick that up too).

**All Boards Rentals (1)** also rents out all sorts of cool, fun bikes; from cruisers to electric Fat Bikes (fat tyres, making it easier on all sorts of tracks and roads, and designed like a low rider motorbike).

**a.** 340 Avenue du Touring Club de France, 40150 Hossegor
**t.** 6 77 968 447
**w.** allboards.surf.location.com

**Nalu Massages** offer a range of mobile massage treatments, from chair, deep tissue and foot to Balinese reflexology massages. They're mobile, so they can, as they say themselves 'transform your space into a calming atmosphere', in and around Hossegor. Only by appointment, 7 days a week. Open from May till October.

**t.** 6 37 646 176
**e.** info@nalumassages.com
**w.** nalumassages.com

**Hossegor Lake Paddle (2)** takes you out onto the Hossegor lake on a SUP, Canadian kayak or outrigger. Open from May to October on Wednesday, Saturday and Sunday. From mid-June to mid-September open every day.

**a.** Plage du Rey – Lac d'Hossegor, Soorts-Hossegor
**t.** 7 84 554 479
**w.** hossegor-lake-paddle.com

**Skate Club Hossegor (3)** has an indoor bowl, street park, offers classes for riders of all levels and longboard cruising tours through the pine forest. Open all year.

**a.** 49 Avenue des Tonneliers, 40150 Soorts-Hossegor
**t.** 6 44 255 800
**w.** skateclubhossegor.fr

If you want, you can do a **yoga** class every day if you time it right. Here are just a few options from the many yoga schools in the area.

Yogini Gabrielle welcomes you in her **Yoga Bikram Hossegor** (**4**) studio. Open all year, every day, on Saturday classes are held in English.

**a.** 407 Avenue de la Tuilerie, ZA Pédebert, 40150 Soorts-Hossegor
**t.** 9 70 359 277 / 6 78 451 403
**w.** yogabikramhossegor.fr

**Samudra Yoga Studio** (**5**) offers vinyasa, power, and surf yoga, with Caroline Beliard-Zebrowski, surfer and yogini.

**a.** 455 Avenue de Pascouaou, ZA Pédebert, 40150 Soorts-Hossegor
**t.** 6 83 658 672
**e.** caroline.beliard@gmail.com
**w.** carolinesyoga.com

**Hossegor Yoga** (**6**), with Barbara Wright, Ashtanga Yogini, teaches at the Quiksilver Boardriders Store. Open all year.

**a.** 36 Boulevard du Docteur Junqua, 40130 Capbreton
**t.** 6 77 734 655
**e.** yogahossegor@gmail.com
**w.** yogahossegor.com

Follow a complete **shaper workshop programme** (**7**) at the OG-Atelier in Capbreton, factory of the Plonka surfboards, with South African National Team coach and former pro-surfer, Kevin Olsen. Expect devotion to creativity, old school techniques and modern ideas in a one-to-one course in design and shaping techniques to shape your own surfboard.

**a.** OG-Atelier, ZA Les Deux Pins, 4 Rue Pitey, 40130 Capbreton
**t.** 5 58 726 008
**w.** plonkasurfboards.com

**Hammam Kafane** (**8**), oh yes, relax-a-lot, the oriental way. Open all year, by appointment only.

**a.** Rue des Resiniers, ZA Les 2 Pins, 40130 Capbreton
**t.** 5 58 481 458
**w.** hammam-kafane.fr

**Spa Dune & Eau** (**9**) is a like a modern temple of well-being, not very personal, but with a lot on offer; like a heated pool, hydro beds, sauna and steam room, massages and facials with essential oils. Open all year, every day.

**a.** 59 Avenue de l'Océan, 40530 Labenne Océan
**t.** 5 59 590 590 / 6 34 263 858
**w.** duneeteau.fr

## EAT/DRINK/HANGOUT

◆

Get your wholesome, happy breakfast or lunch at **Le Deli (10)**. Organic cakes, fresh smoothies, good coffee, wraps and brownies. All served in a sunny atmosphere. Open from May to October. •€• •€€•

**a.** 54 Avenue du Penon, 40510 Seignosse

**Chez Monette (11)** serves different styles of food, tapas-style, in a Balinese-style garden, sometimes accompanied by live music. Open in the evenings from May to September. •€€•

**a.** 5 Avenue Jean Moulin,
40510 Seignosse
**t.** 6 79 589 035

Enjoy a good wine and some tapas at **Chez Béné (12)** while enjoying live music or watching some surf action on screen. Open all year. •€•

**a.** 2 Avenue de la Grande Plage - Résidence Le Trident,
40510 Seignosse

**Heads Beach Brewing Co (13)** is a small craft brewery with home-made brewed beer, fingerfood, tapas, burgers, and maybe some beards and funky hats to go with that. Open from March to October.

**a.** 4 Place des Bourdaines,
40510 Seignosse
**w.** headsbeachbrewingcompany.com

Bar, restaurant and tearoom **Les Mets D'Alice (14)** has got a lot of foodie goodies on the menu; from banana-chocolate crumble pie to a creative mix of French and Thai cuisine. Open from March to October. •€• •€€•

**a.** 20 Place de Castille, 40510 Seignosse
**t.** 5 58 498 148

It's not an easy job for real coffee lovers to get a tasty cup in France. Go try **Little Cove Café (15)**, located opposite Parc Aquatique in Seignosse. A real barista serves not only coffee, but also prepares smoothies and sandwiches. Or choose some fine patisserie to go with that. Open every day from July till mid September, and school holidays. •€•

**a.** 4 Avenue de la Grande Plage,
40510 Seignosse
**w.** littlecovecafe.com

**Café Bleu (16)** is a bit hidden behind shops in the main street of Hossegor centre, which also means it's a little haven of peace amidst summer buzz, both inside and on their shaded terrace. It's a sweet and cosy little place for coffee, breakfast, lunch and light dinner. Open from April to November. •€•

**a.** 74 Avenue Paul Lahary,
Residence La Pierre Bleu,
40150 Hossegor

**Le Mango Tree (17)** is a ' bar á fruits mobile'; a pop-up food truck with fresh fruit juices and healthy, yummie food goodies. Served with big smiles from the two lovely Mango Tree ladies, whose passion for (healthy) food shows in their cuisine. You'll find them in Plage du Parc, next to the lake and children's playground, in the centre of town. Open from May to October. •€•

**a.** Avenue de Rosney / Avenue de Vamireh,
40150 Hossegor
**t.** 6 89 616 870
**w.** lemangotree.com

**L'&tiquette (18)**, this laid-back wine bar will introduce you, in a simple and enjoyable manner, to some quality wines. Local hangout and friendly place in the heart of Hossegor. Open all year.

**a.** 16 Place des Pins Tranquilles,
40150 Hossegor

**Glaces Romane (19)**, oh my, 48 flavours of ice-cream to choose from. And all home-made, with love.

**a.** 31 Avenue Paul Lahary, 40150 Hossegor

**Sushi Stop (20)** offers, as the name suggests, delicious and fresh sushi. You'll be thankful you stopped. Open Thursday to Sunday. •€• •€€•

**a.** 24 Allée Louis Pasteur,
40150 Soorts-Hossegor
**w.** sushistop.fr

Oyster bars line the lake of Hossegor; the lake itself stretches over 5750 metres and is connected to the ocean. You can choose one that appeals to you. There's not really a bad one that we know of but if you want to be sure, try award-winning **Oyster Cabana Chez Jérome (21)**. They also arrange demonstrations and tastings, and you can find them at local markets. •€€•

**a.** 1 Avenue du Tour de Lac,
40150 Hossegor
**t.** 6 73 342 162
**w.** huitres-hossegor.fr

**Market**: Marché de Pays offers local products, every Saturday morning, all year round.

**a.** Fronton de Soorts, Rue de la Fôret,
40150 Soorts

If you're a fan of hop, **L'ile du Malt (22)** is your go-to beer cave. They've got over 400 worldwide beers, dedicated and knowledgeable staff, happy hours and evening concerts. Open all year.

**a.** 51 Avenue des Tisserands,
ZA Pédebert,
40150 Soorts-Hossegor

You'll find **Jack's Burgers (23)** in 3 locations (Hossegor, Capbreton and Soustons). It's fast food-de-luxe, loved by locals and tourists, and definitely in a better setting than the average burger-chain. Open all year. •€•

**a.** Route de Tosse, 40140 Soustons
**a.** 73 Avenue des Charpentiers,
40150 Soorts-Hossegor
**a.** 22 Avenue de Verdun, 40130 Capbreton
**w.** jacksburgers.fr

**Les Caprices de Romane (24)** is a salon de thé, coffee and pastry shop, but of course you're lured in here because of their delicious ice-cream after you've done your shopping in the outlet stores. Open all year. •€• •€€•

**a.** Avenue de Tisserands, ZA Pédebert,
40150 Soorts-Hossegor

**Made with Love (25)** is a salon de thé, an atelier de cuisine, and serves brunch, lunch and cupcakes, made with love of course, in a candy sweet setting. Open all year. •€• •€€•

**a.** 69 Quai de la Pecherie,
40130 Capbreton
**w.** madewithlove-cupcakes.fr

**Veganethik (26)** is a skate store, a skate park, a tattoo and piercing parlour, a place to get organic and vegan products, enjoy jam-sessions, art classes and what-not? It's all the above, and for sure a little more. It's a très cool local hangout that can't be labelled. Go check it out.

**a.** 17 Rue du Hapchot,
Zone Artisinale des 2 Pins,
40130 Capbreton
**w.** veganethik.fr

## SHOP

◆

Many surfers are into fishing and music, but not so many designers take that into consideration, do they? **The Louvine Collective (27)** actually thrives on the feedback of fishermen, musicians and surfers, and their say on design and food. They produce small collections of tees, hats and accessories for fishing and outdoor living, and cook with the use of organic and fresh products. Louvine's menu (at a food-truck for lunch, the restaurant for dinner) has influences from Asian and Mexican cuisine. Open all year at weekends, every day in summer. •€• •€€•

**a.** 45 Avenue du Penon, 40510 Seignosse
**t.** 9 71 571 610
**w.** louvine.com

**Philippine Hossegor Laboutique (28)** is a cute, stylish, mini concept store; seriously bohemian, with original creations, decorations, bags, clothes and accessories. All made in Hossegor!

**a.** 153 Avenue de Paul Lahary,
40150 Hossegor

The jewellery at **Boutique L'atelier des Dames (29)** has this swanky French boho and rock-chic character. Well, that's what we think. All French manufactured jewellery, made from unusual and sometimes recycled, but fine, materials from all over the world. And a very friendly lady in the shop to tell you all about it.

**a.** 58 Place Louis Pasteur,
40150 Hossegor
**w.** latelierdesdames.fr

**Soorts-Hossegor ZA** (Zone Artisinale) used to be an industrial zone and is still outlet store heaven. Lately, more très cool bars, shops and hangouts than we can keep track of are popping up. Some of our favourites you'll find listed here.

**All Good (30)** is a beauty of a store - spacious and smartly decorated. You'll find small and local designer brands, books, jewellery, coffee, boards and more. The shop's got a few of their own brands too, like Woll beer, and Jesus Loves Beer clothing. From home-made cakes to scented candles made out of organic wax, and stylish clothes. You can return to the shop over and over again and there will always be something new to discover. Ask the friendly staff about upcoming events in the shop, such as music, film and art events. Open all year.

**a.** 33 Avenue des Tisserands,
ZA Pédebert, 40150 Soorts-Hossegor
**t.** 5 58 470 486
**w.** allgood.fr

Get your feet rolling at **The Sector 9 Store (31)**. A huge choice of boards, well arranged, and over 30 test boards ready to be checked out. Conveniently, testing can be done in the parking area right in front of the store. Staff are extremely friendly, hence the good vibe, and of course, well-informed and fitted out to give the best advice. So, no matter if you're a pro or a novice, you fit the surf and skate lifestyle, or are just checking for a gift, the Sector 9 Skateboard Store is a fun place. Open all year. Just check the times for the lunch break, it's taken very seriously: the staff have either gone surfing or skating!

**a.** 165 Avenue des Rémouleurs,
ZA Pédebert , 40150 Soorts-Hossegor
**t.** 5 58 479 169
**w.** sector9store.com

**Chipiron Surfboards (32)**, lovely people, lovely crafts. Besides original and authentic boards, they have clothes, caps and accessories, all gathered in their shop. Chipiron Surfboards was set in motion by local, Damien Marly, with the simple idea to make his own surfboards and share know-how. Joined by friends, Antoine Hodin and Julie Pollet, Chipiron became the brand it is today, with a distinguished identity: 'We create boards for an instinctive and pure glide'. You can check them out at their test centre. Open all year.

**a.** 376 Avenue des Forgerons,
ZA Pédebert, 40150 Soorts-Hossegor
**w.** chipiron-surfboards.com

The idea of **Collective Soul Concept Store (33)** is to initiate access to, and emphasis on, original and quality workmanship and materials. So, you'll find unique textiles, interior design, clothes, art and accessories, either made in small series, or unique, vintage items. It's all work from the heart from creative and passionate people collaborating with each other. Open all year.

**a.** 93 Avenue des Tisserands, ZA Pédebert,
40150 Soorts-Hossegor
**w.** collectivesoul.fr

**All Troc Second Hand Shop (34)**: The place to go if you're in need of a used board, wetsuit, bike or skateboard. They've got a big assortment and you can make a rather smart purchase to save some money for travelling. You can also bring your gear, and get your money once they've sold it.

**a.** 34 Avenue des Charpentiers,
ZA Pédebert,
40150 Soorts-Hossegor
**t.** 5 58 417 041
**w.** alltrochossegor.com

**Wasted Talent Boutique (35)** is an initiative of Wasted Talent; creators, curators and distributors of selective brands. They're working with artists, surfers, musicians and photographers. Funky and fine clothes, glasses, and make sure to check out their 'What Youth' magazine. Open Monday to Saturday.

**a.** 165 Avenue de Rémouleurs,
ZA Pédebert, 40150 Soorts-Hossegor
**w.** wasted-talent.eu

Another fine concept store: **Boho Factory Hossegor (36)**. Jewellery, art, decorations, small furniture, clothes, and coffee. Except for the coffee, all items are created by local designers and artists. Open all year.

**a.** Avenue de la Tuilerie (direction Rip Curl),
ZA Pédebert, 40150 Soorts-Hossegor

## SLEEP

◆

**Ocean Shelter (37)** is your ideal natural base camp, located in the forest and with only a 1 km walk to the beach, near surf spot Les Casernes. There's a house (6 persons), tipi tents that can fit 4 persons and 2 retro caravans (2 persons). Bikes are free to use, there's a heated pool, shaded terrace and hammocks to doze off after a surf session. Open from Easter to October. ◆€◆ ◆€€◆

**a.** 196 Route de Vieux Boucau,
Quartier Lamontagne, 40510 Seignosse
**t.** 6 84 356 214
**e.** info@oceanshelter.com
**w.** oceanshelter.com

**Lodge Natureo (38)** is an ecologic, wooden, luxury villa, right on the beach of Estagnots. Very comfortable, and done up in perfect harmony with the surrounding dune landscape. Up to 12 persons can make use of 4 spacious rooms, 1 suite and a dormitory. There's a fully equipped kitchen, big living room, jacuzzi, sauna, swimming pool, terrace and bicycles. Available all year. ◆€€€◆

**a.** 10 Avenue des Gurbettes,
40510 Seignosse
**t.** 7 85 388 737
**e.** lodgenatureolandes@gmail.com
**w.** vacances-estagnots.com

**Seignosse Surf Villa (39)** is located conveniently 500 m from Plage de Penon, backed by pine forest and close to 2 golf courses. It has 6 comfortable rooms and is stylishly decorated in surf-inspired themes, for up to 14 persons. Big peaceful garden with swimming pool, and a small golf putting green, and... howzaboutzat, a yoga studio! The Villa is the brainchild of South African National Team coach and former pro-surfer, Kevin Olsen. You can either book a room, rent the entire villa, including professional surf coaching from Kevin, or do a little bit of both. You can use the yoga studio, or book classes. Check online for availability and packages. ◆€€◆ ◆€€€◆

**a.** 9 Avenue des Chais, 40510 Seignosse
**t.** 5 58 726 008 / 6 26 328 759
**w.** seignossevilla.com

German-owned **Secret Wave Surf Camp (40)** is a B&B for 30+ ocean lovers. It has 5 comfortable rooms, each with their own wooden deck. On offer: delicious home-cooked vegetarian meals, yoga, surf coaching and rental, massages, bicycles and French language courses. Open from April to November. ◆€€◆

**a.** 3 Avenue Jean Moulin, 40510 Seignosse
**t.** 5 58 470 633
**w.** secretwavesurfcamp.com

**Natural Surf Lodge (41)** is an environmentally friendly surf camp for max 16 persons. You can choose between: The Surfers Cocoon Lodge, with room for family and individuals, then there's The Bungalow - what used to be a shelter for, ehm, pigs, is now a comfy nest for surfing lovebirds, and The Fermette, an ancient bread-oven converted into a little surf house! Every lodger has access to the communal room and kitchen, BBQ, tree hut, hammocks, jacuzzi and steam room. Open from April to October. •€€•

**a.** Route Louis de Bourmont, 40510 Seignosse
**t.** 6 74 160 228 (Claire Becret)
**e.** claire@naturalsurflodge.com
**w.** naturalsurflodge.com

The **Lake Loft (42)** is perfectly situated in a calm street in Hossegor, between lake, ocean and city centre. French-German couple Christina and Olivier welcome you to their über-stylish villa. They love to share their knowledge of the surroundings and can provide you with extra services, such as massages, exclusive catering, pilates or yoga classes, surf lessons or SUP tours. The house is spacious and bright because of the perfect use of big windows, wood and metal, and comes with a sunny garden, terrace and swimming pool. Available all year. • €€€ •

**a.** 353 Avenue des Écureuils, 40150 Soorts-Hossegor
**t.** 5 58 739 755
**e.** info@lakeloft.fr
**w.** lakeloft.fr

For a bit of boutique-surf-chic, check in to the **Hotel 202 (43)**, located in the heart of Hossegor, with 22 spacious rooms (as in 25 m2!) and 2 suites. Each room has their own balcony, bath and separate shower. There's a swimming pool and sauna. Open all year (except a few weeks in January). •€€€•

**a.** 202 Avenue du Golf, 40150 Hossegor
**t.** 5 58 432 202
**e.** contact@hotel202.fr
**w.** hotel202.fr

**Wood'n Sea Surf Lodge (44)** is located 400 m from famous surf spot La Piste, in Capbreton. There are 3 dormitory rooms for solo travellers or friends, and two double bedrooms. You can enjoy yoga classes, massages and evening BBQs on the large terrace. Owners Sylvianne & Antoine will happily advise you where to go surfing, dining, or do other activities, so you can enjoy the area in the best way. Open from April to October. •€• •€€•

**a.** 6 Rue de Baye, 40130 Capbreton
**t.** 6 80 830 032 (Sylvianne) / 6 07 721 478 (Antoine)
**e.** contact@woodnsea-lodge.com
**w.** woodnsea-lodge.com

**Campervans (45)** can park and stay overnight, empty toilets and fill water tank at the Aire de Camping Car VVF, at Plage des l'Océanides. Fresh croissants and pains every day from a mobile boulanger. Open from March to November. •€•

**a.** Allee des Ortolans, at the end of La Rue des Allouettes, 40130 Capbreton

At **Board 'n Breakfast (46)** you can choose to stay in either double rooms or bunk beds in the main house, a separate villa or a smaller beach house. All residents can make use of the sunny garden, pool and bar. Welcoming hosts, Ine and Anton, make sure your stay is relaxed and fun-filled. They serve a healthy breakfast (with home-made goodies) and the occasional BBQ. They also offer yoga weeks and coaching weeks. Open from April to November. •€• •€€•

**a.** 3 Allee du Poitou, 40530 Labenne
**t.** 6 48 992 470
**e.** info@boardnbreakfast.com
**w.** boardnbreakfast.com

# SURF

Just off shore at Capbreton, a deep-sea canyon, the 'gouf', causes the waves to be even more powerful and hollow; roughly between Seignosse and Labenne. Because of the gouf, the waves of Hossegor can handle more size before losing their shape, and that's exactly what makes this part so famous and attractive to the surf nation. Paradoxically, the gouf reduces wave movement at the surface and is used by fishermen and boats in trouble, as a natural refuge in rough weather.
For all breaks here: if you're a beginner, never surf alone, always be aware of the strong currents. And keep a close watch over your kids swimming and playing near the shorebreak.

**Les Casernes (I)**, at Seignosse, is a relatively quiet spot. Park your ride at the car park in the woods, walk along the path to the beach and from the top of the dunes, overlook the many breaks, left and right, then take your pick.

Between the breaks **Le Penon (II)** and **Les Bourdaines (III)** are numerous options to walk to if the breaks near the parking area are busy. Best in small to medium nw to w swell. Best tide depends on sandbanks. All levels. Easy parking/campsites/restaurants/surf schools.

**Hossegor (IV)** breaks Bourdaines, Estagnots, Les Culs Nus (= bare arses, yes, this is a nudist beach), La Gravière and Plage Central always attract more crowds, because of their wave quality and ability to keep shape in bigger swells, and also because they're right next to the urbanisation, as in; bars, restaurants, shops and schools. Works in small to medium (Bourdaines, Estagnots) and medium to big nw, w and sw swells. All levels in small swells, level getting higher with building swells, watch out for the heavy shorebreak. Parking on the coast road/restaurants/bars/surf schools.

# SCHOOL RENTAL REPAIR

**Capbreton**'s **(V)** hollow breaks, south of the Hossegor canal, need a bit more swell than the breaks to the north. Much photographed because of the many bunkers - half standing, half sunken - on the beach. Best low to mid, with a nw, w swell. All levels. Parking in summer can be hassle/restaurants/surf schools.

**Hossegor Surf Academy Shop (47)** promises repairs within 24 hours. The shop has all the essentials and includes the shaping bay of Spoutnik Surfboards.

**a.** 284 Avenue des Charpentiers,
ZA Pedebert, 40150 Soorts-Hossegor
**t.** 6 83 078 752
**e.** spoutniksurfboards@gmail.com

**Natural Surf School (48)** teaches with the aloha spirit; sharing and respecting the natural elements, working as ecologically responsibly as possible. They've got over a 100 boards to choose from, from beginner up to advanced surfer – you can swap your board if the surf conditions change, or skill improves. Open from May to September. They operate from a wooden surf shack on Plage des Casernes, Seignosse.

**t.** 6 74 160 228 (Claire)
**w.** naturalsurflodge.com

**Chipiron Surf School (49)** is one of the few surf schools that specialises in longboard lessons; improve your cross stepping and hang five skills. Rental of customised Chipiron longboards and shortboards, and fins to test. Open from May to October. Located at Plage Les Culs Nus.

**w.** chipironsurfschool.com

Besides running a traditional surf school, **Yosurf (50)** organises surf boat trips. You'll leave from the port of Capbreton and be cruising the heart of the Bay of Biscay to reach the best spots. Including a picnic on the beach, video analysis and pictures of your surfing. Half day and full day options. Open in season.

**a.** 106 Avenue des Syngnathes,
40150 Hossegor
**t.** 6 88 791 731
**w.** yosurf-school.com

**Adishat's Surf School (51)** belongs to previous longboard champ Hanalei Lillaz and operates from Plage du Prevent in Capbreton. Open from May to September.

**a.** 11 Rue des Mousses,
(Plage du Prevent),
40130 Capbreton
**t.** 6 74 382 357
**w.** adishatsurfschool.com

**Water Addict Surf School (52)** offers technical training, surf and SUP, throughout the year for all ages and levels with Franck Ehrhard - the permanent coach of Le WASA CLUB and former top athlete. Surf camps and accommodation from June to September.

**a.** 12 Impasse des Oeillets des Dunes,
40130 Capbreton
**t.** 7 83 125 740
**w.** water-addict.com

**Labrador Boards (53)** shapes, sells, repairs; shortboards and longboards, guns, SUPs, also second-hand.

**a.** Avenue Jean Lartigau, 40530 Labenne
**t.** 5 24 335 749
**w.** labrador-surfboards.com

# SEASIDE LOCAL: JUSTINE MAUVIN

Multi-talented Roxy rider, Justine Mauvin, happily shares her love for the ocean, surfing and music with us. Born and raised on Reunion, surfing was part of Justine's life from an early age. The family lived mostly outside, enjoying the ocean, nature, wildlife and the huge melting pot of cultures and religions on the island. "I realise how lucky I am, to have grown up this way," says Justine. After high school she decided to move to France, where she's been living since then, on the Les Landes coast: "For an islander like me, it's the best combo, living between mountains and ocean."

Surfing has made a big impact on the course of her life: "I would never have this life if I didn't make choices around surfing. Along the journey I meet inspiring people, in crazy locations all around the world, and we are all connected by one thing: the ocean. The ocean gets us closer and at the same time it makes you go see what it's like on the other side. It's unique. It's a journey of a lifetime."

Besides surfing, making music became a way to express herself from an early age: "For me, to voice my feelings and inner thoughts through surfing and music is easier than talking, it's always been this way. I feel the need of writing a song because it's the most instinctive way to give my inner birds a chance to speak (sing) out loud."

If she's not travelling the world, you'll find Justine either making music or surfing at her favourite breaks along the Basque country and the southwest of France.

*"I love it when the background is breathtaking. To me, watching mountains or cliffs from the water is the best show. You are surfing, and being part of the beauty of the world at the same time. But my favourite circumstance is when I have friends or family to share it with. That's the trick of the good things in life; it has to be shared!"*

Read the full story about Justine on:
**w.** ilovetheseaside.com

Photos: Roxy

ANGLET (I)
6-10
BAYONNE
ANGLET
11-19
1-5
GRAND PLAGE (II)
D260
BIARRITZ
PLAGE DE LA CÔTE DES BASQUES (III)
20-28
29-46
D810
LA MILADY (IV)
47-51
BIDART (V,VI,VII)
BIDART
52-56
A63
PARLEMENTIA (VIII)
CENITZ (IX)
LAFITENIA (X)
ERROMARDIE (XI)
GUÉTHARY
57-63
E5
D932
ACOTZ
64-67
SAINTE BARBE (XII)
AHETZE
LES DEUX JUMEAUX (XIII)
HENDAYE (XIV)
SAINT-JEAN-DE-LUZ
68-75
Côte Basque
D912
D810
HONDARRIBIA
HENDAYE
87
76-81
E70
D918
84
85
ASCAIN
D918
GI3440
IRUN
D3
88
D4
82
D4
AP8
SARE
83
N121A

# CÔTE BASQUE

The Basque country is like a stunningly beautiful lady, dressed in outdoorsy clothes, with the ocean at her feet and the mountains covering her back. This part, just before the border with Spain, has it all: stylish villages, charismatic people, and of course, a variety of surf breaks. It's here that the birth of French surfing took place and a strong cultural identity is permeated in daily life. You're in Euskal Herria: the land of the Basque language, or simply Euskadi. With the wide range of surf spots on offer for beginner to advanced surfer, and the Pyrenees at such close range, the area is obviously popular. In summer, campgrounds are full, roads blocked and attitudes get edgy. So, pick the right season and you'll find peace and beauty, and some sturdy food to accompany that. Omnipresent around here: the Lauburu symbol, resembling a rounded swastika. Our favourite interpretation of its meaning: it's like a wave in the ocean, a symbol for life itself, a constant wheel of creation and ending.

## TRAVEL INFO

There are good options to use public transport to hop from one place to the other, like free shuttle buses.

### BY AIR

**Biarritz – Anglet – Bayonne Airport**, located between Anglet and Biarritz. The airport's located just off the N10. Several low-cost airlines ensure regular connections from London, Brussels, Dublin and Stockholm.

**w.** biarritz.aeroport.fr

Other airports nearby are Pau (1h15), San Sebastián (about 50 minutes) and Bordeaux (2,5 hrs).

### BY TRAIN

**High speed and regional trains** run several times a day from Paris (5h15), Bordeaux (2 hrs), or Pau (1 h), to Biarritz. Regular trains run between Bayonne, Biarritz, Saint-Jean-de-Luz and Hendaye. Info on schedules:

**w.** voyages-sncf.com

### BY BUS

There are **free shuttle buses** (La Navette) running in Bayonne, Biarritz and Bidart. So you can leave your car and hop on and off to the market, the station, the centre or the beach. Buses from ATCRB run between Hendaye, Saint-Jean-de-Luz and Biarritz. Chronoplus runs between Biarritz, Anglet and Bayonne. RDTL buses run between Bayonne and Vieux-Boucau, crossing all the surf destinations.

# DON'T MISS

## *Les Fêtes de Bayonne*

A series of festivities that lasts for five days and nights; always starts on the Wednesday before the first Sunday in August. Festival-wise, you can't find them any bigger in France. The festival started in the 1930s, when a group of friends from a local rugby team wanted to have a festivity similar to San Fermin in Pamplona (you know, the one with lots of people running through the streets, chased by bulls – well, they have bulls here too, but they're not in the streets). Don't forget to dress in white, wear a red scarf and eat well, because there's a lot of drinking involved...

**w.** fetes.bayonne.fr

## *The game of Pilota or Jai Alai*

Every Basque village has at least one outdoor 'fronton' - a wall with a court - for what must be one of the fastest ball sports in the world (danger - balls travelling at up to 200km/h). The objective is to play a ball, depending on the variation of the game played, with bare hands, a basket, or a wooden bat, against the fronton between 2 designated lines. The opponent has to hit it back off the first bounce, or while it's in the air. Usually played by 2 teams, consisting of 2 players each. It's immensely popular, played by young and old, and you don't need much equipment: a ball and a wall will do. Jai Alai is the variation where a player has a 'cesta', a hook-shaped racket, fastened to the hand. Watch and be amazed.

# USEFUL WORDS

*Hondartza* = Beach
*Eskerrik asko* = Thank you
*Kaixo* = Hello
*Agur* = Bye

# PAYS BASQUE FOOD FACTS & YOU SHOULD DEFINITELY TRY

◆

## ESPELETTE PEPPERS

◆

The deep-red Espelette pepper, apparently introduced to the Basque people by a Basque navigator who had sailed with Columbus, is cultivated in the village of Espelette. It was originally used for medicinal purposes – not quite sure how that worked out, but it did prove to be an excellent means for conservation and flavouring of hams, chicken and fish stews. The mild heat and smoky-sweet flavour is closer to paprika than chillies, and you can purchase them in a string of fresh or dried peppers, and as ground pepper. You'll find them in every market, also sometimes at stalls along the roads leading inland, and of course, in Espelette itself; where an annual festival is organised by the Confrérie du Piment d'Espelette, the Espelete Pepper Brotherhood. Held every last weekend in October, the Piment d'Espelette Festival attracts thousands of tourists. Late summer, families string the peppers into 'ristras' and hang them to dry from windows, balconies, doors and gates for about a month. Once the festival begins, locals dress in traditional clothes, and there's dancing, drinking and, of course, food. That'll be laced with pepper, for sure.

## GÂTEAU BASQUE

◆

Gâteau Basque (or Etxeko Biskotxa, cake of the house, in Basque) is a sweet, buttery cake made from almond flour, either filled with prune or black cherry preserves, or vanilla pastry cream. It's a speciality from this area, Labourd. Ideally, the crust is rich and crumbly, and if filled with cherries, it should be the Basque black cherry that grows in this area. It's their artisanal pride, so there's a museum dedicated to the delicious tart, where you can learn how it's prepared properly.

**w.** legateaubasque.coz

# SURFER-TRAVELLER TYPE CÔTE BASQUE

◆

*You love stylish surf, and stylish surfers (M/F), can tackle mountains and ocean in one day, and, when you realise there's no better place, can deal with the fact that so very many people seem to agree; you're able to eat gateau Basque every day, accept that the coffee's just not that good, and give in to drinking more Txakoli wine or chocolat chaud instead. You can't get enough of red woodwork on white houses, like to choose between surfing reefs, beaches, pointbreaks, big waves or longboard sliders, and don't mind tackling tongue-twisting words that contain more z's, x's and k's than are possible to pronounce.*

# IN AND AROUND BAYONNE

◆

Bayonne, Baiona in Basque, is the capital of the Basque province Labourd (Lapurdi). The main attraction is definitely the old centre, Petit Bayonne - its small streets lined with a fine mix of French and Basque architecture and historic medieval buildings. Many of the ornate structures, like the gothic cathedral, are a legacy of the wealth generated by seafarers: the thriving whale and cod industry, and the Basque sailors who returned from far off lands with spices and exotic riches to trade. Alongside the river Nive - which carries water from the Pyrenees into the Adour, in Bayonne, and finishes at sea in Anglet - the wooden framework and shutters of warehouses are cheerfully painted in all sorts of colours, and terraces look inviting on warm days. Anglet is part of the Bayonne jurisdiction, sandwiched between Bayonne and Biarritz, and is where you find the beaches and the surf.

**Tourist office** at 1 Avenue de la Chambre d'Amour.

Photo: Alexandra Gossink

## TO DO

◆

**Bloom Yoga (1)**, the yoga studio from yogi Zoë Bloom, offers daily classes (also in English) in the centre of Bayonne: vinyasa, hatha, yin, and yoga for beginners. Check the site for their schedule.

**a.** 9 Rue Thiers, 2nd Floor, 64100 Bayonne
**t.** 6 01 343 705 / 5 59 293 313
**w.** bloomyoga.fr

A large **Skate and BMX park (6)** is situated at Plage de la Barre, right next to McDonalds. Open all year. Free entrance.

**a.** La Barre, 299 Avenue de l'Adour, 64600 Anglet

**Atlanthal (11)** is a beauty centre, spa and health club; with pilates classes, cross training and body balance.

**a.** 153 Boulevard des Plages, 64600 Anglet
**w.** biarritz-thalasso.com

**Blank Surf Shack (7)** offers workshops and coaching, and assists in various stages of designing or repairing your own board. Their aim is sharing, therefore making their space available to anyone that's dedicated to the manufacturing of boards.

**a.** 10 Allée du Samadet - Parking de la Brocante Oplus, 64600 Anglet
**t.** 6 16 725 823 / 6 08 147 425
**w.** blanksurfshack.com

**Yogattitude** belongs to longtime yoga teacher Gaëlle Le Corre, offers yoga-courses and workshops in July (hatha, ashtanga, and iyengar). Check site for availability and dates, or private yoga-coaching sessions at your place, in and around Bayonne and Biarritz.

**t.** 6 80 689 813
**w.** yogattitudecoaching.com

## EAT/DRINK/HANGOUT

◆

**Café Théâtre Luna Negra (2)** has live music and performances, and theme nights, from flamenco and chansons to blues. Among the regular artists; 'Betty the Shark' - the electro-pop live band with singer/surfer Lee-Ann Curren, and a magic show from the mentalist Bastian.

**a.** 7 Rue des Augustins, 64100 Bayonne
**w.** lunanegra.fr

When you visit the market at Les Halles, enjoy a glass of wine and lunch at bistro **Chez Pantxo (3)**, sit either inside, or outside on the terrace. Highly recommended by locals. Open all year, from 07:00 to 16:00 hrs. •€•

**a.** Les Halles, Quai du Commandant Roquebert, 64100 Bayonne

**The Beach House (12)**: on cold days, sit inside at the fireplace amid stylish décor and vintage furniture, or relax on the sundeck, next to the pool. Expect a sea and mountain inspired menu. Open from April to October. •€€•

**a.** 26 Avenue des Dauphins, 64600 Anglet
**t.** 5 59 152 717
**w.** beachhouseanglet.com

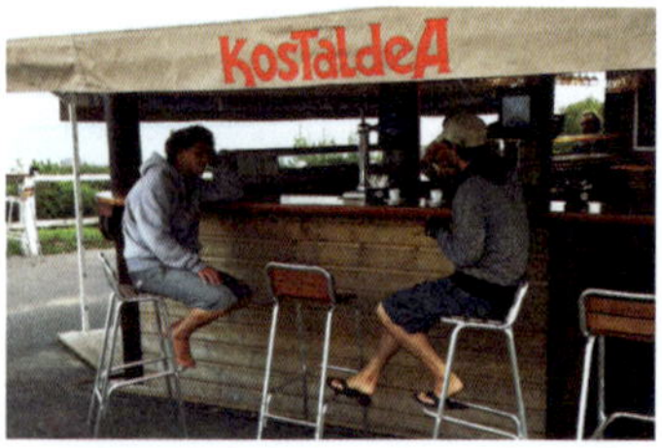


**Kostaldea (13)**, open-air beer garden, great after-surf hangout with view of the beach (Plage Chambre d'Amour). Open: depending on the weather! •€• •€€•

**a.** Esplanade Yves Brunaud, 64600 Anglet
**t.** 5 59 426 697

## SHOP

◆

**Les Halles (4)**: like many French towns, Bayonne has a covered daily market. And at the open-air market, out front on Saturdays, you're in for a treat – try not to miss this. Local traders and producers gather with their fresh products, ham, chocolate and Basque linen. Open all year, from 06:00 to 13:30 hrs.

**a.** Les Halles, Carreau des Halles, (alongside the river Nive), 64100 Bayonne

**Les Jolies Choses (5)** is an eclectic pop-up store, which is renewed by local designers every three months. Expect to see, eat, drink, buy, and be inspired by contemporary art, design, clothes, photos, and some more, without a doubt. Open all year.

**a.** 26 Rue Victor Hugo, 64100 Bayonne

**Bio market Marché Biocéan (8)**, every Saturday, in Quartier Blanc-pignon.

**a.** Parking opposite 99 Avenue de l'Adour, 64600 Anglet

**Notox Surfboards (9)** aim to reduce the environmental impact of surfboard design by developing and manufacturing high performance, eco-friendly boards. You can visit the showroom, where second-hand boards are also on sale. Open all year.

**a.** 6 Rue du Lazaret, 64600 Anglet
**t.** 5 59 523 153
**w.** notox.fr

**La Ruche Moderne (10)** is a mixture of a cultural centre, collective garage, bar, and expo space of vintage motorcycles, art, vintage furniture and whatever treasured object is added to the collection. It's host to events like the Surf Punk Invitational.

**a.** 98 Avenue de l'Adour, 64600 Anglet
**w.** laruchemoderne.net

**Polette Bazar (14)** is a tea and gift shop that sells locally produced items, from skateboards and beer, to oil, herbs and selected teas in a stylish, clean décor. Open all year.

**a.** 11 Rue Paul Courbin, (Halles des 5 Cantons) 64600 Anglet
**t.** 9 86 241 381

**Girl Shop (15)** is an outlet boutique, bringing together a set of original brands in a nicely decorated space. Everything a girl can wish for (if the girl wishes for it); jewellery, jeans, bags, swimsuits, coats and art. Open all year.

**a.** 47 Avenue de la Chambre d'Amour, 64600 Anglet

## SLEEP

◆

One of the best money-saving options in the area must be **Auberge de Jeunesse Gazte Etxea** (**16**), the youth hostel. Located in a green setting near the beach, with bike, surfboard and wetsuit rental available. Open all year.
◆€◆

**a.** 19 Route des Vignes, 64600 Anglet
**t.** 5 59 587 000
**w.** fuaj.org/en/anglet

**Hotel Arguia** (**17**), 500 m from the beach, has 12 rooms in a big white villa with a large garden. Relaxed, clean, simple but tastefully decorated, pets allowed (!), also available for groups, easy access to public transport.

**a.** 9 Avenue des Crêtes, 64600 Anglet
**t.** 5 59 638 382
**w.** arguia.free.fr

**Campervans** (**18**) can park and stay overnight at Aire de Camping Car des Corsaires, right at the beach. Free to empty water and toilet. Open all year. (Free from 7th November to 7th April).
◆€◆

**a.** Boulevard des Plages (D405), Anglet 64600

# IN AND AROUND BIARRITZ

◆

With its funky-chic vibe, 16th century to modern architecture, and many beaches to choose from, this town's a magnet to travellers, surfers, jet-setters and rock 'n' roll stars. Add restaurants, cafés and shops that stand out from the conventional, and it's safe to say there's a good reason why the winter population of a mere 30 thousand permanent residents (les Biarrots) triples its number in summer. Holidaying at the seaside became fashionable in the 19th century, especially after Napoleon built an imperial summer residence for his wife, Eugenie, which is now known as the Hôtel de Palais. One of the first golf courses in France, Golf du Phare, was created here, right under the lighthouse. It's still a main attraction. Well, for those who are into golf. Shaped by storms and the constant pounding of the Atlantic, the coastline has a raw, unpolished beauty. Driving down the N10 from Biarritz towards the green hills and mountains near the Spanish border, it's not easy to see where Biarritz ends and Bidart begins, and before you know it you've passed lovely Guéthary. But there's no doubt you're in Basque country. It's been said that the red woodwork on the white houses used to be painted with blood from bulls to protect the wood from the rain and storms. It's definitely suited to the sturdy Basque soul.

**Tourist office** at Square d'Ixelles.

## TO DO

◆

**Le BIG Festival** in Biarritz, usually held mid-July, running since 2009, is truly something. It's big as in big names, from Pharrell Williams and the Prodigy to Neil Young. It's big as in long – over a week long. And big as in diversity; rock, reggae, hip-hop, house and electro.

**w.** bigfest.fr

Pre-surf warm-up? Climb the 248 steps up in the **Phare de Biarritz (20)** for a view of the ocean, Biarritz and surroundings, all the way to the Pyrenees. The lighthouse stands 75 m above sea level. Open all year in the afternoon, in July and August also in the morning.

**a.** Pointe Saint-Martin, 64200 Biarritz

Taking a stroll from Grand Plage to Plage de la Côte des Basques is the best way to **discover the seaside part of Biarritz (21)**. You'll pass Le Rocher du Basta, which is between Grand Plage and the old harbour, Le Vieux Port; connected by a small bridge from the mainland. Move on to the Port des Pecheurs, which is a good option for lunch if you're into seafood. Taking in the fresh air along the shores is even more beneficial than you'd expect: the large amount of seaweed adds iodine to the water, and that, dear seaside lover, is a good thing. It's also the reason you find so many thalassotherapy resorts in this area, using it for medical and beauty treatments.

Looking for a safe beach to take the little ones, try **Plage de Vieux Port (21)**, it's a small bay protected from waves and strong currents, so one of the safest to play and swim.

**Musée de la Mer (22)**, aquarium in an Art Deco monument. A captivating adventure for kids, that's for sure: sharks, barracudas and stingrays sharing their territory peacefully.

**a.** Rue d'Atalaye, 64200 Biarritz
**w.** museedelamer.com

Whether winding down the streets to Le Vieux Port, surfing Grande Plage, or checking the waves at Plage de la Côte des Basques, you can't miss the **Rocher de la Vierge (23)** - the rock of the Virgin. Legend has it that from this point a mysterious light beamed and saved many whalers and sailors from shipwreck. So, out of gratitude, a landmark was placed in 1865, that could be accessed by a wooden bridge. Of course that didn't stand the test of ocean fury, so in 1887 it was replaced with the iron bridge over which you can now reach the viewpoint; installed by Gustav Eiffel (yes, the very same as the tower).

**Atelier Lolë Côte Basque (29)** is the shop and on-site yoga studio of yoga clothing brand Lolë, with a great view of Grand Plage. They also offer pop-up activities like wellness weekends and bootcamps. Open all year, every day from 10:00 to 19:00 hrs.

**a.** 2 Place Bellevue, 64200 Biarritz
**t.** 5 59 269 898
**e.** lole.bellevue@lolewomen.com
**w.** lolewomen.com

**Pause Yoga Biarritz (30)** is a vinyasa-flow yoga studio, run by yogi Amélie Apparicio-Bernard. Your class will involve balancing the body and breath in perfect harmony. Also on offer: SUP yoga (usually at Plage d'Hendaye, to the south).

**a.** Village Iraty, Bâtiment Halle Darla 49, 14 Rue des Mésanges, 64200 Biarritz
**t.** 6 62 408 815
**w.** pauseyogabiarritz.com

If you're into contemporary art, pay a visit to the spacious **Ateliers d'Artistes des Serres de la Milady (47)**, there are regular exhibitions or you can shop for something special. Open every day from 10:00 to 18:00 hrs.

**a.** 49 Avenue de la Milady, 64200 Biarritz
**w.** lesserresdelamilady.com

**Wheels and Waves festival (48)** is an annual 4-day event held around various influences: bikes, art, music and surfing (at Plage de la Milady). Kick-started (no pun intended) in 2009 by a group of local passionate bikers/surfers, it's getting more and more popular by the year.

Expect races, group ride-outs, surf contests, stands, live music, films and some très cool Yamaha's, Honda's and Nortons. It usually takes place mid-June, around the Cité de l'Océan.

**w.** wheels-and-waves.com

**Cité de l'Océan et du Surf (49)** is dedicated to the discovery of the Big Blue. You can expand your knowledge about how waves are born, Atlantis myths, the state of the ocean today. (A combination with a visit to Musée de la Mer is possible, since the two complement each other perfectly). The building itself is an interesting site, with its curved surface resembling a wave and skate ramp.

**a.** 1 Avenue de la Plage, 64200 Biarritz
**t.** 5 59 227 540
**w.** citedelocean.com

**Club Hippique (50)**, situated next to the ocean, will help you discover, enjoy and perfect your equestrian activities; at both beginner and competitive levels.

**a.** Allée Gabrielle Dorziat, 64200 Biarritz
**t.** 5 59 235 233
**w.** biarritzcheval.com

## EAT/DRINK/HANGOUT

◆

Restaurant **Le Surfing (24)** offers a view over the surf of Plage de la Côte des Basques. Basque, Asian and vegetarian cuisine, but best known for their burgers. Open for breakfast, lunch and dinner. ◆€€◆

**a.** 9 Boulevard du Prince de Galles, 64200 Biarritz
**t.** 5 59 247 872

Bar Restaurant **Côte 57 (25)** is right next door to Le Surfing. Serves tapas, seafood and drinks. The bar is named after that important year, 1957, that the American film crew of screenwriter Peter Viertel brought surfing to Biarritz. Open every day for lunch and dinner. ◆€€◆

**a.** 7 Boulevard du Prince de Galles, 64200 Biarritz
**t.** 5 59 222 783

**Etxola Bibi (26)**, small but very lively bar, overlooking the beaches of Côte des Basques and Marbella, great for sunset beers or watching the old folks playing boule. Open all day. ◆€◆

**a.** Square Jean Baptiste Lassalle, 64200 Biarritz

For a decent coffee, stop in at **Milwaukee Café (31)**; a cosy hangout with an international vibe, run by American Wendy and her daughter Emily. The pastries are American recipes like cheesecake, apple crumble and brownies, but with an undeniably delicious French touch. Also a hearty lunch menu and terrace with street view. Open all year. ◆€◆ ◆€€◆

**a.** 2 Rue du Helder, 64200 Biarritz

If bars are rated 'classic', this is the one for Biarritz: **Bar Jean (32)** serves as a local meeting point and hangout; it's vibrant, stylish in a very uncomplicated manner, and the food's good too. Regional and Spanish dishes, tapas, fine wines. Open Thursday to Monday from 08:30 to 02:00 hrs. ◆€€◆

**a.** 5 Rue des Halles, 64200 Biarritz
**t.** 5 59 248 038

At **Le Comptoir du Foie Gras (33)** you can eat your tapas while standing outside this little restaurant, leaning on the big wooden barrels, watching les Biarrots passing by. ◆€€◆

**a.** 1 Rue du Centre, 64200 Biarritz
**t.** 5 59 225 742

Restaurant **Le Clos Basque (34)**: favoured by locals, tasty regional cuisine, and very good value for your money as well. Open every day (except Monday) for lunch and dinner. ◆€◆ ◆€€◆

**a.** 12 Avenue Louis Barthou, 64200 Biarritz
**t.** 5 59 242 496

**Saline Ceviche Bar (35)**, as the name implies, is the place to go for ceviche, marinated fresh fish, but also some tasty tortillas and other South American, Caribbean and Japanese fusion cuisine. Open all year for lunch and dinner. ◆€€◆

**a.** 62 Rue Gambetta, 64200 Biarritz
**t.** 5 59 436 598

Photo: Helder Supply Store

**Ventilo Café** (**36**), a place for good vibes and good food; mostly seasonal, home-made and done with style, and for drinks, live music, vinyl sessions, and overall cool bar.

**a.** 30 Rue Mazagran, 64200 Biarritz
**t.** 5 59 243 142

For cocktails and nightclubbing check **Le Carré Coast** (**37**), live sets from either resident or visiting DJs, electro and deep-house, near la Grande Plage. Open for night owls only.

**a.** 21 Avenue Edouard VII, 64200 Biarritz

Sit with your feet in the sand at Bar Restaurant **La Plancha D'Ilbarritz** (**52**), right beside the beach of Ilbarritz in Bidart. Open February to October, regular live music in summer. •€€•

**a.** Plage D'Ilbarritz, 64210 Bidart
**t.** 5 59 234 495

**Artisan Boulanger Patissier, Au Fournil de la Licorne** (**53**), our favourite! Get your croissants, gateau Basque, pains, and loads more, fresh from the oven. And repeat.

**a.** RD 810, Quartier du Plateau, 64210 Bidart

## SHOP

◆

**Les Halles** (**38**), the daily market. Find Basque stuff, fresh oysters and local goodies. Open every day from 07:00 to 13:30 hrs.

**a.** 1 Rue du Centre, 64200 Biarritz

**Helder Supply Store** (**39**), our favourite store and art-expo in Biarritz: it's got ocean-related art, books, furniture, clothes and beautiful photos and surfboards, a lot of which is created by local artists and brands. Very friendly staff, drinks, sushi and a regular change in exhibitions and apparel. Don't miss this little gem! Open all year. (You'll find another Helder Supply Store, open between May and October, facing Le Grand Plage.)

**a.** 13 Rue du Helder, 64200 Biarritz
**w.** heldersupply.com

Wouldn't you go for a shirt that says 'Fuck Surf Play Golf'? Get just that and more original clothes, caps and accessories at **Kick Asss** (**40**). The shop sells limited editions of their brand's

creations, made with quality materials. Open all year.

**a.** 37 Rue Mazagran, 64200 Biarritz
**w.** kickasss.com

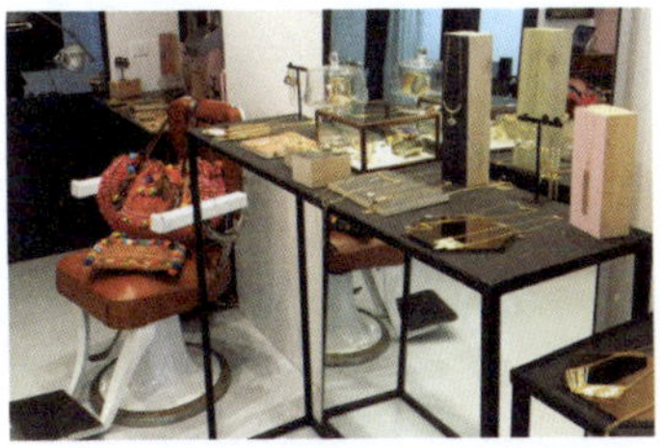

Find French manufactured jewellery collections at **Boutique L'Atelier des Dames (41)**, made from the finest, unusual and recycled materials from all over the world. Open all year.

**a.** 7 Avenue Maréchal Foch, 64200 Biarritz
**w.** latelierdesdames.fr

**More & Less Longboard Shop (42)** sells new and second-hand boards, fish and single fins; fins, books and clothes. Just look in the window at the racks and you'll be overcome with desire to go stroke all those beautiful boards.

**a.** 4 Avenue Reine Victoria, 64200 Biarritz
**t.** 5 59 225 792
**w.** more-and-less.com

**Les Enfants Terribles (43)** is a stylish shop that sells selected trends in clothes and accessories, re-issue vintage or limited series of kitchen utilities, bags and more. Open all year.

**a.** 2 Rue du Port Vieux, 64200 Biarritz
**w.** les-enfantsterribles.com

If you're at all into beautiful hand-shaped boards and surf culture you must visit **Wallako Surf Shop (54)**. The idea was to create a place like the Californian sixties surf shops, where surfers meet and talk about the waves or just have a good time and hang out, and they did a great job. It's a Walhalla of beautiful boards, mostly shaped by the shaper in residence in the workshop next to the shop, or international artisans. You'll find longboards, mid-lengths, shortboards, bonzers, and every other whatnot, in retro-style and modern shapes. But also clothes and accessories from small, mostly French, brands.

**a.** 111 Avenue de Biarritz, 64210 Bidart
**t.** 5 59 243 641
**w.** wallako-surfshop.com

## SLEEP

◆

**Carlina Lodge (27)**, located on the first 2 levels of the Sunset Resident Hotel, has spacious rooms and apartments on offer, overlooking the Plage de la Côte des Basques. Open all year. ◆€€◆ ◆€€€◆

**a.** 9 Boulevard du Prince de Galles, 64200 Biarritz
**t.** 5 59 244 214
**w.** carlina.com

**Hotel de la Marine (44)** is a budget option by Biarritz standards. This little family-run hotel is a short walk from most beaches, simple but clean. They also have a small flat available. Open all year. ◆€◆ ◆€€◆

**a.** 1 Rue des Goélands, 64200 Biarritz
**t.** 5 59 243 409
**w.** hotel-lamarine-biarritz.com

**Design Hôtel de Silhouette (45)** is located in one of the oldest buildings in the centre of Biarritz, now completely renovated. It offers 20 rooms, all uniquely decorated. There are regular art exhibitions, and ballet venues and concerts are held in their garden. Open all year. ◆ €€€ ◆

**a.** 30 Rue Gambetta, Quartier des Halles, 64200 Biarritz
**t.** 5 59 249 382
**e.** reservations@hotelsilhouette.com
**w.** hotel-silhouette-biarritz.com

**Surf Hostel Biarritz (46)** offers accommodation in a spacious 5 bedroom country house with room for up to 15 people. Homely atmosphere, shared or private rooms for 2 to 4 people, bathroom and kitchen are shared. The lounge areas and dining room form the heart of the hostel. Open from April to October. ◆€◆

**a.** Batiment E, Domaine de Migron, 64200 Biarritz
**t.** 6 63 342 745
**w.** surfhostelbiarritz.com

**Campervans (51)** can park and stay overnight at Aire de Camping Car Milady. Electricity, water and toilet emptying facilities. Open all year. ◆€◆

**a.** 65 Avenue de la Milady, 64200 Biarritz

A second **Surf Hostel (55)** is located in a typical Basque villa in the small town of Bidart, a little to the south of Biarritz. At this location there's also a 3-bedroom apartment for rent, on weekly basis only, sleeps up to 6 persons. Open April to October. ◆€◆

**a.** 101 Avenue Chabadenia, 64210 Bidart
**t.** 6 63 342 745
**w.** surfhostelbidart.com

**Maison Bista Eder (56)**, set in a Basque villa, has 3 comfortable and colourful rooms and 2 studios overlooking Plage d'Erretegia (hence, 'Bista Eder' meaning 'beautiful view'). Available all year. ◆€€◆

**a.** 3 Rue Mar y Montes, 64210 Bidart
**t.** 5 59 548 021 / 6 75 173 229
**e.** contact@bistaeder.fr
**w.** bistaeder.fr

# IN AND AROUND SAINT-JEAN-DE-LUZ

It's hard not to see the charm of this little town with its surroundings of little villages and mountains. The old centre of Saint-Jean-de-Luz consists of cobbled streets and timbered Basque villas from the 17th century. Extravagant architecture symbolises the wealth in days gone by, when the town was an important whaling and fishing port; it then also gathered significant income through its pirates, who plundered and looted all that could be plundered and looted at sea. Actually, the pirates did all that with permission of the French King. They were called corsairs and were originally fishermen and traders, working all along the Basque coast, originally only using arms to defend themselves against real pirates. With the official 'go' from the king to chase after his enemies and confiscate their goods, the corsairs would then hand the loot over to the authorities. But a good number of them became pirates themselves, with or without a license to steal. Today it's a laid-back seaside resort with a distinguished vibe. Oh, and go slow now; a great many retired people choose Saint-Jean-de-Luz as their final domicile.

**Tourist office** at 20 Boulevard Victor Hugo.

## TO DO

Don't miss **Guéthary** (**57**): you'll pass this little beauty of a seaside village driving from Biarritz to Saint-Jean-de-Luz. It's classic, it's hip, it's cool, it's non-conventional, it's none of the above, it's entirely its own character. There are stylish old men and women, beautiful girls, strong boys, and kids that look like they're going to grow up like them.

Every café has its own charm, eateries are fun, terraces sunny, streets lined with willows, and the ocean out front's got the heaviest waves.

If you're looking for a beach that's protected from waves, rocks and strong current; just to sunbathe, let kids play or swim safely, the big crescent-shaped bay **La Grande Plage** (**68**) is your best option in the area. The bay is enclosed by a long promenade, and at the far end protected by sea walls.

To get a good idea of what the wealth of the corsairs brought, stroll along **Rue Gambetta** (**69**), the main shopping street, and have a coffee or some at the Place Louis XIV, the square at the westernmost end of the street. Most buildings are built around the 17th century, some by ship owners. From here walk further towards the port, which was once one of the largest fishing ports of France.

Practice paddling a Hawaiian canoe, SUP or sea kayak with **Ocean Paddling Evolution 2 (70)**, usually in the bay of Saint-Jean-de-Luz. Available in season or by reservation.

**a.** Promenade Jacques Thibaud,
64500 Saint-Jean-de-Luz
**t.** 6 74 470 955
**w.** office-des-sports-du-pays-basque.com

**S..Kale 64 (71)** offers yoga and pilates classes, and massages. Contact Jade and Michel for bookings and class schedules. Open all year.

**a.** Résidence Mendi Eder, 465 Chemin d'Aguerria, 64500 Saint-Jean-de-Luz
**t.** 6 86 871 997
**w.** escale64.com

The good thing about this area is that, just half an hour drive inland, the landscape changes, villages are rural, there are hiking and biking opportunities galore, and even skiing and surfing in one day is possible with the Pyrenees at such close range. If you don't want to do all sorts of tiring activities, or your kids are too young for them, but you do want to enjoy the outdoors and the view from above, you can take Le Train de la Rhune all the way up to the summit of **La Rhune mountain (82)**. Towering 905 m above sea level, you'll have a panoramic view over the Basque coast and the peaks of the Pyrenees. The train is a 35 min ride up. You can also hike all the way up, following a path that's quite steep, but do-able for an average hiker. Maybe you'll bump into a 'Pottok', a wild pony, or see Griffon vultures. La Rhune train runs from March to October.

**a.** Col de Saint-Ignace, 64310 Sare

**Centre Equestre Olhaldea (83)** offers guided treks with horses or ponies, from a few hours or a full day, up to 5 days, through the Basque and Spanish landscape and mountains.

**a.** Zalditokia, Chemin de Sainte Catherine,
64310 Sare
**t.** 5 59 542 894
**w.** olhaldea.com

## EAT/DRINK/HANGOUT

◆

The former Kafé Loco, in Guéthary, is now **Le Poinçon (58)**; run by the current owners for a while now, serving quality cuisine with products from fresh markets, some of which is bio produce. Decorated in bright colours with a playing corner for kids, and locally produced items for sale, it's still a place you love to go to. Open from 08:00 to 23:00 hrs. •€€•

**a.** Rue du Comte Swiecinski,
Gare de Guéthary, 64210 Guéthary
**t.** 5 59 265 744

Walking down from the main square of Guéthary, you'll find bar and restaurant **Hétéroclito (59)**. Great place for sunset beers, tapas, good vibes and checking out the famous (big) waves of Parlementia. •€€•

**a.** 48 Chemin du Port, 64210 Guéthary
**t.** 5 59 549 892

**Hotel Le Madrid (60)**, perfectly situated in the centre of the village, you can watch the world of Guéthary pass you by. Or better yet, join them on the terrace. Local cuisine. Open every day from 12:00 hrs. •€€•

**a.** 563 Avenue du Général de Gaulle,
64210 Guéthary
**t.** 5 59 265 212

At Plage de Cenitz, in front of the reef breaks, sits **Restaurant Le C (61)**. Perfect after-surf hangout, friendly staff, free sunsets and regular DJ gigs and live music. Open in season.
•€• •€€•

**a.** 257 Chemin de Cenitz, 64210 Guéthary
**t.** 6 50 732 309 / 5 59 240 147
**w.** le-c-guethary.com

**Xibao (64)** is a mobile restaurant that finds its spot in the parking area for surf break Lafitenia, run by a passionate crew.

You can enjoy home-made cookies, fresh sandwiches and drinks, and intimate concerts, sitting back and relaxing in their deckchairs. Open in season. •€• •€€•

Just opposite the parking of Lafitenia, is the nicely decorated restaurant and bar **Ostalamer (65)**, with a big terrace and a good view of the Basque coast. Menu is varied and you'll find locals and tourists alike. Open from March to December. •€€• •€€€•

**a.** 160 Route des Plages, Quartier Acotz, 64500 Saint-Jean-de-Luz
**t.** 5 59 858 471
**w.** ostalamer.com

**Ocean Coffee Bar (72)** serves great coffee and the finest breakfasts. Great atmosphere, lovely staff, and some delicious sweets to go with that coffee. Open all year. •€•

**a.** Avenue de Verdun 9 - Rue J.I. Harispe, 64500 Saint-Jean-de-Luz (opposite the station)

## SHOP

◆

**Providence Guéthary (62)** is a boutique, a gallery, a coffee bar; a very dynamic place in all. In an intimate space regular exhibitions and music events are held, you can leaf through beautiful books, listen to old-skool vinyl, find your perfect surf fins, skateboard, or clothes. Open all year.

**a.** 548 Avenue du Général de Gaulle, 64210 Guéthary
**t.** 9 80 491 601
**w.** providenceguethary.com

**Les Halles (73)**, the covered daily market. Espelette peppers, gateau Basque, Bayonne ham, Ardi Gasna – sheep's cheese: Basque goodies on offer, next to other local produce and a drink at the bar amongst the locals. Open all year, every day from 06:00 to 13:00 hrs.

**a.** Boulevard Victor Hugo, Saint-Jean-de-Luz

In the headquarters of Quiksilver Europe, located in an interesting building constructed of glass and wood, around five big cabanas, set on stilts and stitched into the slopes, you'll find the **Quiksilver Boardriders Campus 162 (74)**: a shop, a barber's and a coffee bar where sometimes intimate indoor concerts are held. Outside a skate ramp is free to use.

**a.** 162 Rue Belharra, 64500 Saint-Jean-de-Luz

Photo: Alexandra Gossink

## SLEEP

◆

**Balea Hôtel Guéthary (63)** is a former school transformed into a hotel in the heart of Guethary. A place with history and soul that's very welcoming to surfers and their families. They've got 26 rooms, a sunny and quiet garden, and beaches at walking distance. Open all year. •€€•

**a.** 106 Rue Adrien Lahourcade, 64210 Guethary
**t.** 5 59 260 839
**w.** hotel-balea-guethary.com

In the seaside area Acotz, between Guéthary and Saint-Jean-de-Luz, are numerous campsites. A plain but perfectly situated camping is **Camping Playa Acotz (66)**, overlooking point break Lafitenia. Rents out mobile homes and roulettes. Open April to November. •€• •€€•

**a.** 264 Route des Plages - Quartier Acotz, 64500 Saint-Jean-de-Luz
**t.** 5 59 265 585 / 9 63 212 838
**w.** camping-playa.com

**Maison Tamarin (67)** is a characteristic Basque villa, some 500 m from Plage de Lafitenia. It sleeps up to 15 guests, with 8 bedrooms, a heated pool, and a big, lush garden. Available either fully or self catered. Open all year. •€€• •€€€•

**a.** Chemin de la Ferme de Kokotia, Quartier Acotz, 64500 Saint-Jean-de-Luz
**t.** 5 59 475 960
**w.** maisontamarin.com

**Campervans (75)** can park, stay, and fill up water at the Aire de Camping Car next to the station. Free to use facilities to empty water and toilet. Open all year. •€•

**a.** Pont Charles de Gaulle, 64500 Saint-Jean de Luz

# IN AND AROUND HENDAYE

Hendaye may not be as chic as Saint-Jean-de-Luz or charming as Biarritz, but being so close to the border of Spain you can't miss its influences; like pintxos and chipirons on the menu, and a slight disorderly feel to it. Because of the small landing strip on the opposite side of the river, in Spanish Hondarribia, there are planes flying overhead – really just over your head, so close you can almost touch them - adding a surreal air to the place.

**Tourist office** at 67 bis Boulevard de la Mer.

## TO DO

At **Serge Blanco Thalassothérapie** (**76**), you can spend half a day pampering yourself (4 hours in the morning or afternoon) in the spa and use the hammam, swimming pool, saunas and an outside jacuzzi. You'll find the spa at the end of the boulevard, towards the harbour. Open all year.

**a.** 125 Boulevard de la Mer, 64700 Hendaye
**w.** thalassoblanco.com

Just out of town heading towards the southeast, there's this fun survival playground **Wow-Park** (**84**). Cabins in tree tops, big slides, and lots of outdoor fun for families. They recommend that you wear long sleeves, and not to wear plastic and nylon shoes or clothes... Open from May to November.

**a.** 11 Chemin de Bittola, 64122 Urrugne
**w.** wowpark.fr

Discover the outdoor possibilities of the Basque country with **Evasion Rafting and Adventure Sports** (**85**). They'll take you canyoning, climbing, rafting on the river Nive, and on all sorts of adrenaline enhancing adventures. Located near Espelette.

**a.** Maison Errola, 64250 Itxassou
**t.** 5 59 293 169 / 6 16 747 893
**w.** evasion-sports-aventure.fr

**Hiking and biking** (**86**) just over the border of Spain: from Hendaye take the road towards Hondarribia airport. After passing the airport follow the signs for Guadeloupe. You can park your car at the bottom of a long hiking trail, which is also part of the Santiago route. There are two ways up, but unless you are into alpinism, we suggest you take the slowly winding path. Every now and then the green will give way to a grand view over Irun, the river, Hendaye, and the ocean. Besides this path, there are many more hiking and biking trails nearby, going down and along the seaside. Several signs explain the routes and length.

## EAT/DRINK/HANGOUT

All along the **Boulevard de la Mer** (**77**) - and even more concentrated in

and behind the old casino overlooking the beach - are numerous restaurants, cafés, shops and surf schools. The wooden shack (Talarmein & Fils) at the south side sells great paninis and excellent churros. Expect the restaurants to be a little overpriced, but serving a decent meal with a view.

In the **Avenue des Mimosas (78)**, just one street behind the boulevard, there are a few nice places to hang out, like Belharra at nr 17, which serves pizzas and sandwiches, also take-away. For pintxos, tapas or paella there's Arroka Café at nr 10. Get your coffee or Basque lunch at Brasserie L'Océ, nr 9. Just around the corner you'll find the bakery La Chocolatine, that also sells salads and quiches.

**Sokoburu Market (79)**, every Saturday from 08:00 to 13:00 hrs, mouth-watering local goodies.

**a.** Boulevard de la Mer (towards the marina), Sokoburu, 64700 Hendaye

**Bask Rock Café (80)**, great place for drinks. It feels a bit like you're in someone's funny, skull-painted living room. They serve tapas and cocktails and have several Belgian beers to choose from.

**a.** 9 Rue des Figuiers, 64700 Hendaye

If you love your pulpo and chorizo, cross the border to **Hondarribia (87)**. Don't let the dull flats you see from the beach in Hendaye fool you, Hondarribia has a great historic centre. It's easy to find an eatery for pintxos, the Basque version of tapas, at the left riverbank. Or try Singular Food, a popular and very reasonably priced restaurant where they serve old local recipes with a new flair. You'll miss it in a blink of an eye, but you can't miss the big grey building as you drive from Hendaye through Irun to Hondarribia airport. The restaurant is in the FICOBA expo-building, but has its own entrance.

**a.** Avenida Iparralde 43, Edificio Ficoba, 20305 Irun

## SLEEP

◆

**Col d'Ibardin Campsite (88)**, situated in the green hills behind Hendaye and Saint-Jean-de-Luz, with a view of the mountains of La Rhune.

**a.** 220 Route d'Olhette, 64122 Urrugne
**w.** glistencamping.com

# SURF

Depending on sandbank conditions, there are few variations between the **Anglet breaks (I)**, some of which are separated by jetties. Too big or hollow for you? Just watch and learn; there's some high level surfing going on, especially at Les Cavaliers to the north. Anglet beaches work on small to medium nw to w swell, best at mid tide: at high tide some super hollow waves break close to shore. VVF in the south and la Barre at the northern end are sheltered from sideshore winds and bigger swells. All levels. Easy parking/toilet/shower/restaurant/surf school.

In Biarritz you have several beachbreaks to choose from. **Grande Plage (II)**, just in front of the casino (a pain to try park your car here), holds up to 2,5 m and is sheltered by rocks. Despite its name it's not a big beach, the south end is the best option for bigger boards.

Surfers of all levels will have a fun time at the classic **Plage de la Côte des Basques (III)**, a large stretch of beach overlooked by the distinctive Villa Belza. Although this is a popular and usually crowded break, there are several peaks to choose from. The south end, which has rock/sand bottom, is more exposed but less crowded. Works on small to medium nw to w swell, low to mid tide is best. At high tide the beach disappears and it's hard to get out of the water. All levels. Parking (can be a problem in summer)/shower/restaurant/surf school.

From the clifftop at Avenue Notre Dame you can check the surf from above. From here you can also see the spots at Plage Marbella, to the south, and even further south is Ilbarritz, usually producing a hollow wave. **La Milady (IV)** can be good for beginners to intermediate, easy access, best to surf on smaller days. Watch out for big rocks, not a low tide break. Ilbarritz, right next to it, is a favourite for bodyboarders. Beach can be crazy crowded in summer. All levels. Easy parking/toilet/restaurant.

The beaches of **Bidart** have sandy and rocky bottoms, some surrounded by steep hills. **Erretegia (V)** is a beautiful spot in the sense that the backdrop is luscious green and it's usually uncrowded. Walk, skate or bike downhill (parking down is limited, in space and height, 1,80 m). Sometimes mellow and mushy, best on small days. And watch out for big rocks. **La Centrale (VI)**, or Bidart Centre, is a popular beachbreak with tourists and eager local groms alike - who love the fast and sometimes barrelling waves closer to shore. Family beach, but watch your own eager groms in the surf because the current can be strong.

**Uhabia (VII)** can be seen from the D810, driving south. Good spot for all levels, depending on the shifting banks, holds up to 1,5 m. All work best with a clean small to medium nw to w swell. All levels. Easy parking at all spots/restaurant/surf school.

Bring the guns out for **Parlementia (VIII)**, Guéthary. Advanced surfers only on this long-ride, beautiful-to-watch reefbreak that comes to life on big swells. Don't be fooled by the fact that you see a lot of old men with longboards. They're usually local, in shape, and able to hold their breath for prolonged periods. It can be surfed by the lesser gods in smaller swells, but please respect the local folks.

**Cenitz (IX)**, a reefbreak to the south of Guéthary, has a long left and a faster right to choose from.

**Lafitenia (X)** is a popular, always crowded, right pointbreak. The level of surfing is very competitive. It's a beautiful, small beach, surrounded by green hills.

The next one is **Erromardie (XI)**, an open and easily accessible beach where waves break over uneven reef and sand. All spots need medium to big nw to w swell, best mid to high tide. Intermediate to advanced level. Easy parking (but packed in summer)/toilet/shower/restaurant/playground at Lafitenia.

A sheltered break in big winter swells is **Sainte-Barbe (XII)**, in the bay of Saint-Jean-de-Luz. Watch before you go in, and enter at the northern side. It's a long paddle out to the line-up near the jetty, where the take-off is really fast, then slows down to a mellow section (hence the large number of stand-up paddleboards). Although the surf can be a bit funky, the backdrop is classic. Needs big nw swell. Intermediate level. Easy parking/shower/restaurant.

If the spots from Anglet to Guethary are trop grande for your taste, **Hendaye (XIV)** is the best option in medium to big nw swells. It's a huge bay, with several peaks to choose from. Most of the beach in the middle of the bay will disappear at high tide. Surfable at all tides, but low tide and high tide produce a lot of closeouts. All the way to the north end of the bay, where two big boulders stand erect from the water; **Les Deux Jumeaux (XIII)**, a right pointbreak that comes to life during big nw swell, favourable for longboarders and SUPs. Not a beginner spot - it's a powerful wave and a long paddle out. Best at mid tide, more rocks than you'd expect appear at low tide. Easy parking/restaurant/surf school.

# SCHOOL RENTAL REPAIR

**Marty Surf Delivery** is a unique concept offering home delivery of all the surfing equipment you need for your holiday on the Basque coast. From longboards to fish, logs, single fins, shortboards to beginner boards. Marty also offers surf guiding to the best spots in the area, including photos and/or video analysis. And last but not least: he does board repairs!

**t.** 6 95 455 499
**w.** martysurfdelivery.com

To help you make the right choice from all the surf schools in Biarritz, you can check whether they're affiliated with **AESB**, the Biarritz surfing association.

**w.** aesb.fr

**Rainbow Surf School (19)**: lessons, rental of longboards, shortboards, beginner boards and SUPs, as well as the surf school they have a very well-equipped shop at nr 21.

**a.** 31 Avenue de la Chambre d'Amour, 64600 Anglet
**w.** ecoledesurf-rainbow.com

**Jo Moraiz Surf School (28)** started out as the first school in Biarritz and was run from 1966 by none other than Jo Moraiz himself. Jo, one of the first local pros, who represented France in one of the first World Surfing Championships in the sixties, has sadly passed away, but his son, Christophe, took over and so the school lives on with the same spirit. Open from April to November.

**a.** Plage de la Côte des Basques, 64200 Biarritz
**w.** jomoraiz.com

**Gold Coast (81)** is a well-established surf school in Hendaye. Surf and SUP lessons and rental. It has a big shop and a café as well. Open all year.

**a.** 71 Boulevard de la Mer, 64700 Hendaye
**t.** 5 59 203 144
**w.** ecolesurfhendaye.com

Photo: Ananda van Welij

# 3. MINDFUL MEDITATION

*Many of us find ourselves constantly on the move during our day-to-day life, whether physically, mentally, or both. It can be hard to find a moment of utter and complete awareness, of totally being in the present moment.*

*Even while surfing you can find yourself caught up in thoughts and stuck in whatever feeling you took with you into the water. To release this and really be present in the action of surfing, and to improve the experience tremendously, follow this technique.*

*Sitting on your board, take time for a moment to become totally aware of your surroundings, become aware of the rhythmic movement of the water, the colour of the ocean and the clouds in the sky. Then take this awareness into your own body and run through a checklist; pay attention to how are you sitting on your board, whether your spine is erect, your shoulders relaxed away from your ears. Then start taking your awareness inwards, following the movement of your breath. Is it calm & even? If not, start elongating your breaths, feeling how this eases your whole body. Once you have reached this state of total awareness and the next wave is coming, see if you can take the vibe with you into your surf and experience how this total fusion with the wave expresses itself, in this state of mind it's likely that you'll have one of your best rides ever!*

***Benefits:***

*Improves well-being, physical and mental health.*

MUNDAKA (VI)
PLENTZIA (VIII)
BAKIO (VII)
LAGA (IV)
LAIDA (V)
SOPELANA (IX)
45,67
BAKIO
MUNDAKA
43,44,55
ZURRIOLA (I)
ITZURUN (III)
ZARAUTZ (II)
SOPELANA
BI-631
48,52-54
46,49-51,57-59,68
56
LEKEITIO
26
GI-636
AP-8
IRUN
GETXO
GERNIKA
34,41,42
30-33
66
N-634
35
SAN SEBASTIÁN
1-25,60-62
BILBAO
DEBA
ZARAUTZ
27-29,36,38-40,62-65
47
AP-8
Pais Vasco
AP-8
A-15
37
AP-1
AP-68
A-1
AP-1

# PAIS VASCO

Welcome to the southern provinces of Basque country. This part of Euskal Herria, the land of the Basque language, is maybe more outspoken in its culture than their neighbours over the French border. You'll definitely spot the flags and signs of the heart-shaped Basque country hanging from houses, even painted on rocks. Both origin and language of the Basque country are a mystery to this very day; Basque words have similarities with languages in countries as far as Japan.

Encompassed by the Pyrenees and dipping its toes in the Bay of Biscay, expect to be awed by this area in one way or another. Cliffs, inlets, rivers and estuaries magically reflect the light, even on cloudy days. And cloudy days you'll get, for sure. Not too cold, but often you'll feel a drizzle, or rain, or at least the air feeling humid. It makes for the valleys to be green and glorious. And expect waves, in all shapes and sizes. You'll find there's variety enough for everyone from big wave riding thrill-seekers to banana-shaped, curved figures who prefer to hang ten.

## TRAVEL INFO

Either pick one place to stay, like Zarautz, San Sebastián or Sopelana, and make daytrips with public transport, or choose a road trip to discover all, with a van or car. The toll road between Vitoria and San Sebastián is quite expensive, and it only saves you 20 minutes in time.

### BY AIR

**Aeropuerto de Bilbao** is situated 9 km north of Bilbao, in the municipality of Loiu. It serves connections to most European cities.

### BY TRAIN

There are some good connections between Bilbao and Paris, Barcelona and Madrid, check schedules with **RENFE**. More scenic (and time-consuming) local routes can be taken with **EuskoTren**.

**w.** renfe.com
**w.** euskotren.eus

### BY BUS

There's a bus connection to the centre of **Bilbao** and **San Sebastián**.

**a.** 48180, Loiu, Bizkaia
**w.** aena.e

Photo: Marinus Joris

# DON'T MISS

*Las Fiestas de San Fermín*

**Las Fiestas de San Fermín, in Pamplona, is a week-long festival starting every year on the 6th of July, ending on the 14th. If you haven't heard of it, where have you been?**

The festival, dating back to the 13th century, was originally a religious celebration with music, a procession and bullfight. The 2-day celebration has grown to a week of festivities with dancing, street theatre, a lot of drinking, partying, fireworks and, of course, the running of bulls through the streets of the city. There are 8 runs in total and it's not really recommended to participate, just watch. It was Ernest Hemingway who told the whole world about the festival, and made it as grand and widely known as it is today. So, another piece of advice: get there early.

**More info**: turismo.navarra.es

# USEFUL WORDS

*Topa! or, Eskerriska!* = Cheers!
*Barkatu* = Sorry, Excuse me
*Boga Boga* = Paddle Paddle

# BASQUE LOCAL RECIPE

## MARMITAKO

A typical Basque dish, the name means 'from the pot.' What comes from the pot is a delicious stew made from mostly tuna and potatoes. Before it made its way into Basque kitchens, marmitako was a typical meal for Basque fishermen and was prepared while they were on their boats, in search of tuna.

## RECIPE FOR 2 PEOPLE

To fully appreciate this dish, use only the freshest of ingredients and play some traditional Basque folk songs in the background to add flavour, character and depth to your dinner.

## INGREDIENTS

*200g (½ lb) Fresh Tuna*
*1 small Onion*
*1 Green Pepper*
*2 large Potatoes*
*1 maybe 2 cloves of Garlic*
*1 or 2 Dried Peppers*
*(Pimiento Choricero - soak in water before using)*
*1 small Tomato (optional)*
*Fresh Parsley*
*Olive oil*
*Txakoli (white wine)*
*Water & Salt*

## DIRECTIONS

- Peel and 'crack' the potatoes roughly into chunks – they shouldn't be sliced, but if you can't get the hang of it, then cut into big cubes
- Cut vegetables into small pieces
- Lightly sauté the onion in oil till soft and see-through
- Add green pepper, cook on gentle heat for a few minutes
- Add potatoes & garlic, cook for a few more minutes
- Add wine (about a glass full, then pour yourself a glass)
- Peel pre-soaked pimientos choriceros and add to pot
- Add water (to just cover ingredients) and a pinch of salt
- Put the lid on and leave to cook slowly for 20-30 mins (no boiling or bubbling), stir occasionally and top up water if necessary.
- Optional add tomato
- Once potatoes are tender, add tuna (cubes), let cook for 2-3 minutes
- Finish with a sprinkle of roughly chopped/torn parsley

*Serve with a bottle of txakoli, the spare one, that you didn't drink while cooking. Topa! (Cheers)*

## SURFER-TRAVELLER TYPE PAIS VASCO

*You love sturdy men, or devilish handsome gals, your tapas to be pinched, and your wine to sparkle; a bit of rain won't kill you, fishing villages never bore you, your cojones are big enough for some of these waves, and you don't mind eating at midnight or waiting hours for the shops to re-open after siesta.*

## IN AND AROUND SAN SEBASTIÁN

Not many places in the world have their beaches right in the heart of the city. San Sebastián's got several. And they define its vibe. A lively boulevard - even in stormy weather - serves as a vein, transporting its people to and from the old city. People holding tight to surfboards, suitcases, shopping bags and their hats to keep them from sailing away with the wind. And yes, the food's good; one after another pintxos bars in the old centre. The vibe is splendid. But it's the loveable people that make Donostia – the Basque name for San Sebastián – extraordinary.

**Tourist office** at Alameda Boulevard 8.

Photo: Alexandra Gossink

## TO DO

◆

San Sebastián's **Surfilm Festibal (1)** is the longest running surf film festival in the world, and a must-go-to at least once for every surf aficionado. Every year in June you can enjoy exhibitions, performances, concerts, gatherings, workshops, and of course, surf-related movies.

**w.** surfilmfestibal.com

**Single Fin Classic Hawaii x Vans (2)** is an international longboard contest and festival at Playa de la Zurriola in San Sebastián, held every year in June or July since 2014. Organised with soul and passion by Surf Shop Hawaii Donostia, it fuels the spirit of every true longboarder with expression sessions, celebrating the classic ride, and just having fun with friends.

**w.** hawaiidonostia.com

**Surfing Etxea (3)** organise kayak and SUP tours inside the La Concha bay, your chance to see the little island Santa Clara from up close. Tours last about 1,5 hrs.

**a.** Avenida de Zurriola 34,
20002 San Sebastián
**t.** 9 43 011 384 / 6 86 988 706
**w.** surfingetxea.com

Join in the vinyasa-style yoga classes at the amazingly beautiful **802 Yoga Studio (4)**. Classes in Spanish and English (Monday), suitable for all levels, drop-in possible. To book your class it's best to send an email.

**a.** Urdaneta 4, Bajo 20005 San Sebastián
**t.** 6 44 212 456
**e.** info@802yogastudio.com
**w.** 802yogastudio.com

## EAT/DRINK/HANGOUT

◆

San Sebastián has **pintxos and tapas bars** galore; it would take a lifetime to check them all out. Just follow your instincts and do as the locals do, sample the local specialities 'txikiteo' style - a pintxos-bar-hopping food expedition.

But, to suit non-meat or fish eating travellers, we picked out a few vegetarian friendly eateries. We know it's not easy for you out there in southern Europe!

**Kafe Botanika** (**5**) offers juices, shakes, organic meals, a choice of vegetarian dishes and a relaxing vibe, some cool tunes and a readers corner, all in a nice setting, either indoor or in the garden. The café sits alongside the Urumea River. Open all year. •€• •€€•

**a.** Paseo Arbol de Gernika 8, 20006 San Sebastián
**t.** 9 43 443 475

**Restaurante El Tedone** (**6**) believes in serving good, honest food to make the world a better place. So, they strive to use as many biological, seasonal, non-GM and organic products as possible in their cuisine. And, it's no solo comida; regular music and talks. Open all year. •€€•

**a.** Calle Corta 10, 20001 San Sebastián
**t.** 9 43 273 561
**w.** tedone.eu

The best antithesis to the infamous McD is the **Green Break** (**7**), a vegan take-away, right in the old centre. From burritos, salads, pizzas and veggie-burgers to ice-cream and killer tiramisu, it's all 100% vegetable and delicious. Either take-away or eat there. Open all year, closed on Monday. •€• •€€•

**a.** Narrika Kalea 20, 20003 San Sebastián

**La Guinda** (**8**), situated close to Playa de la Zurriola, makes for a great after surf hangout. The café and soul food restaurant serves breakfast, coffee, drinks and food, with love. Open all year, closed on Monday. •€€•

**a.** Calle Zabaleta 55, 20002 San Sebastián
**w.** laguindadelicoffee.com

Tapas bar and restaurant **A Fuego Negro** (**9**) treats their food as a work of art. Delicious food that looks so good it's almost a shame to eat it. But don't let their pintxos with a twist get cold now, while taking pictures, just enjoy it. Good music and art exhibitions on offer as well. Open all year, closed on Monday. •€€•

**a.** Calle de Agosto 31, 20003 San Sebastián
**t.** 6 50 135 373
**w.** afuegonegro.com

Contrary to their neighbours on the French side of the border, coffee tastes perfect almost everywhere. A few addresses we especially like:

**Fam Kafe (10)** is a great little place for take-away coffee and cake or croissant, lovely staff. In the streets behind Centro Kursaal, just before you cross the bridge to the old centre.

**a.** Calle Peña y Goñi 15,
20002 San Sebastián

If you think cupcakes are outdated, think again, the girls from **Sweet Roma (11)** serve an excellent coffee or tea and sweet cake in their nicely decorated cupcakery.

**a.** Calle Sanchez Toca 3,
20006 San Sebastián

**Caffè Terzi (12)** is not just another place for a good cuppa, it's coffee culture that's on offer here. A must for coffee aficionados, or those who need to learn to appreciate it... Open from 07:30 in the morning.

**a.** Calle Andrestegi 8,
20018 San Sebastián

## SHOP

◆

Get your organic food, tea, and other eco essentials at **Supermercado Ecológico Bio Lêku (13)**, in the old centre.

**a.** Calle Aldamar 16, 20003 San Sebastián
**t.** 9 43 359 066

At the north end of Playa de la Zurriola sits the **Patagonia (14)** store. Besides being a well-stocked surf and outdoor shop, it serves as a meeting point for local and visiting surfers. Nice stack of books, friendly staff that are passionate about the outdoors and surf themselves. Open all year, closed on Sunday.

**a.** Paseo de Jose Miguel Barandiarán 24,
20013 San Sebastián
**t.** 9 43 290 126

**Miner Bicis Urbanas (15)** is not just any bicycle shop; alongside beautifully designed bikes and bike accessories, they sell clothes that will fit a day out in town better than a bicycle ride.

**a.** Ronda 7, 20001 San Sebastián
**t.** 9 43 271 050

Surf shop **Hawaii (16)** is one of the earliest surf shops in San Sebastián, they started in 1980 and have opened 3 shops since then. A well stocked shop with surf and streetwear, surf necessities, longboards, single fins, fish and shortboards. They're also the initiators of the Single Fin Classic every year in June. Shops at:

**a.** San Bartolomé 12,
20007 San Sebastián
**a.** Legazpi 8, 20004 San Sebastián
**a.** Avenida de la Zurriola 20,
20020 San Sebastián
**w.** hawaiidonostia.com

**Flow Store (17)**: pretty cool streetwear and skateboard shop in the centre, near the Cathedral. If you want to find out what's on in town, ask the staff. Or check out their own film or music events. Closed on Sunday.

**a.** La Calle Larramendi 9,
20004 San Sebastián
**t.** 9 43 471 945
**w.** theflowstore.com

Although they don't want to be labelled, especially as a surf or skate shop, **The Bohemian Shop (18)**, in the old centre, is well influenced by its culture. Besides clothes from smaller brands, books and accessories they sell retro and vintage decorations.

**a.** Calle Iñigo 1, 20003 San Sebastián
**t.** 9 43 424 573

New and second-hand clothes make a perfect match at **Vintage Closet (19)**. All handsomely styled, you'll find shoes, dresses, shirts and accessories (m/f). Closed on Sunday.

**a.** Calle Zabaleta 43, 20002 San Sebastián
**t.** 8 43 983 281
**w.** vintageclosetss.com

**KaXilda (20)**, it's a bookstore, a café, and an art gallery. So, if you like good books, culture and coffee, this is your spot. Open all year, from 10:00 hrs.

**a.** Bajo, Calle Arroka 1-3, 20006 San Sebastián
**t.** 9 43 571 987

**Pukas Surf (21)**, one of the most well-known surfboard manufacturers of the Basque Country, has several shops and schools along the coast. In the old centre you'll find one of their bigger, well-equipped and nicely decorated surf and lifestyle stores. Open every day.

**a.** Calle Mayor 5, 20003 San Sebastián
**t.** 9 43 427 228
**w.** pukassurf.com

## SLEEP

◆

**Campervans (22)** can park and stay for a maximum of 48 hrs at the Aparcamiento Autocaravanas. Close to the centre and Bahía de la Concha. •€•

**a.** Paseo de Berio 12, 20018 San Sebastián

**Green Nest Hostel Uba Aterpetxea (23)** is the perfect economic choice if you want to enjoy all the fun of San Sebastián, but wake up in the quiet beauty of nature. Green Nest is set in a modern building, using only green energy, such as solar panels and biomass, in the Lau Haizeta park, 4 km from the centre of town. Storage for your boards is provided. Open all year. •€•

**a.** De Uba Bidea, 43, 20014 San Sebastián
**t.** 9 43 457 117
**e.** booking@greenestdonostia.com
**w.** nesthostelsansebastian.com

**Donosti Chill Retreat House (24)** is a surf and yogi friendly house, near Playa de la Zurriola, with 6 comfortable and spacious rooms (sleeps 12 persons), and a multipurpose living room that also fits 10 to 12 people for yoga classes. You can either just book a room to explore the city, rent the whole house to host your own retreat, or join one of the retreats offered. Since well-being is a priority for host, surfer and yogi, Alejandra Romo, they can provide in-house yoga classes, food workshops, surf lessons, and outdoor and culinary tours. •€€•

**a.** Usandizaga Kalea, 20002 San Sebastián
**t.** 6 27 122 148
**e.** info@donostichillretreat.com
**w.** donostichillretreathouse.com

**Etxea Surf House (25)** is located in the heart of the city, in front of Playa de la Zurriola. If you don't mind sleeping in a bunk bed, it's a cheap option to stay within a stone's throw of the surf, the bars and the city. They've got a terrace with hammocks to hang out and make new friends. Open all year. •€•

**a.** Avenida de Zurriola 34, 20002 San Sebastián
**t.** 9 43 011 384/6 86 988 706
**e.** info@surfingetxea.com
**w.** surfingetxea.com

Hostel **Capitan Tximista (26)** sits right next to an 18th century mill, on the southern slope of Monte Jaizkibel. The hostel sleeps up to 40 persons (bunk beds), has bicycles for rent, and is a perfect place to set off on outdoor adventures. The staff can help you organise your trips. •€•

**a.** Barrio Jaizubia 14 – Goikoerrota, 20280 Hondarribia, Gipuzkoa
**t.** 9 43 643 884
**e.** info@capitantximista.com
**w.** capitantximista.com

# IN AND AROUND ZARAUTZ

Most of what makes Zarautz attractive takes place on the boulevard and in the old centre just behind it. And then there's the beach and ocean, of course. It's not your typical surf or former fishing town; it has more grandeur and style, and is far more old-fashioned than you'd expect from such a popular surf and party town, which is what it's known for. The surroundings are breathtakingly beautiful, and home to vineyards producing txakoli, a sparkling white wine.

## TO DO

**Pro Zarautz** (**27**) is an annual surf festival with local, European and international surfers, as part of the World Qualifying Series of the World Surf League. Besides the contest there's live music, skate and BMX shows, surf and yoga classes. It's usually held end of March/beginning of April.

**w.** prozarautz.com

**Lotuz Yoga** (**28**) offer daily classes in Ashtanga, Mysore style, and sukhashanti yoga (a safe and easy way to perform yoga). Up-to-date schedule on the website.

**a.** Calle Torre Luzea Parkea 5, Bajo, 20800 Zarautz
**t.** 6 61 432 238
**w.** lotuzyoga.com

**Spa Malecon** (**29**) overlooks the beach and surf. The small spa and adjoining gym offer a hydro-massage bath and pool, spinning classes and massages.

**a.** Calle Balea 5, 20800 Zarautz
**t.** 9 43 011 240
**w.** spamalecon.com

**Getaria** (**30**), the next village to the south of Zarautz, which you can spot from the boulevard, is a small fishing port. Its genuine character differs from Zarautz like a posh sister and her tough brother. Walk the small winding streets to look for some culinary treats, watch the buzz in the harbour and take a tour through the txakoli wine region in the rolling green hills surrounding Getaria.

**Taste Txakoli** (**31**): If you didn't already have a glass with your pintxos, it's about time you did. This young, fruity white wine is distinctive to this area. Served chilled, with a slight bubble, it's a perfect combo with the salty, oily pintxos. Taste and learn more with a guided tour at one of several vineyards. You can find a map and info for the vineyards open to visit at the Regulatory Board of Getariako Txakolina.

**a.** Parque Aldamar 4, Bajo, 20808 Getaria
**w.** getariakotxakolina.com

The last thing you expect in such a small fishing village is a big museum dedicated to a famous fashion designer. Since Getaria is the birthplace of Cristóbal Balenciaga, son of a sailor and a seamstress, you'll find the **Cristóbal Balenciaga Museoa** (**32**), in an eye-catching modern building on a hill, overlooking the town. Besides the permanent collection, various other exhibitions and workshops are held here.

**a.** Aldamar Parkea 6, 20808 Getaria
**t.** 9 43 008 840
**w.** cristobalbalenciagamuseoa.com

Checking surf breaks and beaches, you'll spot a phenomenon alongside the coast, especially in the area around Zumaia, at Itzurun beach, to the south of Zarautz: **Flysch** (**33**). It's like art: long parallel grooves in the rock, created by ocean and earth, formed over a period of 100 million years. Caused by a collision of tectonic plates, formed by layer upon layer of silt and sandstone sediments, it's like looking into earth and ocean's knowledgeable brains.

Monumental fishing village **Mutriku** (**34**), dotted with old houses, some of medieval age, makes for a nice detour on your search for waves around Deba. Like many villages that used to depend on fishing but got caught up by economic crises, the town now caters to tourists, with restaurants, campsites and holiday homes. But it's still a sight for sore eyes with the old port, narrow streets and tower houses. And the ocean still plays an important role; at the new harbour wall you'll find one of the first wave power plants.

## EAT/DRINK/HANGOUT

Zarautz, like most Basque towns, has so many eateries; we say let yourself be guided by your hunger, instinct and explorer heart. It's really not a difficult job: go into a bar where you like the smiles of the folk, make sure there are locals of all ages, and make a choice of pintxos at the bar, accompanied by a glass of txakolina.

The one you shouldn't miss out on is just a little north of Zarautz, in the fishing village Orio. Grillhouse **Katxiña** (**35**) is a family-run restaurant, serving the most delicious barbecued fish (and meat). It sits right above the estuary so you'll have a great view of the ocean and green hills. Make sure you drink their Katxiña txakolina with that, one of the finest txakolina in the area, straight from the vineyards of their son.

**a.** Barrio de San Martin 8, 20810 Orio
**t.** 9 43 831 407
**w.** katxina.com

Drink, have a good time, enjoy music, and hang out with the local crowd in the bars in small streets behind the south end of the boulevard, like **Sausalita** and **Marmol**. Best days, of course, from Thursday to Sunday.

## SHOP

**Pukas Surf Shop** (**36**), surf and lifestyle shop from the popular Basque surf brand.

**a.** Avenida Navarra 4, 20800 Zarautz
**t.** 9 43 835 821

Check out the handcrafted, custom and locally produced surfboards from **Surftiger Surfboards** (**37**). Shaper Kim Francis, a Basque local, is inspired by the Californian surf from the 1960s and 70s, but feels he's part of the new

creative generation, shaping more radical 'retrofuture'. You can visit him at his workshop and shaping bay.

**a.** Poligono Apattaerreka, Calle Apatta 1, 20400 Tolosa
**t.** 6 63 484 391
**e.** surftigersurfboards@gmail.com

## SLEEP

◆

**Zarautz Hostel (38)** is a good option if you're looking for a simple and affordable place to stay near the surf and meet like-minded travellers. Rooms with bunk beds or double rooms, light, clean and nicely done, with a great view from their terrace. •€•

**a.** Calle Gipuzkoa Kalea 59, 20800 Zarautz
**t.** 9 43 833 893
**e.** info@zarautzhostel.com
**w.** zarautzhostel.com

**Boutique Hotel Zerupe (39)** uses concrete, wood, glass and steel, and large photos to create a spacious and tranquil feel to the place. All 11 rooms are uniquely decorated with themes like forest, marine flora, ocean geology and winter landscape. Besides the beautiful interior, services are what you expect a boutique hotel to offer. Located in the heart of the old centre. •€€•

**a.** Zigordia 24, Bajo, 20800 Zarautz
**t.** 9 43 508 582/688 864 322
**e.** reservas@hotelzerupe.com
**w.** hotelzerupe.com

**Gran Camping Zarautz (40)** is located on the slopes north of town and has some great vistas of ocean, land and Zarautz. They rent out mobile homes. From here you can walk down to the beach of Zarautz. Open all year. •€•

**a.** Monte Talai-Mendi s/n, 20800 Zarautz
**t.** 9 43 831 238 / 9 43 132 486
**w.** grancampingzarautz.com

**Camping Itxaspe (41)** has pitches, bungalows and studios on offer. From the site and their swimming pool, magnificent views over the ocean and Flysch cliffs. •€•

**a.** From the A-8, take Salida 13, 20829 Itziar-Deba
**t.** 9 43 199 377
**w.** campingitxaspe.com

**Camping Aitzeta (42)** is situated in the hills surrounding Mutriku. A peaceful campsite with spectacular views of the ocean and Mutriku's sea port. Open from May to October. •€•

**a.** Lugar Laranga 35, 20830 Mutriku
**t.** 9 43 603 356
**w.** campingaitzeta.es

# IN AND AROUND MUNDAKA

You would think that, with one of the most famous powerful and longest left waves in their front garden, Mundaka would be a living, breathing surf organ. Well, in a way it is, from the tiny symbol of a wave on public trash cans, to surfers from all over the world flying in on a perfect swell forecast. But, you won't come up against surf shop after surf shop. You won't see all the best-known brands all over the place. It's traditional, classic; people of all ages dress up and gather around the restaurants and bars during lunch time, or the water's edge and park at the end of the day. Having a drink, a chat - or a heated discussion, more likely. And the real beauty of Mundaka is its location, within the Urdaibai Biosphere Reserve. The cliffs, bays and inlets all the way up to Sopelana offer spectacular views and hike, bike and surf options.

## TO DO

What a great way to discover nature's ways: paddling a SUP, under the guidance of landscape architects and surfers, **Site of Tides' (43)** Eneko and Eunate. With their Boga Boga ('paddle paddle' in Basque) trips through the Urdaibai Biosphere Reserve, near Mundaka, they share their passion and insight into the changing behaviours of this beautiful landscape. Silently glide along wetlands where you can spot spoonbills and fish eagles.

**a.** Laida Beach, 48311 Ibarrangelu
**t.** 6 56 710 950
**w.** siteoftides.com

**Bosque Animado (44)**, or Oma Forest, was created by Basque artist, Agustin Ibarrola, in the 1980s, uniting the work of ancestral Palaeolithic artists with the modern trend of land art. You can walk round the painted forest, an open-air art installation, and admire the totem-like figures painted on trees. But it's more than just looking at painted trees. Depending on your path, your point of view and your own perception, you can see changes and transformations as you move along. So every visitor gets a customised exhibition. Open all year.

**a.** BI 4244, near Kortezubi, 48315 Barrio de Oma, Urdaibai Biosphere Reserve

**San Juan de Gaztelugatxe (45)** is one of those astounding sites steeped in myths and legends. As one legend has it, you should ring the chapel bell (three times), after completing the climb up the 237 steps (or are there more? we lost count...), and make a wish. The original chapel on top of the little island dates from the 9th or 10th century and – maybe another fable, maybe not – was seemingly built by the Knights Templar. It's been raided, attacked and set on fire, yet there it is, renovated over time but still standing, facing the ocean storms, deeply devoted local fishermen and tourists from around the world. Closed in winter.

**a.** Between Bermeo and Bakio, BI 3101

Fly over the cliffs and reefs of Sopelana with **Parapente Sopelana (46)**, and you can decide whether to add some funky acrobatic moves in the air, or just enjoy the quiet and beauty of the flight. Don't worry, your safety comes first.

**a.** Above Playa La Salvaje – Barinatxe, Sopelana
**t.** 6 07 213 431
**w.** parapentesopelana.com

If it wasn't for the famous Guggenheim museum, designed by architect Frank Gehry, a lot of folks might not bother to **visit Bilbao (47)**. Driving around the city from spot to spot it certainly doesn't look inviting. But trust us, it pays to enter the city, rather than avoid it. Not only the museum, the old centre is pedestrian – and shopping – friendly; they managed to mix modern and old splendidly together, a feast for architecture-loving eyes.

## EAT/DRINK/HANGOUT

◆

Bar **Ibarralde (48)**, great atmosphere, sometimes live music and, of course, a considerable choice of pintxos and vinos.

**a.** Florentino Larrinaga 13, Bajo, 48360 Mundaka
**t.** 9 46 876 348

If you like a creative twist to your meal, you'll be fine at **Milagros Restaurante (49)**. Choose from sushi, Asian and Latin American, and good to know, vegetarian food. Mostly prepared with seasonal and local products. Besides food, there are live music events, DJs and acts on the menu. •€€•

**a.** Carretera Sopelana Plentzia, Calle Bideondo 1, 48650 Barrika (Sopelana)
**t.** 9 46 770 235
**w.** milagrosrestaurante.com

Ok, it's not easy to explain what exactly is going on in **Oficina de Hechos (50)**, but expect to get to know Sopelana's underground scene of surf art, crafts, film making, poetry, writing and soulfood creators. Oficina de Hechos means Office of Facts, a name they acquired by making sure they put their money where their mouth is. For example, they talked about film projects and now they not only showcase surf films, they made a bunch of films themselves (Oficina de Hechos on Vimeo). Check it out!

**a.** Calle Solondota (Etxabea 3) 7, 48600 Sopelana (close to La Salvaje beach - Barinatxe)
**w.** oficinadehechos.blogspot.com

## SHOP

◆

**Styling Surf Shop (51)** has surf and skate shops in a few places in the Basque country. In Sopelana's shop you'll find boards of their own brand, clothes and accessories, and of course all your surf necessities. Friendly and helpful staff.

**a.** Avenida Arrietara 85, 48600 Sopelana
**t.** 9 46 767 000
**w.** stylingsurf.com

## SLEEP

◆

**Campervans (52)** can park and stay at Area de la Pergola in Bermeo, facilities to empty water and toilet. Close to football stadium, so can get noisy.

**a.** Camino de Matxitxako Bide-Zabala, 48370 Bermeo

**Mundaka Hostel and Sports Café (53)** is a renovated hostel with all modern amenities and clean rooms with bunk beds. Their Sports Café is a cool hangout for after surf beers and snacks. Open all year. •€•

**a.** Calle Santa Katalina s/n, 48360 Mundaka
**t.** 9 46 028 477
**e.** info@mundakahostel.com
**w.** mundakahostel.com

**Camping Portuondo (54)** has an area of pitches, bungalows and artfully designed mobile homes. But the best attraction is the views over the Urdaibai estuary. Open all year. •€• •€€•

**a.** Portuondo Auzoa, 48360 Mundaka
**t.** 9 46 877 701
**e.** recepcion@campingportuondo.com
**w.** campingportuondo.com

**Boutique Hotel Restaurante Castillo de Arteaga (55)**: Live like a king in this 13th century rather impressive castle. Located in the Urdaibai Nature Reserve. It offers a gourmet restaurant with a roof terrace boasting fantastic countryside views. Guests will be taken to another century, but with nowadays conveniences. There's also an extensive wine cellar, where you can enjoy tasting sessions. •€€€•

**a.** Gaztelubide Kalea 7,
48314 Gautegiz Arteaga
**t.** 9 46 240 012
**w.** castillodearteaga.com

**Aldori (56)** hotel is set in a rural house, inland from the Urdaibai estuary, blending in perfectly with the area. It has spacious and nicely decorated rooms, and a garden extending into the forest and green hills. •€€•

**a.** Calle Zabale 8, 48392 Muxika
**t.** 9 46 271 509 / 6 71 671 089
**e.** reservas@aldori.es
**w.** aldori.es

**Moana Surf Hostel (57)** specialises in surf and skate camps, and can house up to 75 people. This is one of the few camps that also organises camps in winter! But you can also just stay in the hostel for bed & breakfast. •€•

**a.** Elortza Auzoa 5, 48610 Urdúliz
**t.** 6 35 719 844 / 9 46 764 859
**e.** info@moanasurfhostel.com
**w.** moanacamps.com

**Camping Sopelana (58)** is situated next to Atxabiribil beach, one of Sopelana's surf breaks. Besides pitches they have mobile homes for rent. Open all year. •€•

**a.** Playa Atxabiribil, 30, 48600 Sopelana
**t.** 9 46 761 981
**w.** campingsopelana.com

**Campervans (59)** can park and stay at Área Para Autocaravana. The parking is situated a few kms from the beach, and in walking distance of the metro that brings you to the centre of Bilbao. •€•

**a.** Sabino Arana Kalea 48600 Sopelana
(next to BI634)

Photo: Sander Dijkmeijer, Zaratuz (II)

# SURF

San Sebastián's perfectly crescent-shaped **Playa de la Zurriola (I)** is a beachbreak with several peaks to choose from, depending on sandbars. Surfing in the city brings something of a special feeling to it: straight from beach to bar, but not the cleanest break, and crowds of course. Best on small w and nw swell, works on all tides. All levels. Parking difficult/shower/toilet/bar/restaurant/surf school/surf shop.

The big beach at **Zarautz (II)** offers several peaks and some really high level surfing. You can usually tell the tourists by the not-so-hot-as-the-locals level of surfing, and there are lots of tourists in the line-up during summer, since Zarautz is a popular surf holiday destination.

Best on small n and nw swell, works on all tides. All levels. Parking difficult in summer/shower/toilet/restaurant/surf school/surf shop.

**Playa de Itzurun (III)** in Zumaia is easily crowded, since it's a quite consistent beachbreak with some (natural) jetties. Backdrop of beautiful Flysch cliffs. Works on n and nw swell. All levels. Easy parking but busy/restaurant/surf school.

**Playa de Laga (IV)** is a beauty of a bay, just north of Mundaka, enclosed by cliffs and pine forest. Works best on small to medium nw swell, at mid tide. Can be crowded in summer and at weekends. All levels. Easy parking/shower/restaurant.

**Playa de Laida (V)**, at the Urdaibia estuary, produces usually mellow waves, you can check it from the road. Works best on small to medium n, nw and w swell, at mid tide. All levels. Easy parking/surf school/restaurant.

**Mundaka (VI)**, the famous left-hand riverbreak, is a spectacle to watch when it's on. Steep take-offs, speedy tube rides and unforgiving wipeouts. Works only on big n, nw and w swells, and when working, it's always crazy crowded. Best tide from low to mid. If you feel up to it, first watch for a while how it all works, and where to go in and exit. Experienced surfers only. Parking can be busy/restaurant/bar/surf shop.

The beachbreak of **Bakio (VII)** has a strong local surf community due to its consistency, proximity to Mundaka, and powerful waves. Shifting peaks, depending on sandbanks. Works on small to medium w, nw and n swell, low to mid tide. All levels. Easy parking/restaurant/surf school.

On big swell windy days the small, protected bay of **Plentzia (VIII)** is an option. There's a long lefthander breaking from the rivermouth, perfect for bigger boards – but a small take-off zone. Shorter rides in the middle of the bay, also a good area for learners. This spot doesn't work often, it needs a big n or nw swell and is protected from strong sw wind, best at low to mid tide. Easy parking/toilet/surf school.

The beautiful hilly area around **Sopelana (IX)** offers several reef, sand over reef, and beach breaks. You'll never be alone at these consistently working breaks, but crowds do spread out. Take in the view, enjoy the clean water, make friends. Works on small to medium n and nw swells, best tide depends on what part of the beach or reef you choose to surf. Easy parking/toilets/restaurant/surf school.

Photo: Melchior van Nigtevecht

# SCHOOL RENTAL REPAIR

◆

**Etxea Surf House and School (60)** is located in front of Playa de la Zurriola, in San Sebastián. They offer lessons and equipment for all levels, SUP tours, and rent out bicycles. They also organise surf boat trips! Open all year.

**a.** Avenida de Zurriola 34,
20002 San Sebastián
**t.** 9 43 011 384 / 6 86 988 706
**w.** surfingetxea.com

**Zurriola Surf School (61)**: lessons, rental and other activities, such as yoga and pilates. Open all year.

**a.** Calle Usandizaga 14,
20002 San Sebastián
**t.** 9 43 011 391
**w.** zurriolasurfeskola.com

**Pukas (62)** has shops but also surf schools; offering lessons and rental, for beginners up to high performance, Pukas boards and SUPs. Schools in San Sebastián, Zarautz, Getaria and Sopelana.

**w.** pukassurf.com

**Essus Surf Shop & Surf School (63)**: lessons for beginners to advanced, all ages and they can also combine with yoga.

**a.** Calle Torre Luzea 2, Bajo,
20800 Zarautz
**t.** 9 43 835 024 / 6 61 432 237
**w.** essussurf.com

The **Good People Surf Camp (64)** is situated in campsite Talai-Mendi, with its own facilities, such as tents, hammocks, use of Sector 9 skateboards and a yoga and massage area. You don't have to participate in a camp, they also offer lessons for individuals or small groups, or just rent a board.

**a.** Nafarroa Kalea 64, 20800 Zarautz
**t.** 9 43 536 627
**w.** goodpeoplesurf.com

Photo: Maaike Pays

**Axi Muniain Surf Eskola** (**65**): although he's a big wave surfer, Axi Muniain's still happy to teach you from scratch how to catch waves, or help you improve your level of surfing.

**a.** Calle Trinidad 1, Bajo, 20800 Zarautz
**t.** 9 43 835 648 / 6 49 787 842
**w.** aximuniain.com

Surf Taxi Boat **Getari Charter** (**66**) will take you to surf spots along the Basque coast, depending on where it's best, from Mundaka to the Les Landes breaks in France. They go from spot to spot and beach to beach, trying to avoid crowded peaks. They can carry up to 9 surfers plus full equipment, and start from the harbour in Getaria.

**t.** 6 00 521 822
**w.** getari.es

**Uretan Basque Surf Center** (**67**): surf and SUP lessons, and surf camps in Bakio.

**a.** Calle Erdiko Benta 1, 48130 Bakio
**t.** 6 80 279 526
**w.** uretansurfing.com

**Acero Surf Eskola** (**68**) is the surf school of well-known Basque surfer Eneko Acero (yep, brother of Kepa). Small groups only (max 5 persons), from beginner to advanced, experts and competitors.

**a.** Errementerina Bajo S/N, 48993 Algorta (Sopelana)
**t.** 6 55 935 156
**w.** acerosurfeskola.com

# SEASIDE LOCAL: ALAZNE AURREKOETXEA

Protest team rider, Alazne Aurrekoetxea, is a young, passionate, ocean-loving girl who likes challenges, big waves and the long left of Mundaka. A Basque beauty with cojones...
When she's not surfing; either shortboard or SUP; or racing her SUP (why settle for one sport when you can excel at three), she'll be swimming in the open ocean, just to be in the salty water. Alazne's been competing in surf and SUP championships for some years now: "I love the feeling to compete with the best, it helps me to improve my surfing," she says. Although she sometimes feels nervous about competing, moving up in the rankings keeps her going and makes her train even harder. The motivation becomes stronger than her fear. This attitude, and the fun she gets out of it, earned her position in the European SUP surfing championship, and in her first World Tour competitions.

Combining her study with as much time in the sea as possible, she still finds time to practise the traditional ball sport Esku Pilota and enjoy the beauty of her home town, Sopelana, and its surroundings. "The cliffs and wild beaches are strikingly beautiful, our village is quiet, it's paradise for people who love the outdoors; surfing, paragliding, climbing. And visitors should definitely try our cider and pintxos."

Her daily life revolves around surfing, and to improve her performance in competitions she tries to travel to different spots and circumstances: "I am super happy that I get all the support from my sponsor, Protest, to reach my sportive goals. I'm proud of what they do to help me fulfil my dreams - they feel like my second family."

*"Surfing is a crazy life. I can't help feeling excited every time I'm hitting the water. But besides surfing, my daily goals involve having fun with my friends and family." Alazne's passion is contagious and she fully lives her own motto to 'go confidently in the direction of your dreams'. Leaving us with a final piece of advice: "Live the life you have imagined."*

Read the full story about Alazne on:
**w.** ilovetheseaside.com

Photos: Protest

Styling
PROTEST

PROTEST

MERON, GERRA, OYAMBRE (IX)
LOS LOCOS (VIII)
LIENCRES (VII)
LANGRE (V) SOMO (VI)
BERRIA (III) EL BRUSCO (IV)
LAREDO (II)
BRAZOM (I)
AP-8
30-32,35-43,49,50
34
ST VICENTE
29
COMILLAS
AP-8
CA-131
SUANCES
23,24,28
18,20-22
SANTANDER
TORRELAVEGA
19,25,26
AP-8
27
SOLARES
3,15,16,47,48
SOMO
2
4-6,8-14,45,46
CA-141
17
AP-8
N-634
LAREDO
1,7,44
Cantabria
N-621
A-67
N-629
33

# CANTABRIA

Sloping hills, impressive mountains, cliffs and valleys; you'll have to try your best to find a flat piece of land. Cantabria has 6 protected nature areas, but even the green hills and estuaries without the official label make this area one grandísimo playground for the outdoorsy type. Expect to be awestruck, bobbing in the water on your plancha, looking back inland. Visit in the right season, like early spring, and you'll be paddling in crystal clear (yet cold) waters and seeing the snowy mountaintops of Los Picos de Europa.

Except for Spanish vacationers in summer, Cantabria is far from overrun with tourism. There are, however, many cows. No, really, there are more cattle here than anywhere else in Spain. You'll spot the long horned creatures everywhere, even crossing streets in their own totally relaxed tiempo. Another thing you'll notice a lot of – monasteries. In the Middle Ages these popped up all over the region, with settlements built around them, after huge numbers of Christians sought refuge in Cantabria and Asturia; almost the only part of the Iberian peninsula free from Moorish occupation. In the 17th and 18th century, Santander's location en route to other European ports and America turned the Cantabrian seaside into an important trading place. Nowadays, besides tourism, the main sources of income are cattle farming, agriculture and fishing.

## TRAVEL INFO

Whether you fly in, sail in, or travel with your car or van, you can centre yourself at one place, like Somo or San Vicente de la Barquera and won't have to drive for miles to search for surf, food and culture.

### BY AIR

**Seve Ballesteros-Santander airport** is located 6 km from Santander. There are buses to take you to the centre.

**a.** Carretera del Aeropuerto s/n 39600, Maliaño, Camargo

Low-cost airlines fly on a regular basis to European cities like Brussels, Düsseldorf, London and Lisbon.

**w.** aena.es

### BY BOAT

Brittany Ferries run regular services between Santander and the UK - Plymouth or Portsmouth.

**w.** brittany-ferries.co.uk

# SURFER-TRAVELLER TYPE CANTABRIA

*You're very much into rustic, of any type, or rural, you get into a meditative modus from watching happily grazing cattle, and like to surf all types of beaches and bays, be surrounded by lush green slopes, hills, mountains and valleys, get your feet soaked in wetlands and estuaries, and don't get a lactose intolerant outburst from milk, cheese and pastries.*

# IN AND AROUND SOMO

Of course Santander, the capital of Cantabria, is the place to refer to if addressing the area, but as seaside lovers we'll just narrow ourselves down to the beach. Even if we do recommend a visit to Santander - walk through the old town, nip your cider, enjoy as many tapas as you can - the 5 km stretch of beach at Somo is the perfect place to start from and return to. There are many campsites, hotels and surf camps, yet still you feel its spaciousness and, of course, its northwesterly aspect serves as a swell magnet par excellence.

## TO DO

◆

**Laredo (1)**, situated less than 50 kms east of Santander, is a popular Spanish beach resort. Thing is, the beach - La Salvé, a 5 km stretch of sand - is immense, and the view from it is nothing short of splendid; green cliffs to the left, the old town to the right. It's the seaside part of town that's just plain ugly, full of 20th-century building blocks. Nevertheless, a good chance you'll end up here one day or another to search for surf with wind protection. If you do, make sure you enjoy a little after-surf in Puebla Vieja, the old city at the eastern end of town. Cobbled streets slope down from La Atalaya hill, and there are a satisfying number of bars and eateries, like surf bar **Plural Puebla** at Calle El Medio 24.

*¡Take time to check your spelling on the GPS. Loredo (next to Somo) is much closer to Santander than Laredo, which is halfway to Bilbao!*

**Derby Playa de Loredo (2)**, annual horse racing event, is usually held end of July or beginning of August, and coincides with low tide, as they race along the beach. In years gone by there was also a race for donkeys, but nowadays it's a much grander affair so you'll find a fine selection of Thoroughbred horses racing as the main event of the day.

Learn how to shape your own surfboard at the shaping school of **Ahau Surf School (3)**. They share their knowledge and experience from over the years of surfing and shaping all types of water slides. During the process you'll learn some history about the evolution and development of boards and surfing. Or just check out their beautiful boards, handcrafted with love, made from balsa, red cedar or a combination of different woods.

**a.** Duque Santo Mauro 7, 39005 Santander
**t.** 6 33 785 109
**w.** ahausurfschool.com

## EAT/DRINK/HANGOUT

◆

Bakery **Curros&Co (4)** is so much more than a place to get your daily bread. Of course, you'll find freshly made bread of all kinds, you can also enjoy a coffee, tea, some sweet and hearty pastries, and have a look around for some fine decorative pieces, small furniture and accessories. Very nicely done. Closed in winter. •€•

**a.** Calle Isla de Mouro, 4, 39140 Somo
**t.** 6 64 808 011
**w.** currusco.com

If you feel like a bit of change from the Spanish diet, you should try Italian restaurant **L'ArteSano (5)**. This little place is run by two Italians with extreme passion for serving good food. Everything's freshly prepared and they try to use as many locally grown products as possible. Great coffees too! •€• •€€•

**a.** Calle Isla De Mouro 11, 39140 Somo
**t.** 6 45 076 294

## SHOP

◆

Shaper Stefan, from **Kun_tiqi Surfboards (6)**, has made it his mission to give surfers a chance to contribute to preserving nature and at the same time enjoy her gifts. Kun_tiqi boards are produced from eco-friendly and sustainable materials, using mainly balsa wood, and their resin is made from 55% vegetable oil. "In addition", says Stefan, "Kun_tiqi takes on its social responsibilities by paying a fair price to the producer and ensuring that proper working conditions are constantly maintained and improved. We're proud to produce it with affinity to nature, and hope everyone who choose our boards are proud to surf it." You can visit the shop, which has most surf essentials and stocks Patagonia wetsuits, and rent a board to experience the ride.

**a.** Barrio la Cardosa 11, 39160 Loredo, near Playa De Somo
**t.** 6 22 420 641 (Stefan)
**e.** info@kuntiqi.com
**w.** kuntiqi.com

## SLEEP

◆

**Camping Playa Regatón (7)** is situated in a green setting next to the Regatón beach, by the estuary of the Asón river. Shaded pitches, hikers' cabins and apartments, dogs allowed. Open from April to September. •€• •€€•

**a.** Calle El Regatón 8, 39770 Laredo
**t.** 9 42 606 995
**w.** campingplayaregaton.com

**Latas Surf (8)** offers fun accommodation on campsite Surf Resort Loredo, in cosy, tent-shaped little wooden structures that they call 'the Sheddies'. Located 250 m from the surf break, there's a mini ramp and a nice green space to play volleyball and do yoga. If you don't want to sleep at the campsite, you can also stay in their nearby Surf House. Open in season. •€•

**a.** Calle Arna 131, Latas Somo, 39140 Loredo
**t.** 9 42 509 236 / 6 99 028 629
**w.** latassurf.com

**Wolfhouse (9)** is the brainchild of Italian couple Alessandro and Camilla, longtime dedicated sliders of fish and longboards. Like two young wolves, they wanted to escape the greedy city pack, to live in peace and in contact with nature. In Loredo, with all its perfect surf possibilities, they set up a holiday house for travellers and surfers of all ages and abilities. Their philosophy is to allow everyone to travel cheaply and safely, and in the most fun way. Of course, being stylish boarders themselves, surfing is a serious matter; sharing this passion, and discovering new places and breaks are all on the daily menu. Shared rooms, double or twin rooms and singles available. You can also choose one of their packages to include surf lessons. •€•

**a.** Calle Rumor 9, 39160 Loredo
**t.** 6 10 057 658
**e.** wolfhouse@hotmail.it
**w.** wolf-house.com

**Camping Derby Loredo (10)** is ideally situated close to the 8 km long magnificent beach of Loredo, with direct access to and views over the bay of Santander. They have got pitches, 3 bedroom basic bungalows and a hostel with bunk beds. Pets allowed, surf, SUP, yoga and pilates classes on offer. Closed from mid December to mid January. •€•

**a.** Calle Bajada a la Playa 19, 39160 Loredo
**t.** 9 42 504 106 / 6 69 456 296
**w.** campingloredo.com

**The Loredo Surf House (11)**, established in 2015, is a fresh member of the surf house guild, offering bunk beds, family rooms and double bedrooms with terrace in their villa near the beach. Open all year. •€• •€€•

**a.** Calle Juncal 6, 39160 Loredo
**t.** 6 36 375 263
**e.** info@loredosurfhouse.com
**w.** loredosurfhouse.com

**Campervans (12)** can stay and use facilities at Area de Somo, next to Camping Somo Parque. Close to beach and centre. Open all year. •€•

**a.** Barrio Suesa Mojante, s/n, Ribamontán al Mar, 39150 Suesa (Somo)

Photo: Marinus Joris

**Casa del Surf (13)** was one of the first surf houses in the area. Situated in a tranquil part of Somo, minutes away from the beach, in a classic Spanish building. The 8 spacious rooms are decorated in a mix of traditional and surfy-style. Open all year. •€• •€€•

**a.** Regunil 40, 39140 Somo
**t.** 6 16 382 534
**w.** casadelsurf.es

**La Posada de Somo (14)** has some tastefully styled villas, suites and rooms on offer. Maybe some need a bit of maintenance, but you never know what might happen after the next season, the décor is still a treat. Open all year. •€€• •€€€•

**a.** Barrio de Somo Llosa Sierra 118, 39140 Somo
**t.** 9 42 510 292
**w.** laposadadesomo.com

**Ahau Surf House (15)** is located at the beach of El Sardinero, one of the nicest areas of Santander. Whether you're travelling solo, as a couple, a family or with a whole bunch, the house with garden can accommodate up to 7 people. •€• •€€•

**a.** Duque Santo Mauro 7, 39005 Santander
**t.** 6 33 785 109
**w.** ahausurfschool.com

Being passionate campervan travellers themselves, the initiators of **Surf Cars (16)** rent out VW vans to travel the coast of northern Spain. Nothing too fancy and businesslike, more the idea of 'friends borrowing from friends', but provided with everything a travelling surfer needs. Pick-up and return available from Santander airport (which has direct shuttle link with Bilbao airport).

**t.** 6 93 911 293
**e.** info@surf-cars.com
**w.** surf-cars.com

Hotel and restaurant **Hosteria de Arnuero (17)** was once an estate, built in the architectural style known as 'casa de indiano' – houses built by Latin-American colonists who returned to Spain. Their 12 rooms are decorated in such a way that their style stays true to the original construction and rural setting, but with an original twist. Very child friendly, pets welcome. Open all year. •€€•

**a.** Barrio Palacio 17, 39195 Arnuero
**t.** 9 42 677 121
**e.** info@hosteriadearnuero.es
**w.** hosteriadearnuero.es

# IN AND AROUND LIENCRES

The town of Liencres is actually just a few streets and a few blocks of houses; what really matters here is the surroundings, the natural park, the many surf opportunities and all the other small settlements along the coast.

## TO DO

Walk, bike, hike, surf, get lost, spot migrating birds and try not to step on plant species that have adapted to living in the sandy environment of **Dunas de Liencres Natural Park (18)**. With its 256 hectares of dunes, forest, beaches and cliffs it's one big delicious outdoor heaven. (At night it's outdoor heaven for a whole other sort of species, but let all species live happily ever after.)

**Los Locos Surf Shop (19)** organises SUP tours and lessons on the Cantabrian lakes, rivers and ocean.

**a.** Calle José Felipe Quijano 1, 39300 Torrelavega
**t.** 9 42 808 314
**w.** loslocossurfshop.com

## EAT/DRINK/HANGOUT

Bar and restaurant **La Viga (20)** offers home-made food, coffee, lunch and dinner (also take-away), sit either inside or outside on their covered terrace. Really nice place, originally decorated, friendly staff and regular live music events.

**a.** Carretera de la Arnia 1, 39110 Soto De La Marina
**t.** 9 42 579 809

**Pura Vida Crepes-Burger (21)** is exactly what it says: crêpes and burgers. But not just any; very tasty, fresh, burgers and crêpes, and big as you can dream them, with everything on top. Oh, and they serve mojitos to go with that. Nice little hangout, and you can take your burgers to-go as well. Open in the morning for breakfast and coffee. •€•

**a.** Avenida Marques de Valdecilla 56, 39110 Soto de la Marina
**t.** 9 42 079 729

**Desafinado (22)** is a lively restaurant, wine and jazz bar, serving Cuban food, live Cuban and jazz music, Cuban beer and mojitos. The place is Cuban owned, did you guess? •€€•

**a.** Las Mazas 15, 39120 Liencres
**t.** 9 42 574 326

**Suka Suances (23)** suits vegetarians and non-vegetarians alike. It's one of the few places that has a good choice of meat and fish free dishes on the menu, so vegetarians (and vegans), dig in! Fusion cuisine, sushi and salads. Open from 12:00 hrs. •€• •€€•

**a.** Calle Torrelavega 7, 39340 Suances
**t.** 9 42 810 528

**Rancho Chico (24)** is an easy-going eatery and hangout, serving perfect after-surf food like pizzas and wraps. •€•

**a.** Calle el Muelle 23, 39340 Suances
**t.** 9 42 844 315

## SHOP

◆

**Los Locos Surf Shop (25)** sells surf, skate, and street wear, from known brands and also their own brand. You'll find your surf and SUP essentials, and boards. They have knowledgeable and friendly staff and also organise SUP tours and lessons (they were one of the first in Spain riding the SUP-wave, so to speak).

**a.** Calle José Felipe Quijano 1,
39300 Torrelavega
**t.** 9 42 808 314
**w.** loslocossurfshop.com

Carlos Clavero and Rubén Fuente from **CeCe Longboards (26)** do, as they say themselves, their shaping in the ocean, so don't expect them to be in the shop at all hours. The shop serves actually as their showroom and if you want to speak to them, choose a board or have a look around, they're very accommodating, just make an appointment, that's all. It's very likely you'll meet them in the water at their favourite breaks around San Vicente de la Barquera. It does pay to check their boards out, either in the water, the showroom or on their site; being both classic and stylish sliders themselves, they know exactly what a longboarder's looking for.

**a.** Calle Felix Apellaniz 2,
39300 Torrelavega
**t.** 6 45 960 448
**w.** cecesurf.com

## SLEEP

◆

A cool place to stay overnight with your campervan, is **Parking Lago del Acebo (27)**. Situated in a natural park, near a lake and next to a safari park, so you can watch elephants, giraffes and other animals on the roam. Free facilities, open all year.

**a.** Between Torrelavega and Solares (A8),
Lago del Acebo, 39693 Cabarceno

**Bio Surf Camp (28)** follow the idea that for surfing, there's no need to make any changes to beaches, you 'take advantage of the natural energy of the waves to ride freely'. This is what they strive for with their camp as well; bond with the environment and blend in with nature. They have an organic vegetable garden, bio construction units to sleep in, make use of renewable energy and organise workshops to learn how it all works. You can also join their tours to learn more about sealife and the ocean, or a workshop on ocean movement and surf forecasting. They welcome solo travellers, families, friends and couples, and have accommodation to suit the needs of all. •€• •€€•

**a.** Calle Serapio Beade, s/n,
39340 Suances (Los Locos)
**t.** 6 80 206 552
**e.** info@biosurfcamp.com
**w.** biosurfcamp.com

# IN AND AROUND SAN VICENTE DE LA BARQUERA

The small seaport is getting more popular every summer - mostly by word of mouth within the surf community - because of its many surf spots, view from the water of the mountains - Los Picos de Europa, good food and chilled vibe. Even if we did try to keep it to ourselves, you'd probably hear of it sooner or later. It's not a hip town, doesn't have any bearded hipster joints, healthy juice bars or exceptional pointbreaks and reefs. It's quite traditional, even sleepy off season. The town, built on a flooded river valley, has the essentials; a market with quality local products, tapas bars, and breakfasts with chocolate to dip your churros in. History from as far back as the early Middle Ages still intertwines with day-to-day life, like the 32-arch stone Maza bridge you'll constantly cross to get from town to beach and back, or the towering Castillo del Rey. But it's the constant embrace of nature that, in the end, does the trick of making you fall in love with this place.

## TO DO

The villa **El Capricho (29)**, designed by Antonio Gaudí in the 19th century, is a typical Gaudí work: fairytale like, with cylindrical walls and a tower, dotted with funny little details like animals playing musical instruments and ceramic sunflowers. Open all year, every day.

**a.** Parque de Sobrellano, s/n, 39520 Comillas
**t.** 9 42 720 365
**w.** elcaprichodegaudi.com

**Festival La Folia (30)**, held every year on the first weekend after Easter, in San Vicente de la Barquera. A noisy one, and best you join in. A torch-lit procession takes place, with the statue of Virgin Mary being carried through town, alongside a lot of music, singing, drinking and fireworks.

What a treat: just the sound of hooves and the ocean. **Equus Boria (31)** organises horse trail rides in the National Park of Oyambre. You'll be led by experienced guides, riding a calm-as-calm-can-be horse, and if an inexperienced rider, you'll learn the basics before you set off. A tour takes 1 to 2 hours, during which time you'll certainly be awed by the views of the surroundings and the sea.

**a.** Carretera Boria, s/n, 39582 Santillan
**t.** 6 26 283 570
**w.** equusboria.com

Team rider for CeCe boards, Nienke Duinmeijer, hosts annual **Single Fin Surf Travel (32)** weeks (usually in May) on the beaches of San Vicente. The perfect opportunity to learn or work on your longboard skills, and with the help of video-analysis and special workshops from pro longboarders, Rubén Fuente and Carlos Clavero from CeCe, you'll progress in leaps and bounds (or cross steps and toes on the noses). Nienke shares her love for this area by also offering a selection of optional activities for you to try. We say try them, feel the love.

**w.** singlefinsurftravel.nl

Being so close to the Picos de Europa you can almost touch them, you should really go on an adventure, explore them up close and personal. **K2Aventura** (**33**) takes you on a trail, via Ferrata del Caliz, with horizontal and vertical routes. With the use of cables, zip lines, ropes, railings and hanging bridges (and a safety harness to secure you from any falls) you'll reach areas that you'd probably never get to otherwise. The instructor can pick you up from your place in San Vicente.

**t.** 6 15 497 665
**e.** info@k2aventura.es
**w.** k2aventura.es

**SUP dreamers'** (**34**) base is in the Nansa Valley, west of San Vicente, with direct access to the beach of Sable and the estuary of the river Nansa. You can enjoy paddleboarding in all its forms: head to the beach and get into the waves or do some relaxing SUP yoga & pilates on calm water amidst nature. You can also try out SUP equipment from their specialist shop.

**a.** The pink building on the CA-181, 39548 Pesues (Val de San Vicente)
**t.** 6 76 562 286
**w.** sup-dreamers.com

## EAT/DRINK/HANGOUT

◆

Get your bread and sweet treats at **La Gallofa** (**35**), it's a 'panaderias especializadas', so that's what you get.

**a.** Plaza Jose Antonio 6, 39540 San Vicente de Barquera

Bar restaurant **La Folía** (**36**) serves tapas, pulpo, and lots more seafood in a cosy interior in the centre of town.

**a.** Avenida Los Soportales 7, 39540 San Vicente de la Barquera
**t.** 9 42 711 034

The terrace of beach bar **Dias de Surf** (**37**) is a great place for drinks and snacks after a hard day's surfing, located right behind Camping El Rosal, with a view over the inner bay.

**a.** Avenida Francisco Giner de los Ríos 12, Barrio de la Playa, 39540 San Vicente de la Barquera
**t.** 6 09 282 963 / 6 18 964 263

## SLEEP

◆

18+ Surf **Hostel Llambres H2O** (**38**) is located in the green hills overlooking the Oyambre National Park, in a farmhouse with a big garden. Closed in January and February. •€• •€€•

**a.** La Revilla 11, Carreteira CA-131, 39540 San Vicente de la Barquera
**t.** 6 25 611 449
**e.** escuelasurfh2o@hotmail.com
**w.** escuelasurfh2o.com

**Hospedaje Los Llaos (39)** is perfectly situated in the bay of San Vicente, with standard rural rooms and a shared kitchen. Views of the beach or the mountains, and within walking distance from the beach. •€• •€€•

**a.** Calle Los Llaos 6,
39540 San Vicente de la Barquera
**t.** 9 42 710 758 / 6 76 656 895
**w.** hospedajelosllaos.com

Next door neighbour is **Hospedaje Granada (40)**, at the same perfect location, 10 rooms available, shared lounge, a big garden with BBQ and outside oven. It's like sleeping over at your warm, welcoming Spanish grandma's place (if your grandma was Spanish). •€• •€€•

**a.** Calle Los Llaos 5,
39540 San Vicente de la Barquera
**t.** 9 42 712 113
**w.** hospedajegranada.com

**Surf House Sanvi (41)** is an Italian-owned surf house in the green hills to the west of San Vicente, with views over the ocean, the lagoon, Oyambre Natural Park and the mountains of Picos de Europa. They have 4 shared rooms with either single or bunk beds. Open from April till October. •€• •€€•

**a.** Barrio Boria 13,
39540 San Vicente de la Barquera
**t.** 6 97 522 808
**e.** info@surfhousesanvi.com
**w.** surfhousesanvi.com

**Camping El Rosal (42)** is a very popular campsite, especially during holidays, due to its location right next to the beach, in front of the surf breaks, with the calm water of the inner bay at the back. Pitches are shaded by centenary pines and they also have wooden tent bungalows for rent, each with their own little terrace. •€• •€€•

**a.** Carretera de la Playa, s/n,
39540 San Vicente de la Barquera
**t.** 9 42 710 165 / 9 42 710 011
**e.** info@campingelrosal.com
**w.** campingelrosal.com

**La Peña Casares (43)** sits between the 2 beaches of San Vicente, a bit inland, with a great view and has - and we mean this in a good way - an old-fashioned Spanish interior. A rural and traditional accommodation for sure, at one of the most beautiful spots in the area, in the heart of the Oyambre Natural Park. Friendly reception and service. Open all year. •€•

**a.** Barrio Valles, s/n, 39547 La Revilla
**e.** info@posadacasares.com
**t.** 9 42 712 661 / 6 64 348 399
**w.** posadacasares.com

Photo: Melchior van Nigtevecht

Photo: Alexandra Gossin

# SURF

The coastline east of Santander is afforded some protection from the stormy swells because of its northeast facing position, but not too reliably. And it definitely pays to explore if you want to find quiet, uncrowded beaches. Check beachbreak **Brazomar** (**I**) at Castro Urdiales if it's too big elsewhere.

The best option, however, to hide from strong w and nw wind accompanied by a big swell is **Laredo** (**II**). A 5 km crescent-shaped beach that offers several peaks, with powerful, fast breaking waves that call for acceleration skills. Works on medium to big w-nw-n swell, all tides. All levels. Easy parking in winter, difficult in summer/shower/restaurant/surf school/surf shop.

While many prefer the A-frame peaks at **El Brusco** (**IV**) to the west, the quieter beachbreak at **Berria** (**III**) can also handle a bit of size. It's a rather nice stretch of beach north of Santona, one of the oldest fishing towns of Cantabria. Can feel a bit surreal with the large penitentiary at the east side of the beach, and the fenced campsite facing the ocean, but it's consistent, with several peaks depending on sandbanks. Works with medium nw swell at all tides. All levels. Easy parking/campsite/surf school.

**Langre** (**V**) is an idyllic bay, sheltered by high cliffs from sw winds, works best with medium swell at low to mid tide. **Somo** (**VI**) is a long stretch of sand with room to roam, even on busy days, and many peaks to choose from. Some peaks are excellent for beginners, hence the many surf schools. Good vibe generally. Works best with a small to medium nw swell, at all tides (depending on sandbanks). All levels. Easy parking/shower/toilet/restaurant/campsite/surf school/surf shop.

**Liencres** (**VII**), in the middle of a protected natural park, offers several peaks. Locals from Santander prefer this spot when it's working, and that's quite often. But usually there are plenty of peaks to choose from, just watch out for current and some rocks in the water. Works on small to medium w-nw-n swell, mid to high tide. Easy parking/ toilet/restaurant/surf school.

**Los Locos** (**VIII**), at the village of Suances, is a popular (read consistent) beachbreak, so expect it to be crowded. Its position works like a wave magnet to swell from the nw, and it's protected from ne wind. Works best with small to medium swells, at all tides. All levels, but you need to be able to handle a crowded break. Easy parking/ restaurant/surf school/surf shop.

The beaches at San Vicente de la Barquera, **Meron, Gerra and Oyambre** (**IX**), need a bit of swell. If it's too big, try Oyambre, which is slightly more sheltered. The breaks work best with medium w-nw-n swell, at all tides, but usually better soon before or after high tide. Easy parking/toilet in summer/ shower/restaurant/campsite/ surf school.

# SCHOOL RENTAL REPAIR

◆

**Atlantic Surf Shop and School (44)** offers SUP and surf lessons, and rental of boards, and the shop provides all your surf essentials. They also organise SUP and surf camps in summer, making use of the Camping Playa Regatón. Open all year.

**a.** Calle Marqués de Comillas 2, 39770 Laredo (shop)
**a.** Avenida Enrique Mowinkel, 39770 Laredo (school)
**t.** 9 42 612 213
**w.** atlanticsurfshop.es

**Loredo Surf School (45)** is run by the sons and daughters of the pioneers of Spanish surfing. The team of second-generation surfers are certified and have extensive experience in teaching, and knowledge of the beaches in the area.

**a.** Calle Juncal 6, 39160 Loredo
**t.** 6 36 375 263
**w.** loredosurfhouse.com

**Kun_tiqi (46)** offers high quality and fair priced surfboard repairs. There's nothing they can't fix.

**a.** Barrio la Cardosa 11, 39160 Loredo, Playa De Somo
**t.** 6 22 420 641 (Stefan)
**w.** kuntiqi.com

**Ahau Surf School (47)** teaches all levels of SUP and surfing, in small groups and with personal attention. Experienced and qualified staff. Ahau have their own board brand and shaper, they organise camps and have shaping workshops on offer.

**a.** Duque Santo Mauro 7, 1-A, 39005 Santander
**t.** 6 33 785 109
**w.** ahausurfschool.com

**GO Surfing Shop (48)** is situated in the Zoco Gran Santander shopping mall, close to the A-67. They provide for all your surf essentials.

**a.** Local 222, 3 Avenida Primero de Mayo 64, 39011 Santander
**t.** 9 42 322 525
**w.** gosurfingshop.com

**Buena Onda (49)** is a surf school and shop that's been around since 1990, find them just behind camping El Rosal. Friendly, qualified and knowledgeable staff. Surf, SUP and bodyboard, lessons, rental and surf camps on offer. Open in season.

**a.** Avenida Francisco Giner de Los Ríos 48, 39540 San Vicente de la Barquera
**t.** 6 35 725 832/ 6 46 554 053
**w.** escueladesurfbuenaonda.com

**Costa Norte (50)** surf school, in the same street, offer SUP and surf classes, rental and surf camps. In their shop, alongside the essentials, they've created a little hangout as well.

**a.** Avenida Francisco Giner de Los Ríos 20, 39540 San Vicente de la Barquera
**t.** 6 09 282 963 / 6 18 964 263
**w.** escueladesurfcostanorte.com

Photo: Melchior van Nigtevecht

# 4. ON THE BOARD: PARVATASANA

*Upward Bound Fingers Pose*

***This pose is a very simple and effective pose to do on your board in between sets.***

*It tones the knuckles, palms, wrists and forearms. It also helps open the chest and loosens tightness in the shoulders, so that there will be no restrictions in these areas while paddling for your next wave!*

***Benefits:***

*Stretches and opens chest and shoulders.*

***How:***

*Sit comfortably on your board, inhale, take the arms up at shoulder height and interlock the fingers, slide the hands together right up to the webbing between the fingers. Bring the tips of thumbs together. Exhale and roll the palms out, keeping the tips of the thumbs touching and the fingers well interlocked. Inhale and take the arms up alongside the ears. Hold the position for several breaths. Exhale, bring the arms forward and down. Repeat, changing the interlock of the fingers so that the other index finger is on top.*

***Note:***

*It is important to do both sides to balance out the nervous system.*

PLAYA DE SAN LORENZO (VI)
TAPIA DE CASARIEGO (IX)
XAGO (VII)
SALINAS (VIII)
PLAYA ESPAÑA (V)
RODILES (IV)
RIBADESELLA (II)
PLAYA DE VEGA (III)
SAN ANTOLIN (I)
32,39, 41-46, 56,57
GIJÓN
49,50,58,59
47,48
40
SALINAS
TAPIA
NAVIA
CUDILLERO
AVILÉS
22,38
18,23-31,33
17,35-37,54,55
6,15,16,53
2,3,51
A-8
N-634
19
VILLAVICIOSA
RIBADESELLA
4,5,7-14,52
20
OVIEDO
34
Asturias
N-625
1
21
AP-66

# ASTURIAS

Nowhere else in Northern Spain does the E70/A8 - your highway to swell - run so close and parallel to the coast as in Asturias. Nearly half of the Asturian territory is declared National Reserve, and in addition to all the outdoor fun this obviously brings, Asturias has a cultural heritage that reflects their rich history. It shows its inheritance in ancient Roman routes, Palaeolithic cave paintings, and architecture; like the many 'Indiano' houses and estates that were built by wealthy Asturians who once emigrated to America then returned to their homeland.

So, while enjoying the great outdoors, down a little culture in the same swig. Walk with the pilgrims on their way to Santiago – or offer them a coffee and a chat. Dip your toes in the Cantabrian Sea and reach for the snowy mountaintops of the Picos de Europa, all in one day. And, of course, explore as many of the blue flag beaches as you can along the Costa Verde – the green coast. There are many, and we trust you leave nothing but your footprints.

# TRAVEL INFO

The network of roads in Asturias to get you to even the smallest of towns is perfectly laid out. As a swell hunter, the one you'll be on and off is the E70/A8, running along the coast.

### BY AIR

**Aeropuerto de Asturias**, is situated in Castrillón, near Avilés, and within an hour's drive of the bigger cities Oviedo, Gijón, and the surf beach of Salinas. It serves connections to several European cities. The company Alsa (alsa.es) runs buses between the airport and the cities of Avilés, Gijón and Oviedo. Services to Avilés and Gijón also stop in Piedras Blancas and Salinas.

**a.** 33459 Santiago del Monte, Castrillón
**w.** aena.es

### BY TRAIN

Daily services run between Asturias main cities like Gijón and Oviedo, provided by the national train company RENFE (who also operate the FEVE trains, a narrow-gauge rail line that crosses the coast of Northern Spain).

**w.** renfe.es

# SURFER-TRAVELLER TYPE ASTURIAS

*You adore drinking cider with some rich cheese, and having it poured into your glass from a great height, you agree with taking a pilgrimage once in your life - or fantasise about it; you can distinguish between at least 50 shades of green, and don't mind driving down steep lanes to get to the surf.*

# IN AND AROUND RIBADESELLA

Previously a small fishing village with a busy fishing port, Ribadesella's now an Asturian summer tourist hotspot. And there's some fun surf to be had, with a backdrop of villas in Indiana architectural style. If there's no surf at La Playa de Santa Marina, don't leave town immediately. Take a stroll around the old quarter - cross the Puente del Río Sella bridge to the east of town. Make sure to stock up on chocolate, somewhat a local speciality. Then maybe check out the prehistoric graffiti of Asturia's ancestors at the Tito Bustillo site; there are cave paintings of deer, horses and women, whatever the preference was at the time of painting (between twenty-two thousand and ten thousand years BC). And from Ribadesella you're so close to the mountain range of the Picos de Europa, it would be a shame not to go and see them up close. To the west of town, some fine beaches, like Playa de Vega, lay waiting for you.

**Tourist office** at Paseo Princesa Letizia.

## TO DO

◆

**Picos de Europa National Park (1)**: If you're the type of traveller that prefers 'done that' to 'seen this' but still wants to take the picture, we recommend you walk The Cares Route: a hiking trail through the Picos that follows the gorge carved out by the river Cares, also known as 'the Divine Gorge' for its stunning beauty, hence the need for a camera. The route is 12 km - or 24 if you walk the same route back - and suitable for almost everyone (kids from 6 years on). Don't let the first two rather steep kms up discourage you. Wear boots that can handle a few loose rocks, and don't forget to take enough water, food and sun protection. You can also take your dog, as long as he's on a leash.

**To get there:** follow the AS-114 towards Cantabria, in Arenas de Cabrales take the AS-264 south for 5 kms, to Poncebos. You can park your car at the cable car parking. For a fee you can take a transfer back from Caín to Poncebos.

Driving from Cantabria via the coastal road to the beaches of **Llanes (2)** towards the west, you'll pass the small settlement **Cué (2)** on the outskirts of Llanes. Cute as cute can be. (And it's got an eco store if you want to stock up on health food you won't find in supermarkets.) Driving further, you can check the **viewpoint Boriza (2)**, at the Punta el Pandón, the headland that looks out on **Castro Ballota** (the small island in the middle of the bay), and the whole coast from east to west.

If there's no reason to make the descent down to the beach, park your ride near **Playa de Andrín (2)**. The hinterland is a very peaceful area with lots of rural hostels if you want to spend the night, great views and hiking and biking trails – the E9 coastal trail links all the beaches in the area. There are bars at both beaches.

Explore the caves, cliffs and cenotes of the Asturian east coast with **Escuela Asturiana de Surf (3)** on their guided Espeleo Paddle tours. They'll take you along the coast, predominantly limestone, a continuation of the Picos de Europa. The years of erosion from water, waves, wind and stones have created a landscape of sinkholes, rock arches, and gorges. And there's no better way to reach and discover nature's work than paddling through on a SUP. In the coldest months the school takes tours on the calmer waters of the estuaries, lakes and reservoirs. Or – and this is really something else – paddle through an alpine landscape in the mountain lakes, surrounded by ice on a snow paddle tour.

**a.** Playa de San Antolín, s/n, 33500 Llanes
**t.** 6 70 686 801
**w.** escuelaasturianadesurf.com

The river Sella is one of the major rivers in Spain. The **Descent of the River Sella (4)**, held every year around the first weekend of August, is one of the world's largest canoeing events with over 1000 participants from all over the world. The race starts in Arriondas, at the foot of the Picos mountains, and ends 20 km downstream in Ribadesella, where river meets ocean. But, of course, the Asturians make a party of it, spreading the event over 4 days, with music and family-friendly activities. You don't have to be a pro to participate, but if you want to paddle the Sella on a less crowded and crazy day, there are many companies along the river that rent out gear.

Walking the **Santiago route (5)**, or a part of it, is considered either a religious or spiritual act. You don't have to be religious to feel the need to take the pilgrimage. Walk along with the pilgrims from Playa de Vega, or any point really. You'll find the Camino, and its wanderers, popping up and disappearing from the most unexpected corners and angles and spots.

There are 2 routes passing through Asturias: the original El Camino Primitivo, and the Camino del Norte, the coastal route. You'll know you're on a Camino trail when you see the symbol of the Santiago pilgrimage, a scallop shell, on posts and signs to guide the pilgrims along the way. What really gives it away though, are the lonesome, hunchbacked, and slightly forward stooping figures walking with sticks, their faces lost in thought.

**Motor Beach Festival (6)** is a 4-day long festival, usually in the third week of July. Expect pure Rock 'n' Roll with lots of classic bikes and cars, music, food, surf, and fiesta vibes. Local and national shapers present their single fins and longboards. One of the highlights of the festival is the Single Fin & Logger contest, where the best surfers and craftsmen (m/f) surf, exclusively, on single fin polyester or wooden longboards which weigh at least 7 kilograms. Without a leash. Naturalmente.

**a.** Playa de la Espasa, 33344 Caravia
**w.** motorbeach.com

## EAT/DRINK/HANGOUT

◆

**Ribadesella (7)** has some fine eateries, sidrerías, terraces and some tapas bars. Most of the ones we recommend are in the old quarter, around Plaza Reina Maria Cristina.

For some good quality seafood try **Restaurante Güeyu Mar (8)**, right by the beach. Certainly not cheap, but grand choice of (seasonal) crab, squid, calamares, salmon and much more.

•€€• •€€€•

**a.** Playa de Vega 84, 33560 Ribadesella
**t.** 9 85 860 863
**w.** gueyumar.es

## SHOP

◆

**The weekly market (9)** in Ribadesella is an introduction to the region's finest: from artisanal cheese, wild boar sausage, and home-made fish empanadas, to organic and wild herbs from the mountains. Every Wednesday morning at Plaza de Mercado in the old town.

## SLEEP

◆

Youth Hostel Ribadesella, **Roberto Frassinelli (10)**, is located on the promenade of Ribadesella's beachfront in a refurbished aristocratic Casa de Indianos. They also offer surf lessons and other outdoor activities. Rooms sleep 4 to 6 people. Open all year. •€•

**a.** Ricardo Canga, s/n, 33560 Ribadesella
**t.** 9 85 860 421 / 6 08 025 658
**w.** albergue-ribadesella.es

**Casa Rural Bajo los Tilos (11)** - under the linden trees - is a welcoming rural tourism hotel in the small village Santianes del Agua, just 5 minutes from Ribadesella. It's set in the green valley of the river Sella, in a restored old farmhouse, which retains the original features. The hotel has 6 spacious bedrooms with wooden floors and a great view of the surroundings, lounge with fireplace, small bar, and dining room, where home-made meals and their own ecological cider are served on request. Pets allowed. •€€•

**a.** Santianes del Agua, 33569 Ribadesella
**t.** 9 85 857 527 / 6 69 460 544
**w.** bajolostilos.com

**Camping Playa Sauces (12)** is a family-friendly campsite, with lots of open space and tidy bungalows to rent, 600 m from Playa Santa Marina. Open all year. •€•

**a.** Carretera de San Pedro, La Playa, s/n, 33560 Ribadesella
**t.** 9 85 861 312
**w.** campingplayasauces.es

Close to Ribadesella, at the mouth of the river Sella, you'll find **Los Silos de El Correntíu (13)**. A traditional Asturian farmhouse (sleeps 4 persons) and 2 silos, refurbished to sleep 2 persons each, set on a large plot of land with ancient oaks and fruit trees. The small stream running by, escorrentía, gives the place its name. Available all year. •€€•

**a.** Carretera La Piconera 42, 33560 Ribadesella
**t.** 6 51 582 440 / 9 85 861 436
**e.** aldea@elcorrentiu.es
**w.** elcorrentiu.es

**Camping Playa de Vega (14)** is ideally situated near the 2 km long beach and surf spot Vega. From this beach you'll regularly see pilgrims on their way to Santiago de Compostela, as the coastal route passes the beach. The campsite is surrounded by green, every pitch is hedged so you'll have your privacy, and there are chalets for rent. Open from June to September. •€•

**a.** Playa de Vega, 33345 Ribadesella
**t.** 9 85 860 406
**e.** info@campingplayadevega.com
**w.** campingplayadevega.com

**Camping Arenal de Morís (15)**, is situated 200 m from the beach Arenal de Morís, backed by green hills and mountains. They have open pitches on the grass, fully equipped tents and wooden cabanas for rent that sleep up to 5 persons. Quiet family-friendly campsite with swimming pool. Open from Easter to September. •€• •€€•

**a.** N-632, Viaducto Caravia, s/n, 33346 Caravia (take the turn off in Caravia Alta)
**t.** 9 85 853 097
**w.** arenaldemoris.com

**El Babu (16)** is a small rural boutique hotel, set in a typical 18th century Asturian house, at the foot of the Sueve mountain range. Perfectly nestled between ocean and mountains, it offers views of the countryside and sea. Despite being an ancient building, it's light and spacious because of the huge windows. The owners built (and do their utmost to run) the place with respect to the environment. Open all year. •€€• •€€€•

**a.** Carrales, 33343 Caravia
**t.** 9 85 853 272 / 6 28 402 771
**e.** reservas@elbabu.com
**w.** elbabu.com

# IN AND AROUND GIJÓN

◆

Often called a rough-and-tumble harbour town, that doesn't exactly describe the Gijón city centre. It has an honest and straightforward vibe, and in the streets just behind the boulevard, surrounding San Lorenzo bay, is a little treasure pond of fine shops, original eateries and laid-back cafés. If you look from above, you see that Gijón is just a tiny grey spot in a huge carpet of green. Enjoy the magic ride of rivers, hills, cliffs, beaches and bays, only interrupted by an adorable fishing settlement.

**Tourist information point** at Escalera 4, Playa de San Lorenzo.

## TO DO

◆

**RodiRide Surfboards (17)** offer SUP yoga, SUP tours on the Ria de Villaviciosa, SUP races and learning to surf waves on a SUP. Or you can just rent the equipment, if you prefer.

**a.** Calle Carda 4, 33300 Rodiles / Villaviciosa
**t.** 6 09 890 134
**w.** rodilesup.com

Get your sore muscles treated at **Terma Spa (18)**. They offer sports, hot stone and therapeutical massages. Or take a soak in a roman or algae bath. Open all year.

**a.** Calle Muralla 13, 33202 Gijón
**t.** 9 85 359 448 / 9 85 344 435
**w.** termaspa.es

For some reason the folks of Gijón are really into **yoga (18)**; there's a studio at every other corner. Here are just a couple of suggestions:

**Yoga y Salud (18)** offer restorative yoga and meditation classes (in Spanish).

**a.** Calle Menéndez Valdés 16 (First Floor), 33202 Gijón
**t.** 9 84 032 926
**w.** vitriolyogaysalud.com

Yogi Veronica Trabanco, from **Astur Yoga (18)**, offers vinyasa and ashtanga classes, 4 days a week.

**a.** Travesía del Convento 9 (First Floor), 33202 Gijón
**t.** 6 25 061 228
**w.** asturyoga.com

**Kaos Temple (19)**, originally an ancient temple, is located in Llanera. Today it's an indoor skatepark, and hosts art and cultural exhibitions. Artist Okuda San Miguel painted the walls, domed ceilings and vaults with vibrant murals, 'as it's always been done in churches'. A recurring feature in the paintings, the Kaos Star, is a symbol for Kaos Temple: "No matter what you do, where you come from, have your own reference to achieve your goals". The church is open, not only to skate in a unique setting, but also for contemporary art enthusiasts.

**a.** Polígono de Asipo, Coruño, 33428 Llanera (between Gijón and Oviedo)
**w.** laiglesiaskate.com

Free drinks, on the house, at the **Natural Cider Festival** (**20**). The yearly festival in Nava, dedicated to the drink that's deeply rooted in this region, is held during the second weekend of July, and the week running up to it. There are all kinds of activities, exhibitions, concerts and theatre, leading up to the Saturday, when the sound of firecrackers signals the start of a free tasting session. But, in order to get a drink for free, you'll have to wear a green handkerchief around your neck! Don't miss the pouring competition on Sunday – pouring cider into a glass the proper way, without spilling, is an art form in itself.

**a.** 33520 Nava

With **3 ski resorts** (**21**) (Pajares and Fuentes de Invierno in Asturias, and San Isidro in Leon) within an hour from the coast, you can surf and ski or snowboard in the same day.

Pajares ski resort (80 kms from Gijón) is the highest, situated some 2000 m above sea level. It's the ski resort closest to the ocean in Spain, and probably in Europe. The best time is between November and April.

**w.** valgrande-pajares.com

## EAT/DRINK/HANGOUT

◆

You can tell it's a good day when **Terrazas Ipanema** (**22**) on Playa España is open. The beach bar opens 'solo con sol', only on sunny days, you see. Why else would you bother! Open from April to October (well, when the sun's out).

**a.** Playa España, 33314 Villaviciosa (just east of Gijón, along the VV-3)
**t.** 9 85 894 898

There are many, many, many y mucho fine eateries and tapas bars to find in **Gijón**, here's just a small selection:

Make yourself at home in restaurant and bar **El Siete** (**23**), their interior invites you to. Good food, good service and some fine cocktails to drink to that.
•€• •€€•

**a.** Calle Recoletas 7, 33201 Gijón
**t.** 9 85 341 368
**w.** elsietegijon.com

**El Bello Verano (24)** is a cool little hangout for a beer, fresh juice or home-made food, served in a surfy décor next to the seaside. •€•

**a.** Calle del Doctor Aquilino Hurlé 40, 33203 Gijón
**t.** 9 84 704 818

**Rawcoco Green Bar (25)** serves just about anything healthy, fresh and delicious; juices, shakes, salads, wraps, energy shots, detox lemonades, all made with fresh and organic ingredients and a lot of love and care for your well-being. Highly recommended. Open every day. •€•

**a.** Calle San Bernardo 36, Bajo, 33201 Gijón
**t.** 6 20 963 877

**Blu Café (26)** serves breakfast, a fine selection of coffee and tea, home-made sweets and artisanal chocolate. Very nice vibe and friendly staff. And your pet is welcome too. •€•

**a.** Calle Pedro Duro 9, 33206 Gijón
**t.** 9 84 199 046

Vermutería and tapería, **Cactus (27)**, has burgers, tapas, sushi, vermouths, vodkas and gins on the menu. And by the way they're served, you can tell they love their products. Original and stylish interior, laid-back atmosphere, check out their live music events. •€€•

**a.** Instituto 1, 33201 Gijón
**t.** 9 84 290 541

## SHOP

◆

**Trashville (28)** is an original and funky tattoo shop and gallery, with some real friendly staff, right at the boulevard of San Lorenzo bay. Even if you don't plan on getting a new tattoo, you can check out some nice books, customised skate and surfboards from local shapers, or learn about the local art-scène.

**a.** Calle Carlos Marx 1, 33207 Gijón
**t.** 9 84 289 096

**Tablas Surf Shop (29)** is a long-established surf shop (since 1979) and if there's anything you should or want to know about surfing in Asturias, owner Jaime and his son Jaime are the guys to talk to. The shop has a large assortment of Californian logs, single fins, shortboards, boards from their own brand, TBLS, and from Portuguese shaper Nico of Waveglider. And all your surf, SUP and skate necessities. They also organise surf trips and camps. Closed on Sunday.

**a.** Paseo Muro de San Lorenzo 4, 33202 Gijón
**t.** 9 84 394 144 / 9 85 354 700
**w.** tablassurfshop.com

Get your good and honest food at the alimentación ecológica **Huerta La Vega (30)**. They sell directly from the producer, have a preference for Asturian and organic products, and care about sustaining the biodiversity of the environment. All in all, a healthy choice of fruits, veggies, wine, rice, beans and more. Closed on Sunday.

**a.** On the corner of Calle Ezcurdia 72, and La Calle Premio Real, 33203 Gijón
**t.** 9 85 134 078
**w.** huertalavega.com

**Grandppa (31)** surfboards, relatively new in the shaping guild (since 2012) produce custom resin-tint surfboards; from longboards, alternative shapes, fish to shortboards. Grandppa boards are, as the shapers state 'made out of love for surfing', but are beauties to look at as well, with symmetrical designs and an original choice of colours.

**t.** 6 96 403 188 / 6 99 604 375
**w.** grandppa.com

**Punto Retro (32)** sell objects with a retro touch, almost all pieces you find in their shop are unique. Not very likely that you'll take your old furniture with you, but if you do, Ana and Amelia, the owners, can spice it up for you, sin problema.

**a.** Camino del Curullu 896, Nave 4, 33394 Gijón
**t.** 9 85 338 443 / 6 59 402 824
**w.** puntoretro.com

## SLEEP

◆

**Campervans** can park at the parking **Avenida Eduardo Castro (33)**, close to the harbour and next to Playa Del Arbeyal. Can be a bit noisy at night, but a good place to park and explore the city. Take buses 1, 4 and 6 to get to the centre (2,5 km).

**a.** Avenida Eduardo Castro s/n, 33212 Gijón

**Atlantic Surf Route (34)** rents out campervans, from VW classic T2 and modern T5 pop-top, Nissan to a larger Weinsberg CaraBus 601, providing the opportunity for travellers to take a longer journey along the seaside. They pick you up at either Oviedo or Santander airport, you can return the van in Cádiz or Sevilla in Andalusia (or vice versa), so can literally take the Atlantic surf route.

**e.** info@atlanticsurfroute.com
**w.** atlanticsurfroute.com

Hosts David and Susana love to share every piece of paradise in Asturia. They welcome individuals, families and groups of friends to their friendly rural house, **El Perro Verde (35)** – the green dog. It's the place where they've made their dreams come true, creating a home for everybody to enjoy at an affordable price, and sharing all the activities you can do in the area. They have rooms with bunk beds, family and double rooms. And, your dog can stay for free. Open all year. •€•

**a.** Barrio Santiago, 46, 33314 San Justo, Villaviciosa (close to Rodiles)
**t.** 9 85 990 078
**w.** albergueelperroverde.com

**Camping La Ensenada (36)** is a modest campsite, nicely positioned just behind the beach of Rodiles, opposite the river Villaviciosa. Open from April to September. •€•

**a.** Caraterra N-632, Playa de Rodiles, 33300 Villaviciosa
**t.** 9 85 890 157

**Camping Villaviciosa (37)** is a large campsite with hedged pitches and wooden bungalows for rent. There's also a small sauna, and massages on offer. Open all year. •€• •€€•

**a.** La Rasa, s/n, Selorio, 33316 Villaviciosa
**t.** 9 85 891 529
**w.** campinglarasa.com

**Camping Playa España (38)** is a spacious green campsite with lots of shaded pitches, close to surf spot Playa España, also rents out small caravans with tent (sleeps 3 persons). Open March to September.

**a.** Playa España, Santana 70, Quintes, 33314 Villaviciosa
**t.** 6 20 246 045
**e.** camping@campingplayaespana.es
**w.** campingplayaespana.es

# IN AND AROUND SALINAS

It can take a while to fully take in the charm of Salinas and the adjoining town of Avilés. They're able to show their happy and their sad faces, very much like life itself. But spend some time there; walking, exploring, surfing, eating, drinking and talking to the welcoming folks of the seaside settlements. Forget getting lost in an industrial site full of factories and warehouses. You learn there is more to Avilés, like its cobblestoned medieval centre, or the modern cultural centre designed by Oscar Niemeyer. And fully take in the seaside of Salinas, with its big bay full of potential nice long peelers, beachside cafés and photogenic boulevard. Leave the row of apartment buildings, blocking your view of the beach, for a sad day..

**Tourist Office Avilés** at Calle Ruiz Gómez 21.

## TO DO

The **Salinas Longboard Festival (39)** is an annual event, usually held in the last week of July. There are not only surf competitions with the world's finest longboarders, the 4-day event has music and Spanish-style parties; long, fun and intense. It's one of the most famous longboard festivals in the world, and certainly the largest in Europe. If you're around end of July, make sure to visit.

**Cudillero (40)**, situated between Luarca and Salinas, is a pretty seaside village that is no doubt on the itinerary of many tourist organisations, but that doesn't make it less pretty. And there aren't that many tourists in Asturias all together. Cars aren't allowed in the centre any more – and a good thing that is, we got stuck once, and even though our van's not that big, moving in reverse through the small lanes is nothing short of awkward. So, park your car just outside town and wander along its row of whitewashed houses with colourful woodwork, down to the harbour. In the late afternoon, fishing boats return and sell their catch at the market. There's a street market every Tuesday and Friday.

## EAT/DRINK/HANGOUT

**Aloha (41)** is a happy, easy-going and brightly coloured little bar with lots of Aloha vibes. They serve good snacks, juices, live music, beers and vinos. •€•

**a.** Calle Cabruñana, Bajo, 33400 Avilés
**t.** 9 84 061 377

**Agüita (42)**: great café, bar and hangout, close to the beach, with ocean view. Healthy food, juices, some fine lunches, and of course, the best after surf snack: chocolate con churros. •€•

**a.** Calle Pablo Laloux 14, 33405 Salinas
**t.** 9 84 496 305

Photo: Alexandra Gossink

## SHOP

◆

**Finca Salinas (43)** okay, what to call a place that has good food, is a cool place to hang out, where you can check out surfboards and bikes, or have your bike fixed at their bike workshop. They also make their own surfboards, called Lola Surf, and sell surf essentials at their surf shop. Go check it out! It's located on the way to Salinas, along the N 632.

**a.** Avenida del Campón 51, 33405 Salinas
**t.** 6 07 930 269
**w.** fincasalinas.es

## SLEEP

◆

From **Alamar Surf House (44)** and surf school you can check if you should go out for a surf, or stay in for another coffee till the tide's ok, in their cosy and very nicely decorated guesthouse. A welcoming place, perfect for those who want to be as close to the seaside as possible. In the evening there's usually some live music and a few beers to prolong that lovely salty after surf feeling. They have private double rooms and rooms with bunk beds. Open all year. •€•

**a.** Calle Príncipe Asturias 69, 33405 Salinas
**t.** 6 58 033 494 / 6 33 244 840
**e.** info@alamarsalinas.com
**w.** alamarsalinas.com

**El Pez Escorpión (45)** is a beach lodge and surf school, a stone's throw from the Salinas beach. It has a spacious and comfy communal lounge, kitchen, and clean rooms with bunk beds. Open all year. •€•

**a.** Avenida Marola 1, 33450 Salinas
**t.** 9 85 500 859
**e.** reservas@elpezescorpion.com
**w.** elpezescorpion.com

**Rural Surf** (**46**) is located in a quiet area, surrounded by green hills and close to the beaches of Bahinos, El Sablon and Requexinos. A project created by a group of friends who love surf, nature and adventure sports. The accommodation is set in a typical Asturian rural stone house, fully restored with respect to its original character. There are single and shared bedrooms (with bunk beds) to choose from, and a garden overlooking the ocean. You can also participate in outdoor activities, like rock climbing, or surf lessons, from beginner to advanced. They'll take you to uncrowded spots, and like you to have fun in the water so built a solid base to make you feel safe. Open all year. •€•

**a.** Linares 132, 33457 Naveces (just west of Salinas)
**t.** 6 22 568 351
**e.** info@ruralsurf.com
**w.** ruralsurf.com

You'll be likely to choose **Camping Taurán Agroturismo** (**47**) for its unique location on a cliff overlooking the sea. But there's more to it, like large pitches and fully equipped wooden cabins for 2 to 6 people. Then there's a pool, playground and the farm where you meet all the native Asturian animals, such as ponies, goats, sheep, and chickens. The campsite uses solar energy, recycles waste and water. To top it off, there's an ecological garden, and a greenhouse from which products are sold in their mini market. In July and August there are special activities for kids. Open from May to September. •€•

**a.** Paraje Taurán, s/n, 33700 Luarca-Valdés
**t.** 9 85 641 272
**e.** tauran@campingtauran.com
**w.** campingtauran.com

**Camping Playa Otur** (**48**) is close to a lot of convenient things, like surf beaches, hiking trails, a nature reserve, the town of Luarca and a nudy beach - just so you know, in case you feel the need. Besides 80 pitches, they've got wooden chalets for rent. Open from Easter to September. •€• •€€•

**a.** Carretera de la Playa, s/n, Otur, 33792 Luarca
**t.** 9 85 640 117 / 6 47 074 924
**e.** info@campingotur.com

**Campervans** can park in a designated area just above the beach of **Tapia de Casariego** (**49**), shops and restaurants nearby. Free water, and facilities for emptying toilet. Open all year. (Payment collected by police in morning.) •€•

**Camping Playa Penarronda** (**50**) is a small friendly site, located right at the beach, near Tapia. Informative staff, spacious pitches, and bungalows for rent. Open from Easter to September. •€• •€€•

**a.** Playa de Penarronda, 33794 Barres-Castropol
**t.** 9 85 623 022 / 6 16 602 496
**e.** campingpenarrondacb@gmail.com
**w.** campingplayapenarronda.com

Photo: Alexandra Gossink

# SURF

There are so many little coves and bays along the coast of Asturia, it feels like there's always more to explore, that's what we love about this place. So, it's definitely not just the breaks we mention here.

**San Antolín** (**I**), a beachbreak between Llanes and Ribadesella, is conveniently close to the road, so easy to check. Usually not too crowded, rivermouth beachbreak with several peaks to choose from. Best on small to medium n-nw-w swell, all tides. All levels. Easy parking.

**Ribadesella** (**II**) beach can produce some real fun surf, and there's something to it; surfing a break in the middle of town, with onlookers from the boulevard. Protected from east winds, best with small to medium n-nw-w swell, any time but high tide. All levels. Parking can be a bit of a hassle, best in the small harbour/restaurant/surf school/surf shop.

**Playa de Vega** (**III**) is a beautiful, exposed 2 km stretch of sand, picks up the smallest of swells from the n, nw or w, but easily blown out. Can be busy with beachgoers and surfers alike on sunny weekends and during summer, but several peaks to choose from and good vibes all around. No surf? Follow the Camino de Santiago trails for a hike. Easy parking/shower/restaurant/bar/surf school/campsite.

**Rodiles** (**IV**), the most famous (and infamous) break in the area, heavily localised - as in, you're not really welcome on the main peak at the riverbreak to the west of the beach. Don't worry, beach is big and beautiful, backed by pine trees where families love to picnic, you can collect snapped boards and watch some high level surfing. To the east of the beach surf schools feel it's safe enough to go surfing. The riverbreak produces a long, powerful and barrelling left at low tide. Experts only – or, we may as well say, locals only. Easy parking/shower/restaurant/surf school/surf camp/campsite.

Gijón locals often surf **Playa España (V)**, a very small bay with a backdrop of green hills. Needs a medium nw-w swell, best at low to mid tide. All levels. Easy parking/restaurant/surf school.

**Playa de San Lorenzo (VI)**: the city break of Gijón has, as you can expect, not the cleanest water and can be crowded, but then again, you're in the middle of Gijón. It needs medium n, nw or small n swell, works on all tides (but part of beach disappears at high tide). All levels. Parking is a hassle/shower/restaurant/bar/surf school/surf shop.

**Xago (VII)** is a pretty family beach at Avilés, which picks up almost any swell and is a much sought after spot in summer. The big crescent-shaped bay of **Salinas (VIII)** has a lot to offer for all kind of surfers and all kind of boards. It's famous for the annual longboard festival held in July. This spot, also known as Salinas San Juan, is very consistent, in an urbanised area, so expect crowds on good days. Then again, it's a big stretch of sand. Works with small to medium n-nw-w swell, best from mid to high tide. All levels. Easy parking/shower/restaurant/surf school/surf camp/surf shop.

Between Salinas and Tapia there are numerous small bays that are rarely crowded. We really appreciate the beauty of these spots, and encourage you to explore with respect to their relative anonymity.

**Tapia de Casariego (IX)** was primarily put on the surfing map as a contest venue on the WQS tour. It's a sheltered beachbreak at a rivermouth that works best at low tide. You can check if it's worth changing into your suit from the car park overlooking the break. Needs a medium n-nw swell. All levels. Easy parking/shower/surf school/campsite.

# SCHOOL RENTAL REPAIR

◆

Besides surf and SUP lessons (and rental) **Escuela Asturiana de Surf** (**51**) offers not just surf and SUP lessons (and rental), but all sorts of SUP tours, from descending the river Sella to paddling the mountain lakes in winter. Open all year.

**a.** Playa de San Antolín, s/n, 33500 Llanes
**t.** 6 70 686 801
**w.** escuelaasturianadesurf.com

**Waikiki** (**52**) surf shop and school is based in the old town of Ribadesella. The shop has all your surf, SUP, skate and beach essentials. The school operates from the town's beach, Santa Marina, group and individual lessons. Shop open all year.

**a.** Calle Travesía la Iglesia 1, 33560 Ribadesella
**t.** 9 85 857 783
**w.** waikikisurfshop.es

Five-time Spanish longboard champion and European tour medallist, Ricardo Palomeque, shares his knowledge and experience, with small groups, in his surf and SUP school **Marejada** (**53**). Both at the beach; the school, situated in a traditional 'horreo' (corn shed), and his hostel, where he also hosts surf camps, organises English language classes, yoga and outdoor activities.

**a.** Playa de la Espasa, s/n, 33342 Colunga
**w.** escuelamarejada.com

**Special Surf School** (**54**) and camp is run by brothers and longtime surfers, Dani and Raul García. Dani, Raul and their team make it about more than just enjoying and learning to surf; their surf house and school at Rodiles has a skate ramp in the big garden, they offer additional surf-related stretching and pilates classes, and shaping workshops. Lessons and camps also in English. Camps open in season, lessons all year at different locations.

**a.** La Playa de Rodiles (along the VV-6), Villaviciosa
**t.** 6 16 677 529
**w.** specialsurf.com

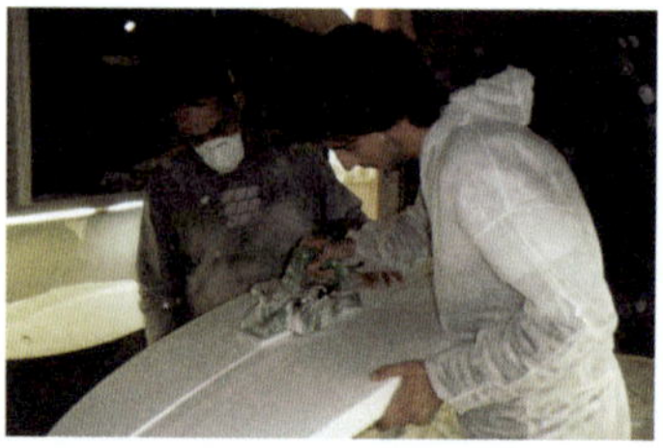

**RodiRide** (**55**) surf and SUP, school and camp, offers SUP and surf lessons, SUP tours, SUP yoga, all equipment rental, also custom-made surfboard shaping workshops, and how to fix your own boards. Open all year.

**a.** Calle Carda 4, Rodiles, 33300 Villaviciosa
**t.** 6 09 890 134
**w.** rodilesurf.com

**Longbeach** (**56**) surf school and surf house offer surf lessons for all levels, and all ages - they run special lessons for adults. Also the occasional longboard clinic (announcements on website and facebook page). Open from March to October.

**a.** Calle Piñole 20, Puerta 'I', 33400 Salinas
**t.** 6 51 958 829
**w.** escueladesurflongbeach.com

**Surf School Las Dunas** (**57**) organises surf camps from 2 to 14 days, for all levels, including video analysis. Open all year.

**a.** Calle Bernardo Álvarez Galán 1, 33400 Salinas
**t.** 9 85 502 244
**w.** escueladesurflasdunas.com

Surf school and shop **Picante** (**58**), founded in 1986, is one of the pioneers of surf schools in Spain. They're located right on the beach of Tapia and offer surf lessons for all levels.

**a.** Playa De Tapia, 33740 Tapia de Casariego
**t.** 6 10 988 683

**Hola Ola** (**59**) surf school, rental and lessons for all levels, in groups or individual.

**a.** Playa Penarronda, Barres, 33794 Castropol
**t.** 9 82 120 064
**w.** holaola.com

Photo: Geert-Jan Middelkoop

# 5. CORE STRENGTH: PARIPURNA NAVASANA

*Boat Pose*

***Core muscles are the basis for the body's actions.***

*They assist overall performance, improve balance, and prevent against injury. Since surfing involves a lot of twisting and rotating, core strength plays a critical part in helping you keep your balance on the board. A strong core is necessary to prevent problem pains, and to enable you to surf better, with additional speed and power. Paripurna navasana, or boat pose, strengthens the whole core from abdomen to back.*

### *Benefits:*

*Core strength.*

### *How:*

*Sit on the floor with your legs stretched out straight in front of you. Lean slightly backwards and place your hands a few centimetres behind your hips on the floor. Lift your chest. Bend your knees and raise the legs until your shins are parallel to the floor. Bring the thighs close to the torso and move your back, ribs and shoulder blades forwards. Keeping the thighs close to the chest, exhale and straighten your legs without rounding the back. Extend from your calves to your heels. Your feet should be higher than your head. Lift your arms and stretch them evenly forward, parallel to the floor, without touching the legs. At this point you will feel your abdomen working but don't let the front of your body shorten. Lift your navel up toward your chest, your ribs up off of your abdomen and roll your shoulders back. Keep your palms extended, facing each other. Stretch the fingers forward and pull your shoulders back and down as you lift your sternum.*

PRAIA DO ESTEIRO
(II)
6
3
AC-862
PANTIN
(III)
ORTIGUEIRA
PRAIA DA
FROUXEIRA (IV)
AC-566
VIVEIRO
N-642
REINANTE
(I)
7-10,16-20,24-26
VALDOVIÑO
AC-862
SAN XORXE (V)
DONIÑOS (VI)
12-14,21,22,27
LU-540
FOZ
5
RIBADEO
A-8
1,2,4,23
North Galicia
O FERROL
AG-64
11,15
N-640
AP-9
A-8
A CORUÑA

# GALICIA

*North Galicia*

Galicia, Galicia, oh all those little corners and inlets and bays and headlands. If there's any place where our motto 'we're here to inspire, now you can go and explore' is spot on, it must be Galicia. Although we've crisscrossed this area of Spain numerous times, you need a lifetime, or two, to get to know it, even a little. And the teeny tiny bit that we know, we love to share. And invite you to discover loads more. The winding roads along the Costa da Morte – the death coast, named after the many ships that wrecked on the shores – lead to deserted stretches of beach. Others seem to take you on an endless journey along green hills and mountains, fields and small towns with farmland and their 'horreos'. These typical granaries, built on pillars to keep stored food safe from rodents, are still largely in use.

# TRAVEL INFO

Although best explored by car or campervan, there are numerous fine surf hostels and camps that provide for all your rides to the surf, food and other activities, and you'll still get a full Galicia experience.

### BY AIR

Numerous airlines, including low-fare, frequent the two main airports in Galicia, Santiago de Compostela and A Coruña. Buses (w. autoscalpita.com) run between A Coruña airport and the town's centre. The same goes for Santiago (w. empresafreire.com).

**w.** aena.es

### BY TRAIN

The national rail company Renfe runs short-distance as well as long-distance services, connecting local towns with bigger cities and the rest of Spain.

**w.** renfe.es

Photo: Marinus Joris

# SURFER-TRAVELLER TYPE GALICIA

*The name Death Coast doesn't scare you off, you're into exploring and not afraid of driving an extra mile to get to know the extremities of every headland and peninsula. You like your reward for going the extra mile to be one of utter beauty, isolation and silencio, love to dive into wifi-free sanctuaries, and wish a sturdy looking local to turn out warm, welcoming and friendly.*

# GALICIA FOOD FACTS

### PADRÓN PEPPERS

You'll find Padrón peppers in tapas bars all over Northern Spain, but originally they're from, as the name suggests, the Galician municipality of Padrón. They're small and very mild, and taste best when lightly fried in olive oil, with some sea salt, pepper and garlic.

# IN AND AROUND ESTACA DE BARES

The green, rocky and hilly headland of Punta de Estaca de Bares is the northernmost point of Spain. Hike, bike, take in the views, and camp out for a few days. Or check the surf at Praia de Esteiro. If you're anything into ornithology, don't miss out on Bares. Especially between September and December, when migrating birds choose the headland as their in-between station, before setting south.

## TO DO

**As Catedrais** (**1**), or the beach of the Cathedrals, is just as its name implies, a beach where the ocean and earth, over time, created rocks and high ceiling caves with such arched formations that they resemble gothic, church-like buildings. You can see them from the cliffs, but it's more impressive walking through the bows, checking the caves out, from down at the beach. Make sure you do this at low tide however, as the beach disappears at high tide.

**a.** Between Ribadeo and Foz, along the LU-P-0610, 27793 Barreiros

If just walking, watching, and taking the pictures isn't enough, join the SUP route along the rock formations of the Cathedrals beach, arranged by **HOLA!OLA** Aventura & Surf (**2**).

**a.** Avenida Calvo Sotelo 30, 27700 Ribadeo
**t.** 9 82 120 064 / 6 09 903 211
**w.** holaola.com

**Acitividades Estaca** (**3**) take you on kayaking tours along the estuary O Barqueiro and surrounding rivers and beaches. You'll enjoy natural sites in their full glory, seeing everything from the water's edge. They offer tours with different levels of difficulty and length. You can also join their hiking tours.

**a.** Puerto do Barqueiro, s/n, 15337 Mañon
**t.** 6 47 536 305
**w.** actividadesestaca.com

## SLEEP

Camping **A Nosa Casa** (**4**) is ideally located right behind the beach of Reinante and 500 m from Cathedrals beach. Plain but clean campsite, rents out bungalows with seaview. •€•

**a.** Carretera de la Playa 42, Reinante, 27794 Barreiros
**t.** 9 82 134 005
**e.** info@campinganosacasa.com
**w.** campinganosacasa.com

**Campervans** (**5**) can stay and use water for free at Area de Foz, along the Ría de Foz, close to the city centre. Open all year.

**a.** Rua do Ru Fondos Curbeiro, 27780 Foz

**Hotel Semáforo de Bares** (**6**) was in use, up to the end of the 1960s, as a communication station for passing vessels, a military observation post and a meteorological station.
So, you can imagine that its location, on a cliff, at 210 m above sea level, adds more than just a little extra to your stay. It was totally renovated as a hotel in 2002. Open all year. •€€• •€€€•

**a.** Santa María de Bares (on the pinnacle of the Bares headland), 15339 Mañón
**e.** infor@hotelsemaforodebares.com
**t.** 9 81 417 147 / 6 99 943 584
**w.** hotelsemaforodebares.com

# IN AND AROUND VALDOVIÑO

ne of the more popular holiday areas in Galicia, because of its proximity to numerous beaches, like famous surf spot Pantín, choice of campsites, and outdoor activities. But besides the month of August - Spain's national holiday month - you can avoid crowds and enjoy the natural sites and beaches and rural villages, almost all by yourself, and some local folks, of course.

## TO DO

**Pantín Classic Pro** (**7**) is held every year at the end of August/beginning of September. It's a high rated World Surf League qualifying series competition with international world cup surfers, earning their points for the World Cup Tour. So, expect to see some spectacles in the great setting of Playa de Pantín.

**w.** pantinclassic.org

Hike, spot wild ducks, migratory and local birds, or find a secluded sand dune protecting you on windy days, at the wetlands of the **Frouxeira Lagoon** (**8**), just behind the large bay of Valdoviño. Herons and hawks, godwits and plovers are among the many birds that can be seen from wooden bird observatories.

Several artisan and food markets are held in Valdoviño regularly, like the **Feira de 1900** (**9**), on the last weekend of September. A market and fiesta at the same time, celebrated with street entertainment, costumes, regional cuisine, and crafts.

Signposted routes for **hiking and biking** (**10**) run along the coast, cliffs and through the forests. And don't forget to check out the avant-garde lighthouse at Punta Frouxeira in the small village of Meirás.

Practice some new skate or BMX tricks at the **Evo Indoor Skatepark** (**11**). Open all year, closed on Monday.

**a.** Avenida Souto Vizoso 68, 15570 Narón (Ferrol)

## EAT/DRINK/HANGOUT

Chiringuito **O Alpendre** (**12**) is a friendly bar at the beach of Doniños for an after surf beer, an early morning coffee, or just good vibes and a snack. Open in season.

**a.** Playa Doniños

On your way up from, or down to Playa de Doniños, you'll find restaurant **Casa Cholas** (**13**), overlooking the bay of Doniños.

**a.** Outeiro 210,15593 Doniños
**t.** 9 81 320 615

On the opposite side, there's tapas restaurant **Casa O Abeiro** (**14**). Different menu, same beautiful view.

Get your hamburgers and good surf food at **Eder** (**15**), even though they serve hamburgers, it's far from being a fast food joint. Also vegetarians can get their fill. Eder serves salads, sandwiches, smoothies, from breakfast to dinner. They've intertwined their passion for food and cooking, travelling and surfing, into what they call 'a factory of experiences'. Open all year. Eder is located in 2 places:

**California's Eder**
**a.** Calle Cataluña 27, 15570 Narón
**t.** 8 81 953 391

**Memories Eder**
**a.** Calle Españoleto 45, 15404 Ferrol
**t.** 9 81 324 928
**w.** eder.gal

## SLEEP

◆

If you want a whole house to yourself, you can rent **Casa Rural Pantín** (**16**), conveniently situated just 1 km from surf break Rodo beach in Pantín. It's plain, easy, spacious and, well, rural; has 3 double bedrooms, fully equipped kitchen and a garden. •€• •€€•

**a.** Lugar Mamela Arriba 18, 15553 A Lagoa
**t.** 6 29 888 008
**w.** casarural-pantin.com

After travelling abroad, Galician owner Augustín Prado returned home to set up the **Surf and Breakfast** (**17**) hotel in the small seaside village Valdoviño. He chose a great location, just 300 m from the beach, with spots like Pantín around the corner.

The house has space for up to 20 guests, with 6 rooms to choose from; 1 double, 2 triple and 3 quadruple rooms. The double room on the first floor is adapted to also be suitable for people with disabilities. •€• (discount on long stay)

**a.** Avenida Ferrol, s/n, 15552 Valdoviño
**e.** sandb@surfandbreakfast.com
**w.** surfandbreakfast.com

**Camping A Lagoa (18)** is located right behind the 3,5 km stretch of beach and lagoon of Frouxeira. Open from mid May to mid September. •€•

**a.** Aldea a Lagoa 9,15552 Valdoviño
**t.** 9 81 487 122

**Camping Valdoviño (19)** is just steps from Frouxeira beach, surrounded by reed beds and dunes. Green hedged pitches and bungalows for rent. Open from April to mid September. •€• •€€•

**a.** Estrada Ferrol-Cedeira, km. 13. Atios, 15552 Valdoviño
**t.** 9 81 487 076
**w.** turvaldovino.com

**Camino Surf Camp (20)** has a choice of accommodations. In summer you can participate in the Surf'n'Roll workshop where sport meets music: jazz musicians from Austria join the Camino Surf Team, and together they offer music- and improvisation-classes in the morning, and surfing classes in the afternoon. •€• •€€•

**a.** Carretera Playa, s/n, 15552 Valdoviño
**w.** valdovino.caminosurf.com

**Onda Root Surf & Yoga Lodge (21)** has a country house, 6 double rooms, and a spacious, sunny garden with hammocks to chill. Situated in the small rural village that surrounds San Xurxo beach. Besides their organic breakfasts, there's surf and yoga on the daily menu. Open from April to December. •€• •€€•

**a.** El Vilar 169, Cobas, 15593 Ferrol
**t.** 6 33 117 480
+43 6 603 122 322 ((December - April)
**e.** info@ondaroot.com
**w.** ondaroot.com

**As Cabazas (22)** is a small campsite, situated right by the beach of Fragata, and close to other surf spots and beaches, such as San Xurxo and Doniños. Open from June to September. •€•

**a.** Carretera Cobas S. Jorge, s/n, 15594 Ferrol
**t.** 9 81 365 111
**e.** info@ascabazascamping.com
**w.** ascabazascamping.com

Photo: Alawa Surfcamp

# SURF

**Reinante (I)** is one of the many beaches easily accessed (and seen) from the coastal road. Works on small n-nw swell, best from low to mid. Beachbreak with some rocks. All levels. Easy parking/shower/restaurant/campsite.

**Praia do Esteiro (II)** at Cabo de Estaca de Bares is a beauty of a bay, with a backdrop of green hills, pine woods, and cliffs. Works with a small to medium n, nw, and w swell. All levels, but beware of current. Easy parking (some free camping allowed off season, if you keep it clean, quiet and stay on the paved roads)/bars near the port.

**Pantín (III)** is a well-known contest site and popular beach, with powerful waves, several peaks to choose from and some high level surfing. Go early in the morning to avoid the crowds. Works at all tides, best with small to medium n, nw and w swells, but also holds bigger swells.

All levels, but beware of rips and current, watch closely before entering. Easy parking/showers.

The big stretch of dune-backed beach at Valdoviño, **Praia da Frouxeira (IV)**, picks up any small n, nw and w swell, but is easily blown out. All levels. Easy parking/shower/toilets/surf school/restaurant/campsite.

The west facing crescent-shaped beach of **San Xorxe (V)** picks up lots of swell and has potential in small to medium nw-w swell. Best from low to mid tide, depending on sand banks. There are lots of smaller bays worth checking north of San Xorxe.

The other large beach, south of Xorxe, is **Doniños (VI)**, very popular with beachgoers in summer and surfers all

# SCHOOL RENTAL REPAIR

year. Best with small to medium w-nw swell, all tides. All levels. Easy parking/showers/beach bar.

**HOLA!OLA** Aventura & Surf (**2**) has all your surf essentials, and the shop at number 9 has a large collection of shoes and street wear.

**a.** Avenida Calvo Sotelo 30, 27700 Ribadeo
**t.** 9 82 120 064 / 6 09 903 211
**w.** holaola.com

**Alawa** (**23**) surf school and camp, 100 m from the beach, offers surf lessons from beginners' up to high level competition training, and is run by pro women's longboard champion Estitxu Estremo. 'Alawa' means 'to the water', in the sense that there are good waves – which sums up the positive spirit of the school. Open in season.

**a.** O Ariño 24, 15553 Pantín
**t.** 6 46 790 554 (Estitxu Estremo)
**w.** alawasurfcamp.com

**Valdo** (**24**) surf school gives all level surf and bodyboard lessons.

**a.** Paseo Lagoa 9, 15552 Valdoviño
**t.** 6 76 433 929 / 6 07 320 382

In need of repairing your board? **Toma Goma** (**25**) is your go-to place. Also shaper of their own brand Toma Goma boards.

**a.** Travesía Carreira 5-A, 15552 Valdoviño
**t.** 6 25 941 508 / 6 26 207 104

**The Camp Doniños** (**26**), set between pine forest and beach, offers surf lessons (and camp) for all levels.

**a.** San Jorge de la Marina 8, 15590 Ferrol
**t.** 6 05 182 537
**w.** thecamp.es

**With Ferrol Surf School** (**27**) you'll stay in the rural town of La Cabana, within reach of surf beaches such as Doniños, San Xorxe, Ponzos and Campelo. They offer yoga classes and you can stay in single, double or triple rooms, so it's not so much of a 'camp'. Surf lessons include video analysis.

**a.** Lugar de la Cabana Montecoruto 120, 15591 Ferrol
**t.** 6 47 419 284
**w.** ferrolsurfschool.com

Photo: Marinus Jons

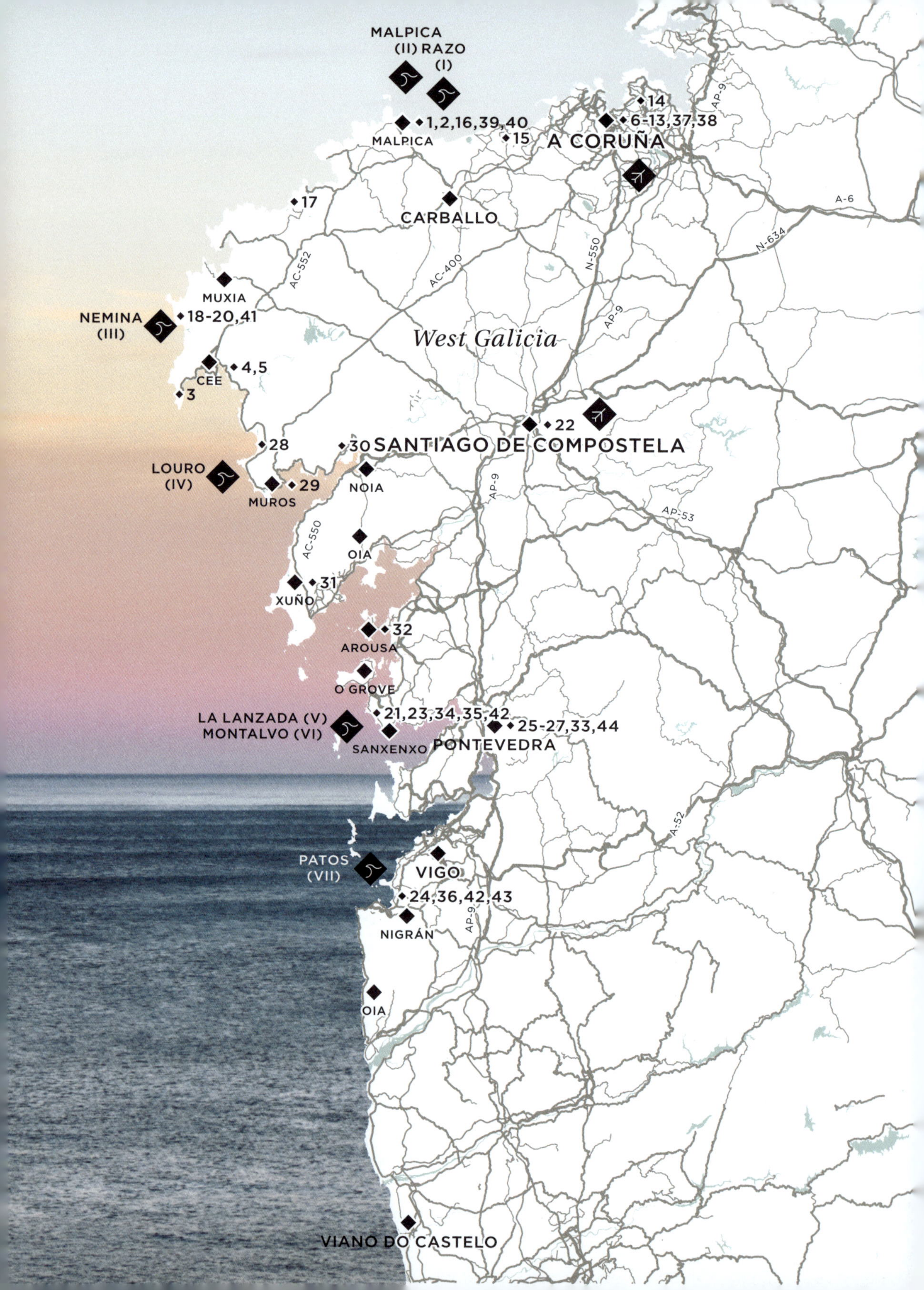
MALPICA
(II) RAZO
(I)
14
1,2,16,39,40
6-13,37,38
MALPICA
15
A CORUÑA
AP-9
17
CARBALLO
A-6
N-634
N-550
AC-552
AC-400
MUXIA
NEMINA
(III)
18-20,41
AP-9
West Galicia
4,5
CEE
3
22
28
30
SANTIAGO DE COMPOSTELA
LOURO
(IV)
MUROS
29
NOIA
AP-9
AP-53
AC-550
OIA
31
XUÑO
32
AROUSA
O GROVE
LA LANZADA (V)
MONTALVO (VI)
21,23,34,35,42
SANXENXO
25-27,33,44
PONTEVEDRA
A-52
PATOS
(VII)
VIGO
24,36,42,43
NIGRÁN
AP-9
OIA
VIANO DO CASTELO

# GALICIA

*West Galicia*

## IN AND AROUND A CORUÑA

The city's boulevard runs the length of a large bay where you can surf with a big swell. But surely you're not here for the surf, but to eat, drink, shop, see the sites. Numerous bike rentals can fix you up with a ride to explore the city and boulevard. Why not cycle all the way up to the tower of Hercules, ancient Roman lighthouse, on the headland to the north, for some fresh air and a seriously good vista. Or say hi to the two silver surfers at the other end of the bay. From A Coruña, the coastal road south - to Razo, and Malpica - offers views over the ocean, passing by small villages and swathes of hilly green. And if you're all eaten drunk and shopped out, beaches and surf spots can be easily checked from the road.

**Tourist office** at Jardines de Méndez Núñez.

## TO DO

◆

**Malpica Longboard Classic** (**1**) is held annually at the beginning of May in the small town Malpica. Descending towards the harbour, where you can park, you may agree that the town's nothing too fancy or picturesque, but that's part of the charm - a working fishing town that goes about its business. Once a year the big bay of the town, fringed by the promenade and a few friendly cafés and eateries, fills up with logs, rock 'n roll music, BBQs and fiestas while the Longboard Classic is on. A brilliant feel-good festival that skipped holding serious competitions years ago, because the party was too hard the previous night. So, expression session it is, so much more fun!

**w.** malpica.longboardclassic.es

From Malpica you can hike or bike south along a coastal path towards the pretty bay of **Praia de Seaia** (**2**), and further towards the 16th century chapel at **Cabo de San Adrián**. Adrián (Hadrian) is the Saint that rid the area from a plague of snakes. Make sure you drink some of the water from the source Fuente Novenllos, it's believed to be holy by the faithful.

Faro de Finisterre sits 'at the end of the world' at the **Cabo Finisterre** (**3**). Many Santiago pilgrims come here to burn a piece of cloth, their hiking boots or a personal note in a fire pit, to end and begin an era, or for lessons learned. Sometimes pods of dolphins can be seen from the cape. It's the westernmost point of Spain, coloured by myths and legends from since the times it was believed the sun died here every night. You can go on a magical mystery tour to sit or lie on - or just touch if they're not too comfy - the stone chairs, benches and holy stones around Cap Finisterre; leftovers from a Celtic past, said to be fuelled with spiritual power…

**Atlantis Adventure** (**4**) takes you climbing, canyoning and/or abseiling down waterfalls, caves and mountains. You'll be jumping, sliding and swimming - releasing some serious amounts of adrenaline! They have something on offer for every member of the family.

**a.** Xallas 27, 15270 Cee
**t.** 9 81 706 087
**w.** atlantisaventura.com

Some 10 km from Cee you'll find **Cascada Ézaro** (**5**), the waterfalls of Ezaro, where the water of river Xallas cascades into the ocean.

## EAT/DRINK/HANGOUT

◆

**Migas Dulces Bocados** (**6**) serves American inspired breakfasts, desserts and sweets, like brownies, cupcakes, muffins and cheesecakes. However, in a very un-American way, they make use of artisanal and high quality ingredients. Find them near the Hercules tower. •€• •€€•

**a.** Calle Torre 102 Bajo, 15002 A Coruña
**t.** 9 81 214 132

For a nice hangout, good coffee and a (sweet) bite, check **Five Elephant** (**7**) or **Miss Maruja**, also take-away. •€•

**a.** Calle Fernando Macías 23, 15003 A Coruña (Five Elephant)
**a.** Calle Zalaeta 20, 15002 A Coruña (Miss Maruja)

Restaurant **RootS** (**8**) mixes Galician food with an Asian touch in a fine setting. •€€•

**a.** Calle Emilia Pardo Bazan 20, 15005 A Coruña
**t.** 9 81 918 782

Restaurant **Bio Bania** (**9**) is a good option for those longing for a varied vegetarian and biological menu. •€€•

**a.** Calle Cordeleria 7, 15003 A Coruña
**t.** 9 81 221 301

Photo: Marinus Joris

Restaurant **El Valentín** (**10**) is lovingly managed by the brothers Silva, fond believers in healthy cuisine, and adding an international flavour to their dishes. They've got some fine pastry as well and changing exhibitions of local artists on the walls. •€• •€€•

**a.** San Agustín, 30, 15005 A Coruña
**t.** 8 81 873 704
**w.** elvalentin.es

## SHOP

◆

Get your stack of gluten-free and ecological goodies at **Pura Vida Ecocentro** (**11**).

**a.** San Agustín 28, 15001 A Coruña

**MAOW** (**12**) is a fun studio & shop run by inspired lady Lydia: bags, decorations, books, stationery and what-not.

**a.** Calle San Andrés 104, 15004 A Coruña

**Lataya** (**13**) is concept store, filled with beautiful design, vintage, clothes and more.

**a.** Calle Picavia 5, 15004 A Coruña

## SLEEP

◆

Camping **Los Manzanos** (**14**) has shaded pitches, bungalows for rent and is decorated with sculptures from Galician artists. Open all year. •€•

**a.** Rúa Maceiras, 15179 Oleiros,
**t.** 9 81 614 825
**e.** informacion@campinglosmanzanos.com
**w.** campinglosmanzanos.com

**Campervans** can park and are allowed to stay at **Praia Salseiras** (**15**), water facilities 2 km further, next to Pavillón de Deportes, on Avenida Laracha. (Good surf on small w-nw swells too!) Open all year.

**a.** 15145 Caión (between A Coruña and Malpica)

Photo: Marinus Joris

**Camping Sisargas (16)** is ideally located near the ocean and forests of pine and eucalyptus trees. Open from June to September. •€•

**a.** Calle Filgueira 12, 15113 Malpica
**t.** 9 81 721 702
**e.** info@campingsisargas.com
**w.** campingsisargas.com

**Campervans** can use the parking Mórdomo at **Playa de Traba (17)**. No facilities, just (cold) showers on the beach. But the beach is beautiful and picks up all available swell.

Friendly family-run **Hotel Rural Fontequeiroso (18)**, close to Cape Touriñán and surf spot and beach Nemiña, has 6 rooms, all with terrace and bathroom, a communal living room with fireplace, a reading room with a view, and big garden. Open all year. •€€•

**a.** Lugar de Queiroso, s/n, 15124 Nemiña
**t.** 9 81 748 946 / 6 17 490 851
**e.** correo@casafontequeiroso.com
**w.** casafontequeiroso.com

**Nemiña apartments (19)** are not the most original in decoration and style, but their location and direct access to the beach of Nemiña are undeniable perks. Available all year. •€€•

**a.** Playa de Nemiña, 15124 Muxía
**t.** 6 89 293 380 / 6 19 373 050
**e.** vbaamil@gmail.com
**w.** nemina.com

The cosy wooden log cabins of **Cabañas de Lires (20)** sleep up to 5 persons and are surrounded by trees. There are big hammocks in the garden, a pool and a stable with domestic animals. Open all year. •€€•

**a.** Lugar de Lires 99, 15138 Cee
**t.** 9 81 748 393 / 6 96 029 810
**w.** cabanasdelires.com

Dare to stay at the end of the world with your camper? Campervan parking at the **Lighthouse at Cape Finisterre (3)** has no facilities, but a killer view (can be packed in summer). Watch out in heavy rains when the road gets slippery.

# IN AND AROUND PONTEVEDRA

◆

The most attractive part for a visitor to Pontevedra, the city, not the province, is of course, the medieval town centre, on the south side of the river Lerez. Especially when you're in the mood for a night out in town, the bars and eateries come to life in the evening. And it's all on a smaller scale than A Coruña.

**Tourist office** at Plaza Verdura.

## TO DO

◆

At the end of every September, the **Rock & Long Festival** (**21**) celebrates the arrival of winter waves with a longboard and retro board competition. To add to the fun of the 3-day festival, there are rock concerts and a surfer's market.

**a.** Playa de Montalvo, Sanxenxo, 36970 Pontevedra

If you're not a pilgrim, walking or biking to **Santiago de Compostela** (**22**), you can still check out the city to witness what all the fuss is about (although, of course, it's really more about the journey) and check out their worn shoes, relieved faces, and the big cathedral, where every pilgrim places his hand on the pillar (oh, even you, here by hired car, can do this, but it's just not the same, is it?).

## EAT/DRINK/HANGOUT

◆

**Kannion Surf Bar and Restaurant** (**23**) hosts regular live concerts and music events on the beach. They also organise the annual Rock & Long surf festival at the end of September.

**a.** Praia de Montalvo, 36970 Pontevedra
**t.** 6 61 580 009

Watch the sunset at **Pénjamo SunBar** (**24**), join in for a morning yoga class, or have a cocktail with some Mexican food. •€€•

**a.** Playa de Patos, Rúa Cansadoura 29, 36340 Nigrán
**t.** 6 98 191 734

## SHOP

◆

**Playground Store (25)** is a skate and street wear shop in the medieval heart of Pontevedra.

**a.** Calle San Román 10, 36002 Pontevedra
**t.** 9 86 841 750

**Carballo Estrela (26)** has some funny, funky supplies for the great outdoors. From picnic baskets, knives and sleeping bags, to bird houses.

**a.** Calle San Román 22 Bj, 36002 Pontevedra
**t.** 6 55 545 061

If you're in the mood for a little urban vibe after all the outdoor fun: **Éxfico Concept Store (27)** offers art expos, photography, vinyl, clothes and bicycles, all in a cool décor.

**a.** Julián López 20, La Guardia, 36780 Pontevedra
**t.** 9 86 611 601
**w.** exficoconceptstore.com

## SLEEP

◆

**Bed & Breakfast San Cibrán (28)** is set in a farmhouse near the surf break of Louro, in a quiet area, with a pool and a killer view. Open all year. •€€•

**a.** Aldea San Cibrán s/n, 15293 Carnota
**t.** 6 27 277 361
**e.** info@sancibranrural.com
**w.** sancibranrural.com

**Ancoradoiro (29)** is a small campsite, close to the ocean, pitches with lots of privacy, enclosed by trees and bushes. Open from Easter to September. •€•

**a.** Ancoradoiro 6, 15250 Muros
**t.** 9 81 878 897 / 6 59 600 861
**e.** wolfgangh@hotmail.es
**w.** rc-ancoradoiro.com

Sleep among the trees, (luxury) monkey style: **Cabañitas del Bosque (30)** are unique log cabins, hidden in the forest, between the branches of trees, either overlooking the estuary of Muros and Noia, or the woods. Fully equipped luxury and a hot tub on the terrace to top it off. They also offer all sorts of activities. Open all year. •€€€•

**a.** Areal, s/n, 15237 Outes
**t.** 9 81 850 903
**w.** cabanitasdelbosque.com

Photo: Alexandra Gossink

**Surfhouse As Furnas (31)** has five rooms with double beds, and a room with two single beds, each with a private bathroom. There's a communal kitchen, dining and living room, a laundry room for free use, sunny terraces and garden with hammocks. Ask for activities such as Spanish language course, yoga, and surf lessons. •€• •€€•

**a.** Agra, 66, Xuño, 15995 Porto do Son
**t.** 6 34 690 455
**e.** info@surfhouseasfurnas.com
**w.** surfhouseasfurnas.com

Campervans can park and stay at **Arosa Surfcamp (32)**, it's like a small campsite, with a bar and windsurf and SUP rental, close to the beach. •€•

**a.** Playa de Concerrado, 36626 A Illa de Arousa
**w.** arosasurfcamp.es

**Slow City Hostel (33)** is a fine option if you want to spend some time in Pontevedra. Very friendly staff welcome you to their hostel in the historic centre. They promote interaction and cultural exchanges between guests with comfy communal areas. •€•

**a.** Rua da Amargura 5, 36002 Pontevedra
**t.** 6 31 062 896
**w.** slowcityhostelpontevedra.com

**Campervans** can stay at **Area de Besadoiro (34)**, facilities for water, a washing machine, electricity, no toilets or showers. Near the beach. •€•

**a.** Rego Dos Besadoiros, 36990 Sanxenxo

There are plenty of campsites around the Portonovo/Sanxenxo area, all close to the beach, like **Camping Rias Baixas (35)** at Playa de Montalvo, with some shaded pitches. Open from May to September. •€•

**a.** Montalvo 73, 36970 Sanxenxo
**t.** 9 86 690 015
**w.** campingriasbaixas.com

**Camping Playa América (36)** (at surf spot Patos) is a large campsite with plenty of pitches and wooden cabanas for rent. Open all year. •€•

**a.** Calle Canido 7, 36350 Nigrán
**t.** 9 86 365 404
**w.** campingplayaamerica.com

Photo: Alexandra Gossink

# SURF

There are so many inlets and headlands worth checking, depending on the swell size and direction. Making a little study of the map, wind and swell conditions can be very rewarding.

The little holiday village of **Razo (I)** only gets summer crowds - the rest of the year, its beautiful stretch of beach, backed by dunes and protected by cliffs at the south end, is rarely busy. If there's no surf you can go for endless hikes, and behind the dunes is Laguna de Baldaio, home to otters and many types of birds. Works with small to medium n and nw swell. All levels. Easy parking/shower/surf school and bar in summer/toddlers playground.

**Malpica's (II)** city beachbreak, home to the annual Malpica Longboard Classic in May, is well protected from southerly wind. Works with medium n-nw swell, all tides except high. All levels. Parking can be a problem in summer, best to park at the port and take a short walk to the boulevard/shower/restaurant/bar.

**Nemiña (III)** is a popular, big beach with a grand backdrop of dunes, hills and a rivermouth to the south end of the beach. Very consistent, crystal clear (cold) water, sometimes dolphins drop in... Works best with medium to big w-nw swell, all tides. You can see Playa Rostro from here, another beauty of a beach, but a bit of quest to get there. All levels. Easy parking/shower/restaurant in summer.

# SCHOOL RENTAL REPAIR

Picturesque **Louro** (**IV**) is a southwest facing beach, a good option with strong north winds. Needs medium to big w-nw swell. All levels. Parking close to the spot can be a problem on busy days/shower/campsite.

**La Lanzada** (**V**), near Sanxenxo and Pontevedra, is a popular beachbreak with several peaks to choose from.

Another option is **Playa de Montalvo** (**VI**), home to the Rock & Long festival in September. Both beaches offer some protection from north winds and need medium nw-w swell. All levels. Easy parking/shower/toilets/beach bar/surf school in summer.

Although reefbreak **Patos** (**VII**) is northwest facing, the headland to the north and some small islands block incoming swell, so needs a bigger n-nw or w swell to work. Can be crowded with Vigo and Nigrán locals. Easy parking/beach facilities in summer (toilet, bar, surf school).

**Surf shops** in A Coruña (**37**):
**Pure Surfing Co** offer beach, mountain and city essentials, and have a range of longboards, shortboards and fins.

**a.** Marcial del Adalid 15, A Coruña
**w.** puresurfing.es

**Raz Surf Gallery** has surfboards, skate and street wear.

**a.** Rúa Pondal 2, A Coruña
**w.** raz.es

**Sandspit**, surf, skate and street wear.

**a.** Estrecha de San Andrés 2, A Coruña
**w.** sandspit.es

**New Wave Store**, surf, street, skate and outlet.

**a.** Cordeleria 6, A Coruña
**w.** nwstore.es

Check out local shaper **DelMar SurfCo** (**38**) for some original and soulfully shaped boards. Also for repair of your board.

**a.** Os Mariñeiros, 15010 A Coruña
**t.** 6 09 985 186

**Raz surf camp**'s (**39**) been around since 1991, sharing their knowledge of surfing and the ocean. Operating from Playa de Razo, with their camp nearby.

**a.** Playa de Razo, 39 Arnados, 15107 Carballo
**t.** 9 81 752 408 / 6 59 381 300
**w.** razsurfcamp.com

**Art surf camp and school** (**40**) operates from Razo beach, offering surf, SUP, and longboard skateboarding lessons.

**a.** Rúa Paseo Praia 14, 15107 Carballo
**t.** 6 38 123 496 / 6 29 203 284
**w.** artsurfcamp.com

Surf camp and school **Surf Costa da Morte's** (**41**) main goal is providing fun in learning how to surf better every day, without too much stress and pressure.

Their school and camp are located right at the beach of Nemiña. They also offer rentals, kayak tours and yoga classes. Open in season.

**a.** O Saburil, Playa de Nemiña, 15124 Muxía
**t.** 6 55 578 544 (Rubén) / 9 81 556 265 (Celme surf shop)
**w.** surfcostadamorte.com

**Prado** (**42**) surf school offers surf, SUP, longboard and bodyboard lessons.

Open all year, operating from the beaches of Patos (Nigrán), and A Lanzada (El Grove).

**a.** Rúa Praia de Patos Nigrán
**t.** 6 36 024 702 / 6 53 929 347
**w.** pradosurfescola.com

**Patos** (**43**) surf school offers courses and rental.

**a.** Camiño da Praia, s/n, Playa de Patos, 36350 Nigrán
**t.** 6 38 724 917
**w.** patossurf.com

Surf shops in Pontevedra (**44**) for all your surf requirements: **Walls Surf Shop** and **Mission Surf Shop**.

**a.** Calle Echegaray 21, 36002 Pontevedra (Walls)
**t.** 9 86 861 078
**a.** Rúa Peregrina, 48, 36001 Pontevedra (Mission)
**t.** 9 86 845 524

Photo: Camino Surf House

THERE'S NO
SUCH THING
AS A LITTLE MARINE
POLLUTION
HELP US KEEP THE OCEAN CLEAN
Surfrider
Foundation
EUROPE
Y&R France 2010 - Crédit photo : Ben Stockley
www.surfrider.eu

# 6. BACK STRENGTH: SHALABASANA

*Locust Pose*

***To be able to lift your chest off the board.***

*An important part of surfing and the foundation for a good paddling technique, you need to have strong back muscles that can endure an arched back paddle position. If you can't do this for the length of your surf session then the shoulders, neck, and lower back will start to suffer and become exhausted. Shalabasana, or Locust Pose, is a great exercise to strengthen the back.*

***Benefits:***

*Strengthens the back and abdomen. Opens shoulders and neck. Eases upper backaches.*

***How:***

*Lie down on your front. Extend both legs firmly away from the trunk. Press the tops of your feet into the floor. Press your tailbone down towards the floor so that the buttocks and the front of your pelvis stay grounded. Rest your arms along the sides of the body, palms facing up. Lift your shoulders up and away from the floor, roll the shoulders back, reach the wrists back and broaden the chest. Exhale and lift your chest, head, and hands, so that the arms extend parallel to the floor. When you're able to work the upper back without lower back strain, you're ready to lift into the final pose. Lengthen your legs on the floor, as before. Lift the outer shoulders away from the floor to help the upper back and shoulder blades move away from the neck. As you press the tailbone and buttocks toward the floor, lengthen your abdomen toward your head. On the exhalation, simultaneously lift the chest, arms, head, and legs. Reach the chest forward and up while lengthening the arms and legs back and up.*

1
AP-4
24,25
A-4
JEREZ DE LA FRONTERA
AP-4
2
CÁDIZ
A-381
A-48
CHICLANA DE LA FRONTERA
Andalusia
A-381
N-340
A-48
26
FONTANILLA
(I)
9,10,13,14,35,36
CONIL
3,4,18-21
VEJER DE
LA FRONTERA
EL PALMAR
(II)
EL PALMAR
5
N-340
12,15,16,27-29,37-40
6,11,
23,33,34
CAÑOS DE MECA
(III)
17,22,
30-32
BARBATE
BARBATE (IV)
7
TARIFA
8
TANGER

# ANDALUSIA

Andalusia in our guide is really just a small part of the region. After all, we're here first and foremost to surf, right? The southwest facing Costa de la Luz on the Atlantic coast, especially the area between Cádiz and Barbate, is your best option to catch waves. It's Moorish influences give it a strong Arabic feel, the natural parks and many green hills are topped with windmills, but most of all, it's the white beaches, baking in the sun, that make for a perfect winter swell-a-vacation.

## TRAVEL INFO

The cheapest way to travel is by bus or coach. Many private companies run between every village and city in Andalusia. Ask a local for the main bus station in town. For the coastal area, best try Los Amarillos (**w.** losamarillos.es), Comes (**w.** tgcomes.es) or Alsa (**w.** alsa.es).

### BY AIR

The airport of **Jerez** is 8 km northeast of the town centre. It's growing rapidly with the increase of low-cost airline connections. Buses run regularly between the airport and the centre of Jerez de la Frontera and Cádiz. The C-1 train line runs between the airport, the centre, Cádiz and Sevilla. The distance from airport to Conil de la Frontera is 75 km.

**a.** Carretera de Sevilla N-IV, km 631, 11401 Jerez de la Frontera
**w.** aena.es

Or **Sevilla Airport**, bus EA Especial Aeropuerte runs regularly between airport and city centre. Distance to Conil de la Frontera is 160 km.

**a.** A-4, Km. 532, 41020 Sevilla
**w.** sevilla-airport.com

## SURFER-TRAVELLER TYPE ANDALUSIA

*You just can't get enough of absorbing bright sunlight, love a good western décor, don't mind being blown away by the Levante – a strong easterly that can continue for days. You like your fellow surfers to be friendly and laid-back and even let you in on a secret spot or two, and love to be pleasantly surprised by the many options to use everything within your quiver's reach; shortboard, mid-length and longboard, all in one week.*

## IN AND AROUND EL PALMAR

You might think, driving alongside the ocean on the Avenida de la Playa in El Palmar, where's the town centre? Well, actually, you're in it, on it; this is it. The boulevard and some side streets, fields with grazing cows, big cactus plants and Moorish white houses, wooden sheds, some bars, restaurants and surf shops. That's El Palmar. And the endless stretch of beach, of course. Some days, when everything's closed and the wind's blowing dust off the streets, you can almost hear Ennio Morricone's tune 'Once upon a time in the West'. Except for the crazy crowded summer months, you'll have the beaches to yourself, some dog walkers and surfers. There are 2 small grocery shops in El Palmar selling the bare essentials and fresh bread; if you need to load up, best go to Conil de la Frontera where you have a choice of supermarkets.

## TO DO

◆

Go to **Sevilla** (**1**), less than 2 hours drive from El Palmar, where in summer, it can get hot, hot, hot. But any other season, and especially in winter, it's a delight. The two main universities in town attract students from all over the world, adding a vibrant and lively buzz to the historic centre. You'll hear lots of languages being spoken in the many eateries, shops and bars. You can tick off 'things to do in Sevilla' from a list, like visiting the Moorish palace Alcázar, or Sevilla's cathedral, the third largest in the world. But really, just wandering around Barrio Santa Cruz, getting lost in the old part of town, eating some tapas here, downing a sangria there, will feed your Sevilla experience better than seeing all the sites. Maybe make a little detour on the way back, to down one more drink at Jerez de la Frontera, the city of... you guessed that right: sherry. (But no drink-drunk-driving now, one of you just stick to coffee, ok?)

*A little tip for vegetarians: look for 'Pisto' on the menu - a meatless dish, similar to the French 'Ratatouille', made of zucchini, peppers, tomatoes, eggplant and olive oil, with optional poached egg topping.*

If you think Sevilla's too far, or if you just can't get enough of the Andalusian city vibes, opt for **Cádiz** (**2**). First of all, it's ultra tranquilo for a city, and a constant sea breeze blows off any city dust you gather. The old city – the place you want to be – is almost entirely surrounded by the ocean. Drive all the way to the end of the Avenida Andalucía to reach the old part. And if you're anything into local cuisine, don't miss Mercado Central, the daily market, what a treat! Every stall has the name of the owner on it, making it a very personal business, and easier to chat and get your samples of sausage, olives and fruits. Outside, alongside the walls of the historical market building, are several eateries, some will even prepare your freshly purchased goods!

Okay, no city dweller at all? **Vejer de la Frontera's** (**3**) your go-to town. El pueblo blanco, on top of a hill, a little inland from El Palmar is uber cute, quite photogenic, but most of all, not too touristy and a change from beach life without being too far from the ocean.

If you have some time to spend at the Costa de la Luz, why not try to speak the language? At **La Janda Language School (4)** you'll be immersed in the Spanish language in a fun way, going on cultural outings, tapas tours, or participating in cookery classes. You can even combine classes with hiking, swimming or surfing!

**a.** José Castrillón 22,
11150 Vejer de la Frontera
**t.** 9 56 447 060
**w.** lajanda.org

The CA2143, between Caños de Meca and Barbate, runs through the **Breña National Park (5)**. From the road you can stop at several points and take one of the paths into the pine forest – as in many coastal areas, pines were planted here to control the spread of sand dunes. For a grand view of the area, walk towards the tower on top. Or hike along the cliffs by taking the coastal path that connects Caños de Meca and Barbate.

Josef Fuchs and his horses, from **Trafalgar a Caballo (6)**, are keen to share the scenery of Caños de Meca, Barbate and surroundings with you, on varied riding routes during a week's holiday. Maybe your partner surfs and you'd rather go riding, then get together in the evening and share your daytime adventures.

**a.** Pago de Zahora 367, 11159 Barbate
**t.** 9 56 437 309 / 6 76 689 870
**w.** wanderreiten-andalusien.com

The long stretch of beach is known as a kite and windsurf heaven, but even if you're not into sports that require lots of wind, **Tarifa (7)** itself is well worth a visit. It's actually a funky little town, with strong Moorish influences and a good vibe - maybe because of the many travellers that like to stay on a while (those who can handle the constant wind without going loco) and get all entrepreneurial. If you want a taste of the town and its locals, some surf, kite and other activities, check in to the Girls Love Boards house. You have to be a girl though...

**w.** girlsloveboards.com

You're so close to **Morocco (8)**, it's possible to take a daytrip to Africa if you want. Get on the boat to Tanger from Tarifa in the morning, stroll through the medina, get lost in the souk, enjoy a generous helping of tajine, and be back in Tarifa in the evening. Two companies run daily ferry services and the journey only takes about 45 minutes. There's a car park at Tarifa (around 20 € a day) if you want to go by foot. You can buy tickets at the port.

**Yoga** is as hot in Andalusia as it is elsewhere. Here are a few of our recommendations:

Find **Shala Virabhadra (9)**, in Conil, in the middle of a row of houses - it doesn't look like a studio from the outside, but once inside, it's a haven of peace. The studio is run by local yogi Curro Arroyo, offering daily Ashtanga yoga classes. Drop-in classes possible.

**a.** Calle Mirador de Castilnovo 2,
11140 Conil de la Frontera
**t.** 6 65 588 801
**w.** shalavirabhadra.com
**w.** ashtangaconil.com

Petra from **Ocean Yoga (10)** offers massages and twice weekly hatha vinyasa yoga classes in Conil, core vinyasa yoga classes for kiters and oceanlovers in Tarifa, and organises regular yoga retreats in Vejer de la Frontera. You can also book private yoga classes at your holiday address.

**t.** 6 55 281 666 (Petra)
**w.** oceanyoga.es

Indira, from **Yoga Soul Retreat (11)**, offers regular yoga retreats, and also Ayurvedic and balancing massages. The retreats are held in Zahora, in a small green oasis near the beach.

**t.** 6 22 346 022 (Indira)
**w.** yoga-soulretreat.com

The wooden yoga lodge at **A-Frame Surf & Yoga Camp** is a fine place to have a yoga class, looking out over the green fields. There are special yoga camps, and also drop-in classes by **Yoga Conil (12)**. Contact for availability and times.

**a.** Avenida de la Playa (opposite the stone tower at the beach), 11159 El Palmar
**t.** 6 57 885 665 (Yoga Conil)
**w.** aframe.de / yogaconil.com

## EAT/DRINK/HANGOUT

◆

From **Feduchy Lounge (13)**, you can look at all the passers-by, or at the clientele, or at the handsome waiter, but keep your main focus on the food. The cook really knows how to handle that you see – and won some awards with it. •€€•

**a.** Calle Pascual Junquera 2, 11140 Conil de la Frontera
**t.** 9 56 440 992
**w.** feduchy.com

Get your sweets and treats and cupcakes and cookies at **Canela & Miel (14)**.

**a.** Calle General Gabino Aranda 8, 11140 Conil de la Frontera
**t.** 9 56 113 432

Live music at night, laid-back terrace by day, **Cortijo El Cartero (15)** is a fine before and after surf hangout. •€•

**a.** Cortijo El Cartero, 11159 El Palmar
**t.** 6 51 493 144

Get your tapas, salads and pizzas with a view of the ocean and the surf at **La Dolce Vita (16)**. Open in season. •€• •€€•

**a.** Avenida de la Playa, s/n, 11159 El Palmar
**t.** 6 27 681 339

**El Chiringuito de Juan (17)** at Playa de Zahora is open on summer, sunny days. Good for watching sunsets while munching your tapas. •€€•

**a.** Playa de Zahora, 11159 Caños de Meca
**t.** 6 67 644 287

**El Poniente (18)** is set in an old windmill, with killer views over a green valley and the ocean in the distance; make sure you're here around sunset. Good food, cocktails and sometimes live music. Open every day, in winter only at weekends. •€€•

**a.** Carretera de los Militares,
11150 Vejer de la Frontera
**t.** 6 38 054 434

For some freshly prepared Moroccan and Middle Eastern goodies, check in at deli and food bar **Califa Express (19)**. Eat in or take-away. Open every day. •€• •€€•

**a.** Plaza de España 15,
1150 Vejer de la Frontera
**t.** 9 56 447 730
**w.** califavejer.com

Cafeteria and restaurant **La Piccolina (20)** is a treat. Friendly, nice décor, delicious breakfast, coffees and teas, lunch, tapas, home-made desserts, and most veggies used are from their own crop. Open from March to December. •€• •€€•

**a.** Plaza de España 20,
11150 Vejer de la Frontera
**t.** 6 08 034 300

Taste some rural cuisine at **Valvatida (21)**: recommended by locals, should be good right? Small and cosy restaurant with a creative menu, mostly prepared with local ingredients. •€€•

**a.** Calle Juan Relinque 3,
11150 Vejer de la Frontera
**t.** 6 69 719 129

**Bar Las Dunas (22)** must be the most relaxed bar, hangout and restaurant, that we love to return to, over and over again. Of course, its location, at the beach of Cabo de Trafalgar has something to do with it, but it's the laissez-faire yet friendly approach in the running of the place that really grabs you by the ankles, from their simple but excellent breakfast - café con leche with tostada - to spontaneous dance and music nights.

**a.** Calle Cabo de Trafalgar 258,
Caños de Meca
**t.** 9 56 437 203
**w.** barlasdunas.es

Bar and restaurant **Jaima Meccarola (23)**, in looks and vibe, is certainly different from Las Dunas. But we're all about trying new things every now and then. The view, we can assure you, will not disappoint.

**a.** Avenida de Trafalgar, s/n,
11160 Los Caños de Meca
**t.** 9 56 437 362

## SLEEP

◆

**Caracolvan (24)** rents out campervans, from VW classic T2 to modern T6 pop-top. Pick up at Sevilla or Jerez airport, or Cádiz train station. You can even return the van in the north of Spain (or vice versa), so you can take the full Atlantic surf route. •€• •€€•

**e.** info@caracolvan.com
**w.** caracolvan.com

If you want to go basic, but well equipped to camp out, **Puzzle Campers (25)** rents out exactly what you need: small and medium sized Berlingo vans. Pick up from Cádiz station, or Sevilla or Jerez airport.

**w.** puzzlecampers.com

**Campervans (26)** can use facilities, empty toilet and fill up water, plus washing machines and wifi at Auto Caravanas Conil. Gate open during shop hours (10:00 to 14:00 and 16:30 to 19:30). •€•

**a.** Polígono Industrial La Lobita, N-340,
11140 Conil de la Frontera
**w.** autocaravanasconil.com

**La Luz Surfcamp (27)** is lovingly run by German couple Moni and Tom, longtime residents of El Palmar. Besides being friendly hosts, they'll share all the tips, to-dos and go-tos you could need. Healthy local food, yoga and surf classes, and rental of boards can be provided. And since Moni is a very creative lady, the interior of the house has an interesting combination of funky seventies and authentic Schwarzwalder décor. Their house is within walking distance of the beach. •€• •€€•

**a.** Apartado No 117 AP E, 11140 El Palmar
**t.** 6 20 779 844
**e.** info@laluzsurf.com
**w.** laluzsurf.com

**A-Frame Surf & Yoga Camp (28)** is located directly on the boulevard, overlooking the surf at El Palmar. You can choose to stay in single or double room, apartment (max 4 persons) or studio (2 persons). Their communal kitchen, lounge, terrace and garden have a homely atmosphere, and all guests can join in surf, yoga and lots of other activities, like climbing and horse riding. •€• •€€•

**a.** Avenida de la Playa (opposite the tower at the beach), 11159 El Palmar
**t.** 6 26 935 771
**e.** info@aframe.de
**w.** aframe.de

**El Palmar Camping (29)** is 1 km from the beach, reached by a dirt road. A surprisingly green, hedged oasis, with a swimming pool and wooden bungalows for rent. •€•

**a.** 11151 El Palmar
**t.** 9 56 232 161
**w.** campingelpalmar.es

Family-friendly **Hacienda Sajorami (30)** offers houses, rooms and apartments. The apartments all face a large garden and the ocean, from where you can watch the sunset through the palm trees. Open all year. •€• •€€•

**a.** Playa de Zahora, 171
**t.** 6 70 991 126
**e.** info@haciendasajorami.com
**w.** haciendasajorami.com

**Camino Surf Lodge (31)** is a 10 minute walk from the Trafalgar cape and Caños de Meca beach. You can choose accommodation only, or to participate in their surf courses, from beginner to advanced. Open from October to April. •€• •€€•

**a.** Carril de la Aceitera 260, 11159 Zahora
**w.** andalusia.caminosurf.com

**Macondo y Los 4 Vientos (32)** rents out several houses and apartments - the best is La Casa Blanca, because of its location, looking out over Trafalgar cape and the beach. •€• •€€•

**a.** Carretera del Faro de Trafalgar 261, 11159 Los Caños de Meca
**t.** 6 26 591 247 / 6 49 173 850
**w.** canosmeca.com

**Casas Karen (33)** offers about the nicest places to stay in the area: scattered throughout a large garden are their rental properties: converted farmhouses, a beach apartment and 'chozas', the traditional thatched straw houses. Your host, Karen, has been around here since 1988 and is a good source of knowledge about the area. At Casas Karen they do their best to be as environmentally friendly as possible, and you'll see that their garden is living proof of this philosophy. Open all year. •€• •€€•

**a.** Camino del Monte 6, 11159 Los Caños de Meca
**t.** 9 56 437 067 / 6 49 780 834
**e.** info@casaskaren.com
**w.** casaskaren.com

**Camping Camaleón (34)** is set in the middle of La Breña Natural Park, some 500 m from the beach at Trafalgar cape. With lots of shaded pitches, nature lovers will like it here, waking up to the sound of birds, the ocean and the wind. •€•

**a.** Calle Camaleón, s/n, 11159 Caños de Meca
**t.** 9 56 437 154
**e.** info@campingcamaleon.com
**w.** campingcamaleon.com

# SURF

Late autumn, winter and early spring are the best months to find surf in Andalusia. There are more spots to find up and down the coast from El Palmar than mentioned below. But let's leave a bit to explore…

**Fontanilla (I)**, in Conil, is a good beach for learners, works best with small to medium sw-w swell, low to mid tide. Exposed to strong wind. All levels.
Easy parking/restaurant.

The 5 km long windswept beach of **El Palmar (II)** offers peaks galore, and can handle some size, but is easily blown out. It is, however, the most consistent beach in the area, and a good indicator of how the surrounding beaches or reefs are working. At its best with small to medium sw-w swell, all tides except high. All levels. Easy parking along the boulevard/no beach facilities but plenty of bars and restaurants/surf school/surf shop.

**Caños de Meca (III)** has several peaks. There's the **reef** in front of the old apartment building (that seems out of place here), with fast hollow waves, a small take-off zone and usually a crowd of skilled surfers, not too keen on sharing their spot. Works best at low tide. Experienced surfers only. The **middle of the bay** can produce some real fun and powerful waves, for all levels and usually a good vibe going on. **Trafalgar**, near the lighthouse, is a reefbreak that suits longboarders just fine. But you'll seldom be alone out there and the level when it's on fire can be pretty high. Vibe's good though, you

# SCHOOL RENTAL REPAIR

can always enjoy seeing a perfect hang ten, even if it's not you with your toes on the nose. Usually needs a bit more swell, works best from low to mid tide. Intermediate to experienced surfers. Parking can be difficult on busy days - at the beginning of the road is a bigger area to park/restaurant/beautiful hiking area towards Cabo Trafalgar.

**Barbate** (**IV**), between the secluded beach Hierbabuena and the port of Barbate, needs a bigger swell to start working properly, and if you do paddle out, you won't be given a grand welcome by the local surf community because it's not that consistent, so a treasured spot when it's on. Experienced surfers only. The parking area up the hill has a bit of a reputation for car theft, so best park in town. When El Palmar is too big or blown out, beginners and intermediates can also try the stretch of beach in front of Barbate's boulevard, sheltered from the seaport. Easy parking/restaurants.

**Trafalgar Surf School**'s (**35**) run by surfer, yogi and surf teacher Laura. She knows the area well and guides you to the best spots for your level of surfing. You can also enquire about her yoga classes.

**a.** Carretera de la Florida 43,
11140 Conil de la Frontera
**t.** 6 57 885 665
**w.** trafalgarsurf.com

**Wall** (**36**) surf shop for all your surf essentials and clothes, in the centre of Conil.

**a.** Calle San Sebastián 10, Bajo,
11140 Conil
**t.** 9 56 440 410

**9 Pies surf camp and shop (37)** is a friendly and welcoming place to get your surf essentials, info on tide and forecast, surf lessons or rentals. They also organise surf camps.

- **a.** Ubicada en Avenida de la Playa, s/n, 11150 El Palmar (look for the sign)
- **t.** 6 20 104 241 (shop)
  6 22 780 262 (camp)
- **w.** escueladesurf9pies.com

Along the same **Avenida de la Playa** you'll find:

**Kotadalu (38)** Surf Shop and Camp.

**Homies Surf and Skate (39)**, they have a skate ramp where you can test their boards (or show off your skills).

**Olavida Surf School (40)**: lessons, rental, smaller shop items, sports activities and cinema in summer. Find them in a small side street just off the boulevard.

- **a.** Playa el Palmar, Camino de Guerrero, 11159 El Palmar
- **t.** 6 78 36 09 25

Photo: Melchior van Nigtevecht

# SEASIDE LOCAL: ARTIST DROOG79

◆

Meet Ed, or rather, Droog79: artist, illustrator, designer, surfer, skater, dad, husband, and suburbia-fleeing long-term resident of hilltop village, Vejer de la Frontera.

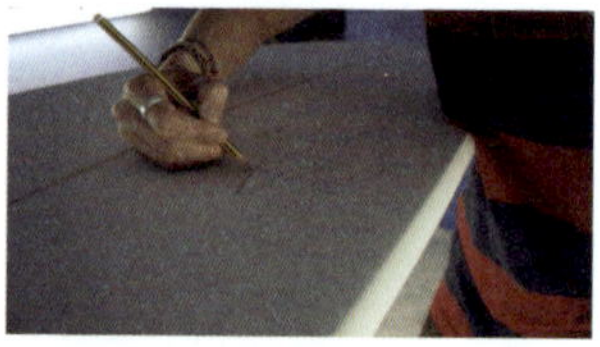

In 2011, after months of travelling in their van through southwest Europe, Ed and his girlfriend arrived in Vejer de la Frontera and instantly clicked with the whitewashed Andalusian village. They stayed on a bit to learn Spanish, and they were offered teaching jobs. They never left after that, got married, had a baby and here they still are, feeling quite settled. "We met some really great folk in our first few weeks here and were made to feel very welcome. With such a perfect location, between beaches and natural parks and a laid-back pace of life, it really was a no-brainer. Since then we've explored near and far, in the province of Cádiz and beyond, and it just gets better and better as we find new people, places and things going on to get involved in."

Looking at some of his artwork you can see where the inspiration is coming from, but it's not as obvious as just skating and surfing. "Sometimes, to quote Paul Klee, you are just taking a line for a walk. Surfing taught me about moments of 'flow', to do something for the pure joy of the moment and nothing else, and lose yourself completely in what you're doing. I rarely have a fixed design of a completely finished piece in my mind when I start, and even if I do it never turns out exactly that way. Of course, this way of working means a lot of pieces don't turn out well or don't fit the brief (if there is one) but it's worth it for when those little gems pop out!"

*"It's like life really; you start out with a rough overall design for it, but the dream is always changing, evolving and you have to be open and adaptive to the unexpected. I think from the outside I can be seen as a bit of a drifter, but I think it's more like tacking a boat: You have a destination in mind but it's not that simple, you have to make a lot of seemingly wayward manoeuvres to get there. And in these detours lies the magic."*

◆

You can find (and order) the work of Droog79 at the A-Frame surf camp in El Palmar, or online: **w.** droog79.org.uk
Read more about Droog79, his art, life in Andalusia and surfing on: **w.** ilovetheseaside.com

◆

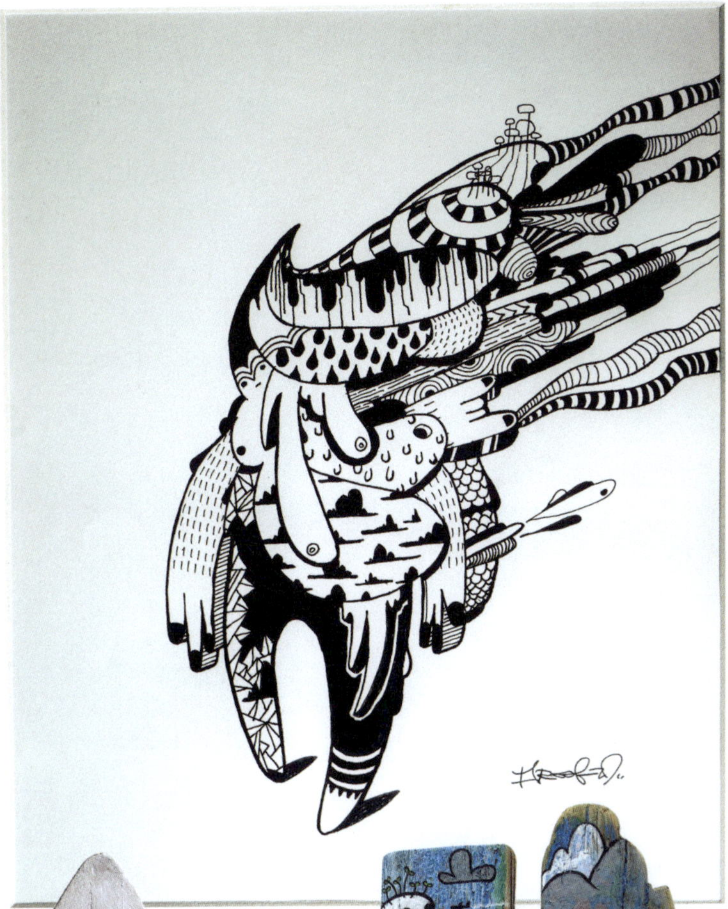

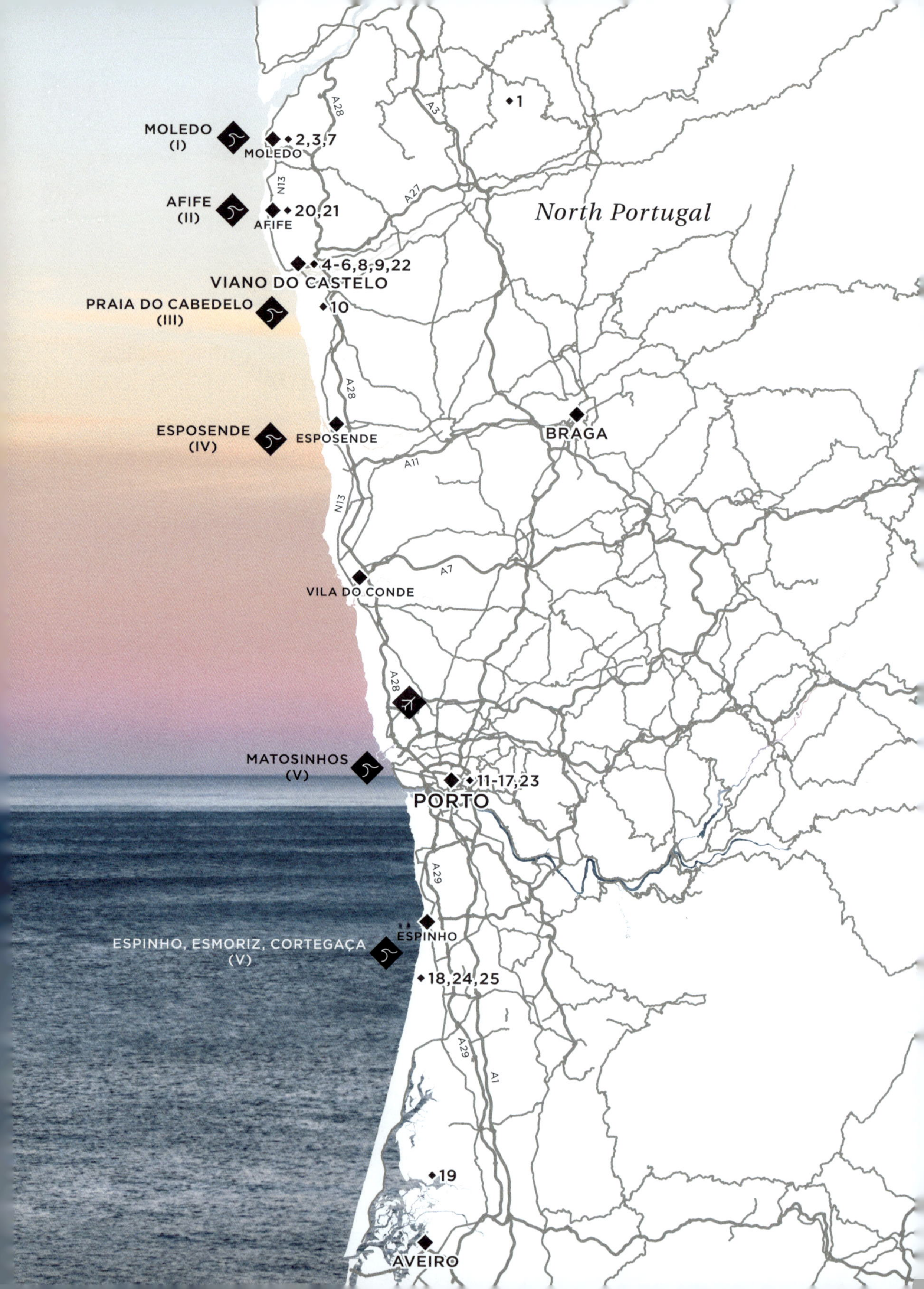
North Portugal
MOLEDO (I)
MOLEDO
2,3,7
1
A28
A3
N13
A27
AFIFE (II)
AFIFE
20,21
4-6,8,9,22
VIANO DO CASTELO
PRAIA DO CABEDELO (III)
10
A28
ESPOSENDE (IV)
ESPOSENDE
BRAGA
A11
N13
A7
VILA DO CONDE
A28
MATOSINHOS (V)
11-17,23
PORTO
A29
ESPINHO
ESPINHO, ESMORIZ, CORTEGAÇA (V)
18,24,25
A29
A1
19
AVEIRO

# NORTH PORTUGAL

*Norte*

The area's well known for its many vineyards and the Douro estuary, but the main attraction, in our humble opinion - the variations in the landscape. Not far from the buzzing cities are small villages that seem to have stood still in time, with a deep sense of community and old traditions still intact. Just drive the coastal routes from Porto down to Peniche and you'll see what we mean. It's the most green and mountainous part of Portugal, hence a bit of unstable weather. If you're into seafood, you're in the right place, and can add some of the catch from the river to top it off, like trout, salmon, and eels.

## USEFUL WORDS

*Handy phrases to keep things friendly and gentle in the line-up;*
*Desculpe – Sorry*
*Não faz mal – It's nothing bad/no problem*
*Com licença– With your permission/excuse me*

## TRAVEL INFO

It would be a waste not to take in the changing landscapes outside of the main cities, and they're best explored by car.

### BY AIR

**Francisco Sá Carneiro International Airport** is 12 km west of Porto. Many airlines, from all over Europe's main cities, have regular flights. Both metro and bus (also at night) connect the airport with the city.

**a.** Pedras Rubras, 4470 Maia
**w.** ana.pt

### BY TRAIN

There's a good and very economical network between the major towns in the north all the way south to Lisbon. Trains are either regional (R) or interregional (IR), the latter being faster, of course, and a bit more expensive.

**w.** cp.pt

# SURFER-TRAVELLER TYPE NORTH PORTUGAL

*You love your Vinho to be Verde, mountainous landscapes, uncrowded beaches, empty line-ups, friendly local folks, and to see some of Portugal as it was many years ago. You can hold down a good port or unusual local drink, enjoy rivers just about as much as you do the ocean and like to alternate city life with unexplored natural territory.*

## IN AND AROUND VIANA DO CASTELO

Seaside towns, can't get enough of 'em. Even, or maybe especially, when they're not too big and can be covered by foot or on bike. Viana has a bit of a sophisticated air about it, probably due to its many historic buildings. Sophisticated it may be, but definitely not reserved; every time we visit town, people spontaneously start chatting with us, telling us about food we should eat or places we should visit. Viana do Castelo is sandwiched between mountains, ocean, and the Lima river, and has a seafaring history that goes back to the 15th century, when explorers set sail to unknown regions. To get an idea of what's on offer, landscape-wise; drive up to Basílica de Santa Luzia, on the Santa Luzia hill, overlooking city, river and ocean. One thing's for sure, the people of Viana are proud of their surroundings, and so they should be. The area consists of green hills and valleys, nature parks and beaches, and surprisingly, it's not on the hotlist of many tourists or surfers.

**Tourist office** at Praça da Liberdade (bike rental available).

Photo: Geert-Jan Middelkoop

## TO DO

◆

Do as the locals do? Eat **Lampreia**, preferably grilled with lots of garlic and oil, or in a stew with rice. It's a mean-looking fish that looks like an eel, which sucks the blood of other fish (still hungry?), a delicacy in the north of Portugal. To drink, try **Champarrião**, a strange mixture of wine (sometimes red but usually vinho verde) with beer, sugar and cinnamon. Drink it from a ceramic mug, and you're in!

The **Vinho Verde**, literally green wine, is usually a white wine, often lightly sparkling, though can be red, rosé, or even a brandy. The green does not apply to the colour or type of grape, but rather the fact that the harvest takes place early in the season (early summer), therefore it's a 'young wine'.

The granitic soil in this region is high in acidity, adding to the wine's mineral content and fresh character. Visit (and taste at) one of the many vineyards in the Alto-Minho - like the award-winning Quinta das Pereirinhas in Moncão (w. foraldemoncao.com), or one of the organic farms of ViniBio (**w.** vinibio.pt).

Walk, hike or bike, and try not to get lost in the **Peneda-Gerês National Park (1)**, with its highest peak of 1500 metres, on the border of Spain. Granite rocks are scattered throughout the mountainous landscape, shaped by wind and water. Even if you don't spot the otters, deer, wild boar or rare grey wolves that roam the park, you're still likely to meet the Minho horses and Cachena cows. Information available at the visitor centre in Arcos de Valdevez.

**a.** Rua Padre Manuel Himalaia,
4970-462 Arcos de Valdevez

Enjoy some heavy riffs at the 2-day **Sonic Blast Music Festival (2)** in Moledo. Expect psycho blues, serious rock and stoner music combined with sun, sea, surf, skate and pools to cool down. Usually held in the middle of August.

**w.** sonicblastmoledo.com

## EAT/DRINK/HANGOUT

◆

**P'ra lá Caminha (3)**, nothing too hip, just a nice place to sit down and enjoy a beer or two, in the middle of the boulevard. Try their sandwiches! •€•

**a.** Avenida 25 de Abril 434,
4910-232 Moledo
**t.** 2 58 722 606

Biological restaurant **Leve (4)** serves a Mediterranean-inspired menu in a colourful setting. They like to share what they prepare and serve, so they offer regular workshops. •€€•

**a.** Largo 5 de Outubro 58,
4900-515 Viana do Castelo
**t.** 9 65 526 692
**w.** restauranteleve.com

**República Caffe Bar (5)** is a lively bar in the centre of Viana, with open-air concerts in summer. •€•

**a.** Praça da Erva, 4900 Viana do Castelo

**Aquário Bar (6)** serves some fine, freshly prepared dishes and is a place where you find yourself hanging out maybe a little longer than planned. Great terrace, good vibe, nice music, friendly staff. •€€•

**a.** Avenida do Cabedelo, 4935-160 Viana Do Castelo (Cabadelo beach, next to Viana Locals surf shop)
**t.** 2 58 371 022

## SLEEP

◆

As if the whole area's not peaceful enough already, **Casa da Eira (7)** tops it off with absolute tranquillity. They offer 1 large and 2 small rural houses, near Moledo beach, situated in a lush garden and orange orchard, with use of a swimming pool. The original lodgings have been completely refurbished. Open all year. •€€•

**a.** Rua do Ingusto 274, Gateira-Moledo,
4910-255 Caminha
**t.** 9 65 039 277
**e.** info@casadaeira.com
**w.** casadaeira.com

Hostel **Ó Meu Amor (8)** is located in a classic building in the centre of Viana, with double rooms, twin rooms and shared bathrooms. All rooms are decorated with a theme, for example: the Colonial, the Romantic and the Viana rooms. The hostel also offers guided hiking tours in the area. •€•

**a.** Rua do Poço 19, Santa Maria Maior,
4900-519 Viana do Castelo
**t.** 9 62 652 512/2 58 406 513
**w.** omeuamor.com

**Fábrica do Chocolate (9)** are at their most happy when a sweet tooth enters their chocolate-themed boutique hotel, restaurant and interactive museum. The hotel has 18 themed rooms, from Willy Wonka to Dark Chocolate. Guests can indulge, relax and even nourish and regenerate with special chocolate treatments. Yum. •€€€•

**a.** Rua do Gontim 70-76,
4900-474 Viana do Castelo
**t.** 2 58 244 000
**e.** reservas@fabricadochocolate.com
**w.** fabricadochocolate.com

**Dias Rural House (10)** is a good option if travelling with your family or a group of friends. Inside is rather old-fashioned Portuguese décor, but it's perfectly located, close to the beach, and there's a skate pool in their huge garden! There are 4 rooms, with shared bathrooms and kitchen. •€€•

**a.** Rua do Reguengo 452,
4935-414 Vila Nova de Anha
**t.** 2 58 323 750/9 37 965 065
**e.** info@diasruralhouse.com
**w.** diasruralhouse.com

# IN AND AROUND PORTO

One of the largest surf cities in Europe, with a passionate surf community, but not on the list of many travelling surfers. The city is, however, registered on UNESCO's list of World Heritage. And rightly so: what a grand city, in many ways. Built on hills surrounding the river Douro, you'll get a good leg workout wandering around town. There's a saying that goes: 'Porto works, Braga prays, Coimbra studies, and Lisbon gets the money.' Not sure if it's more affectingly used in Lisbon or in Porto, but it sure gives an idea of Porto's spirit and vibe. A working town, no lazing about: 'Yeah, we got impressive buildings, drinks and tiles (check out the main train station!), but let's not pat ourselves on the back over it now, shall we? Move along now, and let us get back to work.'

## TO DO

Well, what's the first thing that comes to mind to do in Porto? Yep, **tasting port (11)**. There are many options to do so in Porto. Some come with complete tours, workshops and chocolate and cheese tasting too (**Espaço Porto Cruz: w.** myportocruz.com), others turn all theatrical and have a guide dressed as Don - cape and sombrero included - explaining Porto's wine history and offering tastings of Ruby and Tawny (**Caves Sandeman: w.** sandeman.com).

At the beginning of September, **SALt Matosinhos (12)** - Porto's own surf film festival - takes place right in front of Matosinhos beach. It's the younger brother of SAL (Surf At Lisbon Film Fest), and hosts 3 days of film screenings, workshops, surf gatherings and talks. And, of course, there's live music, DJs, Portuguese craft beers and street food stalls throughout the event. For events info and updates check their FB page (/SALtmatosinhos).

**a.** Avenida Norton de Matos, 4450-208 Matosinhos

## SLEEP

**Campervans (13)** can park in allocated parking area, half an hour walk from downtown Porto, following a footpath along the river. Good place to park and visit the city for a day. No facilities.

**a.** Cais do Cavaco, Vila Nova de Gaia, 4400-076 Porto

**The Getaway Van (14)** rents out new and sturdy Ford Transit mini campervans, decorated with graffiti art, with the option to rent additional items. •€€•

**a.** Rua do Barroco 174,
Centro Empresarial da Arroteia (Poente),
Fracção O, 4465-591 Leça do Balio
**t.** 2 29 514 904/9 25 324 341
**w.** the-getaway-van.com

**The Poets Inn (15)** was created by (surf) travellers for (surf) travellers. They offer 9 originally decorated rooms, a great view over downtown Porto, books to read, art to admire and enough comfort to feel at home. Poets Inn is located close to 'Torre dos Clérigos', which can be seen from almost every part of the city; hard to get lost! The Inn recommends visiting Porto ex-Librium and Lello, 'the most beautiful bookshop in the world.' •€• •€€•

**a.** Rua dos Caldeireiros 261,
4050-142 Porto
**t.** 2 23 324 209
**e.** info@thepoetsinn.com
**w.** thepoetsinn.com

**Surfivor Porto Surf Hostel (16)** is located in one of the oldest city quarters, Foz do Douro, with an ocean view and within walking distance of Porto's surf spots. They have private single and double rooms and dorms. Yoga, surf lessons and rental available. Open all year. •€• •€€•

**a.** Avenida do Brasil 816, 4150-154 Porto
**t.** 9 39 336 434
**e.** info@surfivorcamp.com
**w.** surfivorcamp.com

Located downtown, **Porto Alive Hostel (17)** is ideally located for a little city exploring by day and by night. Private rooms and dorms, with balconies and views. Open all year. •€• •€€•

**a.** Rua das Flores 138, 4050-263 Porto
**t.** 2 20 937 693
**e.** portoalivehostel@gmail.com
**w.** portoalivehostel.com

**Oporto Surf Lodge (18)**, right next to Praia de Cortegaça, a few km south of Espinho, is a lovely home to surfers, their families and partners. The lodge, done up with lots of wood, offers double rooms with private bathroom, communal kitchen and sunny patio with (warm!) outdoor shower. There's also an apartment (sleeps 6) and the studio (sleeps 2). Option to rent surfboards and wetsuits, take yoga and surf lessons or surf guiding, SUP tours or book a massage. Open all year. •€€•

**a.** Rua do Clube de Campismo os
Northenhos 69, 3885-278 Cortegaça
**t.** 9 65 228 145
**e.** oportosurfcamp@gmail.com
**w.** oportosurfcamp.com

**Camper Van Parking Murtosa (19)** is a very, very nice place to rest your van and wandering spirit for a night or two. Tranquil, views over the water, watching the fishermen and their colourful boats sail in, walking through fields, feels like someone pressed the pause button on time, just like in all the surrounding villages. Some water taps at the picnic area and toilets at the entrance to the port. Opposite Aveiro, 1 km from Murtosa.

**a.** Rua Vasco da Gama, 3870 Bico

# SURF

The beaches along the Costa Verde, the green coast, stretch for miles and miles, wide open to receive any swell.

**Moledo (I)** is a consistent spot, partly backed by pine forest, at the estuary of the Minho river - the natural border between Spain and Portugal. Works with nw to sw swells, and can handle some size. All tides. Intermediate+ surfers (near riverbreak because of strong rips). Easy parking/surf school in summer/restaurant/campsite.

**Afife (II)** picks up any available swell. Long stretch of beach, backed by dunes, fields and bushes. Several peaks spread along the beach. Works best with small to medium nw to sw swell, best from low to mid. At high tide it's better near the rocks to the north. Friendly vibe in the line-up. All levels. Easy parking, several parking areas and entrances to the beach/shower and toilets/surf school at south end (Praia da Arda)/beach bar.

**Praia do Cabedelo (III)** is a large crescent-shaped bay, just south of Viana do Castelo, popular with kite and windsurfers. Get there by crossing the Eiffel Bridge from Viana and turn right. Works best from low to mid tide with small to medium nw to sw swell. Near the lengthy breakwater, bigger nw swells produce beautiful long rights. Almost perfect spot, backed by woods and dunes, but the wind...ouch! Go early. All levels. Easy parking/surf school and shop/restaurant.

The beaches around the fishing village and seaside resort, **Esposende (IV)**, offer fun, uncrowded, clean water surf, but they're easily blown out. Driving along the N13 you can check several beaches. Doesn't need much swell to work just fine. All levels. Easy parking/surf school and shop/ bar/restaurant near town.

Porto's got a few quite polluted city breaks, but surfing the break at **Matosinhos (V)**, to the north of the city, can be very rewarding. It's an urban

# SCHOOL RENTAL REPAIR

break, so you never surf alone but there are several peaks and wave sizes to choose from.

The north side's usually a bit smaller than the south and is protected by a large breakwater. Needs a medium nw to sw swell. All levels. Parking's not easy/surf school and shop/restaurant/bar.

From **Espinho (VI)** to **Esmoriz** and **Cortegaça**, to the south, are many breaks that usually work with small to medium nw to sw swells. There are several breakwaters; the longest one in Espinho, so with bigger nw swells you can still surf here. All levels. Easy parking/near the villages there are some surf schools, camps and restaurants.

**Surf Tree (20)** surf shop and school is based at Afife beach, offering board rental, surf and SUP lessons. Open all year.

**a.** Urbanização Bouça Cabrita, 4900-012 Afife
**t.** 2 58 983 165
**w.** surftree.pt

**ABC Surf School (21)** offers surf and SUP lessons at Afife beach (in summer) and all the other surrounding beaches of Viana do Castelo, depending on the wave and wind conditions. Rui, the founder, is also a great help, giving insider tips on the area. Open all year.

**a.** Praia De Afife, 4900-012 Afife
**t.** 9 63 922 964
**w.** abcescoladesurf.com

**Viana Locals (22)** shop and school offers lessons and rental of wind, kite and surf gear. They also organise SUP tours on the river Lima.

**a.** Avenida do Cabedelo, Aquário Bar, 4935-160 Viana do Castelo
**t.** 2 58 325 168
**w.** vianalocals.com

**Feelflows Surf & Lifestyle Company (23)** is based in Porto, creating handcrafted surfboards, skateboards, art and design pieces. They're inspired by the alternative surf scenes from the US and Australia, and aim to get the easygoing mood of the 60s and 70s back, when it was all about having fun!

**e.** feelflows.surfboards@gmail.com
**w.** feelflows-surfboards.tumblr.com

**Surfer's Camp (24)** guesthouse and surf school is located near the beach at Esmoriz. On offer: empty line-ups, forests to hike and bike, flat day adventures and learning not just the knowledge, but also the fun of surfing. Open all year. •€•

**a.** Rua Senhor dos Aflitos 433, 3885-624 Esmoriz
**t.** 9 12 100 078 (Rui)
**e.** bookings@surferscamp.com
**w.** surferscamp.com

**Surfivor Surf Camp (25)** in Esmoriz offers surf lessons and guiding, yoga classes (June to September) and free use of bikes. Single and double rooms and dorms. Open from March to October. •€• •€€•

**a.** Rua de Pêro Alenquer 555, 3885-607 Esmoriz
**t.** 9 39 336 434
**e.** info@surfivorcamp.com
**w.** surfivorcamp.com

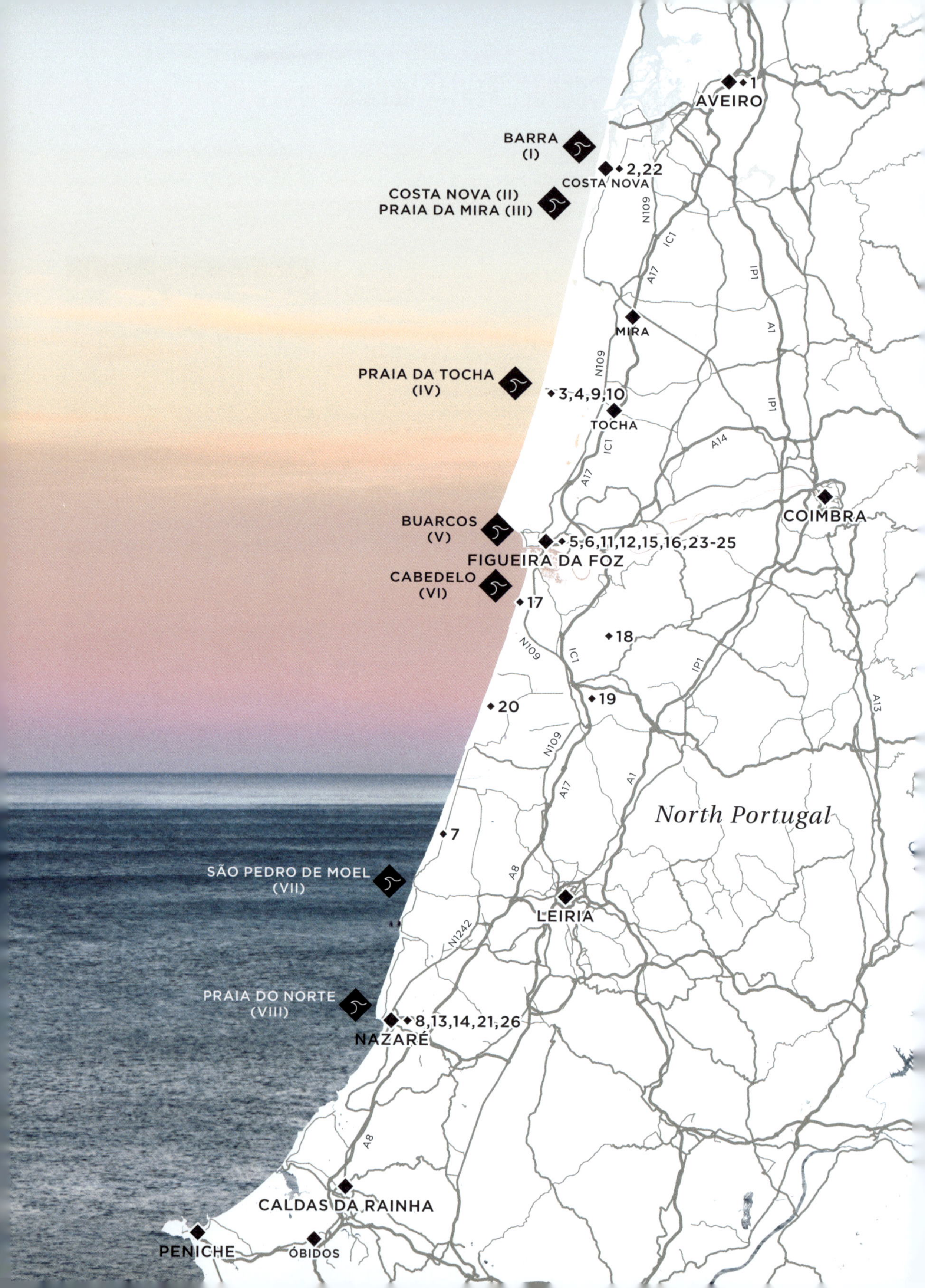
1
AVEIRO
BARRA
(I)
2,22
COSTA NOVA
COSTA NOVA (II)
PRAIA DA MIRA (III)
N109
IC1
A17
IP1
MIRA
A1
PRAIA DA TOCHA
(IV)
3,4,9,10
TOCHA
A14
COIMBRA
BUARCOS
(V)
5,6,11,12,15,16,23-25
FIGUEIRA DA FOZ
CABEDELO
(VI)
17
18
19
20
A13
North Portugal
7
SÃO PEDRO DE MOEL
(VII)
A8
LEIRIA
N1242
PRAIA DO NORTE
(VIII)
8,13,14,21,26
NAZARÉ
CALDAS DA RAINHA
PENICHE
ÓBIDOS

# NORTH PORTUGAL

*Centro Norte*

## IN AND AROUND FIGUEIRA DA FOZ

Sheltered by hills and surrounded by woods and endless stretches of beach, Figueira's outskirts are actually more attractive than the seaport town itself. Although the old centre's got its charms, and you should probably check out the daily fish market, have your coffees and eat out in some gems of restaurants, we think you'd be best to use your time wisely by exploring the greater area of Figueira.

**Tourist office** at Rua Doutor Mendes Pinheiro 2.

### TO DO

**Aveiro (1)** sits at the estuary of Rio Vouga and is often compared to Venice because of its many waterways, and moliceiro boats. The boats were originally used to collect kelp from the river, and goods and cattle (oh, imagine that, cows and sheep sailing downstream in those colourful boats). Nowadays, the moliceiro boats are mainly used as visual props - great features for your photos. You'll also find some fine architectural examples of the Art Deco era throughout the historical centre, so don't forget to look up now and then. If you're on the hunt for an authentic Portuguese souvenir, check the Flea Market, in the streets around Praça do Peixe, on the 4th Sunday every month; from vinyl records and books, to furniture and kitchen utensils.

The brightly coloured striped houses of **Costa Nova (2)** make even the cloudiest of days seem luminous. Like some of the settlements along the Silver Coast, the palheiros, typical wooden houses, were first used by fishermen.

When tourists discovered the blessings of the seaside, at the end of the 19th century, the fishermen – clever chaps – painted their palheiros as colourfully as their boats, and rented them out.

**Campervans**: at the Intermarché in Mira (town) there's a facility to empty your toilet and waste water.

The weekly **Market (3)** in Tocha (the town, not the seaside resort) is a delight: it's big, traditional, and has a great choice of local products on offer. You'll see stalls with an old woman selling solely lemons, her neighbour solely onions, and another with homemade sweets and cakes. Not only food, but clothes, furniture and plants are on sale. Every Sunday in the central square.

Check in to the 1,5 hour **Ashtanga Yoga** classes of yogi Claudia at **Ticket2Surf (4)**, and feel completely rejuvenated. All levels welcome, drop-in classes available, ask for their schedule. Open all year.

**a.** Rua dos Pescadores da Nossa Senhora da Tocha 33, 3060-691 Tocha
**t.** 9 68 144 048 / 9 27 293 073 / 2 31 442 120
**w.** ticket2surf.com

**Serra da Boa Viagem (5)**, Bon Voyage Mountain Range, is situated some 3 km north of Figueira da Foz. You can take endless hikes or bike routes through old eucalyptus forests and mountain ridges, or check out the treetop adventure park. If you want to get an idea of what old rural Portugal looked like, take the - sometimes steep - hiking paths that pass the 'Aldeias de Xisto', villages built with schist rock, starting in Lousã.

Annual surf festival **Gliding Barnacles (6)** is usually held end of August or beginning of September, in Figueira da Foz/Cabedelo. Expect to witness some fine noseriding, single fin longboarding, art, music and good vibes.

**w.** glidingbarnacles.com

Follow the **coastal route (7)** from Figueira da Foz to Nazaré, by taking the N109 from Figueira, and then turn right towards Praia da Vieira.

Along the road you can stop and check the surf, take strolls in the woods, enjoy empty beaches for miles. You'll pass small seaside resorts, like São Pedro de Moel, an upmarket, rather pretty town and surf break.

*The fertile grounds around Alcobaça, just inland from Nazaré, are used to grow grapes for wine, and cherries, ginja, for ginjinha, a typical Portuguese liqueur.*

**Nazaré (8)**, renowned as the big wave spot, with images of the likes of Garrett McNamara taking off on waves the height of skyscrapers. Traditionally a fishing village, and holiday resort for the Portuguese since holidays were invented, it's now akin to a pilgrimage for surfers from all over the world, checking in even on flat days, just to get the picture of the point where on the famous big days the wave towers over the lighthouse. It was a local schoolteacher who set the wheels in motion, some years ago, by sending pictures of the big wave to surfer McNamara. The town itself is still the seaside and fishing resort, where local women in tradi-

tional costume sit with their 'paneiros' – nets laid over wooden structures on which fish are left to dry in the sun. The women dressed in layers of black are widows, who often lost their husbands to the same relentless ocean waves.

## EAT/DRINK/HANGOUT

◆

**Chez Lapin** (**9**) is a friendly local hangout, perfect for sunset beers, steaks on a hot stone, good pizzas, and, the best treat ever: fresh barnacles (in season). Open all year. •€•

**a.** Avenida Doutor Silva Pereira, 3060-692 Praia da Tocha

**Bar Ti Chico** (**10**), also known as Piolho, is a quaint little bar in the seaside resort Praia da Tocha. For over 60 years it's been the place to be for a good night out, usually starting slowly but - depending on who the party's instigator is - can go on till sunrise. Praia da Tocha was a hippy magnet in the seventies, and the bar was known as The Embassy then, because it was a safe haven for the hippies' passports and money while they slept on the beach or in the forest. The name Piolho (meaning lice) is what many bars in Portugal are called; a place crawling with youngsters, like lice. But Ti Chico, or Piolho, is popular with all ages, locals and tourists, who come to drink, dance, listen to live music, and in summer use the street as an extended version of the bar.

**a.** Avenida dos Pescadores da Nossa Senora da Tocha, 3060-691 Tocha

Restaurant and bar **Praça 18** (**11**) serves tasty food, and has small decorations and exhibited pieces of art, some of which are to enjoy, some for sale. Open all year. •€• •€€•

**a.** Praça General Freire de Andrade 18, 3080-058 Figueira da Foz
**t.** 9 14 418 757
**w.** praca18.tumblr.com

Restaurant **Volta & Meia** (**12**) is another gem, serving a diverse menu with vegetarian options, a 'sharing menu' to experience all sorts of flavours, and home-made desserts. Open all year. •€• •€€•

**a.** Rua Doutor Francisco António Diniz 64, 3080-157 Figueira da Foz
**t.** 2 33 418 381/9 68 352 674
**w.** voltaemeia.com

For some good traditional Portuguese food, head to **Tosca Gastrobar** (**13**). Open all year. •€€•

**a.** Rua Mouzinho de Albuquerque 4, 2450-255 Nazaré
**t.** 2 62 562 261 / 9 65 345 521

Get the freshest seafood at **Restaurante O Casalinho (14)**, situated close to the beach, of course! Open all year. •€€•

**a.** Praça Sousa Oliveira 6, 2450-159 Nazaré
**t.** 2 62 551 328

## SLEEP

◆

Small-scale beach hostel **Ticket 2 Surf (4)**, within walking distance of Praia da Tocha, is run with the loving and personal touch of Portuguese-Dutch couple Claudia and Brian. From surfing the uncrowded breaks of Tocha and surroundings, activities like SUP tours on the river and yoga classes, showing off their excellent cooking skills or just sending out good vibes, the welcoming hosts do anything in their power to make sure their guests have the best time. You can choose to stay in single, double or shared room, take surf lessons, guiding and safaris, and join in yoga classes. Also special yoga weeks and 'surf and food' workshops on offer. Open all year. •€• •€€•

**a.** Rua dos Pescadores da Nossa Senhora da Tocha 33, 3060-691 Tocha
**t.** 9 68 144 048 / 9 27 293 073 / 2 31 442 120
**e.** ticket2surf@gmail.com
**w.** ticket2surf.com

**Meeting Hostel (15)** has colourfully decorated single, double, family and dorm rooms. •€• •€€•

**a.** Rua da Fonte 39, 3080-177 Figueira da Foz
**t.** 9 19 200 705
**e.** meetinghostel@gmail.com
**w.** meetinghostel.com

Watch the waves rolling in from the balcony of **Janga Surfcamp (16)**, situated in the hills of Figueira da Foz. A quiet and relaxed place, run by former pro surfer Yoyo Terhorst, where you can also use the gym to work out, take yoga classes, book a massage or relax in the large garden. Single, double and dorm rooms on offer. Open all year. •€• •€€•

**a.** Rua Envolvente do Monte Alto 60, 3080-214 Buarcos
**t.** +49 15 154 697 553
**e.** info@janga-surfcamp.com
**w.** janga-surfcamp.com

**Campervans (17)** can park, stay or use the facilities at Aguiar de Carvalho parking area, with direct access to the beach and village, in season you can get fresh bread in the morning.

**a.** Rua 25 de Abril, 3090 Costa de Lavos

**Termas da Azenha (18)**, formerly a spa resort (from 1711), completely rebuilt and turned into a property with 6 holiday homes and 4 guest rooms, decorated with wall mosaics and murals. Family-friendly place with mosaic workshops on offer and loads to do for the kids. The thermal spa water, believed to have healing properties, still runs through the old baths, and you can use the steam pools and spa baths. There are also two terrains for camping, surrounded by fields and forested hills.

**a.** Rua João Henriques Foja Oliveira 30, 3130-433 Vinha da Rainha, Soure
**t.** 9 16 589 145
**e.** info@termas-da-azenha.com
**w.** termas-da-azenha.com

**Campismo O Tamanco (19)** offers alternatives to regular lodging, such as yurts with wood-burning stoves, outdoor bucket showers and eco-toilets. And really something else; round tubes made from reclaimed materials, surrounded by rich vegetation, designed to have maximum comfort in a minimal amount of space. Also fully equipped cabanas, and camping pitches on offer. Open from March to October. •€• •€€•

**a.** Rua do Louriçal 11, Casas Brancas, 3105-158 Outeiro do Louriçal
**t.** 2 36 952 551
**e.** tamanco@me.com
**w.** campismo-o-tamanco.com

**Campervans** can park at **Parking Praia do Pedrogão (20)**, no facilities, but free parking and immediate access to the surf.

**a.** Rua Maré Viva, 7960 Pedrogão

**North Spot (21)** is located in the northernmost part of Nazaré, some 500 m from Praia do Norte. It's stylishly decorated and peaceful, has 8 bedrooms and 1 suite on offer and comes with a communal garden with swimming pool, kid's playground, and use of BBQ.

**a.** Estrada do Areeiro, 2450-065 Sítio da Nazaré
**t.** 2 62 084 767
**e.** info@northspot.pt
**w.** northspot.pt

Photo: Jop Hermans

# SURF

**Barra (I)**, just south of Aveiro, is where the endless stretch of the Costa Prata beaches begins. This beachbreak is offered a little protection from north wind and bigger swells near the large breakwater. Works best with small nw to sw swells, all tides except high. All levels. (Check out the Barra lighthouse, it's the biggest in Portugal). Easy parking (except maybe on busy summer days)/ shower/toilets/surf school/bar/restaurant.

The length of beach from **Costa Nova (II)** to **Praia da Mira (III)** has some small jetties, and all the way up to **Praia da Tocha (IV)** you can find deserted surf spots.

The breaks here work best with small to medium swell from nw to sw, from low to mid tide, depending on sandbanks. All levels, but be aware of strong currents. Easy parking/shower/ toilet/surf school/bar/restaurant.

Partly sand-covered reef, **Buarcos (V)**, works best with a medium to big nw to w swell, from mid to low tide. It's a big paddle out to the line-up, but a long right ride is your reward. Intermediate to experienced level. Easy parking along the boulevard. No facilities but it's only a short walk to the bars and restaurants.

The consistent break **Cabedelo (VI)**, sheltered by a long breakwater, is a popular local spot and usually crowded, but the vibe is pretty friendly, if you don't show up with a crowd of your own. Works best with a medium nw to

# SCHOOL RENTAL REPAIR

sw swell and offers protection from bigger north swells. (More spots to be found to the south at Praia da Cova Gala). All levels. Easy parking/surf school/bar/restaurant.

**São Pedro de Moel (VII)**, and the expanses of beach to the north and south of it, work best with a small, clean nw to sw swell. Easy parking/restaurant/bar near town.

The oddly big, famous waves of **Praia do Norte (VIII)**, in Nazaré, are caused by a deep underwater trench which channels swell towards the headland with such power that they build up to really, really freaking huge fat waves, only to be ridden by XXL big wave surfers. But it's a spectacle for all levels, that's for sure! The city bay is protected from big swells, but usually doesn't offer many quality waves. Expect it to be crazy crowded when the surf is on fire, and parking can be a problem then too. But on most days there's plenty of space to roam around, and maybe buy a sticker and a mug at the souvenir stalls.

**Riactiva (22)** offers surf, kite and windsurf lessons, and SUP tours; in sea, on lakes and through the channels of Aveiro.

**a.** Avenida José Estevão,
s/n Extremo Sul - Praia da Costa Nova,
3830-453 Gafanha da Encarnação
**t.** 9 19 943 595 / 9 38 744 393
**w.** riactiva.com

**Ticket 2 Surf (4)** offers surf lessons, guiding and safaris, taking you to the best spots in the wider area. You'll be in the good hands of knowledgeable and enthusiastic Brian, working one-to-one or in small groups. They also run river SUP tours, yoga classes and surf hostel.

**a.** Rua dos Pescadores da Nossa Senhora da Tocha 33, 3060-691 Tocha
**t.** 9 68 144 048 / 9 27 293 073 / 2 31 442 120
**w.** ticket2surf.com

**iSurf Academy (23)** is the surf school of former longboard champ Eurico Gonçalves, located at Cabedelo beach. Surf lessons and clinics, rental of surfboards, SUP, bodyboards and all the other surf gear you might need.

**t.** 9 18 733 143
**w.** isurfacademy.wordpress.com

**Surfing Figueira (24)**, school and shop at Cabedelo beach, for all your surf essentials.

**t.** 9 18 703 363
**w.** surfingfigueira.com

**Careca Surfcamp (25)** is located in a rural area, 5 km from the beach. It's an all-inclusive idea, but in proper camping spirit: sleep, eat, surf and repeat. For those less than fond of camping, there's also the option to stay in a surf house in the centre of Figueira da Foz. Open from April to October.

**w.** carecasurfcamp.com

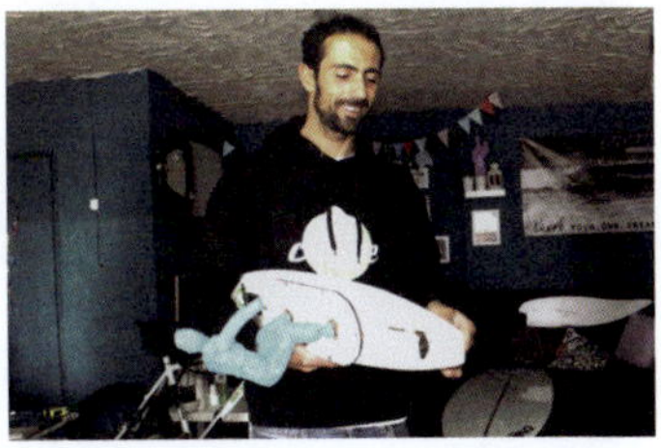

Shaper João Vidinha, of **Crave Surfboards (26)**, has his shaping bay at the colourful site of the port of Nazaré. The good-humoured, friendly João shapes his boards from big blocks of foam, cutting them in two to put the stringer in himself. This way he can decide exactly how much rocker it needs. His knowledge and technical insights stem from a background of building motor-controlled mini boats and planes. But of course his best experience comes from surfing. He likes to surf all kinds of boards, from performance shortboards, single fins and longboards, to SUP: "If I have to build it, I have to know how to surf it." Check out his boards on FB: /cravesurfing.

**a.** Porto de Abrigo da Nazaré, 2450 Nazaré
**t.** 9 17 011 847

# PORTUGUESE LOCAL RECIPE

### BACALHAU ESPIRITUAL

*(with a little twist)*

Claudia Pereira, host and co-owner of Ticket2Surf, kindly shared with us one of her family's Bacalhau recipes. A traditional bacalhau (salted cod) dish, handed down over generations: nutritious, filling and full of Portuguese deliciousness.

### RECEITA FOR 4 PEOPLE

We recommend that (failing the option of making this in your camper, overlooking the ocean), you load up some online videos of Portuguese travel documentaries and gaze at the imagery longingly as you eat.

### INGREDIENTES

*2 ½ kilo Bacalhau (salted cod)*
*4 Potatoes (1cm slices)*
*1 large Onion (chopped)*
*3 cloves of Garlic (chopped)*
*4 Carrots (grated)*
*1 large Courgette (chopped)*
*Olive Oil*
*Salt and Pepper*
*Piri piri*
*Breadcrumbs*

### BÉCHAMEL SAUCE

*4 cups Milk*
*4 tbsp Butter*
*4 tbsp Flour*
*Salt*
*Pepper*

### PREPARAÇÃO

Soak the bacalhau in cold water for 1-2 days to remove excess salt and rehydrate the fish, changing the water at least every 12 hours. After 12 hours, test for saltiness - it should be only mildly salty. !Remember! you can always add salt later, but can't remove it if the fish is under-soaked.

Photo: Geert-Jan Middelkoop

## INSTRUÇÕES

- Make the Béchamel sauce
- Melt butter in a saucepan and add flour. Cook, stirring constantly, for a few minutes, then slowly add milk, whisking constantly to avoid lumps.
- Continue cooking over medium heat until the sauce thickens.
- Remove from heat and season with salt and pepper.
- Boil the bacalhau for around 15-20 mins, and boil the sliced potatoes (in a different pan).
- Drain bacalhau, remove any skin and bones, then shred.
- Heat olive oil in a skillet over medium heat and sauté the onion, garlic, carrot and courgette, with a pinch of salt, pepper and piri piri, until soft (but not brown).
- Add the bacalhau and potatoes, stir to combine.
- Transfer ingredients to a baking dish, cover with béchamel sauce, then sprinkle with breadcrumbs.
- Bake for 25 to 30 minutes, 250 degrees (preheated oven) or until topping's brown and mixture's hot and bubbly.

*Serve immediately, with wine, of course. A herby red pairs well with this dish, or a fragrant white with a high acidity and a bit of what you fancy on the side - green salad and some olives too? Enjoy!*

Photo: Mannus Jons

Photo: SurfEars

# SURFER'S EAR

◆

*On surfer's ear, Tom Carroll, earplugs, and why we should use them!*

At least one of our team, and several of our friends, suffer from surfer's ear. Whether you're a coldwater surfer, or travelling and surfing a lot in waters that aren't all blue flag beaches, infection of the ears is a painful by-product of spending so much time in the water. Excessive exposure to cold water and air, or polluted waters – of which we're often unaware – can lead to ear problems and eventually to surfers ear. Pursuing your passion can, in the case of frequently chasing waves, lead to bone growth inside the ear, narrowing the ear canal. It's a freakish thing our bones do, to try and protect us from the cold water, and it's called exostosis ('new bone' in Greek).

Once your ear canal's narrowed, it's harder to drain (sea)water, or dry out after a surf session. And since seawater isn't as clean as we'd all like it to be, and bacteria really appreciate the warm damp environment of your ear canal, the ear can get infected very easily. To protect your ears, and prevent developing exostosis, it's definitely wise to wear earplugs.

SurfEars were developed by Swedish surfers (who happen to be product designers as well) looking for the perfect device to protect the ears from water, cold air and contaminants, but also let the sound in: a very important aspect of surfing, to stay balanced and connected to the surroundings. The development team of SurfEars worked closely with 2-time surf champ and waterman, Tom Carroll, to make improvements to their product. The result being earplugs that are truly experience-based and tested, practical products, which work!

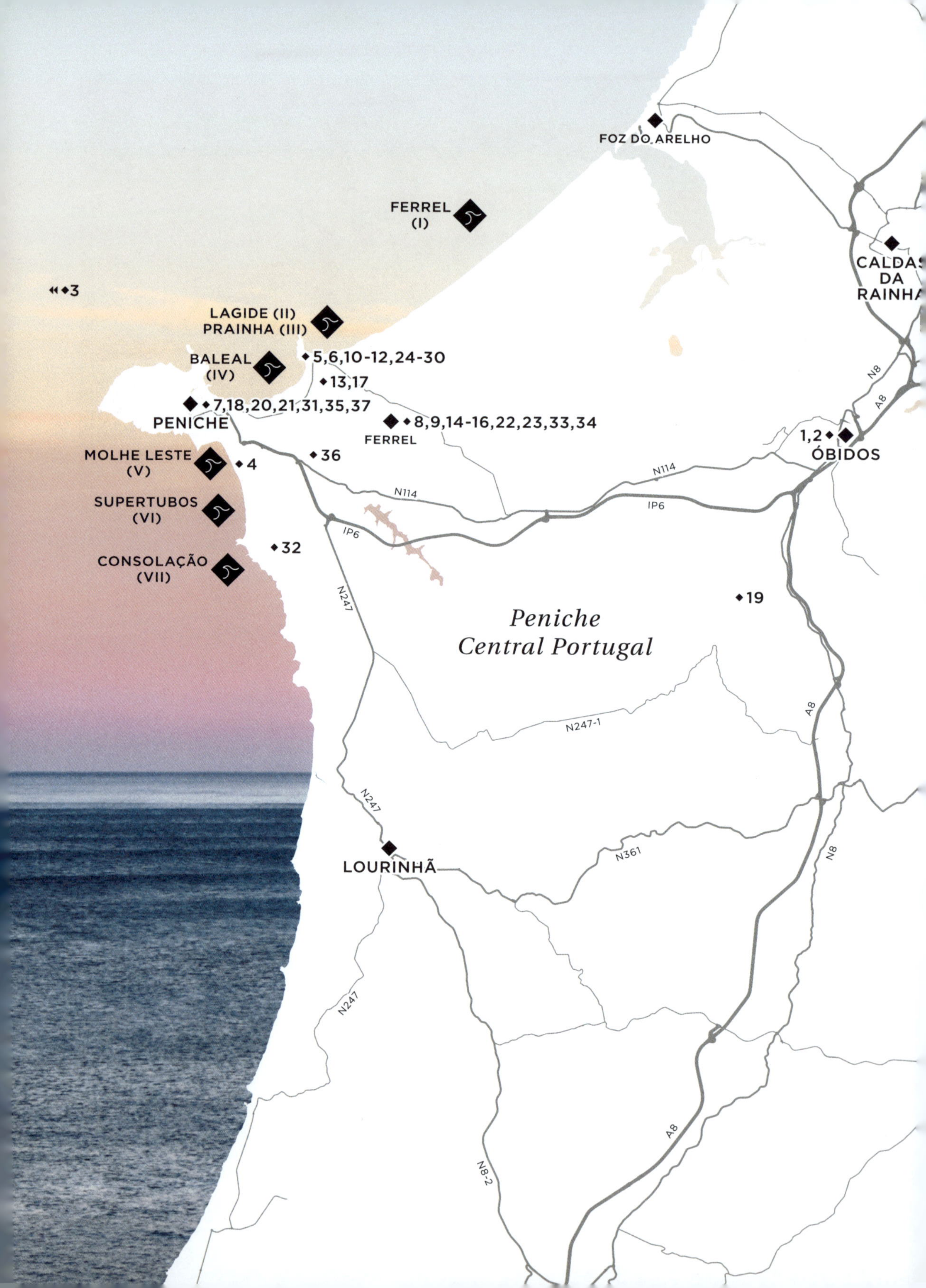
FOZ DO ARELHO
FERREL (I)
CALDAS DA RAINHA
3
LAGIDE (II)
PRAINHA (III)
BALEAL (IV)
5,6,10-12,24-30
13,17
PENICHE
7,18,20,21,31,35,37
8,9,14-16,22,23,33,34
FERREL
1,2
ÓBIDOS
MOLHE LESTE (V)
4
36
SUPERTUBOS (VI)
32
CONSOLAÇÃO (VII)
19
Peniche
Central Portugal
N8
A8
N114
IP6
N247
N247-1
N361
LOURINHÃ
N8-2

# CENTRAL PORTUGAL

*Peniche & Ericeira*

Put the words Portugal and surfing in the same sentence and the first places that spring to mind are Peniche and Ericeira. And rightly so. If they had pores, drops of ocean would ooze out. Ericeira has all the attractions of a fishing village turned seaside resort, and will charm every traveller whether they surf or not. And to add to that - there's hardly a town in Europe with that many breaks within a reach of 4 kilometres. Peniche's old centre is less charming in looks and style, but is as genuine as an older hardworking woman without make-up. She didn't make the effort to put up a façade for all the surf tourists. Because they hardly bother to visit her anyway, probably for a good reason; the surf's up, at any given moment, somewhere around the peninsula.

## TRAVEL INFO

If there's any surf destination where you can do well without a car (although it would still be handy, of course) it's Peniche, and to some extent Ericeira, too. Just check into one of the many camps, schools or retreats and your food, lodgings and rides to the beach are all provided for.

### BY AIR

**Lisbon Airport** is 6 km from the city's centre, which is easily accessed by public transport. From Lisbon centre you can take the bus to Ericeira or Peniche.

**w.** ana.pt

### BY BUS

To get to **Peniche** you have 2 options. Rede-Expressos (**w.** rede-expressos.pt) run regular lines from Sete Rios bus terminal in Lisbon. The journey takes 90 minutes, and you need to make a reservation. On weekdays there's also the Rapida Azul (**w.** rodotejo.pt) from Campo Grande bus terminal, no reservation required.

**Ericeira** can be reached within an hour from Lisbon with Barraqueiro.

**w.** barraqueirotransportes.pt

Or take the public bus, leaving from Campo Grande.

**w.** mafrense.pt

# SURFER-TRAVELLER TYPE PENICHE AND ERICEIRA

*You're passionate about making the most of a surf holiday, and excited at the thought of spending every hour you can in the water, throwing BBQs with friends, going out and about in town and jumping out of bed to press repeat each day. You like your waves to be world class, can handle an angry look from a local surf hotshot, and still show him or her respect. You love reef, river and beachbreaks to the same extent, and have a daily craving for fresh seafood washed down with a cold beer and a couple of shots in a lively bar.*

# IN AND AROUND PENICHE

When talking about Peniche, it's rarely the town Peniche that comes to mind, it's the headland that sticks out from the almost uninterrupted west-facing coastline of Portugal that we all know. Because of its shape, making it surfable in all sorts of swell and wind conditions, it's a hugely popular surf destination. Some might argue that it's too popular, too crowded, and that the vibe's not great because of tension between local surfers, the many, many surf schools, surfing travellers, and tourists that do a bit of surfing on the side. We'll leave that up to you to decide. Meanwhile, we do have a few tips on what's to love about the area, and besides our small collection of favourite places, you'll find truckloads more – especially so, with such an ever-expanding, fast-changing surf magnet as Peniche.

**Tourist office** at Rua Alexandre Herculano (in the Rendas de Bilros building).

## TO DO

◆

**Óbidos** (**1**), once listed as one of the seven wonders of Portugal, is likely on every tourist's tick-list. But, even if you'll never be alone, it's definitely worth the little detour inland. The town's surrounded by a stone wall which you can use as a path and look down on the red-tiled, whitewashed houses, before you descend to the cobblestone streets to wander through the maze-like town. Parking's easy, just outside the town walls, and there's also a car park for campervans with facilities. (And be sure to buy or try the Licor de Ginja - Ginjinha - while you're there, their sour cherry liqueur's known for being one of the best in Portugal.)

With the **Shape and Stay** package of **Yoni Eco Surfboards** (**2**) you can build your own wooden surfboard, under the guidance of Yoni boards shaper Zé. Stay at their Eco Lodge, work on your board and enjoy the company of your fellow shapers at the communal dinners.

**a.** Bairro Encosta do Sol, 2510-441 Óbidos
**t.** 9 64 264 319
**w.** yonisurfboards.com

Three small islands just off the coast of Peniche form **Berlengas Archipelago** (**3**), a nature reserve, and the perfect refuge for migrating birds and endangered species, like the puffin - a bird with some similarities to a penguin. There are walking paths leading to grottos and a fortress. Between May and October boats from Peniche Marina leave daily, to and from the reserve.

The beach of Supertubos is the site for the annual World Surf League **Championship Tour** (**4**) (Rip Curl Pro), usually held between the middle and end of October.

**w.** worldsurfleague.com

At **Yoga Center Peniche** (**5**) you can attend daily yoga classes, from hatha to ashtanga and yin yoga, or book a massage: Ayurvedic, Thai, Lomi Lomi, Reiki and more.

**a.** Avenida do Mar 170-M, 2520-051 Baleal
**t.** 9 61 410 293 (Sabina)
**w.** yogacenterpeniche.com

Join one of the **SUP tours** to Barragem de São Domingos, organised by **3House (6)**.

**a.** Rua da Praia do Baleal, 2520-051 Baleal
**t.** 9 25 310 525
**w.** 3housesurfportugal.com

**SUPxscape (7)** take you for SUP adventures on the Óbidos Lagoon, and can teach you to surf on a SUP, or practise yoga on it.

**a.** Rua da Pragueira 72,
2520-331 Peniche
**t.** 9 37 842 410
**w.** supxscape.com

## EAT/DRINK/HANGOUT

◆

**A Ferreleja (8)**: probably the best bakery and pastelaria in town - and far beyond. But that's our humble opinion. We'd go back for their Broa de Milho, corn bread, any time. In the morning you'll find the town folks enjoying their coffee and sweet treat, and sometimes party people who just finished, well, partying. Open all year.

**a.** Largo Doutor Manuel Pedrosa 5,
2520-106 Ferrel
**t.** 2 62 083 253

**Tables (9)** serves healthy food, made with love; from tapas, traditional Portuguese dishes and energy-boosting post-surf food, to take-away sandwiches, salads and coffee. •€• •€€•

**a.** Largo Doutor Manuel Pedrosa 10,
2520-106 Ferrel
**t.** 2 62 380 026
**w.** tablesferrel.com

**Taberna Do Ganhão (10)** is a small restaurant on your right just as you enter the Baleal peninsula. Fresh food is good food, right? Tasty fresh fish, meat and salads are served here. Open for lunch and dinner. •€• •€€•

**a.** Largo dos Amigos do Baleal,
2520-001 Baleal

It's hard to miss **Bar da Praia (11)**, by the parking area right on the beach of Baleal. Great spot to watch the surf(ers), check your mail, or post your view on Insta, from either inside, behind the large windows, or on their sunny terrace. Open all year, from mornings till late. •€• •€€•

**a.** Largo Amigos do Baleal,
2520-001 Baleal
**t.** 2 62 086 385

**Bar do Bruno (12)** sits at the quieter end of Baleal beach, a little south of the parking area. Nice atmosphere with regular live music and BBQs, good place to hang out and get away from the crowds. Open all year. •€• •€€•

**a.** Avenida da Praia, 2520-001 Baleal
**t.** 2 62 184 212

**The Base (13)** could very well become your base, for pre and post surf drinks, snacks and beats. Friendly hangout, delicious drinks, occasional parties and overall good vibes. Open all year. •€•

**a.** Rua Infante Dom Henrique Lote 2,
2520-160 Ferrel
**t.** 9 67 561 332

## SHOP

◆

As well as your surf essentials, **Peniche Surf Shop (14)** has some real goodies, like the Lisbon Crooks boards.

**a.** Largo Doutor Manuel Pedrosa,
2520-131 Ferrel
**t.** 2 62 103 575
**w.** penichesurfshop.com

Need to do some washing? **Sunshine Lavanderia (15)** is a self-service laundry, with free wifi to use while waiting for your clothes to get shiny and bright.

**a.** Rua 25 de Abril 68, 2520-112 Ferrel

If you want to get an idea of what's going on in Portugal's world of small designer brands, taste locally brewed or

Photo: Geert-Jan Middelkoop

exotic beers, get your hands on a handcrafted surfboard, a good book or some funky artwork, don't miss **Hang Five** (**16**). We believe it's one of nicest shops in Portugal, with a constant supply of things that are made with love, from clothes to all natural granola and wraps. Be warned, you'll probably find yourself coming back to this store and friendly cool hangout over and over!

**a.** Avenida do Mar 97 (behind the cocktailbar), 2520-101 Baleal
**t.** 9 12 292 857
**w.** hangfive.pt

Surf shop **58 Surf** (**17**) has a comprehensive selection of surfboards, wetsuits, clothes and other surf gear to choose from.

**a.** Sol Village, Rua Infante Dom Henrique Lote 4 Loja 1, r/c, 2520-102 Ferrel
**t.** 2 62 769 207
**w.** 58surf.com

If you're into SUP, check out **Paddle and Surf Co** (**18**). From gear to excursions and clinics.

**a.** Rua da Prageira 72, 2520-331 Peniche
**t.** 9 37 842 410
**w.** paddleandsurfco.eu

## SLEEP

◆

Yoga and surf retreat **Buddha Retreats** (**19**), set in a quinta in the village of Columbeira, offers a place to recharge, slow your pace and give your body and mind some TLC. Indoor and outdoor yoga classes, healthy meals and a spacious garden with swimming pool to enjoy. Comfortable single and double rooms and special week retreats: yoga, or yoga & surf, from 4 days to 8 days. •€€• •€€€•

**a.** Rua Salvador Carvalho dos Santos 7-9, 2540-608 Columbeira
**t.** 9 25 283 912
**w.** buddharetreats.com

**Wild Side Campers** (**20**) rents out several models of campervans. Based in Peniche, but pick-up and return from any of the 3 main airports in Portugal. •€€•

**a.** Avenida Monsenhor Bastos 33, 2520-206 Peniche
**t.** 2 62 785 318/9 27 003 884
**w.** wildsidecampers.com

Peniche has 2 campsites, neither of them the most idyllic, green setting that you'd like, but they're open all year, and have all facilities you might need as a camper. You're best option would be **Peniche Municipal Camping** site (**21**), close to the surf. •€•

**a.** Avenida Monsenhor Bastos, 2520-206 Peniche
**t.** 2 62 789 529/2 62 789 696
**e.** campismo-peniche@sapo.pt

**Sail Hostel** (**22**) faces the ocean, and is within walking distance from the beach. It's a very friendly and tranquil place, set amidst a natural surrounding, where the waves are omnipresent, in sight, sound and smell. Comfy double and shared rooms (up to 4 persons). Open all year. •€• •€€•

**a.** Rua do Catalo 10, 2520-141 Ferrel
**t.** 9 27 391 589
**e.** infosailhostel@gmail.com
**w.** sailhostel.com

The name **Surfers Lodge** (**23**) might fool you into thinking it's a low-key, basic place to stay. The lodge is actually a beautifully designed, boutique-style hotel. If you like a little luxurious twist to your surf trip, this could well be your place. The Surfers Lodge was set up by Swedish surf champ, John Malmqvist. Suites, twin, double and dorm rooms, a rooftop infinity pool and hot tub, and optional surf lessons or rental. •€€• •€€€•

**a.** Avenida do Mar 132, 2520-050 Ferrel
**t.** 2 62 700 030
**w.** surferslodgepeniche.com

The **Highway to Swell Motel** (**24**) in Baleal is a small family-run place for surfers. Simple but sweet, and with lots of vintage and driftwood used to make their personalised décor. The garden comes with a pool - for skateboarding, that is. Choice of twin, double or dorm rooms. Open all year. •€• •€€•

**a.** Rua Casal dos Ninhos 12, 2520-053 Baleal
**t.** 9 69 213 179
**e.** info@highway-to-swell.com
**w.** highway-to-swell.com

**Captain's Log House** (**25**) is known for its great atmosphere, and is perfectly located within walking distance of a number of surf spots. Communal kitchen and garden, double, twin and shared rooms (max 4 persons), all with private bathroom. Open all year.
•€• •€€•

**a.** Avenida do Mar 142, 2520-101 Baleal
**t.** 9 14 602 183
**e.** captainloghouse@gmail.com
**w.** captainloghouse.com

The **Surf Castle**'s (**26**) hard to miss - the distinctive whitewashed castle is set atop the cliff overlooking the Baleal peninsula. There are rooms (with a view) in the main house, studios inside the castle and the Casa da Guarda, next to the main house, offers self-catering accommodation for families or groups. •€€• •€€€•

**a.** Avenida do Mar 186, 2520-010 Baleal
**t.** 9 12 526 151
**w.** surfcastle.com

**Apura** (**27**) offers surf, yoga and meditation retreats, run in a holistic way, focusing on both body and mind. Practise yoga in the mornings and work on your surf skills in the afternoon, with hosts Donovan and Yvonne - both certified surf coaches and yoga teachers. It's also possible to participate in the yoga classes only, if you don't want a full retreat. Open from May to October. •€€•

**a.** Rua do Catalo, 2520-141 Baleal
**t.** 9 16 588 550
**e.** info@apura-yoga.com
**w.** apura-yoga.com

The idea of **The Girls Surf House** (**28**) is to open the doors for people who want to feel at home while visiting Baleal. Jeanne, who runs the house, loves sharing her knowledge of the area. You can book your own comfy room and make use of the communal areas - living room, kitchen, and gar-

den. The house is situated opposite Baleal beach. Open all year. •€•

**t.** 9 63 108 475
**e.** thegirlssurfhouse@hotmail.com

**Casa das Marés (29)** is situated on the tip of the small Baleal peninsula, completely surrounded by the ocean. It's run by a local family, and has been since 1930, as the business has passed on to children, and then grandchildren. Open all year. •€€•

**a.** Rua Raul Brandão,
2520-009 Ilha do Baleal
**t.** 2 62 769 200
**w.** casadasmares1.com

**Surf Atlantic (30)** is a spacious private house, perfect for families or groups of friends. Sleeps up to 8 people, and is situated in a quiet street near the beach of Baleal. Storage for boards, sunny terrace with hot tub, and all the comforts you might need on your holiday. You can either book a room or the whole house. •€• •€€•

**a.** Travessa Da Cruz Das Almas 26,
2520-060 Baleal
**t.** 9 16 566 097 / 9 11 849 260
**w.** surf-atlantic.com

Staying amidst the surf schools and camps in Baleal a bit too much for you? Maybe you should check these out:

**Casa d'Arriba Guesthouse (31)** has 3 very sweet little studios for rent, (sleeping 2 to 4 people), with terraces overlooking the ocean, near Praia da Consolaçao. Open all year.
•€€• •€€€•

**a.** Largo Nossa Senhora da Consolação 7,
Praia da Consolação,
2525-433 Peniche
**t.** 2 62 759 333
**w.** casadarriba.com

A few km south of Peniche, **Silver Coast (32)** offers 3 fully equipped apartments (4 to 6 persons) with communal use of roof terrace, garden and swimming pool. Available all year, also for long stay. •€• •€€•

**a.** 58 Rua El-Rei Dom Dinis,
2525-127 Geraldes
**t.** 9 13 127 167/2 62 769 188
**w.** silvercoast-apartments.com

Photo: S.House

# SURF

The series of beaches from **Ferrel (I)** heading north are beachbreaks with rocky bottoms and difficult access, and are popular with the local crew. These breaks work with a small to medium n to w swell, at all tides, but beware of rocks at low. We only recommend for experienced/advanced surfers. Difficult access/no facilities.

You'll find the more accessible spots around Baleal and, therefore, also surf camps, hostels and holiday houses galore. The beachbreaks of Baleal, except **Lagide (II)**, are suited to all levels.

**Praia do Baleal**, or Praia Norte, **(IV)** is the expansive crescent-shaped bay to the southwest of the Baleal headland, with many peaks to choose from, though very changeable depending on wind, swell and sandbank conditions. It picks up all n to w swell. The southwest end of this bay is a good option with a larger w swell, best at low to mid tide. **Prainha (III)**, at the other side of the road to the headland is sand over rocks, works with small to medium nw to w swell, all levels. Lagide, to the south, is a reefbreak, advanced level only and please do respect the locals. Easy parking/toilet/shower/
surf school/bar/restaurant.

South of the harbour from Peniche is **Molhe Leste (V)**, a right-hand pointbreak alongside the harbour wall, fast and tubular, popular with bodyboarders and quick-on-their-feet locals.

# SCHOOL RENTAL REPAIR

The sandbanks of the famous **Supertubos (VI)** beachbreak, in front of the car park, create super fast, hollow waves with steep take-offs. Works with sw to nw medium to big swells. If the wind's not howling and the smell of the fish factory doesn't make you screw your face up till your eyes disappear, it's a great place to kick back and watch the surf. Advanced level/experts only. Easy parking except summer/bar/ restaurant.

**Consolação (VII)** reefbreaks are at the headland south of Supertubos. Difficult access. Advanced level.
Easy parking/restaurant.

**Yoni Wooden Eco Surfboards (2)** produce their boards with sustainable materials and strive to make minimum impact on the environment. The brand was born out of shaper Zé's love for nature and craftsmanship; the outcome being that for every 20 boards produced, only one tree is used, and one is planted back. Yoni Surfboards is located between Óbidos and Peniche.

**a.** Bairro Encosta do Sol, 2510-441 Óbidos
**t.** 9 64 264 319
**w.** yonisurfboards.com

**Baleal Surf Camp (33)**, a family-run business, is one of the longest established surf camps in Portugal, teaching aspiring surfers since 1993. Surf lessons for all levels, accommodation in hostel or apartments, and rental of boards and wetsuits.

**a.** Rua Amigos do Baleal 2,
2520-052 Ferrel
**t.** 2 62 769 277
**w.** balealsurfcamp.com

**Surfguiding Peniche (34)** have a large collection of (mostly Fatum) surfboards and wetsuits, to test or rent. From shortboards and fish to midlength and longboards. If you stay with them you can change and test boards as often as you wish, and you can still rent boards or other surf gear independently if not staying in their accommodation.

**a.** Rua Amigos do Baleal 46,
Casais do Baleal, 2520-052 Ferrel
**t.** 9 11 963 413
**w.** surfguidingpeniche.com

**3House Surf Portugal (6)** is located between the surf spots Lagide and Cantinho da Baía, both consistent and popular breaks. Surf and SUP lessons, and SUP tours on offer.

**a.** Rua da Praia do Baleal,
2520-051 Baleal
**t.** 9 25 310 525
**w.** 3housesurfportugal.com

**Mahalo Surf Experience (35)** will take you to spots suitable for you, whether you're a beginner or stoked to improve your surfing technique, under the guidance of experienced Felippe Bonella Dal Piero, longtime surf coach, ASP judge and life-saving rescue guard. Mahalo also offers shaping workshops.

**a.** Avenida do Mar, 2520-052 Peniche
**t.** 9 25 967 096
**w.** mahalosurfexperience.com

Contrary to what you might assume, having seen the amount of Fatum boards being surfed all over Europe, **Fatum (36)** is not a big factory with loads of people doing production work. It's just 3 people, producing around 60

boards a month. Shaper Gero, originally from Germany, moved to Portugal over 20 years ago, pursuing his dream to live the surfing lifestyle. Although now he actually spends more time in the shaping bay than the ocean, he likes it like this. "I can't do any more production than this, if I did, I'd have to make changes I don't like", he says. He works with a shaping machine: "Once you get into it, it's more precise, 100% of what you had in mind. The evolution of boards goes quickly, if a surfer wants a design from 5 years ago, slightly changed to his present abilities, working with a machine is just so much more precise and easier."

**Fatum** produce boards that suit the Atlantic as well as North Sea conditions, which is what make his boards popular with Northern European surfers. You can order custom-made boards, or visit their shop at the factory to check out a grand choice of shortboards, fish, and longboards.

**a.** Estrada Nacional 114, No 22, 2525-553 Peniche
**t.** 2 62 750 280
**w.** fatumsurfboards.com

**Crowdless Adventure** (**37**) aims to do just that what their name implies: drive you off on exciting off-road adventures, in their Defender, to uncrowded surf spots. Take your own board or rent from a choice of boards, from beginner to expert, and wooden eco boards.

**t.** 9 27 329 294 (Marco)
**e.** casinhadosurf@gmail.com

FATUM
SURFBOARDS
CUSTOMMADE IN PENICHE
FATUM
COME VISIT US:
ESTRADA NACIONAL 114, NO 22
2525-553 PENICHE
PORTUGAL
WWW.FATUMSURFBOARDS.COM

# SEASIDE LOCAL: LIZZY

Lizzy is actually Lisa Marques, a French-born artist who grew up on the Silver Coast of central Portugal and now lives in Peniche. Her daily life here is peaceful, as Lizzy says herself: "I do my illustrations at home, usually before or after work. I help out at Hangfive, a great shop of some friends - selling surf art, retro boards and supporting local projects. Usually I can surf every day. Being in the ocean feeds my soul and inspires me in all the areas of my life. And surfing is the perfect excuse to be in the water any time, sometimes I just need a dip or a long walk by the sea."

After finishing her masters degree in Environmental Tourism, she continued to work on finding an area that balanced the desires of the surf community, surf industry and touristic exploration. This search led to her working for MY Destiny; a non-profit organisation who aim to increase the sustainability of shore communities through surf and travel, but also to another discovery: "At the same time I found my mission by the sea - drawing."

As long as she can remember, art, pencils, paint and ink were part of her life. Lizzy attended a graphics course, but only started drawing again after finishing her degree.

*"Captains, mermaids, mythical characters, tribal patterns. It was like a 'click' for me. I truly believe that where our heart is, is our mission. And we do need more soul in things!"*

Her main inspiration is the ocean, and what it represents. "I see surfing as a way for spiritual and self improvement, and the ocean as the great master. 'I love the sea, because it teaches me', as writer Pablo Neruda said. We always search for perfection, and waves are the best metaphor for life. The perfection depends on how willing you are to catch waves. If you go out often, no matter how the waves are, you will find some perfect days, because you did the preparation in 'bad' days. On the other hand, if you are only waiting for those perfect days of surfing, maybe when you're out there, you won't appreciate it. We need the bad experiences to give significance to the good ones."

Check out Lizzy's Surf and Soul Art on: **w.** cargocollective.com/lizzyartwork and on the walls of Hangfive.
Read more about her projects, art and surfing on: **w.** ilovetheseaside.com

EST.
1964
THE GOLDEN AGE

SANTA CRUZ (I)
1,9-11,20-22,33
SANTA CRUZ
N9
N247
28
SÃO LOURENÇO
2
RIBAMAR
COXOS (II)
29,30
SANTO ISIDORO
RIBEIRA D'ILHAS (III)
Ericeira
Central Portugal
37
3,4,7,8,12-19,23-27,31,34-36
ERICEIRA
N116
PRAIA DO NORTE (IV)
A21
FOZ DO LIZANDRO (IV)
5,6
CARVOEIRA
MAFRA
32

# IN AND AROUND ERICEIRA

With dozens of reefs, beaches and pointbreaks, the living breathing surf organ that is Ericeira attracts surfers of all levels and ability. But it doesn't have the flashy show-off attitude that some seaside surf resorts exhibit. It's rather classic; the old part of the original fishing village still very much intact and slow-paced, Portuguese-style. Announced in 2011 as a World Surfing Reserve, 7 spots in Ericeira can count on the protection of the Save the Waves Coalition from the threat of development.

**Tourist office** at Casa de Cultura Jaime Lobo e Silva, Rua Mendes Leal.

## TO DO

**Ocean Spirit** (**1**) is an annual 10-day international festival, celebrating all kinds of water and wave sports, usually starting mid July, on the beach of Santa Cruz, Torres Vedras. On the menu: surfing, bodyboarding, kite and windsurfing, waveski, SUP and skimboarding. During the festival there are all kinds of activities, live music and, of course, drinks and food.

**w.** oceanspirit.pt

**Yoga Ericeira Shala** (**2**), located between Coxos and São Lourenço, teaches different styles of yoga, like hatha and vinyasa. Drop-in classes available for all levels, lessons held in Portuguese, Spanish and English. Check their schedule on the site. Open all year.

**a.** Rua do Facho Histórico, Lote 14,
2640-017 Ribamar
**t.** 9 17 074 826
**w.** ericeirayoga.com

At the Quiksilver Boardriders store you can use the large **skate park** (**3**). Find the store on the hillside on your right-hand side when leaving town towards the north, close to the campsite, along the N-247. There's also a restaurant, where the rest of your family can hang out while you're having fun.

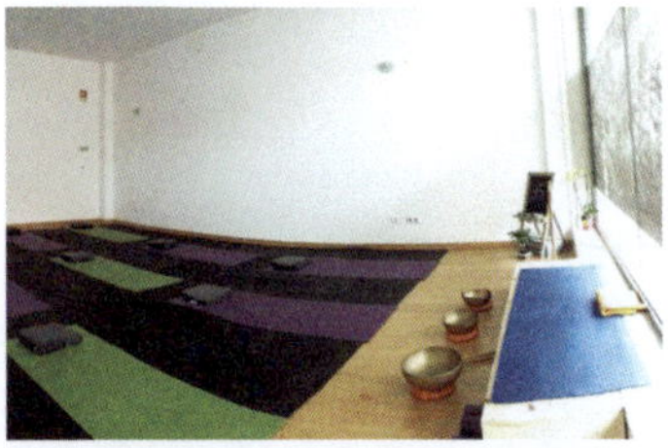

Maphalda Sophia of **Espaço Yoga** (**4**) teaches hatha yoga with a dynamic approach, drop-ins welcome. Classes are held in Portuguese and English. Open all year.

**a.** Rua dos Pocinhos, 6 Loja 6D,
São Sebastião, 2655-333 Ericeira
(close to 58 Surf Shop)
**t.** 9 61 132 836
**w.** espacoyogaby.wix.com/maphalda-sophia

**Here and Now** (**5**) uses the Foz do Lizandro beach as their playground for SUP Yoga and yoga on the beach. Also, special yoga for surfers classes, held at the Rapture Surfcamp, on the same beach. Had enough of exercise? Victor brings his massage table to your place. Available from June to October.

**a.** Rua Pinhal Semana 9,
2655-477 Ericeira
**t.** 9 27 215 805
**w.** here-and-now.eu

**Ericeira SUP Experience (6)** takes you on a SUP along the Lizandro river, the harbour, and on the ocean. You can also book a full board SUP & Yoga package.

**a.** Rua dos Pocinhos, Edificio Rosa dos Ventos, 2655-333 Ericeira
**t.** 9 16 009 498
**w.** ericeirasup.com

**Liquid Earth Adventure (7)** is into adrenaline-enhancing tricks. Join them rock climbing, mountain biking, surfing, or wake-boarding.

**a.** Rua Doutor Eduardo Burnay, nº2 Loja 2, 2655-369 Ericeira
**t.** 9 14 222 428
**w.** liquidearthadventure.com

**Go Out (8)** rents out bikes and scooters, including a surf rack, so you can easily check the spots from areas that are not accessible by car. And way cheaper than renting a car anyway!

**a.** Rua Prudencio Franco da Trindade 1, 2655-344 Ericeira
**t.** 2 61 867 182
**w.** goout.com.pt

*Going to Lisbon, and not necessarily in a hurry? Take the N247, the route passes Sintra and Colares, cliffs, woods and beaches, ending up in Cascais.*

## EAT/DRINK/HANGOUT

◆

Watch a sunset in style, get your laptop out on the shaded terrace, or just chill all day in **Noah Surf House (9)**, at Praia da Física in Santa Cruz. Regular live music and DJs in summer. Open all year. •€€•

**a.** Avenida do Atlântico, 2560-451 Santa Cruz - A Dos Cunhados
**t.** 2 61 932 355
**w.** noahsurfhouseportugal.com

For snacks, tapas, seafood, cocktails and live music with a view, check **Boca Santa (10)** at Santa Cruz beach. •€• •€€•

**a.** Esplanada Antero de Quental 7, 2560-455 Santa Cruz
**t.** 2 61 931 514

**Bronzear Bar & Deli (11)** is a stylishly decorated beach restaurant at Praia de Santa Helena in Santa Cruz. They serve home-made traditional Portuguese and fusion cuisine, using quality and fresh ingredients. Open all year. •€€•

**a.** Praia de Santa Helena, 2560 Santa Cruz
**t.** 2 61 313 474

The Lovely Bay **KFÉ! (12)**: coffee house (as in, great coffee, with blends from all over the world) during the day, then it's time to get the cocktails and wine out in the evenings. Highly recommended hangout, with friendly staff. Open all year. •€• •€€•

**a.** Rua de Santo Antonio 12A, 2655-360 Ericeira
**t.** 2 61 861 237
**w.** lovely-bay.com

**Sunset Bamboo Bar (13)** serves some tasty, big and healthy, natural lemonades, shakes, tostadas, wraps and salads. And then there's happy hour, with cocktails of course. Closed in December and January. •€• •€€•

**a.** Travessa do Jogo da Bola, 3, 2655-297 Ericeira
**t.** 2 61 864 827

Tapas and wine bar **Mar das Latas (14)**, 'sea of cans', is a little treasure,

located near the harbour, serving good wines and creative tapas, and using artfully decorated seafood cans (you can buy them, they make a sweet souvenir). Perfect place for watching the sun go down. Open all year. •€• •€€•

**a.** Rua Capitão João Lopes 24B, 2655-295 Ericeira
**t.** 9 12 218 423

Wine bar and shop **Vira Copos** (**15**) serves and sells a fine selection of quality wine, and serves tapas, either inside, outside, or on the rooftop terrace. Open all year. •€€•

**a.** Rua do Caldeira, 62, 2650-349 Ericeira
**t.** 9 11 516 832

**Adega Bar 1987** (**16**) is a popular hangout with regular live music sessions, from Fado and Flamenco to reggae and rock. Open all year. •€•

**a.** Rua Alves Crespo 3 (near Largo de Santa Marta), 2655-252 Ericeira
**t.** 2 61 861 220

## SHOP

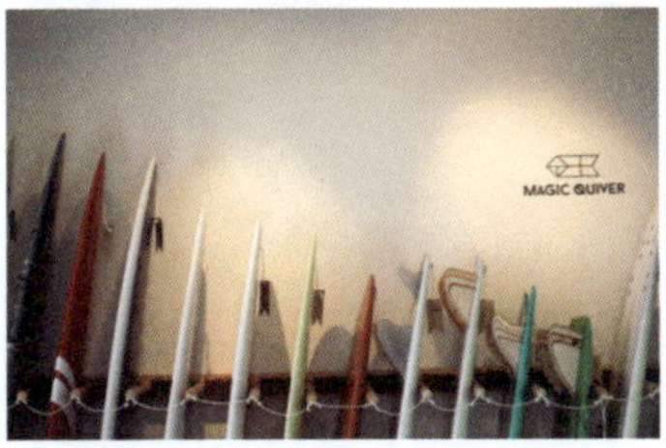

Located in the heart of the old village, **Magic Quiver**'s (**17**) a surf shop with a twist, curating hand-shaped boards, offering surf literature, fins and wetsuits, clothes and accessories from selected brands, and specials brews of coffee and beers.

**a.** Rua Mendes Leal, 24 A, 2655-305 Ericeira
**t.** 2 61 867 798
**w.** magicquiver.com

Get your stack of granola, health bars, and other organic goodies at **Be U** (**18**) market.

**a.** Rua Manuel Ortigão Burnay 1, 2655-304 Ericeira
**t.** 2 61 861 987/9 18 585 501

Need some washing done? At self-service launderette **Lavandaria do Norte** (**19**) they like to minimise the environmental impact of cleaning products, so you can use their ecological and biodegradable products.

**a.** Avenida São Sebastião, Lote 6A, Loja, 2655-210 Ericeira
**w.** lavandariadonorte.com

## SLEEP

◆

Okay, it's far from the cheapest accommodation in our guide, but it is a treat. As in; a treat for you, staying at Charm Hotel **Areias do Seixo (20)**. A place done with muito amor and sophistication, and in harmony with the surrounding landscape of sea, dunes and pine trees. The rooms are uniquely decorated, aiming to create a different sensation in each. And, yes, of course there's a spa and a fine restaurant, all in that same beautifully styled décor. Open all year. •€€€€•

**a.** Praceta do Atlantico, Mexilhoeira, Povoa de Penafirme, 2560-046 A-Dos-Cunhado
**t.** 2 61 936 340
**e.** info@areiasdoseixo.com
**w.** areiasdoseixo.com

**Santa Beach House (21)** is located near the beaches of Santa Cruz. If you're wondering how the hostel managed to collect all the vintage furniture, it was already there! Most of the family's furniture that was left in the old house was included in the refurbishing process, giving the Beach House its homely atmosphere. Double rooms and shared rooms, small pool and sunny garden, friendly and welcoming staff. •€• •€€•

**a.** Rua Pedro Álvares Cabral, Lote 11, 2560-503 Santa Cruz
**t.** 9 17 258 479
**w.** hostelsantacruzportugal.com

Surf camp and school **Surf2Smile (22)** applies Feng Shui design to create the ultimate positive and happy vibe for their guests. Great! As if you weren't already over the moon to be on a holiday, surfing and chilling out. The camp's got double and shared rooms. Open all year. •€• •€€•

**a.** Rua do Juncal, Vivenda Miro, 2560-046 Santa Cruz
**t.** 9 25 428 129
**e.** aloha@surf2smile.com
**w.** surf2smile.com

One of the most stunning views you can get from a surfhouse must be from **Laneez Ericeira (23)**, set on a clifftop overlooking Ericeira's Praia do Sul and the coastline to the north and south. Add a homely atmosphere, beautiful furnishings and comfy, spacious rooms, and a pure dedication to surfing. It must be the synergy between the creators of Laneez Ericeira surfhouse that gives it such an intense surf vibe - Portuguese Miguel Ruivo and Jersey's Mark Durbano - both avid, legendary and longtime surfers who appear to be fearless when it comes to big waves. Double, twin and dorm rooms, surf lessons, guiding and rental available. Open all year. •€€•

**a.** Rua Doutor Eduardo Burnay 5, 2655-368 Ericeira
**t.** 9 68 555 744
**e.** laneezericeira@gmail.com
**w.** laneezericeira.com

**Lovely Bay Lodge (24)**, from the owners of coffee shop KFÉ, is a spacious apartment with 4 bedrooms (sleeps 4 to 10 persons), decorated in traditional style with a twist, located in the heart of the old centre. Available all year. •€€•

**a.** Rua Fonte do Cabo nr 44 1° Andar, 2655-285 Ericeira
**t.** 2 61 861 237
**w.** lovely-bay.com

**Chill in Ericeira (25)** is run by former national surf champ and longtime Ericeira local, Joana Rocha. Choose from 11 brightly coloured double, twin or dorm rooms, filled with genuinely creative details. Located within walking distance of beaches and the old centre. Open all year. •€• •€€•

**a.** Rua Manuel Pereira Santa Rosa 8, 2655-293 Ericeira
**t.** 9 18 439 462 / 9 16 580 881
**w.** chillinericeira.pt

**Camping Ericeira** (**26**) is a large green site offering pitches, wooden bungalows, mobile homes and tent-shaped huts for rent. Open all year. •€• •€€•

**a.** Estrada Nacional 247, Km 49,4, 2655-319 Ericeira
**t.** 2 61 862 706 / 2 61 862 513
**w.** ericeiracamping.com

**Blue Buddha Hostel**, **Blue Buddha Lone Surfer Hostel** and **Blue Buddha Beach House** (**27**) are located near each other on the north side of the old town, overlooking the ocean. Guests from Blue Buddha Hostel can use the communal kitchen, living room and balcony at the Lone Surfer Hostel. Single, double and shared rooms on offer. Open all year. •€€•

**a.** Urbanização Moinhos do Mar 1, 2655-000 Ericeira
**t.** 2 61 869 885
**e.** bluebuddhahostel@gmail.com
**w.** bluebuddhahostel.com

**Quinta dos Raposeiros** (**28**) is set on an 11-acre piece of land near São Lourenço beach, surrounded by orchards and pine trees. There are 4 self-catering apartments with ocean view, a big communal lounge area and garden, kids playground and skate park. Open all year. •€€• •€€€•

**a.** Caminho dos Raposeiros, 2640-065 Santo Isidoro
**t.** 9 67 536 267
**e.** reservas@quintaraposeiros.com
**w.** quintaraposeiros.com

**Casa Paço D'Ilhas** (**29**) is the place of Belgian-born surfer Jelle, who set up camp here in 2015, refurbishing and renovating the over 100 year old traditional house into a welcoming guesthouse, set on a hill overlooking surfbreak Ribeira D'Ilhas. 4 deluxe rooms, 2 budget rooms, and 1 cabana on offer, and a large garden with space to withdraw and have a moment for yourself, a swimming pool, and in-house bar and optional surf, SUP or kite lessons and rental. Open all year. •€€•

**a.** Estrada do Zimbral, Estrada da Junceira Paço de Ilhas, 2640-825 Ericeira
**t.** 9 38 880 186
**e.** info@casapacodilhas.com
**w.** casapacodilhas.com

At surf and yoga retreat **Omassim** (**30**) you can either book a double, single or shared room and make occasional use of the massages, yoga and surf lessons on offer, or book a full retreat package to include either surf, yoga or both. All meals are vegetarian. Open all year. •€€•

**a.** Rua das Taipas, 2640-068 Palhais - Santo Isidoro
**t.** 9 62 826 842
**e.** omassim@gmail.com
**w.** omassim.com

Quinta **EcoNature Dagaio** (**31**) has self-catering apartments, done up in an unmatched style and decorated with the owner's handmade furniture and sculptures. Communal garden and swimming pool. The old town and beaches are just minutes away from the property. Open all year. •€€•

**a.** Rua dos Eucaliptos, Outeirinho, 2655-440 Ericeira
**t.** 9 39 251 244
**e.** dodagaio@gmail.com

**Campervans** can make use of the facilities at **Area Santa Susana** (**32**).

**a.** Estrada Á-dos-Serrados, 2705-841 Santa Susana (on the N247 road between Ericeira and Sintra/Lisbon)

Photo: Gijs Hardeman, Next Destination

# SURF

The beachbreaks of **Santa Cruz (I)**, between Peniche and Ericeira, will give you plenty room to roam without the crowds. Work best with small n to sw swell, but easily blown out. All levels. Easy parking/bar/restaurant.

Pointbreak **Coxos (II)** is for the experienced only. A beautiful site, seen from the cliffs overlooking the break, with a high level of surfing. Long, but fast, powerful and hollow waves that are produced from the depths offshore. Best with a big clean nw swell. Park and hike a bit/no facilities.

**Ribeira d'Ilhas (III)** usually looks deceptively easy to surf, but does take some skill, being a reefbreak, popular spot with small take-off points. Very consistent, working with small to medium nw swell on all tides (reef exposed at low). Beware of the current, watch carefully how other surfers enter and exit. Intermediate to advanced level. (Great hiking options up the cliffs to the north from the parking area.) Easy parking/toilet/shower/restaurant.

**Praia do Norte (IV)**, right in the old centre, is a consistent, partly sand-covered reef. Usually has a few sections, so different levels can surf at the same time. Works best with a medium n to sw swell on all tides except low. All levels. Parking outside the city's centre and walk/surf school/surf shop/bars/restaurant.

Rivermouth spot **Foz do Lizandro (V)** is a nice beach that can have real fun surf, depending on the sandbank conditions, and is usually not that crowded. Works best with small sw swell, from low to mid tide. All levels. Easy parking/surf school/bars/restaurant.

# SCHOOL RENTAL REPAIR

With such a concentration of world class waves, it makes sense that there are plentiful surf schools in Ericeira; almost every accommodation is connected with one, or can recommend one.

**3S Surf Camp** (**33**) is located near the beach of Santa Cruz. They take you to the point and beachbreaks between Peniche and Ericeira to suit your level.

**a.** Avenida do Atlântico, Praia da Fisica, 2560-451 Santa Cruz
**t.** 9 65 385 945
**w.** 3ssurfcompany.com

**Activity Surf Center** (**34**) obviously offers surf lessons, but also some other activities like SUP tours, mountain biking, karting and wine tastings.

**a.** Rua de Santo António 3A, 2655-340 Ericeira
**t.** 9 14 301 500

**Insane Surfboards** (**35**) shapes and repairs.

**a.** Rua Alto da Boa Vista 16 4D, 2655-346 Ericeira (behind the bus terminal)
**t.** 9 18 820 732

**Board Culture Surfboards** (**36**) is a shop, shaping bay and repair centre. Situated next to the São Sebastião shopping centre.

**a.** Urbanizacão Fórum São Sebastião, 2675-270 Ericeira
**t.** 2 61 862 000
**w.** boardculturesurfboards.com

Longtime shaper, Nico, from **Wavegliders** (**37**) makes quite an impression when you first meet him; a tall, outspoken man with big hands that create up to 300 boards a year. No use of a shaping machine, mainly resin-tinted, handcrafted and beautiful boards. But when he starts explaining about his designing, blanks, sanding papers, glassing, ideas and influences, surfing and happy clients, it's like you're talking to a very, very enthusiastic little boy. He started his shaping career as far back as 1988, his references and influences being Greg Noll, Nat Young and the old skool fifties surfing style. "I've always had a passion for the old: old motorcycles, old cars, and old boards." He says, "Old things are made to last. My boards are made like this, influenced by the past, working in the present, taking it to the future." After shaping in production for others for 9 years, he wanted to do his own work, at his own pace. "I do what I love to do, it's a good life and I can go surfing. If expanding my business means selling my soul, it's not for me." You can check out what's in stock or order a custom-made board.

**a.** Rua Vale Carreira 7, N-116, behind garage Anselmo de Castro, 2640-401 Achada/Ericeira
**t.** 9 34 051 150
**w.** wavegliders.blogspot.pt

Photo: Melchior van Nigtevecht

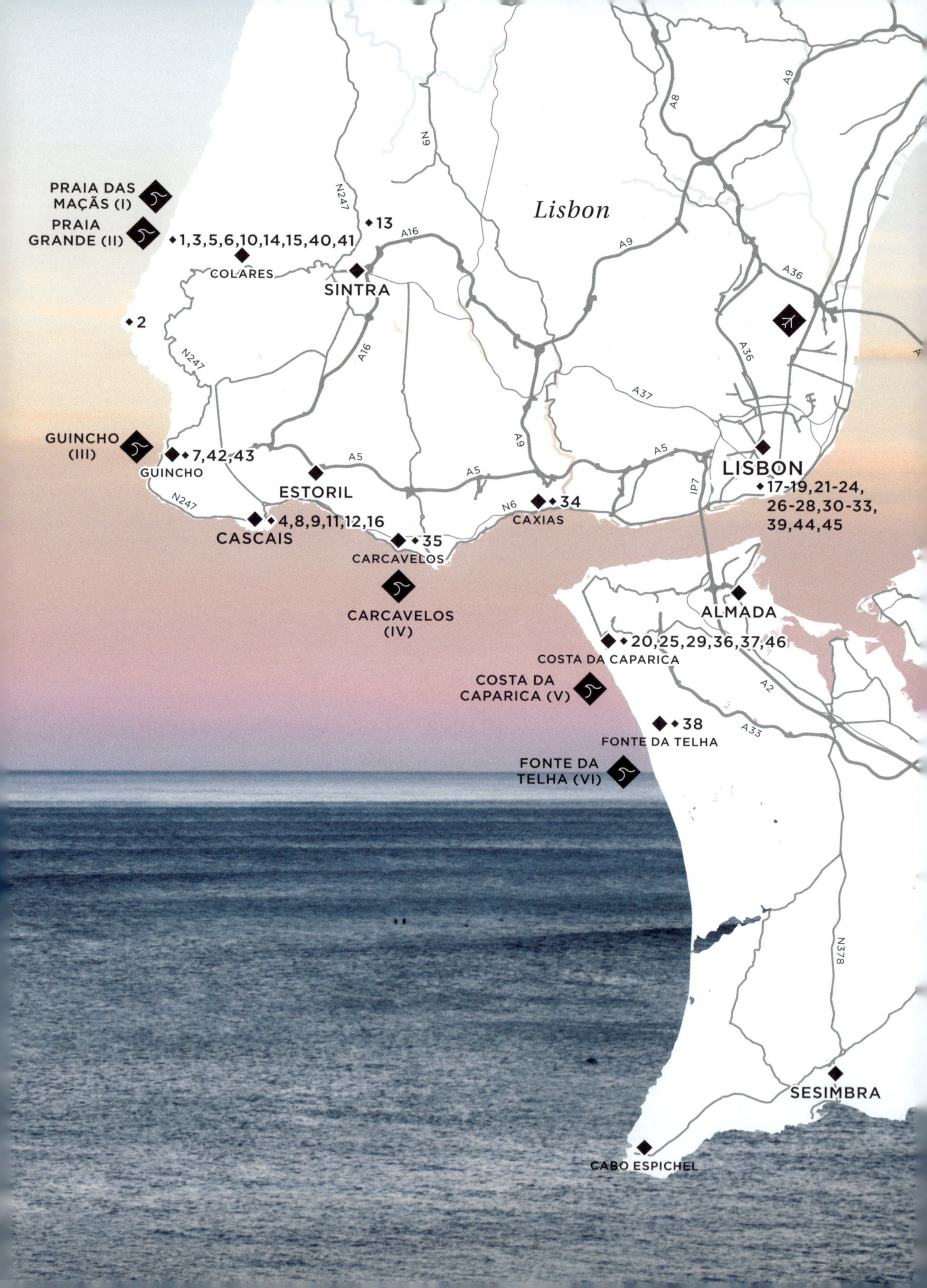
Lisbon
PRAIA DAS MAÇÃS (I)
PRAIA GRANDE (II)
1,3,5,6,10,14,15,40,41
COLARES
13
SINTRA
2
GUINCHO (III)
7,42,43
GUINCHO
ESTORIL
CASCAIS
4,8,9,11,12,16
35
CARCAVELOS
CARCAVELOS (IV)
34
CAXIAS
LISBON
17-19,21-24, 26-28,30-33, 39,44,45
ALMADA
20,25,29,36,37,46
COSTA DA CAPARICA
COSTA DA CAPARICA (V)
38
FONTE DA TELHA
FONTE DA TELHA (VI)
SESIMBRA
CABO ESPICHEL
N247
N9
A16
A9
A8
A36
A37
A5
N6
IP7
A2
A33
N378

# LISBON AREA

With many beaches and nature parks close by, the city of Lisbon makes an excellent base for a surfing and seaside expedition, offering the best of both worlds. Even for the most outdoorsy person with a dislike for cities, Lisbon and its neighbouring villages and sites are a delight. Structured on a very hilly landscape (7 hills to be precise) you'll get all the workouts you need, and just a short drive north or south takes you to green and airy landscape. It's said that Portugal's surfing history started at the popular beach of Carcavelos, but there's a Surf Museum to check and find out!

## TRAVEL INFO

Within the city you really don't need a car, public transport is perfectly arranged, with trains, trams and metro systems that don't need a rocket scientist to figure them out. For most you can buy day tickets.

### BY AIR

Lisbon Airport is 6 km from the city's centre, which is easily accessed by public transport, with both metro and bus services. There are 2 terminals: Terminal 1 handles arrivals and international departures, Terminal 2 handles low-cost airline departures and is connected with Terminal 1 via free shuttle buses.

Bus and metro connections to the city are from Terminal 1.

**a.** Alameda das Comunidades Portuguesas, 1700-111 Lisbon
**w.** ana.pt

### BY TRAIN

There are local trains within the city, called 'urbanos': regional (R) and inter-regional (IR), which are used for shorter distances - they're cheap and there's no need to make reservations. They do make a lot of stops. The intercity trains (IC) connect all Portugal's major cities.

# SURFER-TRAVELLER TYPE LISBON AREA

*You dig the city life, but like an escape route that takes you outdoors within the hour. You get a kick out of downhilling and have enough energy to clamber back uphill again. You're into old trams, graffiti and castles, cry tears of longing for something you didn't know you longed for when hear a good Fado song, and you love to enjoy a pastel de nata and galão on a sunny terrace overlooking the Tejo river, then go for a surf in the afternoon and be back in town before happy hour.*

# IN AND AROUND SINTRA

Just north of Lisbon is this whole area that's surprisingly green and hilly, with lovely ancient villages and some fine beaches and bays. Strolling through Sintra - which is what you should do to take it all-in - you'll find yourself in a mixture of a Disney-like fairytale and ancient times. Steep cobbled streets, castles, gardens, ancient manors; the village and its surroundings are so well preserved, it's like a time machine just dropped you into some bygone era. Depending on your taste, you can visit ornately decorated palácios (Nacional de Peña and Monserrate), a mysterious site (Quinta da Regaleira - taking a guided tour's recommended), or a sober, forested monastery (Convento dos Capuchos). There are regular trains running between Sintra and Lisbon, a 40 minute ride. And from Sintra there are buses going to most sites, like the Parque e Palácio da Peña.

**Tourist office** at Avenida da Republica 23.

## TO DO

◆

From Sintra it's just a few km up towards the sweet village of **Colares** (**1**). From here take the winding road through the green hills towards Guincho - from this road you have several options to drive up to **Parque Convento dos Capuchos**, where you'll find many hiking and downhill mountain bike paths. Or watch a magical sunset. You'll pass the quaint little village of **Penedo**, where famous and fortuned Portuguese hide amongst the villagers in exquisite villas overlooking the hills and ocean. You can also make a little detour to the utmost western point of the European continent, **Cabo da Roca** (**2**).

Nothing better than getting a good **massage** (**3**) after days of frothing in the water, surfing your arms off. Five-time female Dutch surf champ and almost non-stop surf traveller and surf photographer, Renate Moerman, resides in the Cascais/Sintra area and specialises in massage therapy for surfers. Get your muscles relaxed to the core by dropping her a line to either book a visit, or book her and her massage table to come to your accommodation. She's also available for yoga therapy (and surf photographer, whoop whoop, 3-in-1!).

**t.** 9 13 862 418
**e.** comonovo.massagens@gmail.com

Masha Kovacs from **Yoga Masha** (**4**) specialises in yoga and strength programs; by first working on body strength and awareness, then transferring that condition into mental, emotional and spiritual strength. Classes in her studio and on Praia Grande. Check her website or give her a call for the exact times. All levels and drop-ins welcome.

**a.** Rua José Florindo 622, 2750-642 Cascais
t. 9 26 735 786
**w.** yogamasha.com

## EAT/DRINK/HANGOUT

◆

We simply love this place: restaurant **Refúgio Do Ciclista** (**5**), owned by a local former cycling pro (hence the many posters and shirts on their wall). The front side is a very typical small bar, behind is a big canteen-like room where you can order the menu of the day, with a choice of seafood or meat. Very friendly local place with excellent food. Open all year. •€•

**a.** Largo do Chafariz 10,
2705-262 Penedo
**t.** 2 19 280 088

**Bar do Fundo** (**6**), perfectly located at the end of Praia Grande, stands out in style and décor from the usual beach bar, but more importantly, serves some fine meals to match the outstanding views. Friendly staff, open all year for lunch, sunset drinks and dinner. •€€•

**a.** Avenida Alfredo Coelho, Praia Grande,
2705-329 Sintra
**t.** 2 19 282 092

Beach bar **Duna Da Cresmina** (**7**) serves salads, crêpes and juices with a panoramic view over the beaches of Guincho. Open all year. •€€•

**a.** Rua da Areia, Cresmina,
2750-089 Guincho-Cascais
**w.** dunadacresmina.com

**Dona Flor Café & Bistrô** (**8**) has a cosy and colourful lunchroom with many vegetarian and vegan options on the menu. Open all year. •€• •€€•

**a.** Rua do Poço Novo 180,
2750-642 Cascais
**t.** 9 32 962 728

Restaurant **Local**'s (**9**) tagline is 'Your Healthy Kitchen'. And rightly so; serving fresh, biological and vegetarian goodies with a very nice ambience. Open all year, situated in the Mercado da Vila de Cascais (they also have a restaurant in Lisbon in Palácio Chiado). •€€•

**a.** Rua Padre Moisés da Silva,
Loja 13, 2754-529 Cascais
**t.** 9 11 114 190
**w.** localkitchen.pt

## SHOP

◆

The **Coolares Market** (**10**) is a 'Hippie Chick Garage Sale', held every last weekend of the month, using special seasonal themes, set in and around a historic winery. Find the best in small and local design, food, vintage clothes and furniture, workshops, massages

and fun events. Located at the Quinta de Cima do Pé da Serra, along the N247, in Colares.

Find some treasures at **Happy Sardine** (**11**); gifts, souvenirs, small furniture and home décor, cards. Everything is handcrafted, recycled or painted with love, by various artists. And you can get your treasures fully personalised if you so wish!

**a.** Travessa dos Navegantes 12A,
2750-443 Cascais
**t.** 9 66 683 762
**w.** happysardine.eu

**House of Wonders** (**12**) is a concept store where art, workshops, live music and vegetarian food all blend into 4 floors filled with good stuff, and a terrace on the roof to top it off. Open all year.

**a.** Largo da Misericórdia 53,
2750-642 Cascais
**t.** 9 11 702 428
**w.** house-of-wonders.eu

## SLEEP

◆

**Odrinhas Parque (13)** is a small site for campers, with some basic facilities, a bar and a lovely view. ◆€◆

**a.** Rua do Castanhal, 2705-705 Sintra
**t.** 2 19 611 435

**Star Pine Lodge (14)** is the second venture of the owners of The Lodge (w. thelodge.pt), a stylish guesthouse that's quite popular already, so doesn't need our recommendation – although we do recommend it... The Star Pine Lodge is set in a quiet area, beautifully decorated and have a swimming pool, garden and covered yoga space with sea view on offer. They can arrange several activities: surfing, yoga, climbing, and biking. ◆€€◆

**a.** Estrada do Rodízio 145, Vivenda Stella Matutina, Praia Grande, 2705-335 Colares
**t.** 9 60 388 338
**w.** starpinelodge.com

Perfectly located between Almoçageme and Praia das Maças - between ocean and mountains – you'll find the **SaltyWay House (15)**. Lovers of surfing, yoga and climbing will love it, the camp offers climbing courses, routes for advanced climbers, and yoga, surf and climbing combinations. 3 rooms can accommodate up to 12 guests. ◆€◆ ◆€€◆

**a.** Estrada do Rodízio 76, 2705-340 Colares
**t.** 9 11 946 086
**e.** info@saltywaytravel.com
**w.** saltywaytravel.com

Sleeping in a tent, on a five-star hotel mattress, falling asleep to the sound of crickets and frogs, and waking up to the chatter of birds, at glamping camping **Cascais Oasis (16)**. Set on the terraces of an ancient vineyard, there are 5 individually decorated safari tents and a small wooden chalet to rent, a playground and spring water pool and lots of nature surrounding the site. ◆€€◆ ◆€€€◆

**a.** Terceira Circular, 2755-009 Cascais
**t.** 9 61 111 631
**e.** cascaisoasis@gmail.com
**w.** glampingportugal.blogspot.pt

# IN AND AROUND LISBON

This is not a city where you go from one must-see to the other. It's much more refined and has many less obvious precious finds, which you'll find just walking, getting lost, wandering up and down steep lanes, crossing neighbourhoods, contemplating along the shores of the river Tejo. Definitely check out Cais do Sodré and its waterfront boulevard. The once shady neighbourhood, where drunken sailors used to roam the brothels and bars, is now a lively and creative area. Of course, the city's filled with stylish shops, bars, restaurants and places to stay, too many for us to mention here, so we just give you some of our hand-picked favourites. Lisbon is, first and foremost, a seaside town, with a big surfing community and many breaks to choose from. Just a little north and south you'll find dozens of peaks waiting for you.

**Tourist office** at Praça do Comércio.
'**Turismo**' in Palácio Foz Building on Praça dos Restauradores.

## TO DO

With or without a guided tour, there's no escaping the **street art and graffiti** (**17**) in Lisbon. Not just tags; stories on the walls, telling tales of the city's history, and more often than not, about its current state. When jobs were scarce, wages low and rents high, a lot of Lisbon's buildings and apartments were abandoned and used by artists as a canvas to express their vision, or just their art. Sometimes funny, sometimes provoking, and sometimes inspirational but almost always artfully done. There's more to it than meets the eye, and once you take some time studying and admiring them, Lisbon's stories will speak from its walls. Be quick though, one piece can be painted over by another, or gone the next day. There are several small operators offering guided tours, most of them work with Facebook pages - pick one that appeals to you from those that take only small groups.

Not just your ordinary tour operator, but offering extraordinary tours, the crew from **We Hate Tourism Tours** (**18**) - splendid name! They want you to explore and see the city in a different manner, to love the streets of Lisbon like the locals do on their city tour, to experience a cultural exchange on their food trip, and much more.

**a.** Rua da Silva 27, 1200-201 Lisbon
**t.** 9 13 776 598
**w.** wehatetourismtours.com

**Bike along the river Tejo** (**19**), a 16,5 km easy route along a shared bike-pedestrian path, enjoying the views and passing different parts of Lisbon. Several companies rent out bikes; along the river you'll find Bélem Bikes (in Bélem, at the waterfront, near the Electricity Museum, **w.** belembike.com) and Bike Iberia (at the waterfront in Cais do Sodré, **w.** bikeiberia.com).

Check out the annual **Longboard Festival (20)** powered by Lufi, usually held mid June at the beach of Costa da Caparica. National, international and junior longboarders (m/f) gather for contests like Noserider, Expression Session and Legends.

Lisbon's flea market, **Feira da Ladra (21)** ('thieves fair'), held every Tuesday and Saturday, is the oldest market in Lisbon. Find peculiar items, obscure books, a gardening tool you can't live without... Haggling is allowed. The market spans several streets in the Alfama district.

**a.** Campo de Santa Clara, 100-472 Lisbon

## SHOP

◆

The huge **Mercado da Ribeira (22)**, right next to the Cais do Sodré station, is your place to find daily fresh veggies, fruits, fish and locally produced food goodies.

**LX Factory (23)** is not just one shop, it's a creative hotspot set in an industrial environment, with room for fashion, art, design, music, food, drinks and photography. Go see, shop, eat, drink, read and admire.

**a.** Rua Rodrigues de Faria 103, 1300 Lisbon
**w.** lxfactory.com

Get an old-school haircut at **Figaros (24)**, a men's only barber shop which specialises in classic haircuts from 1920s to 1950s and hot towel straight razor shaves. Not in need of a shave? Go get the cool t-shirts.

**a.** Rua do Alecrim 39, Lisbon
**t.** 2 13 470 199
**w.** figaroslisboa.com

In the same building as the Lufi Surf Shop, in Costa da Caparica, sits the **Surf Museum (25)**. Its mission is to preserve and document Portugal's surf history. A very interesting go-to for every curious surfer!

**a.** Avenida General Humberto Delgado 47 Loja I, 2825-337 Costa Da Caparica
**w.** ahms.pt

## EAT/DRINK/HANGOUT

◆

Excellent vegetarian and organic food is served at **The Green Room** (Rua do Cais do Sodré 16) and restaurant **Quinoa** (Rua do Alecrim 54), both situated in the **Cais do Sodré (26)** quarter, near the river and station.

**Pensão Amor (27)**, located in a former brothel in the Cais do Sodré quarter, near the river and metro station, is a real treasure. Announcements of Burlesque shows, antique porn artefacts and vintage furniture make up the décor, live music, and pole dance workshops sums up just half of this lively bar and hangout. Open from 12:00 hrs till late.

**a.** Rua do Alecrim 19, 1200-292 Lisbon

Even though they are mentioned in every guide, site and blog, we can't risk you missing **Fabrica dos Pastéis de Belém (28)**, so here you go. It's always crazy crowded, for a very good reason, they serve the most delicious pastéis de nata you can get your hands on. Go early and you'll be fine, finding a spot inside one of their many rooms, or taking just a pastel to go. Open from 08:00 hrs.

**a.** Rua de Belém 84-92, 1300-085 Lisbon

Pirates, sailors and mermaids, you're going to love **AHOY Coffee & Bar (29)**. Enjoy healthy breakfasts, lunch or a coffee in the daytime, or drinks in the afternoon. Natural juices and gin, home cooking and good vibes. Open from 08:00 hrs.

**a.** Avenida General Humberto Delgado 27 B, 2825-280 Costa Da Caparica
**t.** 9 10 241 298/9 33 881 058

## SLEEP

◆

**Surf Around Portugal (30)** is a young and passionate local company that aims to share the surf potential of Portuguese shores; not only the continent, but also Madeira and the Açores. They organise a ready or custom-made surf trip, where a specialist guide takes you to the places suiting your budget, ability and wishes. Just like I Love the Seaside, they like to make all the connections between the local businesses and the traveller. Being longtime surfers and travellers themselves, they've created a big network throughout the country, so you can count on them to take you to the right places and people - not only surfing-wise, you'll also get your shot of culture and cuisine.

**t.** 9 63 889 279 / 9 12 842 220 / 9 13 891 232
**e.** info@surfaroundportugal.com
**w.** surfaroundportugal.com

**Campervans** can park in the middle of town, right at the river Tejo at **parking Belem (31)**. Situated next to the ferry station Porto Brandao, near the train station Belém that takes you to the centre, a view of the famous 25 de Abril bridge and close to the Statue of Explorers.

**a.** Avenida Brasília, 1300-598 Lisboa

**Lisbon Poets Hostel (32)** is located close to Bairro Alto, and in the middle of the arts district, surrounded by museums, street art, small galleries and live music venues, and lots of cafés, like A Brasileira, right underneath the hostel. (It's one of the most famous Lisbon cafés.) There's a choice of private rooms, studios and dorms. Open all year. •€€•

**a.** Rua Nova da Trindade 2 - 5th floor, 1200-302 Lisbon
**t.** 2 13 461 241
**e.** lisbonpoetshostel@gmail.com
**w.** lisbonpoetshostel.com

**Alfama Patio Hostel (33)** is one of the 3 pretty funky hostels from Destination Hostel. It's located in the Alfama district, the oldest part of Lisbon. They have private rooms, mixed dorm rooms and girls-only dorm rooms. Nicely decorated, and the communal terrace has a view over the city and the river Tejo. Open all year. •€€•

**a.** Escolas Gerais 3, Patio dos Quintalinhos 1, 1100-213 Lisbon
**t.** 2 18 883 127
**w.** alfamapatio.com

**Lisbon Surf House (34)** is set in a 19th century house, a typical summerhouse from the old days. It's a comfortable, boutique-style guesthouse with ocean view, surf lessons and rental (and repair), yoga, massage and lots of other activities on offer in and around Lisbon. Private and shared rooms to choose from. Open all year. •€€• •€€€•

**a.** Rua Direita de Caxias 38, 2760-042 Caxias
**t.** 9 17 326 613
**e.** info@surflisbon.com
**w.** surflisbon.com

**Carcavelos Surf House (35)** has private and shared rooms and a cosy studio, situated within walking distance from the surfbreaks at Carcavelos beach. Guests can enjoy the outdoor pool, the hammocks in the garden, and daily info on where to surf. Rental and repair of boards and wetsuits.
•€€• •€€€•

**a.** Rua Almirante Matos Moreira 72, 2775-609 Carcavelos
**t.** 9 26 873 529
**w.** carcavelossurfhouse.com

It's girls only at **Wave Sisters (36)**. The camp's located conveniently near the beach of Costa Caparica. It's self-catering accommodation, though most meals are cooked together or enjoyed in the village. You can either learn or improve your surfing in the camp, (8 wavesisters max in shared rooms, or double rooms available) or join the Surfari, surfing with other girls at different spots. Communal kitchen, garden and living room, and yoga. Open from March to October. •€€•

**w.** wavesisters.com

At **Old School Surfcamp (37)** you'll have a pretty unique stay. Owner Filipe set his guesthouse in the old home of his grandparents. Filipe is a local surfer,

surf coach and fisherman, how's that for a combination in a host! The house is within walking distance from the endless beach of Costa da Caparica, and has been in his family since 1925.

The cosy little house has 3 bedrooms, which can be used as double or shared rooms, with a communal kitchen and garden. Filipe prepares Portuguese dishes and of course, catches fresh seafood for that. You can use bicycles and skates, and make use of Filipe's knowledge of the area, history, food and culture. Open all year. •€•

**t.** 9 62 561 247
**e.** oldschoolsurfcamp@gmail.com

**Sul** (**38**) hostel and surf school, right at the beach of Fonte da Telha, has double and shared rooms. They use their central location, close to vineyards, Cascais and other parts in Lisbon, to offer guided tours to some of the most beautiful places. •€• •€€•

**a.** Descida da Fonte da Telha 209, 2825-494 Almada
**t.** 9 19 123 770
**e.** sulsurfhostel@gmail.com
**w.** sulsurfhostel.com

Back to the good ol' days, but with all modern amenities: with the vintage VW campervans from **SurfinPortugal** (**39**) you can crisscross your way along the beaches and surf breaks between Nazaré and Sagres. You can choose your van, each with their own travelling past and story, and then add any extras you need to suit your trip.

**e.** info@surfinportugal.pt
**w.** surfinportugal.pt

Photo: Surf Around Portugal

# SURF

◆

**Praia Grande (II)**, backed by impressive cliffs, is a beachbreak with several peaks to choose from. Works with small to medium nw-sw swells, best from low to mid tide. All levels, but heavy shorebreak. At the north end of the beach is a saltwater swimming pool, safe to go with kids if the shorebreak's dumping into the sand.

**Praia das Maçãs (I)**, just to the north, is a tiny bay, sand and rock bottom, best at low tide with a small nw-sw swell. All levels. There's a quaint electric tram running between Sintra and Praia das Maçãs. Parking can be a hassle in summer, but easy off season/toilet/shower/surf school/surf shop/restaurant.

**Guincho (III)** is known best as a windsurf spot. A beautiful stretch of beach with a backdrop of green hills, cliffs and dunes. Picks up loads of swell and can handle some wind, but usually in the afternoon it's windsurf heaven and surf hell, so surf early. Powerful waves that work well with small to medium nw to sw swell, at all tides, strong current. Intermediate and advanced level. Easy parking/surf school/surf shop/toilet/shower/bar/restaurant.

**Carcavelos (IV)** is a long sandy beach that's very popular with the local Lisbon crew. Although sandbanks shift and there are several peaks, you'll never surf alone. Works best with medium nw to sw swell, at all tides. All levels. Parking can be as crowded as the peaks but there's good public transport to the beach/surf school/toilet/shower/bar/restaurant.

Heading south, crossing the water, **Costa da Caparica (V)** offers a never-ending stretch of beach, getting less crowded, less urbanised, and cleaner water as you continue further south.

# SCHOOL RENTAL REPAIR

Some small breakwaters have formed good sandbars and every section will have it's own crew on it. Works with small to medium w-sw swell, and a big nw swell. All levels. Paid parking/ toilets/surf school/surf shop/bar/restaurant.

**Fonte da Telha (VI)** is less organised, less urbanised and less crowded than Caparica, but still a popular spot. Peaks spread out and the beach can produce anything from fun surf to epic waves. Best with small to medium nw to sw swell from low to mid tide, although can work with all tides. All levels. Easy parking/toilets/bars/restaurant.

**Surf At Surf School and Camp (40)** offers private or group surf and bodyboard lessons, and surf camps from 4 to 7 days. Operating from Praia das Macãs and Praia Grande.

**a.** Praia das Maçãs (at Restaurante Neptuno)
**t.** 9 17 854 579/9 66 421 811
**w.** surfatsurfschool.com

**Adraga Surf School and Camp (41)**: individual and group lessons from experienced coaches. Operating from the beautiful bay of Adraga, between Praia Grande and Cabo da Roca.

**a.** Praia de Adraga (near Colares)
**t.** 9 13 612 692
**w.** adragasurfcamp.net

Choose between personal surf coaching, surf and stay, or just bed and breakfast at **Guincho Surf House (42)**.

**a.** Avenida Nossa Senhora da Assunção 1111, 2755-140 Guincho
**t.** 9 14 994 659
**w.** guinchosurfhouse.com

**Moana Surf School (43)** has daily surf and SUP lessons, and other outdoor activities like climbing, mountain-biking, sightseeing tours and fishing trips. They're located at their restaurant, Bar do Guincho, at the beach.

**a.** Praia do Guincho
**t.** 9 64 449 436
**w.** moanasurfschool.com

**Lisbon Crooks** (**44**) is a Lisbon-based surfboard company, delivering quality hand-shaped surfboards and, they add; 'happiness'. If you're interested in one of their boards, drop them a line, feel welcome to visit them, or better yet: have dinner with them or a drink – as long as it's your treat. They're a funny and friendly lot, far from boasting how great they are, they simply state that the boards are a result of love, honesty, experience and friendship. In short, what they do is 'make, sell, rent and destroy surfboards'.

**a.** Rua da Silva 27, Armazém Geral
**t.** 9 13 776 598
**w.** lisboncrooksandsurfers.com

Keep a keen eye on the crew of **Blood Brothers** (**45**). Not only producing some fine handmade surfboards, bikes, Frisbees and skateboards, but adding new projects regularly, using their knowledge as shapers, designers and marine biologists to teach younger generations how to preserve the ocean, while learning the art of a handcrafted surfboard, using biodegradable materials.

**t.** 9 18 847 701
**w.** bloodbrothers.pt

**Lufi Surf School and Shop** (**46**) offers all level surf lessons at Caparica beach and surf trips throughout Portugal. The shop has a big range of Lufi longboards, fish, single fins and all surf essentials. It also serves as a test centre for their boards.

**a.** Avenida General Humberto Delgado n.° 47 Loja I, 2825-337 Costa Da Caparica
**t.** 9 25 892 363
**w.** lufisurfschool.com

Photo: Lisbon Crooks

ROXY

# 7. LOWER BACK RELIEVE: DWI PAVANAMUKTASANA

*Knees to Chest Pose*

***There are many causes for lower back issues.***

*Incorrect posture in day-to-day life and while surfing can both present these issues, as there is often a tendency to over arch the lower back, or to do the opposite and slouch - thus not creating enough length in the lower back. Whichever you do, the Knees to Chest Pose is a great relieve for the lower back as it lengthens the back extensor muscles evenly, on both sides of the torso, and decreases compression of the lower back. By moving the buttocks away from the waist you lengthen the lower back.*

***Benefits:***

*Opens the iliopsoas muscles (hip flexors and lower back stabilisers) and stretches the lower back.*

***How:***

*Lie on your back and bring both knees in to your chest. Hold on to the top of the knees. Keep the back of your head on the floor, with your chin slightly tucked in towards your chest, so that the back of your neck lengthens. Now while holding onto the top of your knees, slowly start moving the knees and upper legs away from your trunk, until your legs are at about a 90 degree angle to your trunk and your sacrum reaches the floor. Your legs should push strongly into your hands, while your hands pull your legs. Move your buttocks away from your waist to create the extra length for your lower back.*

SETÚBAL
CABO ESPICHEL
1
COMPORTA
IC1
A2
COMPORTA
MELIDES
SANTO ANDRÉ
(I)
GRÂNDOLA
A2
A26
Alentejo
2
SANTIAGO DO CACÉM
SINES
N120
SÃO TORPES
(II)
5
N120-1
PRAIA GRANDE
(III)
3,4,6-8,29
PORTO COVO
ILHA DO PESSEGUEIRO
(IV)
N262
IC1
A2
9
CERCAL
N390
MALHÃO
(V)
MILFONTES
(VI)
10,12-23,30,31
VILA NOVA DE MILFONTES
N263
ALMOGRAVE
(VII)
24,25
N120
N393
26
ODEMIRA
ZAMBUJEIRA
DO MAR (VIII)
11
ZAMBUJEIRA DO MAR
27,28
SÃO TEOTÓNIO
IC1
ODECEIXE
A2
ALJEZUR
IC1

# ALENTEJO

◆

O Alentejo! Literally 'beyond Tagus' (beyond Tejo – the river), where only about 5% of the country's population live, although the region makes up almost 30% of the country's land. Got to love a place with lots of empty space. The light seems brighter than elsewhere, especially reflecting the rice fields in the northern areas. Well known for its cork production: cork-oak trees, 'sobreiros', stripped bare of bark (by hand-axe, no machine as good as man for this job) stand all around, alongside olive groves, wheat fields, and our favourite, grapevines. Grapes are good. The two sections of the Alentejo are Alto and Baixo - upper and lower - we stay baixo, and on the coast, where the Atlantic wind keeps the summer from getting crazy hot, away from the inland extreme degrees.

# TRAVEL INFO

◆

Buses running in the area but we highly recommend hiring a car or bike if you don't already have one, so you can explore properly. To see how difficult it is to get around by bus check:

**w.** rodalentejo.pt

## BY AIR

◆

International flights to Lisbon Portela Airport and Faro, each about 2 hours drive away from Alentejo coast.

**w.** ana.pt

## BY BUS

◆

The Rede-Expressos connects once a day by the RX line, several places between Lagos and Sines to Lisbon, in combination with EVA.

In summer there's a daily direct service to/from Sagres via Odemira.

**w.** rede-expressos.pt

## SURFER-TRAVELLER TYPE ALENTEJO

◆

*You love the simple pleasures of life, need nothing more to look at than the ocean, soft rolling hills, and a clear starry sky that's free from light pollution, while knowing you're still safely on Portugal's wine route, and you're happiest when served with fresh fish or seafood. You enjoy the warm waft of citrus fruits, lavender, rosemary and wildflower meadows, feel relaxed with a backpack, hiking into no man's land, and know how to slow down and enjoy nature, rather than getting anxious about how comatose your surroundings and their inhabitants appear to be.*

## ALENTEJO FOOD FACT

◆

### PERCEVES (GOOSE BARNACLES)

◆

Resembling deformed mini elephant feet, these grow in clusters on 'extreme' rocks that can only be reached by experienced, knowledgeable sea-warriors. Perceves fishermen scamper down precarious crumbly cliffs, hanging onto ropes tied to, well, other ropes, with knives and string bags, and venture out to remote places where there's a high risk of being battered against the rocks by waves that appear to be protecting the harvest. A seaside delicacy, requiring a knack to eat without saltwater squirting in your eyes.

# IN AND AROUND PORTO COVO

In the Sines municipality, with a view of, but a safe distance from the industrialised buildings and belching smoke emissions of the city's power plant, lies the traditional-style once seaport now holiday village of Porto Covo. A 'covo' is a type of fishing net or pot used to catch lobsters and crabs, so if you have a taste for salty crustaceans, you're in the right place. Set amid swathes of fields and dunes, with tiny secluded coves and one good surf break.

**Tourist office** in the Market Square.

## TO DO

Take a little drive north to visit **Comporta** (**1**): the village on the heel of the Troia peninsula is home to many wealthy Portuguese people and celebrities, a fact reflected in the prices, from the supermarkets to the independent boutique shops and amazingly beautiful hotels, guesthouses and villas, some restored from traditional farmers houses. Once a popular hippy haven, with illegal parties, raves and beach huts, only a couple linger these days as it's gone a bit more upmarket. You'll feel the shift to more authentical Portugal once you take a drive on the back roads towards Carrasqueira, through unique landscape with dotted areas of singular architecture, rice fields and fishermen's cottages.

At **Santiago do Cacém** (**2**) most hikers and bikers begin their **Rota Vicentina** journey. There are 2 sections of the route through the Natural Park of Alentejo and western Algarve, which ends at Cabo de São Vicente, Algarve: the Historical Way - inland through the cork-oak forests, villages and 'vales', and the Fisherman's Way - staying along the coast for grand cliffs and low-flying stork. You can choose smaller routes within, obviously, or… save yourself the blisters, and walk around the Moorish castle instead.

Join bundles of world music enthusiasts and musicians from all continents for **FMM Sines - Festival Músicas do Mundo**, a world music festival held in Sines and Porto Covo every year, usually at end of July.

**w.** fmm.com.pt

Choose between one day of horse riding or a 7-day Atlantic Trail with **Herdade do Pessegueiro** (**3**). You'll spend some time with the horses, grooming and feeding them, as well as riding, which all makes for a more fulfilling time. Suitable for all ages, and all levels of experience.

**a.** Herdade do Pessegueiro,
7520-421 Porto Covo
**t.** 2 69 959 036 / 9 63 320 898
**w.** herdadedopessegueiro.com

## EAT/DRINK/HANGOUT

◆

Visit the **Mercado Municipal** (**4**), the daily covered market, for your fruit and veggie requirements, fresh fish, flowers and local products, at the same time you can absorb the cultural ambience of the Alentejo local hangout and observe social networking as it was done in the olden days.

**a.** Rua Conde Bandeira (next to the large parking just as you enter Porto Covo)

Restaurant and beach bar **Kalux** (**5**), named after the owner, with a beautiful view of São Torpes beach, has a large terrace, friendly staff, bright décor, and tasty food. They also run surf lessons and provide rentals here, so it gets very busy in the summer. •€• •€€•

**a.** Praia de São Torpes, 7520-089 Sines
**t.** 9 69 176 076

Bar restaurant **A Petisqueira do Primo Xico** (**6**) is a Casa de Vinhos e Petiscos (House of Wine and Snacks) with nice décor and terrace, where regular Fado (traditional Portuguese music) and other live music nights are held. •€€•

**a.** Rua Vasco da Gama 11, 7520 Porto Covo
**t.** 9 39 033 009

## SLEEP

◆

**Campervan Area Porto Covo** (**7**), next to camping and the Mercado Municipal, provides all water facilities and overnight stay for free.

**a.** Rua da Teimosa, 7520-437 Porto Covo

**Pig Dog Surf Camp**'s (**8**) set up perfectly for families and large groups, with 8 bedrooms and spacious communal areas: lounge, kitchen, dining area, outdoor sunbathing space and a BBQ area. Surrounded by nothing but nature and a seaview, you can choose from double, triple or bunk rooms (2-8 persons) and make yourselves at home. •€•

**a.** Estrada Nacional 120. N 44, 7520-049 São Torpes
**t.** 9 67 477 695
**w.** pigdogsurfcamp.com

15 km from Malhão beach, not too far from Vila Nova de Milfontes, **Herdade da Matinha Country House & Restaurant** (**9**) is a treasure. The décor and cosy, intimate atmosphere are offset by the incredible scenery and surroundings to create a tranquil haven where, in their own words, the "mixture of styles gives you a touch of lightness, life and timelessness." It does. Activities on offer include picnics, yoga, surf lessons, hiking, horse riding. Meals are infused with love, carefully prepared with fresh local ingredients, in an open kitchen so you can watch and learn (or watch and drool - in anticipation!) as your hosts cook your dinner. This really is the place to 'relax and enjoy life, as simple as life is'. •€€€•

**a.** Herdade da Matinha, 7555-231 Cercal
**t.** 9 33 739 245
**e.** reservas@herdadedamatinha.com
**w.** herdadedamatinha.com

# IN AND AROUND VILA NOVA DE MILFONTES

Milfontes (let's not splurt out the whole name every time) is a charmer of a town, with a strong sense of local community and individual character, despite the tourist trade of the summer. Positioned almost exactly halfway between Lisbon and Faro, it's not at the top of the list for easy to get to destinations, yet still proves popular for its traditional sleepy feeling, ideal location for surfing and exploring nature, and its rugged beauty. It's the kind of place that makes you want to live in a house on a cliff and write books, eating seafood and drinking wine, overlooking the town, the estuary, and the Atlantic ocean.

**Tourist office** on Rua António Mantas.

## TO DO

Child-friendly shallow and calm waters can be found (great for parents who'd like to relax without constant fear of shorebreak and surfboards) at **Farol beach (10)**, along the estuary, also a good spot for finding crabs under the rocks at low tide.

Visit the cute little fishing village, **Zambujeira do Mar (11)**, which sleeps and fishes in peace for most of the year, attracts some backpackers and campervans in the summer, suddenly comes vibrantly alive with the arrival of the **Festa do Sudoeste** at the beginning of August (**w.** meosudoeste.pt), and then promptly goes back to sleeping and fishing.

You can join Tarik and Lea from **Love Ashtanga Yoga (12)** for a traditional ashtanga yoga class every morning at Herdade Do Freixial, or for a Yoga, Surf & Sun week from May to September. Every year a gathering of yogis from all around the globe meet here, to practise together, surf, and enjoy the stretches of beach. Find out more on their website.

**t.** 9 14 094 330
**e.** loveashtangayoga@gmail.com
**w.** loveashtangayoga.com

Kayaking in the Mira river, hiking, yoga, nature and kayak combinations, tours and wine tasting are all available from **Kayak & Nature Activities (13)**.

**a.** Urbanização Arneiro do Gregorio 32D, 7645-223 Vila Nova de Milfontes
**t.** 9 67 225 122 / 9 18 189 025
**e.** kayaknatureactivities@gmail.com
**w.** kayaknatureactivities.com

**SUP Alentejo (14)** offer SUP lessons with plenty of choice: river or sea, and flat water or wave courses. Also SUP tours and equipment rental.

**a.** Praia da Franquia, 7645-281 Vila Nova de Milfontes
**t.** 9 18 133 801

## SHOP

◆

**Mercado da Freguesia (15)**, the daily covered market, can feel a bit touristy in the summer, but is big and beautiful, and the best place to get your fresh local produce. Next to the football stadium.

**a.** Rua Casa do Povo,
7645 Vila Nova de Milfontes

## EAT/DRINK/HANGOUT

◆

Typical Portuguese tasty food, friendly service and good value meals at **Pátio Alentejano (16)**. •€•

**a.** Rua do Pinhal 4,
7645-238 Vila Nova de Milfontes
**t.** 2 83 997 164

Restaurant and wine bar **Porto das Barcas (17)** is near the harbour, so of course you'll have plenty of fresh fish to choose from, overlooking the sea with perfect sunsets. •€€•

**a.** Estrada do Canal,
7645-239 Vila Nova de Milfontes
**t.** 2 83 997 160

**Tasca do Celso (18)**: in a "restaurant where people can see the kitchen", Celso spoils his customers, preparing traditional Portuguese food and indicating a good wine, one of the best qualities of the house. Celso has one of the most interesting wine cellars in the region, with wines from all over the country, particularly from Alentejo and Douro. •€€•

**a.** Rua dos Aviadores,
7645-225 Vila Nova de Milfontes
**t.** 2 83 996 753
**w.** tascadocelso.com

**Ritual Restaurante & Tapas-Bar (19)** is a cosy place, colourfully decorated with yellow and terracotta, earth tones and wood, serving varied 'world food' dishes, right in the centre of town. •€€•

**a.** Rua Barbosa Viana, 4,
7645-230 Vila Nova de Milfontes
**t.** 2 83 998 648

**Mabi (20)** is a modern-style café serving breakfast, delicious ice-creams, all kinds of coffee and pastries. Open from early till late evening. •€•

**a** Largo de Santa Maria 25A,
7645-313 Vila Nova de Milfontes
**t.** 2 83 998 677

## SLEEP

◆

**Casinhas dos Aivados (21)** is located just 1 km from Praia dos Aivados, in the small village Ribeira da Azenha, between Porto Covo and Vila Nova de Milfontes. Sleeps 4 persons per house, with 4 houses available and a large communal outdoor area filled with fruit trees and chirping birds. BBQ and outdoor dining area, safe space for children to play. •€€•

**a.** Brejos de Baixo, Ribeira da Azenha,
7645-065 Vila Nova de Milfontes
**t.** 9 67 189 963
**e.** info@casinhasdosaivados.com
**w.** casinhasdosaivados.com

**Hike & Surf Lodge (22)** was designed to give the best options for combining surf trips with outdoor activities available in the area. Their philosophy's all about connecting with nature and working alongside it, while having fun too, and you'll fit right in here if you're a lover of nature and outdoor sports who wants to stay in town. Private rooms or shared rooms to suit your budget, friendly helpful local hosts who've created a personal and welcoming atmosphere in a central location with lots on offer: surf lessons, SUP, yoga, fishing and hiking. •€• •€€•

**a.** Rua São Sebastiao 24,
7645-314 Vila Nova de Milfontes
**t.** 9 65 839 839
**e.** stay@surfmilfontes.com
**w.** surfmilfontes.com

**Camping Milfontes (23)** offers bungalows, mobile homes, modern teepee tents and pitches, less than a km from the beach, surrounded by pine forest. •€• •€€•

**a.** Estradas das Pousadas, 7645-300 Vila Nova de Milfontes
**t.** 2 83 996 104
**w.** campingmilfontes.com

The **Herdade do Amarelo Natura & Spa (24)** is a rural tourism unit synonymous with luxury and well-being, between the mountains and the sea, in the South-west Alentejo and Costa Vicentina Natural Park. Offering relaxing spa baths and spa with a unique landscape, and a fabulous view. •€€•

**a.** Estrada Nacional 532, ao km 7 Apartado 5338, 7630-440 São Luis
**t.** 9 17 587 882
**e.** geral@herdadedoamarelo.pt
**w.** herdadedoamarelo.pt

**Portugal Nature Lodge (25)**: created by a Dutch couple to be the place you dream of. Accommodation offerings are special and spacious tents: American Tipi, Mongolian Yurt, or South African Safari. All beautifully furnished and supplied with a private bathroom as well as an outside cooking area. Every tent has a terrace for you to lounge and soak up the tranquility surrounding you, and if that tires you out, you can move along to relax by the pool instead, surrounded by hammocks and lazy chairs. Dreamy... •€€•

**a.** Monte Malhadins, Apartado 2646, Troviscais, 7630-488 São Luis
**w.** portugalnaturelodge.com

**Camping São Miguel (26)**, ecological 'Parque de Campismo' just 4 km from Praia de Odeceixe, is set in 4 acres of pine forest with tents, caravans, wooden bungalows (2 person or 5 person), and plenty to do. Facilities include: restaurant, bar, pizzeria, pool, tennis courts, supermarket, children's corner and games room. Cooking, surfing and walking courses/workshops are available also. Despite all this going on, it's a pure-feeling, peaceful 'parque'. •€• •€€•

**a.** Montes de Azenha do Mar (EN 120), 7630-592 Odemira
**t.** 2 82 947 145
**w.** campingsaomiguel.com

**A Terra (27)**, Eco camping with comfort, is a luxury ecological camping ground set in a beautiful area of natural wildlife. Yurts, Romantic Rajasthani tents or Auspicious Indian teepees are next to a large freshwater lake. Aiming to bring people back to the land and move away from the world of materialism and technology, A Terra have made a relaxing, eco-friendly environment where you can shower under the stars, chill out in a family atmosphere and cool off in the huge freshwater lake. Yoga lessons twice a week, massages and Ayurvedic treatments, and riding lessons are all available on site. Open from April till October. •€• •€€•

**a.** Carvalhal Das Figueiras, Corgo Da Casca 5707, 7630-635 São Teotonio
**t.** 9 36 914 279
**w.** aterra.pt

The **Cerro da Fontinha (28)** country houses were built more than a century and a half ago using traditional taipa (rammed earth) construction methods, with wood and stone structures. The 6 houses (4 with 2 bedrooms, a 1 bedroom and a studio) have been completely renovated, yet are still fully integrated into the natural surroundings. Available activities: canoeing, body and mind therapies, surfing lessons. Free use of wifi, mountain bikes, canoes and fishing rods. •€€• •€€€•

**a.** Cerro da Fontinha, 7630-575 São Teotónio
**t.** 2 82 949 083 / 9 17 802 588
**e.** info@cerrodafontinha.com
**w.** cerrodafontinha.com

# SURF

The endless empty peaks of **Comporta** down to **Melides** and **Santo André** (**I**) are sandy-bottom beachbreaks, with a few small rivermouth sections.

Breaks work with small to medium nw-w swell and bigger s-sw swells, all tides depending on sandbanks. Parking's never a problem/some beaches have facilities and restaurants.

You'll find a consistent break at **São Torpes** (**II**), with some protection from north wind and the huge northerly winter swells, especially at the peak next to the breakwater. A popular wind and kite surf spot, with a warm water current travelling down from the Sines power plant. Not the prettiest backdrop, by any means, but the wave quality makes up for that. Works best with small to medium w swell, can handle more size from n-nw and s-sw swells, all tides, all levels. Parking/surf school/bar/restaurant/toilets.

You'll find a few breaks among the small bays of Porto Covo, with some nice coves to the north, and of course, the central beach **Praia Grande** (**III**). Suitable for all levels in the middle of the beach, with some rocks to each side - for more experienced surfers. Best with small to medium n-nw-w swells, also bigger s-sw. From low to mid tide but works at all tides depending on sandbanks.

# SCHOOL RENTAL REPAIR

To the south, the reefbreak (experienced surfers only) at **Ilha do Pessegueiro (IV)** offers some long smooth rides. Easy parking/surf school/bar/restaurant/toilets.

To the north of Vila Nova de Milfontes, **Malhão (V)**, just behind Orbitur camping, is an isolated beachbreak with sandy bottom and consistent waves. Works with small to medium n-nw-w swells, and handles a big s-sw swell. Best from low to mid tide, not recommended for beginners: rocky areas and strong currents. Parking at top of cliff/no facilities.

The classic wave at **Milfontes (VI)** gets pretty crowded at weekends, with a regular group of locals owning the peak. Beachbreak with some rocky bottom and reef, not ideal for beginners but with a reputable surf school you'll be in safe hands. Works with small to medium n-nw-w swell, and bigger s-sw, best from low to mid tide. Parking/surf school/bar/restaurant/toilets. Large rivermouth break, **Almograve (VII)**, is a beachbreak with some rocky areas at the Rio Mira estuary. Works best with n-nw-w small to medium swell, all tides depending on sand levels, usually hollow faster waves from low to mid tide. Parking can be difficult, or choose the south side of the river/surf school/bar/restaurant/toilets.

The small bay of **Zambujeira do Mar (VIII)** offers protection from persistent north winds but can feel crowded quickly on a windy day when everyone seeks shelter. Works with small to medium n-nw-w swells from low to mid tide. Parking limited/surf school/bar/restaurant/toilets.

**Costazul Surf (29)** have surf schools at Praia Da Vieirinha and São Torpes, offering lessons and guiding, a surf shop with all your surf essentials and a surf house, too, with 6 rooms.

**a.** Rua Vasco da Gama Lote 48,
7520-437 Porto Covo
**t.** 9 32 665 269
**w.** costazulsurf.com

**Surf Milfontes Surf School and Eco Camp (30)** offer lessons and courses for all levels, and SUP, one of the first schools in this area to get their paddles out. The eco surfcamp is a project that follows the principles of permaculture, which allows the creation of functional, sustainable circulations within the natural environment (say what?).

**a.** Rua António Mantas, n° 26,
7645 Vila Nova de Milfontes
**t.** 9 69 483 334 / 9 14 732 652
**e.** info@surfmilfontes.com
**w.** surfmilfontes.com

Opposite the Tourist office you'll find the very nice shop from **Surf Milfontes (31)**, with clothes, accessories, surf essentials and the beautiful Retro Movement boards from shaper Dan Costa.

**a.** Rua António Mantas 26,
7645-221 Vila Nova de Milfontes
**t.** 9 69 483 334 / 9 14 732 652
**e.** info@surfmilfontes.com
**w.** surfmilfontes.de

Photo: Melchior van Nigtevecht

# 8. PRE SURF: PARVATASANA IN ANJANEYASANA

◆

*Upward Bound Finger Pose in Low Lunge*

***Sitting a lot, especially on your surfboard, can cause your hip flexors to tighten.***

*These muscles allow you to lift your knees and bend at the waist, both essential movements for surfing. This low lunge opens the hip flexors which improves your movement. Adding the arm movement is not only great to tone them but also helps train the mind to move legs and arms separately from each other.*

### *Benefits:*

*Opens hip flexors, quadriceps and groin. Aids mental focus. Opens chest and keeps wrists and forearms toned.*

### *How:*

*From a standing position, step your left leg back, bend your right knee (make sure that at all times your knee is above and in line with your ankle), and place your hands on the floor on either side of your right foot, or on top of your knee. Slide your left leg back with the top of your foot on the floor. Once you are stable in your low lunge, clasp the hands in front of you with completely straight arms. Turn your hands inside out and bring arms overhead. It's more important that you keep the arms straight than to bring them overhead.*

### *Note:*

*If you're not doing this pose on the beach, use a blanket for your back knee.*

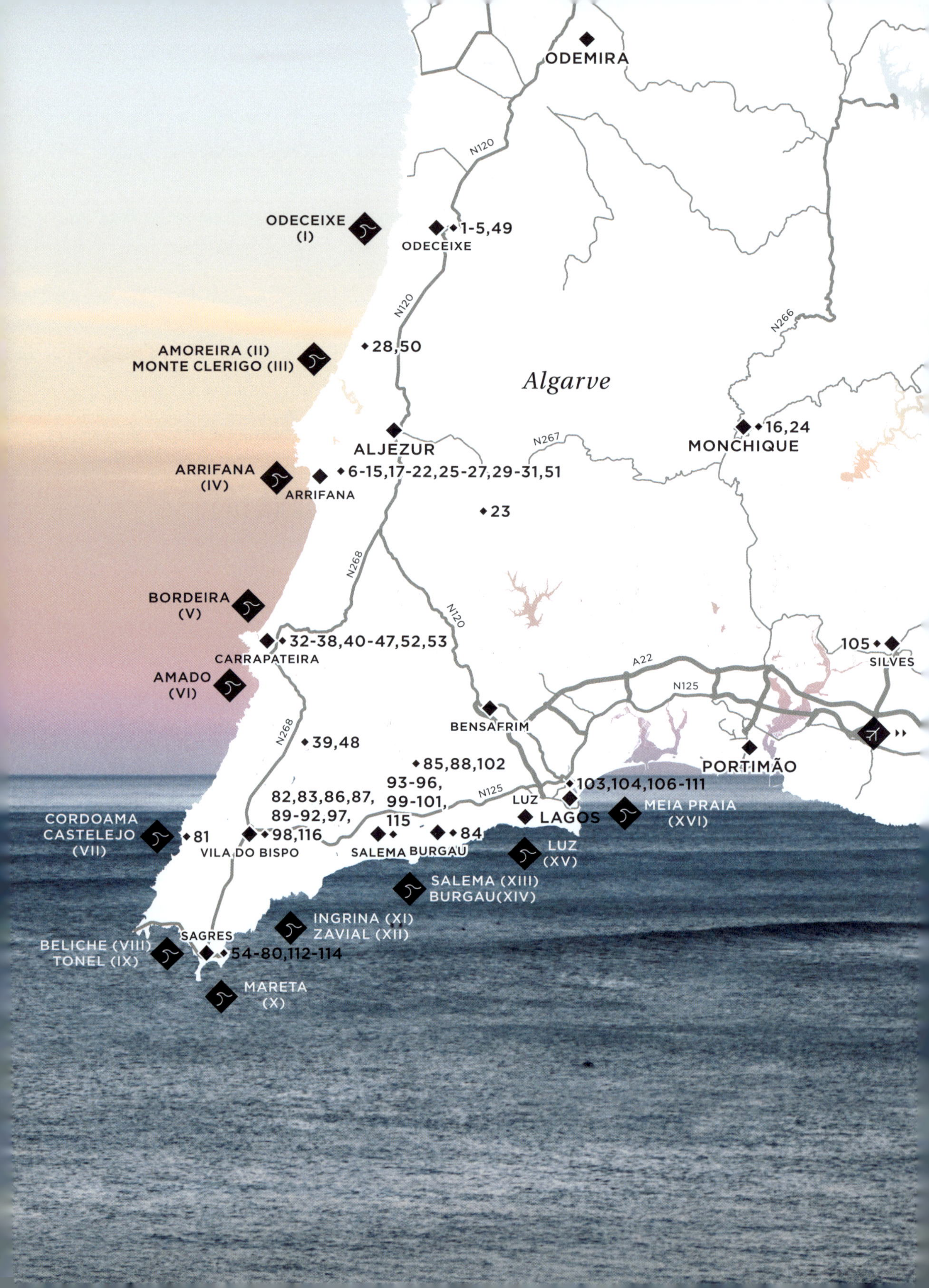
ODEMIRA
N120
ODECEIXE
(I)
1-5,49
ODECEIXE
N120
28,50
AMOREIRA (II)
MONTE CLERIGO (III)
Algarve
N266
ALJEZUR
16,24
MONCHIQUE
N267
ARRIFANA
(IV)
6-15,17-22,25-27,29-31,51
ARRIFANA
23
N268
BORDEIRA
(V)
N120
32-38,40-47,52,53
CARRAPATEIRA
105
SILVES
AMADO
(VI)
A22
N125
BENSAFRIM
N268
39,48
85,88,102
PORTIMÃO
93-96,
99-101,
115
82,83,86,87,
89-92,97,
98,116
N125
103,104,106-111
LUZ
LAGOS
MEIA PRAIA
(XVI)
CORDOAMA
CASTELEJO
(VII)
81
VILA DO BISPO
SALEMA
BURGAU
84
LUZ
(XV)
SALEMA (XIII)
BURGAU(XIV)
INGRINA (XI)
ZAVIAL (XII)
SAGRES
BELICHE (VIII)
TONEL (IX)
54-80,112-114
MARETA
(X)

# ALGARVE

Long associated with tourism, the southeast Algarve's jammed with resorts, apartment blocks, and golf courses. But head west, to the Parque Natural de Costa Vicentina e Alentejo, covering over 100 kms of protected coastline and you'll find the surroundings feel natural and wild. On the west coast, giant swells in winter make walls of impenetrable whitewater with the ocean smashing into cliffs. You'll still find fisherman perched on the cliffs during Atlantic storms, despite the risks. There are reports almost every winter of at least one getting swept away, never to be seen again. Doesn't seem to stop them though, the chance of a good catch clearly outweighs the dangers. The south coast, a run of small beaches and coves, is sheltered from the big winter swells and the northerly wind. On a no swell day it's the perfect playground for SUP, kayak, snorkel and or clifftop hiking. The Algarve surf scene gets busier every year, but if you time it right you can occasionally enjoy an uncrowded break and rollick in the feeling that you're 'away from it all'. Locals are generally friendly, but as with anywhere, it pays to show respect. And if you find a bumpy dirt-track leading to a remote surf spot, think twice before you share your 'secret discovery' online.

## TRAVEL INFO

If ever there was a place you need wheels for surf checks, it's here, unless your accommodation includes transport to the surf. Bus services run between Faro and Lagos, Lagos and Sagres or Odeceixe, but there aren't many surf spots on the schedules.

**w.** eva-bus.com & algarvebus.info

### BY AIR

Faro Airport, 4 km west of Faro city centre, international flights and low-cost airlines. You can take bus or taxi to the city's train or bus station, or pre-book a shuttle bus direct to your accommodation (good value services starting from €15, search 'faro shuttle bus').

**w.** faro-airport.com

### BY BUS & TRAIN

There are train (**w.** cp.pt) and bus (**w.** eva-bus.pt) routes between Faro and Lagos, and good routes to and from Lisbon. Also a direct bus between Lisbon and Sagres, summer service only (**w.** rede-expressos.pt)

# SURFER-TRAVELLER TYPE ALGARVE

*You love to see little white villages dropped in between wide open spaces, sweeping beaches with crumbly cliffs, and old men on dilapidated motorbikes with baskets of fish strapped to their saddle. You don't mind stopping in the road for sheep and goats, getting lost on bumpy dirt-tracks, or driving behind 'mata velhas' (tiny cars nicknamed 'kill old people'), and you're not in a hurry, for anything, anywhere, ever, so won't get stressed by the strength of the 'relaxada' vibe, or the roundabouts with only 2 exits.*

# IN AND AROUND ODECEIXE

Odeceixe consists of 2 parts really; the old town with white stone houses, and a photogenic old windmill stacked upon a hillside. 4 km west of the main town, following the river Seixe - which divides Alentejo and Algarve - into the valley towards the ocean, you find Odeceixe beach and its small settlement with a surf school, some bars and restaurants. The bay is enclosed by cliffs, and an absolute beauty, with endless hiking options along the clifftops.

## TO DO

◆

SUP the river Odeceixe with **SUP Pleasure Odeceixe** (**1**), tours and rental.

**a.** Praia De Odeceixe
**t.** 9 10 735 037
**e.** sup.pleasure@gmail.com

Yoga, daily classes at **Vida Pura** (**2**), where yoga teachers from the area come to teach. Lovely yoga deck with, really it is, the most captivatingly tranquil view over the valley.

**a.** Moinho das Canas, 8670-320 Odeceixe
**t.** 9 18 376 497
**w.** vida-pura.com

## EAT/DRINK/HANGOUT

◆

**Bar da Praia** (**3**): right above the Odeceixe surf school, popular chill-time hangout overlooking the beach: 'a vista, é fabulosa'. Juices and cocktails, tapas, soups and a dish of the day. Open for brunch, lunch and dinner from April, 10:00 till 22:00 hrs. •€• •€€•

**a.** Rua do Posto, S/N, Praia de Odeceixe, 8670-325 Odeceixe
**t.** 2 82 947 228
**w.** bardapraiaodeceixe.com

**Kiosk Agapito** (**4**), beach bar in the main street of the seaside part of town, serves home-made meals, (also vegetarian), coffee and cold drinks. Regular live music, and gourmet food or drink tastings. In summer their yellow-green road train shuttles from Odeceixe to the beach and back several times a day. Open from April, 09:00 to 23:00 hrs.
•€• •€€•

**a.** Rua da Praia, 8670-325 Odeceixe

## SHOP

◆

Artesanato **M de GourMet** (**5**) is decorated with vintage furniture, and has all sorts of local organic products like honey, olive oil and cookies, and cosmetics in arty packages.

**a.** 16a Rua Nova, 8670-320 Odeceixe

## SLEEP

◆

At 'Eco Retreat & Inspiration Land', **Vida Pura** (**2**), everything feels peaceful. The retreat, set in an idyllic valley, is based on bio-dynamic principles. Activities are all linked with health and well-being, like surfing, yoga, and all kinds of workshops. Donkeys, dogs, cats, ducks and chickens wander around happily. Robin, one of the owners, explains, "It's our wish to give people an opportunity to experience inner peace just being here, and at the same time share our idea of living a pure lifestyle, ethical and eco-friendly." Looks like the wish came true. A must visit place – if you already have other sleeping arrangements, try a yoga session or book a workshop just so you can see this for yourself. Open all year.

•€€• •€€€•

**a.** Moinho das Canas, 8670-320 Odeceixe
**t.** 9 17 997 109 (Robin) / 9 18 376 497 (Bela)/9 17 997 106 (Ole)
**e.** bookings@vida-pura.com
**w.** vida-pura.com

# IN AND AROUND ALJEZUR

Alzejur, one of the four Algarve municipalities, has all sorts of archaeological sites, including the castle - built by Berbers in the 10th century - that peeps politely over the quaint, historical town. In olden days of pirate raids, the fort at Praia da Arrifana protected the fishing port, and thereby the locals from being kidnapped and sold into slavery. Nowadays, it's more surf and yoga mixed with traditional cuisine, grilled fish, ceramics and donkeys. What you will notice, is that the town's divided by a river; old town on the castle side, and new town, where building began during the 18th century, to try and move inhabitants away from a malaria outbreak (long since eradicated, just like the pirates).

There's a regular **bus service** to Lagos or Lisbon. **w.** algarvebus.info or eva-bus.com
**Tourist office** at Rua 25 de Abril, 62.

## TO DO

Lunch, walk, relax at the beach, watch the sunset, and if you're lucky, surf at **Praia do Monte Clerigo (6)**, or maybe sit on the terrace and write a song about this take-your-breath-away blue flag beach.

Yoga classes and retreats: Shaini from **Yogaion (7)** - and I Love the Seaside's yoga specialist - gives weekly Iyengar-based yoga classes at different locations, and offers regular yoga, surf, nourish retreats; with emphasis on healthy lifestyles and healthy food. Retreats are held at the Oceanview Beach House on a beautiful secluded beach. Contact Shaini for class hours and dates.

**t.** 9 60 240 584/6 51 987 503
**w.** yogaion.com

After all that healthy activity-filled time, treat yourself to a wine-tasting session of Georg's organically produced wines from ecological vineyard **Adega da Craveira (8)**. Take note that fruit-based + natural = more healthy activity. We really do look after you. Softly spoken but passionate about wine making in an all-natural manner, Georg will explain all you want to know, and make sure you get a full taste of his wines and some local food tasting to go with that.

**a.** Adega da Craveira, Apartado 1007, 8670-909 Aljezur
**t.** 9 11 571 291
**w.** craveira.com

You'll find **Horseriding Aljezur (9)** on the way from Aljezur to Arrifana. Wooden signposts direct you all the way there. The perfect location for a sit-in-the-saddle wander about in the natural park. Lessons are also available.

**a.** Craveira, Vales, 8670 Aljezur
**w.** horseridingaljezur.wix.com

Rock climbing with **Algarve Adventure (10)**: Get your hands all chalky and listen to the sound of the sea blend with your jangling gear. Nothing like an adrenaline-boosting workout on the sea cliffs. If you're into rock. Beginner to advanced. Sport-climbing, bouldering and deep water soloing.

**t.** 9 13 533 363
(Peer, German-as-good-as-local)
**e.** info@algarve-adventure.com
**w.** algarve-adventure.com

Pedro, from **Em Boas Mãos Natural Therapies (11)**, is a surfer who set up business over 10 years ago with the idea of helping the local community to access high quality therapy. Clients range from travellers to locals, from fishermen and firemen to café workers and, of course, he supports many local surfers with his knowledge and wonder works. Massage therapy - sports and remedial, physiotherapy and osteopathic techniques, shiatsu.

**a.** Varandas da Arrifana, Sitio Picão 105, 8670-111 Aljezur
**t.** 9 33 420 203
**w.** boas-maos.com

**Sandytoes (12)** organises bicycle tours, hiking tours and has MTB for rent (they also offer delivery of bikes to your place - up to 10 bikes). The bike tours are a mix of off-road and quiet back roads, swimming in a secret lake, passing through a typical Portuguese village and countryside views. Bring swimming gear and sunblock.

**t.** 2 82 998 063 / 9 16 563 513 / 9 15 167 024
**w.** sandytoes-algarve.com

Donkey trekking: from a day out to a week-long trek (or ask if you want to go for longer), with **Burros Artes (13)**. The rhythm and pace a donkey companion brings to hiking is the perfect accompaniment for communing with nature; it creates a whole new level of relaxada. And the donkey(s) can carry your water, bags, child and whatnots. Join a short tour, a guided trek, or self-guide with map and notes. There's even a moonlight hike in August. Also possible to combine your hike with an art workshop – details on website.

**a.** Vale das Amoreiras, Apartado 19, 8671-909 Aljezur
**t.** 9 67 145 306/2 82 995 068
**w.** burros-aljezur.blogspot.pt

**Arrifana Sunset Festival (14)**, held once a year at the fishing port, end of July. Could well be called the sunrise festival; the music starts early evening and usually goes on until the dawn of the new day. Local food and drinks help party-goers keep their strength up. First held in 2004, it's getting bigger every year as increasing numbers of revellers make sure their return trip plans coincide with the event.

If you're in the area around the end of October, make sure to drop into the Aljezur **Festival da Batata Doce (15)** (sweet potato). Usually held over a long weekend, it celebrates not only the culinary delights and very many ways to cook the batata doce, but also, and it's more about this really, the way of life. Craft stalls, cakes and sweets, books and information stands, bar and live music, all in a big hall that would feel cold if it wasn't filled with the warm glow of a very close-knit and quite lovely community. Ahhh.

Head off for a day-trip to visit the beautiful windy roads of the **Monchique mountain village (16)**. Some lovely walks and bike rides in the area, mingled scents of pine and eucalyptus, and chestnut trees aplenty. From the top of Mount Foia you can ignore the concrete pillars and posts, and not very aesthetically pleasing café, and instead take in the stunning vista - on a no clouds day - of the Algarve region. Wander through local craft shops, drink some medronho (local fire-water) and fill up your bottles with deliciously fresh cool water at one of roadside springs. You'll spot these with ease as there'll be a queue of people and their cars nearby.

## SHOP

◆

For the best fresh local produce, visit the **Weekly Farmers Market (17)**: local produce on offer, and try the 'amendoins', peanuts grown in this area. Held at Igreja Nova (a huge hall at the east top of Aljezur, next to the cemetery) every Saturday morning.

Ok, so your board's broken, your clothes are all dirty and you need to check your mail. You definitely want to check in at **The Washout (18)**: a self-service laundry and a shop, where you can sit down for a coffee, or even book a SUP tour and rent a bike. Open 09:30 till 18:00 hrs.

**a.** Rua 25 de Abril 130, Aljezur
**t.** 2 82 994 100
**w.** thewashout.com

## EAT/DRINK/HANGOUT

◆

Italian restaurant and take-away **Arte Bianca (19)** is a great place for pizzas, and a good option for vegetarians as well. Passionate cook at work! ◆€€◆

**a.** Rua 25 de Abril, 8670-088 Aljezur
**t.** 9 67 519 011
**w.** facebook.com/artebianca.aljezur

Although a bit reluctant to give away their little gem, **Restaurant and Pizzaria Vicentina (20)** was tipped as a favourite by some trusted locals. A pequeno restaurant you'd miss in an instant when you pass by, just along from the tourist office. Besides pizzas, there's a daily 'Prato do Dia' - dish of the day, typical Portuguese food, and local menu with a choice of fish or meat, prepared with love. ◆€◆

**a.** Rua 25 de Abril 76, 8670-088 Aljezur
**t.** 2 82 995 046

**Restaurante Cervejaria Pont'a Pé (21)**, low key, great Portuguese food, 'Catch of the Day' fish, outdoor seating and a busy buzzy local vibe. ◆€◆

**a.** Largo Da Liberdade 12, 8670-066 Aljezur
**t.** 2 82 998 104

Photo: TipiValley

**Restaurante Hello Sailor (22)** serves 'good mood food' overlooking the beach Arrifana, lovely terrace with tasteful driftwood-style decor. Not a big lunch menu but beautifully presented, flavour-filled dishes, home-made with everything fresh! and served by happy people; soups, salads, tortillas, wraps and burgers. Evening-fine-dining menu and a kids' 'mini-me' menu too. Out of season: open for lunch and dinner. High season: 11:00 till 23:00 hrs. •€€•

**a.** Praia da Arrifana, 8670-111 Aljezur
**t.** 2 82 994 289
**w.** hello-sailor-arrifana.com

**FridayHappiness Pizza Party (23)**, all you can eat pizza with drinks deal, DJs and dance in an, err, agricultural outdoor kinda place. How to find it? Here's the thing: you have to ask someone, a local or a surf camp for directions, or to take you. You can check their FB events page. With unofficial after-party. •€•

**a.** Tojeiro, 8550-145 Marmelete
**w.** pizzanightalgarve.com

**Barlefante (24)**, definitely check this place out, for an evening out or to have a home-made tasty snack. Great interior, games room with pool table, live music acts, DJs.

**a.** Travessa das Guerreiras 14, 8550-456 Monchique
**w.** barlefante.blogspot.pt

## SLEEP

◆

**Analogue Apartments (25)** is where you press escape, tune out, log off: in the wifi free apartments, with views over the fields and hills of Aljezur. Record player, drawing stuff, board games, terrace and woodburner. Here it's all about appreciating the finer choices in life; like flip-flops or walking boots, surfboards or bikes, and which beach... •€€•

**w.** analogueapartments.wordpress.com

**Tipi Valley (26)**: this small tented retreat is tucked away in a secluded valley between Monte Clerigo and Amoreira beach, the perfect sanctuary for a peaceful escape. Organic and eco-friendly camp, with proper beds in well spaced-out tipis, offers 5 or 7 day stays, yoga and surf, healthy meals and eco living. •€€•

**a.** Tipi Valley, Monte Branco, 8670 Aljezur
**w.** surfalgarve.com

Stay at **Atlantic Riders** (**27**), with Rene and Helen, and make the most of the west coast with surf and kitesurf options alongside free yoga classes, music nights, BBQs and a great place to chill out. A good place to go solo, romantic or family-style. The Surf Lodge is 5 natural stone houses, built around a central terrace and bar area. You can choose from hostel-style bunk room, double room or private apartment. And some very comfortable tipis are also available in summer. Your non-surfing partner will enjoy this place as much as you do. There are endless hikes to make, the town of Aljezur and some beautiful beaches nearby, and we definitely recommend the healthy and delicious food, prepared by Helen. Open all year. •€• •€€•

**a.** Apartado 62, 8671-909 Aljezur
**t.** 9 18 819 646 (Helen)
**e.** info@atlanticriders.com
**w.** surflife.eu/atlantic-riders

**Monte da Xara**'s (**28**) an awesome little house in characteristic architecture of the region, in the middle of natural surroundings, great views, about 6 km from the nearest beaches. Sleeps up to 4 persons. Open all year. •€• •€€•

**a.** Monte Velho da Seiceira,
Caixa Postal 208 C, 8670-446 Rogil
**t.** 9 65 337 214 (Isabel Lombato)
**e.** montedaxara@gmail.com
**w.** montedaxara.com

Combine your stay in Arrifana with an out-of-this-world view and a relaxed and friendly atmosphere at **Arrifana Point View** surf lodge (**29**), positioned in a quiet street right above the beautiful beach of Arrifana. Add a bit of partying, bit of surf, options for a shaping workshop, biking, rock-climbing, a massage, some yoga, anything else you can think of, just ask - all customised to your personal needs! Open all year. •€€•

**t.** 9 13 533 363 (Peer)
**w.** algarve-adventure.com

**Arrifana Surf Lodge** (**30**), luxurious-style surf camps in 'your home away from home', with great home-made cooking, a relaxed atmosphere and less than a 5 minute drive to Praia da Arrifana. The lodge is a modern build with 4 large private bedrooms, 1 shared bunk room, communal lounge, kitchen and 2 huge terraces with views of the ocean. Also a plunge pool, yoga terrace, hammocks, and bean-bags and you can use the bikes for free. There's a bar directly opposite, so no need for cycling under the influence in the evenings. •€€•

**a.** Sector B Lote 58, Vale da Telha,
8670-156 Aljezur
**t.** 2 82 997 428 / 9 26 511 637
**e.** arrifanasurflodge@gmail.com
**w.** arrifanasurflodge.com

**Rural Hotel Muxima** (**31**), run by welcoming hosts Sofia and Jorge, is set amid 28 ha of cork trees and arbutus (medronho trees). There's a natural swimming pool, hammocks hanging under 100 yr old trees, and an eco-exercise circuit that doubles as a walking trail if you prefer to take it easy. Muxima means 'Heart', in the Angolan dialect Kimbundu; the name's how Sofia and Jorge best express their huge passion for Africa. Bedrooms are themed with exquisite details and décor, in ethnic style; influenced by their travels. Double/twin rooms with private bathrooms, and family suites with kitchenettes; ranging from Junior to Grand (with wood burner). All have heated floor. Breakfast's a beautiful experience and so is the philosophy of the owners: "Here, the nature grows freely at the mercy of the seasons." Open all year. •€€€•

**a.** Muxima - Montes Ferreiros,
8670-000 Aljezur
**t.** 9 16 012 830 / 9 17 059 969
**w.** muxima-montesferreiros.com

# IN AND AROUND CARRAPATEIRA

Small treasures are the big pleasures of travelling, and Carrapateira is small indeed. When you stop here for fresh groceries from the Mercado, take the time to get a coffee, or something stronger, on the terrace with the local 'boys' (that's the bunch of older men that move with the rays of the sun from terrace to benches), and you'll feel how it's very much acceptable to slow down. So do just that - adjust your pace, and your thoughts. Even the wifi connection at the Municipal is slow. Time just takes on a different rhythm in the small communities of Portugal, especially in Carrapateira.

## TO DO

◆

**Explore**: rent a bike and get lost on the trails, ramble along cliff paths, breathe in the sea air. Visit Praia do Amado and take in the spectacular scenery. Relax.

**Holistic Riding (32)** is far less about riding, and much more about the experience. Beginning with some balance and relaxation exercises, you're then gently led into communicating with the horses, before a whole different kind of riding lesson. Here is where you learn something about yourself, and as trainer Andreas says, "This knowledge doesn't become invalid as soon as we get off the horse." Courses and workshops include: individual riding lessons, beautiful trail rides, fear-free learning, general respect and responsible horse treatment, and body language as means of communication. Everyone has something to learn from Andreas and his offerings – we highly recommend that you go and find out what!

**a.** Holistic Riding Center, Monte Velho, 8670-230 Carrapateira
**t.** 9 16 269 813
**w.** holistic-riding.com

Take a wander up the steep little streets to the top of the town and visit the little **Museu do Mar e da Terra da Carrapateira (33)** for a (little) peek into the locals' way of life – we'll give you a clue; it's all about living from the sea and land. Which we like. Lots. Not much information in English but very helpful and informative staff and a great view. Open 10:00 till 12:00 and 13:30 to 16:30 hrs, Tuesday to Saturday.

**a.** Rua do Pescador, 8670-230 Carrapateira
**t.** 2 82 970 000

'Free your motion' with a therapeutic massage, from Angela of **Hasta Elements (34)**, in the Beach Hut at Praia do Amado. Rejuvenating, relaxing, pre-sport dynamic or post-sport muscle recovery. Angela's a licensed massage therapist and qualified to use osteopathic techniques, so can identify and treat to suit your individual requirements, while you lie down and listen to the sea. What better way to relieve any lingering stress that Carrapateira itself hasn't already sorted out. Every day from July to September, no booking required.

**w.** hastaelements.com
**t.** 9 17 003 655

## EAT/DRINK/HANGOUT

◆

Restaurant **Trigo Vermelho (35)**: since it's a quest for vegetarians to find tasteful meals and a bit more choice than green salad, when you do find one, what a prize! This one's even got vegan choices, gluten-free meals, using fresh, local and - where possible - organic ingredients. •€€•

**a.** Rua dos Quintais, 8670-230 Carrapateira
**t.** 2 82 973 908

**Micro Bar (36)**, hamburgers deluxe, and again, good option for vegetarians, they have a veggie version. •€€•

**a.** Largo do Comércio, 8670-230 Carrapateira

**O Sítio do Rio (37)** is almost always busy with local people, which is a good sign. Situated on the river (that's like a little Portuguese lesson, right there) that meets the sea at Praia da Bordeira, there's no view of the beach but it's the perfect spot to start or finish a good walk. Half-shade half-sunny sheltered courtyard. Booking advised, especially in summer.

**a.** Estrada da Praia da Bordeira, 8670-230 Carrapateira
**t.** 2 82 973 119.

**O Sítio do Forno (38)** sits out on the cliff between Amado and Bordeira; once a little cabana used by fishermen, it's one of the best restaurant ocean views you can get. The menu doesn't boast anything exceptional, but fish so fresh you can stare out to sea and imagine it jumped up the cliff itself and tumbled straight onto the grill. Open from 12:00 till 21:00 hrs, Tuesday to Sunday, from April to October. •€• •€€•

**a.** Praia do Amado, 8670-230 Carrapateira
**t.** 2 82 973 914.

**Restaurante Pizza Pazza (39)**, in the tucked away hilly village of Pedralva, has a colourful, friendly, informal atmosphere and unforgettable pizzas. Nice balcony with a view over the village, if you get there early enough to secure a top table. And apparently the pizza's good enough for Princes, but you can find out all about that when you get there. Open Thursday to Sunday from 6pm. And for lunch on Sunday. Closed in winter.

**a.** Aldeia da Pedralva, Pedralva
**t.** 2 82 639 173

Photo: Alexandra Gossink

## SHOP

◆

**Mercado Municipal (40)**, daily market in the main square, small but with all the provisions you need; veggies, fruits, nuts and fish. Seasonal, local, lovely.

## SLEEP

◆

Rent a camper from Tim and Nout; originally from Holland, they spent a few years living campervan life before being inspired to settle in the west Algarve and share the joy of waking up to the best view in the world, simply by opening the curtains in the van. **Hangloose Campers (41)** are fully equipped and ready to go, from salt & pepper to bed sheets, and a roof rack for your surfboards. Surfboard rentals and other extras available, easy booking and super friendly service, with no hidden charges.

**t.** 9 26 214 347 / 9 20 203 065
**e.** info@hangloosecampers.com
**w.** hangloosecampers.com

**Sandy Toes (42)** holiday homes have a 3 bedroom (5 person) very pretty cottage in Bordeira village. Close to Praia da Bordeira and Carrapateira. Recently restored to make it extra beautiful.

**t.** 2 82 998 063 / 9 16 563 513 / 9 15 167 024
**e.** info@sandytoes-algarve.com
**w.** sandytoes-algarve.com

**Pensao das Dunas (43)** has 4 double rooms with private bathroom, and 6 apartments with 1 or 2 double rooms, kitchen and bathroom. Run by a very friendly Dutch couple who do a great job of making you - and your kids! - feel at home. Flowery and half-shaded patio, generous breakfast and a great start for hikes to Bordeira beach. •€•

**a.** Rua da Padaria 9, 8670-230 Carrapateira
**t.** 2 82 973 118 / 9 25 593 955
**e.** pensao.das.dunas@gmail.com
**w.** pensao.das.dunas.pt

**L-Colestorol Bed & Breakfast (44)** is withing walking distance of Bordeira beach, has a homely relaxed vibe, veggie garden and restaurant. Casual, comfortable rooms with twin or double bed - 2 with private bathrooms, 4 with shared bathrooms. Lovely balconies with garden or sunset view, sunny patio, and warm, welcoming hosts. •€•

**a.** Horta do Rio, 8670-230 Carrapateira
**t.** 2 82 998 147
**w.** l-colesterol.wix.com/bedandbreakfast

**Casa Bamboo** (**45**): bed & breakfast in a beautiful location right next to the dunes and beach of Carrapateira. It's got 4 rooms and 1 studio apartment, a lovely garden, and a relaxed, cosy atmosphere. •€€•

**a.** Estrada Da Praia Da Bordeira, 8670-230 Carrapateira
**t.** 9 69 009 988
**e.** casabamboo@gmail.com

**Monte da Cunca** (**46**) consists of restored stone building apartments, using only natural materials. Although situated close to the N268, every apartment has a sunny terrace and from here you can walk the endless hiking paths into the hills behind Carrapateira. •€• •€€•

**a.** N268, Carrapateira, 8670-230
**t.** 2 82 973 102 / 9 66 463 886
**w.** montedacunca.com

**Monte Velho Eco Retreats** (**47**): absolutely yogalistic retreat, where everything's designed to avoid leaving more than a footprint on this wonderful land. Take a walk out to the point and view the never-ending span of ocean; Bordeira to the right and Amado along to the left. Henrique and his wife have created the most magical-feeling natural haven of tranquility up here in the hills. As they say, "Here we become conscious of the vast natural space around us." We do, and it's beautiful. Check out their retreats on offer. •€€•

**a.** Monte Velho, 8670-230 Carrapateira
**t.** 2 82 973 207 / 9 66 007 950 (Henrique)
**w.** montevelhoecoretreats.com

The **Aldeia da Pedralva** (**48**) is up a long winding road from Carrapateira, then down a short winding hill into a tranquil valley. This tiny village was once so deserted that only 9 of the original inhabitants remained. In 2006, a project began to buy and renovate as much of the village as possible, successfully retaining the rustic feeling and creating a very special kind of place.

Here you can experience 'living a unique rhythm' in the cutest holiday cottages, with the sound of chattering birds and softly braying donkeys tinkling in the background. And slow, unreliable wifi - a great excuse for not replying to emails! Restaurant, bar and outdoor pool, gourmet grocery delivery service.

**a.** Rua de Baixo, 8650-401 Pedralva
**e.** reservas@aldeiadapedralva.com
**t.** 2 82 639 342
**w.** aldeiadapedralva.com

Photo: Alexandra Gossink

# SURF

Winter swells are a sight to behold along the west coast, but it's on small to medium days you'll have the most fun. Exploring from beach to beach, you won't find a huge difference in the waves, but still, it's good to have a little variety and save on fuel by working out what happens where, depending on winds and tides. Most beaches have lifeguards in summer.

The beautiful beach of **Odeceixe** (**I**) can have its perfect, glassy days, even in medium swells, but shifting sandbars and outgoing current from the river mess it up easily. Except for summer it's never too busy, and the backdrop makes up for even the worst of waves. On some days it pays to go across to Praia das Adegas, on the south side of Praia de Odeceixe, where the waves break with more power. It's a small bay, officially a naturist beach. Both work best with medium n-nw-w swell, at low tide. All levels, but beware of strong currents. Easy parking up the cliff/toilet/shower/restaurant/surf school.

**Amoreira**'s (**II**) a charming stretch of beach with natural dune area. Depending on sandbanks (which very much depend on recent storms), it can throw a real classic wave, and on its finest days, a nice long right. Not much protection from west wind, works from small to medium n-nw-w swell. Can get busy, especially at weekends. All levels. Easy parking/surf school/bar/restaurant.

**Monte Clerigo**'s (**III**) a fine break and a blue flag beach, with a beautiful longboard wave on a peeling day. Easily messes up though, so you have to be a bit lucky for this one. Works from small to medium n-nw-w swell. All levels. Easy parking/toilet/restaurant/surf school.

**Arrifana** (**IV**) is a shell-shaped bay with a sheltered harbour to the right, the most protected spot from the north wind on the west coast and can handle a bit more size. Sand with some rocks, works from small to medium n-nw-w

swell, usually best mid to high tide, depending on sandbanks.

Gets crowded but a few peaks to choose from, go left for a bit more space. Beachbreak: all levels. Right pointbreak: experienced surfers only, long paddle out and rocks exposed. Parking a bit of a hassle (best to park on top of cliff)/toilet/shower/restaurant/bar/surf school.

**Bordeira (V)** is a wandering stretch of beach with plenty of peaks, so you can walk along to the right till you find some space when crowded. No wind protection, works from small to medium n-nw-w swell.

All levels, but be very, very careful of rips and currents that take you out. Never surf alone if you're a beginner, watch how other surfers get in. Easy parking. No facilities.

**Amado (VI)** offers slight protection from northwest wind and a consistent wave that works at all tides, but as with everywhere round here, this can change with shifting sandbanks. Works from small to medium n-nw-w swell. All levels. Easy parking/restaurant/surf school.

You can check **Cordoama (VII)** and **Castelejo** to the left, from the miradouro and catch your breath at the view of the west coast from a height. Works best with small to medium n-nw-w swell, easily blown out by west wind, gets hollow with an offshore. Low tide can be dumpy, depending on tidal range and sandbanks. Beachbreak with occasional sneaky rocks that appear suddenly. Gets crowded quickly. All levels. Easy parking (except on weekends in summer)/restaurant/surf school.

Photo: Alexandra Gossink

# SCHOOL RENTAL REPAIR

◆

**Odeceixe Surf School (49)** have a small hut on Odeceixe beach where you can get lessons and rentals. Instructors are local surfers certified by the Portuguese Surfing Federation, max. group size: 8 people. Knowledgeable staff can also tell you all about the area.

**a.** Praia de Odeceixe, 8670-320 Odeceixe
**t.** 2 82 949 152 / 9 63 170 493
**w.** odeceixesurfschool.com

**Waterproof Surf School (50)** is the surf camp and school of Nuno Rendeiro, who has over 20 years experience and is certified by the Portuguese Surfing Federation. Surf lessons with a focused but fun teaching method, adaptable to all ages and styles, from beginner to advanced. Work from different beaches in the area, stationed in Rogil.

**t.** 9 10 290 308
**e.** info@waterproofsurfcamp.com
**w.** waterproofsurfportugal.com

**Atlantic Riders (51)**: surf, kite or SUP; individual or group; course or package to include accommodation – just about every option you could think of is catered for. Oh and add some yoga to that. Rene operates lessons from Amoreira and offers rentals of wetsuits, as well as boards, from soft-tops to shortboards, mini-mals, longboards, bodyboards and even skimboards.

**t.** 9 18 819 646
**w.** surflife.eu/atlantic-riders/atlantic-riders-lodge

**Amado Surf Camp (52)** offers daily lessons and rental of boards, operating from Amado, their surf camp is based in a nearby secluded valley, in natural surroundings, next to the village of Carrapateira.

**t.** 9 27 831 568
**w.** amadosurfcamp.com

**Pipe Spot (53)** surf shop's on the main road, providing all your surf essentials, some beautiful (locally produced) surfboards, well informed staff. Open from March to December.

**a.** Edifício Carrapateira, Loja H Cerca da Alcaria, 8670-211 Carrapateira
**t.** 9 34 892 585
**w.** pipespot.com

Photo: Geert-Jan Middelkoop

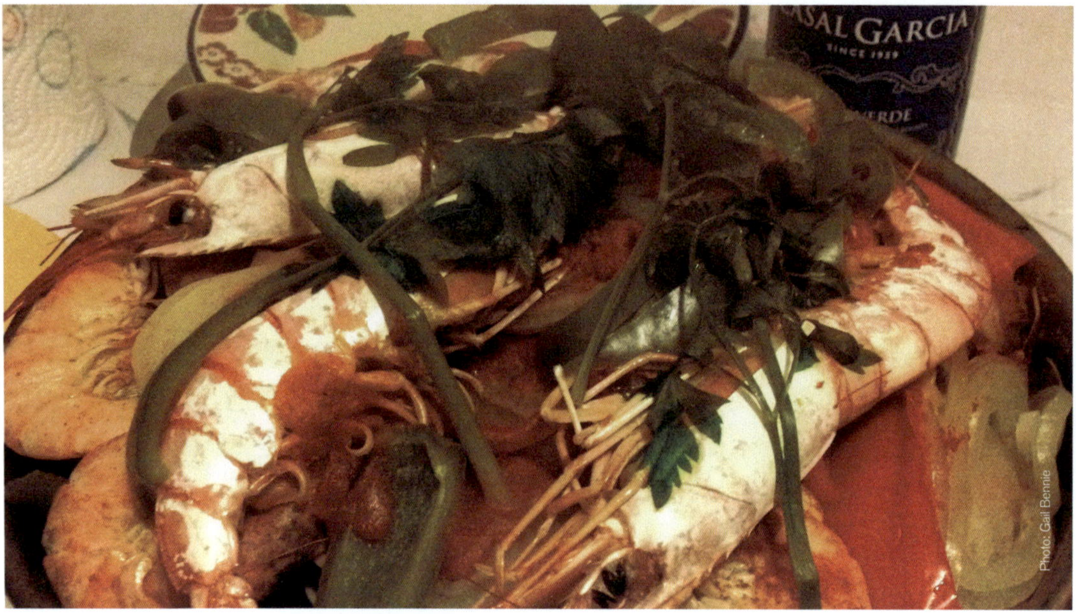


Photo: Gail Bennie

# PORTUGAL LOCAL RECIPE

### CATAPLANA RELAXADA DO NORBERTO

Beloved local Norberto's cataplana's based around the very many varieties of this popular dish, so go ahead and experiment with ingredients. The big deal here, that makes the difference to flavour, is your cooking vibe. No dashing around. Do it the Portuguese way and take your time, relax, smile, Norberto-style.

### RECEITA FOR 4 PEOPLE

Pull up a chair or a stool in the kitchen while this dish is cooking. Snack on chouriço and some fine goat or sheep's cheese. Drink a glass of wine along with that, and fully appreciate the heady scent of the cataplana cooking, as you do some relaxada.

### INGREDIENTES

*500g cubed pork (fatty shoulder)*
*4 Bay Leaves*
*2 or 3 cloves of Garlic (chopped)*
*Fresh Parsley*
*1 Red and 1 Green Pepper (sliced)*
*500g Clams*
*½ a good Chouriço 'picante' (sliced)*
*2 big ripe Tomatoes (chopped)*
*300g frozen King Prawns (entire)*
*1 large Onion (sliced in rings)*
*Pimentão Doce*
*(sweet/bonnet chilli pepper)*
*Tomato Puree & Tomato Ketchup*
*Cup of Tomato Pulp*
*1 big glass of White Wine*
*Sea Salt & Olive Oil*

*Serve with some fresh crusty bread and wine depending on your taste – Vinho Verde (green wine) for a seafood focus, a good red if you want to enhance the pork. Either way, wine is good. Boa appétit, e saúde - cheers!*

### INSTRUÇÕES

- Cook the pork slowly in its own fat, for 5-10 mins on low heat without stirring. Use a good pan with a heavy base. Then add a sprinkle of salt and 2 bay leaves, stir and cook for another 10 mins. Take off the heat and let stand while you:
- Pour a good splosh of olive oil in your cataplana dish (use a good non-stick pan with lid if you don't have the real thing). Add garlic and a scattering of parsley and cook for a couple of minutes.
- Add the meat, stir, add peppers and clams, scatter the chouriço on top. Cooking slowly as you add ingredients, don't forget to have a sip of wine now and then.
- Put chopped tomatoes over the top, then another 2 bay leaves, mix it all in a little.
- Place king prawns on the top, onions over those, chuck a generous spoonful of pimentão doce over it all, and a decent dollop of tomato puree.
- Drink a little more wine and nibble on some cheese, or dig out those olives you forgot you had.
- Pour over the tomato pulp, then the wine, turn up the heat and leave it to do its thing, with the lid on, for about 10 mins.
- Splodge a squirt of ketchup on it and put the rest of the parsley on the top, cook for another 10 mins or so.

# IN AND AROUND SAGRES

The lively (in summer) little fishing town of Sagres sits on the peninsula, just before the 'End of the World' (those Romans found them everywhere), Cabo São Vicente. The surroundings are quite desolate, wild and windy in winter, changing dramatically with the seasons, when Easter brings surf buses from all over, the bars and restaurants spin their 'fechado' signs around and summer fun's in full swing. Until November, when it all goes back into hibernation.

**Tourist office** in Rua Comandante.

## TO DO

Hike, cycle, bus or drive to the lighthouse, **Farol do Cabo de São Vicente (54)**; visit the Bratwurst stall to get your 'I had a Bratwurst at the End of the World' certificate, or go in the evening and watch the summer sunset spectacle (the spectacle being the hoards of people all come to watch the sun set).

If you're around at the end of May, take a wander to Memmo Baleeira Hotel, overlooking the fishing port and soak up some surf culture alongside a get-together of filmmakers, musicians, writers, thinkers, creators, visual artists, photographers, designers and shapers; all, most importantly, surfers with a passion for the ocean.

Exhibitions, conferences, presentations, music and movies, and the great vibe founded by the spirit of sharing and friendship, are the main features at the **Sagres Surf Culture (55)** event. Organised by Surfactory Studio, the event runs over 4 days, has a different theme each year and has been held annually since 2012. Events are all free but you need to reserve your seat, see website for info.

**w.** sagressurfculture.com

The 4-day **Annual Birdwatching Festival**'s held at end September/beginning October. A good selection of activities, some free, revolving around nature and the environment. The main focus, obviously, birdwatching. There's no better place to spot such a variety of species gather for migration, or pass briefly by - quick stop for a last snack 'n' snooze before heading out over the ocean. Also craft and educational workshops, dolphin/whale observation, boat trips, nature walks, horse and donkey rides. A small train circulates daily throughout the festival, providing free transport around Sagres to link the meeting points.

**w.** birdwatchingsagres.com

**Pura Vida Dive House (56)** love to share the underwater world with you. You can either learn to scuba dive, or if you're a certified diver, explore the best dive sites with their experienced dive masters. They also offer snorkelling, hikes, bike and kayak tours, and super relaxing yoga sessions.

**a.** Rua Da Pedra Negra, Baleeira, 8650-362 Sagres
**t.** 9 13 210 716 / 9 18 426 721
**w.** puravidadivehouse.com

Join friendly and knowledgeable Carla, of **Walkin' Sagres** (**57**), for a guided walk enriched with local historical, geological and cultural information. During your hike in the wild landscape you'll observe and learn about all sorts of native fauna and flora; including edible and medicinal plants and some with other uses. And we can assure you, it's far from boring! Walks range from 2hrs to 4hrs. Family-friendly options, small groups (max 10 persons).

**t.** 9 25 545 515
**w.** walkinsagres.com

Yoga classes and courses with Michaël Bijker of **Pure Flow Motions** (**58**), in a light, spacious room overlooking the ocean. Daily classes from Monday to Friday at 08:00 hrs, private sessions and beach yoga also available, contact to confirm availability.

**a.** Hotel Memmo Baleeira, Sítio da Baleeira s/n, 8650-357 Sagres
**t.** 9 20 438 451
**e.** info@pureflowmotions.com
**w.** pfmyoga.com

Book a SUP course - flat water or waves, or a tour to discover the cliffs, caves and sea-side aspect of Sagres as you glide along the unspoiled coast, with the inimitable Jean-Louis, of **SUP Sagres** (**59**). Family-friendly options and rentals also available. Bring sunscreen, cap, towel and water to drink. Equipment provided, and a good mood is included with all activities!

**t.** 9 19 100 529
**w.** supsagres.com

**Mar Ilimitado**'s (**60**) run by a small team of marine biologists with the dream to explore the ocean, and to share the opportunity. Seabird and dolphin watching boat tours, and a range of diving activities are available. Dive options from complete beginner (really completely beginner, they even have a 'Bubblemaker' diving introduction course for children age 8 and over) to advanced. They also run research projects and support those of other institutions.

**a.** Porto da Baleeira de Sagres, 8650-368 Sagres
**t.** 9 16 832 625
**w.** marilimitado.com

## SHOP

◆

Feel the community vibe and take in the colourful sights and earthy smells of the small but friendly morning **Market** (**61**), on the other side of the roundabout from the church. Fresh veg, fruit and herbs, barrels of olives, nuts and beans, still warm bread and cakes, some local cheese and fresh fish. Hungry already? The lovely market ladies can also give advice on how to cook any odd-looking veggies that you're not familiar with. Open until 12:30, closed on Sundays.

**a.** Mercado Municipal, Rua Mercado, 8650-372 Sagres

One of the best pastelarias of Sagres, **Vila Mareta** (**62**), sits round the corner from the bar Dromedario, in a yellow house, no address, no website, no nothing, just the best almond cakes, sweets, and of course pasteis de natas. You'll find it…

**Retro Sailor**'s (**63**) a little homage to the sea with sustainability in mind. It's a small shop but stuffed with goodies, from surf wear and homeware to art, books, prints and postcards, alternative surfboards, handmade skateboards and some original and locally made crafty things too. And it comes with very friendly staff! Closed in winter.

**a.** Praça da República, 8650-356 Sagres
**w.** retrosailorsagres.com

## EAT/DRINK/HANGOUT

◆

The must-go-to in Sagres is **Alice Gelateria** (**64**), real Italian-made Italian ice-cream made by real Italians. Gluten-free, sugar-free, dairy-free and vegan varieties, new flavours daily – you gotta try pastel de nata flavour! Coffees, cakes, brioche and pastries that make you want to fill your bags, boxes and boots. Open from 09:00 till 21:00 hrs, April to November, closed on Tuesdays.

**a.** Rua De São Vicente, 8650-370 Sagres (just along from Sagres Natura Surf Shop)

'Delights for the hungry surfer', lovely vibe, tasty plates of home-made fresh food, sweet treats, coffee, smoothies and regular events, jam sessions and the like, at **The Hangout** (**65**). •€• •€€•

**a.** Rua Comandante Matoso, 8650-370 Sagres
**t.** 9 64 959 903

It's not the easiest place to find, tucked away behind a small cluster of houses, so follow the locals (or your nose) to **Adega dos Arcos** (**66**) for traditional Portuguese-style food. Great value simple meals, generous portions! Grilled fish or meat with salad or veg, potatoes or fries, and a daily special 'prato do dia' are served alongside the normal menu. Friendly staff who'll advise you if the prato do dia is big enough for two, which it often is... Closed on Mondays. •€•

**a.** Roça de Veiga, 8650-387 Sagres
**t.** 9 60 294 290

**A Sagres Restaurant** (**67**) serves traditional regional dishes, with a homely warm feeling. Or if you're in the mood for something a little different, like the biggest bowl of that's-what-I-call-a-salad you ever saw, freshly made pasta, or a bomba burger with hand-cut fries, pop next door to **A Sagres Café**. All home-made with Italian flair and food passion, from the secret recipes of Emilio. Café open all year from midday till midnight, kitchen open for lunch and dinner. Closed on Wednesdays. •€• •€€•

**a.** Ecovia do Litoral (on the corner of the Fortaleza roundabout), 8650-327 Sagres
**t.** 2 82 624 171 - Restaurant/Café

Overlooking Praia da Mareta, **Chiringuito's (Last Chance)** (**68**) is the perfect spot to sit outside on driftwood and pallet board furniture, listen to some chill tunes and drink a coffee, smoothie or caipirinha, with a view of the ocean on the side. Breakfasts, burgers, snacks and tapas are all on the menu. Open March to November, closed Mondays. •€• •€€•

**a.** Praia da Mareta, 8650-361 Sagres

For friendly service, fresh catch of the day seafood, and a little twist on most of the traditional dishes, **Restaurant Carlos** (**69**) has it all. Indoor and outdoor seating area, with recently refurbed modern design, a cabinet full of home-made desserts that make your mouth water, a great selection of wines (trust their recommendation, really) and they're family-friendly too. Closed on Tuesdays. •€€•

**a.** Avenida Comandante Matoso (towards Port of Baleeira), 8650-357 Sagres
**t.** 2 82 624 228

A delightful surprise in such a small town! The lovingly created menu is inspired by years of the owners being travelling foodies. Vegetarian and vegan dishes in a class above all expectations, and some quirky, entertaining décor and staff at **Mum's** (**70**). Expect to relax and take your time over a very enjoyable meal. Booking can be a problem in season, best to book ahead by going there, and you can check out the menu at the same time. Open evenings only, closed in winter. •€€• •€€€•

**a.** Rua Comandante Matoso, 8650-370 Sagres
**t.** 9 10 835 541
**w.** mums-sagres.com

**Terra** (**71**) is relatively new in town. Marta & Morris, from northern Italy, together with their 2 Italian chefs have created a menu with fresh local organic food, and some classic ingredients imported from Italy (pasta and cheese).

The menu's filled with a creative, mouthwatering blend of Portuguese/ Italian dishes. They serve good sandwiches too, and the coffee passed our test não problema . Closed in winter. •€€•

**a.** Curva do Beliche, Urbanização São Vicente, 8650-390 Sagres
**t.** 2 82 625 089

**Dromedaria** and **Pau de Pita (73)** are on a little row of bars on the 'main' street of the town. Spend an evening hopping in and out of all the bars in the row, the way the locals do it. Pau de Pita's got regular live music at weekends, friendly staff and a nice relaxed vibe.

**a.** Rua Comandante Matoso, 8650-370 Sagres

## SLEEP

◆

**Campervans** can empty their toilets at the gas station for Intermarché, on road straight along from the entrance to town. Also washing machines.

**Campsite Orbitur Sagres (74)**, set in the midst of pine woods, surrounded by green, in a quiet location only a short drive from the beach. Pitches, tents, chalets and bungalows, from basic mini lodges to 'Marte' (for up to 7) persons. Open all year. •€• •€€•

**a.** Cerro das Moitas, 8650-998 Sagres
**t.** 2 82 624 371
**w.** orbitur.com/campsite-orbitur-sagres

Choose your accommodation style; lodging in the hostel, in dorm or private room, or book the studio (for up to 4 people) at **PuraVida Dive House (56)**, beautifully decorated and with a peaceful and loving energy throughout. Add activities from a selection of dive or snorkel, explore nature on hike, bike or kayak, surf, yoga and reiki. Also new on the menu is the free-diving week retreat. Trust us, you want to find out more! •€• •€€•

**a.** Rua Da Pedra Negra, Baleeira, 8650-362 Sagres
**t.** 9 13 210 716 / 9 18 426 721
**w.** puravidadivehouse.com

**Algarve Cycling Holidays (75)** offer all-in cycling holidays with a choice of three accommodations to suit your budget and your style, from economy class to 5 star luxury, and offers an optional extra activity day. Everything's organised for you, so relax, ride, repeat. Great guided rides to explore the remote areas of the Costa Vicentina on two wheels - it looks even better on a bike!

**t.** 9 64 785 794
**w.** algarve-cycling-holidays.com

**Mareta Beach Boutique B&B (76)** is a 4 star hotel offering panoramic views over Praia da Mareta. 18 double or twin rooms; 4 of which have seaview, 4 with private balcony. Adjoining Italian-style coffee shop and Pizzeria D'Italia are part of the same group and guests can use tropical garden and jacuzzi at Mareta View, the sister hotel just around the corner. Staff are top notch friendly and helpful too. •€€• •€€€•

**a.** Praça Da República, 8650-356 Sagres
**t.** 2 82 620 040
**w.** maretabeachhotel.com

**Pure Flow Motions (77)** offer surf and yoga holiday retreats; their focus is on healthy and conscious living, and connecting with your inner self and nature. What are you waiting for? Need to recharge your batteries? Do it with a lovely team of people who have a huge amount of passion for what we do and why we do it. 2 yoga sessions a day, nature walks, surfing, meditation, QiGong, mindfulness classes and delicious food that's good for you! Retreats are run from Hotel Memmo Baleeira.

**a.** Pure Flow Motions Retreats, Memmo Baleeira, Sítio da Baleeira, 8650-357 Sagres
**e.** info@pureflowmotions.com
**w.** pureflowmotions.com

Sitting above the fishing port of Sagres is **Hotel Memmo Baleeira (78)**, a surfer-friendly 4 star Design Hotel with a clean, modern and elegant interior. A good position to walk into town for drinks and dinners, or to chill out by the pool and enjoy the view. •€€€•

**a.** Sítio da Baleeira, 8650-357 Sagres
**t.** 2 82 624 212
**w.** memmohotels.com

**Martinhal Family Resort Hotel (79)** has a whole heap of awards for being family-friendly, because it is. Swimming pools, daycare, kids' club, kids play areas, bikestation and pumptrack, a choice of restaurants and the calm shelter of Martinal beach (the least windy and wavey bay of Sagres) on the doorstep. 5 star hospitality in a stunning location creates 'Europe's finest luxury family resort'. •€€€• •€€€€•

**a.** Quinta do Martinhal, 8650-908 Sagres
**t.** 2 18 507 788
**w.** martinhal.com

**Tonel Cottage Holiday Rentals (80)** are perfectly located just across from Praia do Tonel, in a quiet street, close to the town but far enough removed for some tranquil 'relaxada'. Choice of beautifully restored 2 bedroom fisherman's cottage or stylish and spacious studio apartment with own patio garden. •€€•

**a.** Rua do Tonel, 8650-376 Sagres
**t.** 9 26 752 012
**e.** tonelcottage@hotmail.com
**w.** tonelcottage.com

Photo: Alexandra Gossink

# IN AND AROUND VILA DO BISPO

The Vila do Bispo municipality goes from just south of Carrapateira, on the west coast, to Sagres and then along the south coast to Burgau; the only municipality in Portugal with 2 coastlines and the extreme southwest corner of continental Europe. Ranging green hills and off-road dirt-tracks break up the spattering of small towns and villages, farming and fishing continue alongside the ever-growing surf industry, and campervans crowd the car parks year round. However, being within the natural park means there's always a place to get lost, to feel removed from the 'developed world'. All you have to do is: wander away from the path a bit, switch off your wifi gadgets and phone, and breathe in the heady perfume of the Atlantic, mixed with rock rose, eucalyptus or pine, depending on where you end up.

## TO DO

Drive out to the **Miradouro (81)**, in between Cordoama and Castelejo, for a view of the west coast. Signposted from the market in Vila do Bispo. Definitely worth the bumpy drive.

Experience the magnificent coastline from the sea side and explore hidden caves with **Algarve SUP Tours (82)**. Suitable for all ages and abilities, all equipment provided. Optional rock jumps for the brave.

**t.** 9 68 485 186
**w.** algarve-sup-tours.com

Join Nicolau, of **Atalaia (83)**, for a walk on the wild side of the natural park. Local nature lover, fisherman and beekeeper turns storyteller, and shares his passion and knowledge with you about the landscape, geology, indigenous wildlife, what we can do to protect it and lots more. Bee observation optional (and very interesting so we recommend it!).

**e.** info@atalaia-walking.com
**w.** atalaia-walking.com

In the evening and morning, all level **yoga classes (84)**, lasting between 75-90 mins, held throughout the year.

**a.** Urbanização Recantos de Burgau, Lote 9, 8600-120 Burgau
**t.** 9 13 202 621
**w.** fit2lovelife.com

Longtime yoga teacher Diane, from **Algarve Yoga (85)**, runs regular retreats at different locations and gives weekly classes at Monte Rosa in Barão Sao João. She teaches a gentle, but intense form of yoga with room to adjust, for all levels to enjoy.

**t.** 9 62 492 607
**w.** algarveyoga.com

Treat your body's needs with a therapeutic, holistic, relaxation or intensive sports/surf massage from Angela of **Hasta Elements** (**86**). Services all year round in Clinica Vicentina, and Tourism Lodgings service at a selection of accommodations. By appointment only.

**a.** Clinica Vicentina, Sitio das Eiras, Edificio Santa Casa da Misericórdia, 8650-405 Vila do Bispo
**t.** 9 17 003 655
**w.** hastaelements.com

Feel in total harmony with nature and local life, horse riding in the natural park with **Equivicentinos** (**87**).

**a.** Sitio da Penina, 8650 Vila do Bispo
**t.** 9 65 561 377
**e.** equivicentinos@gmail.com
**w.** facebook.com/Equivicentinos

The **Barão de São João Flea Market** (**88**) is held every 4th Sunday of the month, it's something of an experience... Barão de São João's also the place to be at the weekend for all the surrounding villages because of its lively bars and restaurants. It's a place that attracts people who aren't so keen on living a conventional life, and here they can be themselves. Walking around with your camera, like you would do in any other rustic Portuguese village will get you stern looks. 'Just leave me to it' can very well be the mantra of the new age inhabitants of Barão de São João.

## SHOP

◆

Hang out at the daily morning **Mercado** (**89**) and practise some Portuguese with the stall-holders. Mostly locally grown veggies and fruit, organic produce and bread at the bio-stand, and fresh fish. Big jars of local honey, oodles of nuts, beans, figs, freshly cut herbs. Open 09:00 till 13:00 hrs, closed on Sundays.

**a.** Estrada EM1265, 8650 Vila do Bispo

## EAT/DRINK/HANGOUT

◆

Restaurant **Ribeira do Poço** (**90**) has a cool shaded interior back room, sunny window seats at the front, and outdoor tables too – but get there early or reserve a table if you want to have a choice. Traditional Portuguese dishes, good seafood and unbeatable desserts. Recommended by locals, and they're usually right. Closed on Monday. •€€• •€€€•

**a.** Rua Ribeira do Poço 11, 8650 Vila do Bispo
**t.** 2 82 639 075

**Café de Pasto Rodrigues** (**91**) is very much a locals' place, with quite informal service. There's a sunny, sheltered marquee seating area at the front for a laid-back indoor-outdoor feeling, cakes and coffees, a good value prato do dia (dish of the day), bar, and live music most Saturday nights from local talent (usually traditional Portuguese music). •€•

**a.** Largo da Igreja, 8650-290 Raposeira

**Pizza Point**'s (**92**) a lovely little place, just by the school on the corner to Zavial. Open evenings only, but will open for lunchtime group reservations if you call at least a day ahead. Ana uses organic and fresh ingredients wherever possible, and offers vegetarian and gluten-free options in a relaxed atmosphere - almost always busy, with locals popping in for a drink, take-away or slice of cake. •€•

**a.** Rua de Escola 9, 8650-282 Raposeira
**t.** 2 82 639 226

**Água Na Boca** (**93**) has a romantic charm and cosy ambience. Traditional dishes, beautifully presented, and friendly service, close to the sea. Open evenings only, closed on Sunday. •€€• •€€€•

**a.** Rua dos Pescadores 82, 8650-199 Salema
**t.** 2 82 695 651

Family-run business, **Restaurante Lourenço** (**94**), with typical Portuguese food and really good fish! is a cute little place, slightly hidden in a small street to the side of Praia da Salema. Good value, hence always busy. Lunch and dinner, Monday to Saturday. •€•

**a.** Rua 28 de Janeiro, 8650-200 Salema
**t.** 2 82 698 622

**PizzaMobile (95)**, eat in or take-away pizza, salads, cocktails and good selection of beers, including Belgian. Nice décor, relaxed atmosphere and friendly staff. Open every night during season, with occasional live music/open mic events. •€• •€€•

**a.** Rua 28 de Janeiro 3, 8650-200 Salema
**t.** 2 82 697 676

**Restaurante O Sapinho (96)**, on the 'main street' in Figueira (tiniest village ever!) has a little outdoor seating area - good place to sit and watch the village go by while you take a coffee, beer or wine in the sun. Lunch and dinner served by Rui, the owner, with a warm welcome, care and attention to flavour and fresh ingredients, in a friendly, intimate dining room. Traditional Portuguese, great calamari. Closed on Tuesdays and from mid January to mid February. Booking advised, popular with locals and tourists. •€• •€€•

**a.** Rua das Escadinhas 10, 8650-165 Figueira
**t.** 2 82 695 445

## SLEEP

◆

**The Good Feeling (97)** hostel has a good feeling indeed! Portuguese owners, Miguel and Hugo, provide a relaxed atmosphere and a friendly vibe. Free beach drop-offs and lots of local knowledge about which spots to go to when. They also organise SUP tours, surf lessons, yoga classes on the terrace, and have the added bonus of Carlos in the team: he serves up amazing dinners and cocktails alongside breakfasts and snacks, and runs a well-stocked bar, with a sense of humour and a giant smile. Dorms, private rooms and private studios at the back with own terrace areas. Shared kitchen and lots of lounging around space. Fireplace for winter warmth, and hammocks on the terrace for days when you need a cool shady hangout. •€• •€€•

**a.** Sitio Eiras De Cima, 8650-282 Raposeira
**t.** 9 14 658 807
**w.** thegoodfeeling.com

**Camping Ingrina (98)** is a very very basic, very informal, off on a very narrow rutted dirt-road, but very friendly place with a (very!) smiley-faced owner, Manuel. Worth dropping in to see whether it suits you. Great views, totally hidden away, with several permanent residents who make it feel homely and welcoming. •€•

**a.** There doesn't appear to be one. Drive up from Ingrina beach, look for hand-painted sign with arrow.
**t.** Apparantly not.
**w.** Are you kidding?

**One Life Lodge (99)** is an eco resort B&B in Salema offering special surf and yoga weeks, or yoga and hiking. Special weeks for girls only (w. chicksonwaves.com) and dedicated Family Week packages too. Healthy breakfasts, beautiful location and friendly service. •€€•

**a.** One Life Lodge, 8650-192 Salema
**t.** 9 67 580 530
**w.** onelifelodge.com

Oh **Casa Meranka! (100)** In the tiny village of Figueira hides a beautiful little oasis of tranquility and calm. Dutch/English couple, Margo and Josh, had the dream of creating a little space to raise their family living in freedom, connected with nature and with a steady pace of life. So they did. They've really created this place with love, and the care and attention that have gone into handcrafted décor and little details make it a very special space indeed. 4 cottages are available, centred around a sunny sheltered courtyard with shaded chill out space, swimming pool and total sense of 'calma.' •€€•

**a.** 1, Rua do Rossio, 8650-172 Figueira
**t.** 2 82 695 432
**e.** casameranka@gmail.com
**w.** casameranka.com

15 mins walk from a quiet secluded beach is **Figueira Caravan Park (101)**. Created especially for caravans travelling through the south of Portugal, it's a comfortable, quiet and safe park with wifi, water supply, electricity and waste facilities. Small restaurant, bar and mini-mercado nearby. •€•

**a.** Rua da Fonte 6A, 8650-161 Figueira
**w.** figueiracaravanpark.com

Just outside the Vila do Bispo area, but with the same kind of vibe: Barão de São João is where you'll find the beautiful rural guesthouse, **Monte Rosa (102)**. Activities and workshops include raw food, yoga and meditation, and singing. •€€•

**a.** Lagoa da Rosa cx. 9Y, 8600-016 Barão de São João
**w.** monterosaportugal.com

# IN AND AROUND LAGOS

Lagos was originally named 'Zawaia', meaning 'lake', by the Moors, whose influence still remains in architecture, art and - you can't miss it - the castle, built around the 8th century. The region wasn't reclaimed until the 13th century, by the King of Portugal. In the 15th Century it became the first gateway for the European slave trade, and you can still see the 'Mercado de Escravos', the first slave market which opened in 1444. Lagos was then known as the centre for 'The Age of Discovery' as Infante (Prince) Henry - very well known in these parts, lots of statues - set sail to discover and colonise sections of the African coast and its islands. The Lagos in Nigeria was named by these European settlers. These days, however, it's much more about tourist-friendly beaches, rock formations (Ponta da Piedade) and vibrant summer party-hard nightlife, a great variety of restaurants, happy hours and dancing till dawn.

**Tourist office** in Rua Vasco da Gama (near the ship roundabout).

## TO DO

Every year on the 29th August, the bathing festival, **Festa do Banho**, is held, when people from all the neighbouring towns and villages come to swim at midnight. You'll find people and their picnics, accompanied by music and a firework display, all along the beaches, especially Meia Praia and Batata.

**Inlight Lagos (103)** studio offers daily drop-in yoga classes, hatha, vinyasa, kundalini and more, check the schedule on their website.

**t.** 9 13 127 421
**w.** inlight.pt

Drop into the daily **Market (104)** to stock up on your fresh fruit, fish and vitamin-filled veggies, get your senses all a tingle with the smell of local produce, and check out the huge array of freshly caught fish brought in from miles around.

**a.** Mercado Municipal, Avenida dos Descobrimentos, 8600-668 Lagos

**Visit Silves (105)** any time of year, it's remarkably beautiful, but especially during the annual **Feira Medieval de Silves**, in August, when the castle and its surrounding cobbled streets are transported back into the middle ages, with street entertainers and food and drink stalls just like back in the days of old. Outside of the medieval fair, it's still a place well worth a detour inland.

## SHOP

There's a small health food store in Lagos, **Natur Boticae** (Rue Infante de Sagres 22), but for a bigger bio shopping experience, take a drive to Luz and get your bags full of goodness at **Harmony Earth (106)** (open Monday to Friday and Saturday morning) in Luz.

**a.** Rua Joaquim Teixeira 10, 8600-168 Luz
**t.** 2 82 788 353

## EAT/DRINK/HANGOUT

◆

**Nah Nah Bah** (**107**), a burger joint with a tropical twist and good vibes. Even vegetarians will like this place, besides a veggie burger they have various salads, hummus starter and veggie pastas. Closed in winter (open from March). •€• •€€•

**a.** Travessa do Forno 11, 8600-632 Lagos
**t.** 9 66 207 702 / 9 25 736 570
**w.** nahnahbah.com

**Serge & Satoshi Pâtisserie Francaise** (**108**) opens from Tuesday to Saturday, 08.30 to 16:00 hrs and you best schedule that into your trip planner because you don't want to miss out on the croissants, quiches, tarts, pies, scones and cakes, cakes, oh so many cakes...

**a.** Rua Helena do Nascimento Baptista, 8600-160 Praia da Luz
**t.** 9 63 891 542

Having made it to Luz for your fresh croissants and healthy food stocks, why not spend the day on the beach, then take a seat with a sunset view over the praia, at **Endless Summer beach bar & pizza** (**109**).
Note: this is no grab-a-pizza joint, it's a relaxed, slow food restaurant with good vibes and great food! Open every day in summer from 10 till 10. •€€•

**a.** Avenida dos Pescadores, Edifício Luz Loja 4, 8600-130 Luz
**t.** 2 82 098 201
**w.** endlesssummerpizzariabar.pt

## SLEEP

◆

**Tag Hostel** (**110**), situated in a 200 year old building overlooking the sea, is a recently opened, funky yet surprisingly tranquil place. A boutique hostel aimed at travellers and surfers, it's friendly, comfortable and calm, the perfect place to rest and recover from (or altogether avoid) any Lagos partying, which isn't far from the door. •€•

**a.** Rua da Porta de Portugal 63, 8600-657 Lagos
**t.** 9 18 780 198

Rent villa **Casa da Praia** (**111**), in Luz, if you want to be close enough to Lagos for some nightlife, with Luz restaurants, bars and beach (winter surf bonus) on your doorstep and the west coast not too far away to do a surf check drive-by round all the favourite spots. This 3 bedroom fisherman's house with pool has been beautifully converted into a romantic cottage with a secluded garden and shady terrace, and sleeps 6.

**w.** casadapraia-algarve.com
**e.** info@casadapraia-algarve.com

Photo: Mannus Joris

# SURF

**Beliche** (**VIII**) throws a hollow wedge with a good size swell and is a popular break with the locals, especially favoured by bodyboarders. Gets crowded quickly. Steep steps are a good pre and post surf workout, and another benefit of the big cliffs - shelter from north wind. Works with medium to big swell from n-w-s and everything in between. Can work with small to medium s-sw swell. It's a powerful wave so unless you're an experienced surfer, watch for a good while before going in - currents are strong and it can surprise you with a sneaky set. Best mid to high tide, depending on banks and tidal range, beach can disappear at high. Parking gets busy/café in summer at bottom of steps.

Another powerful wave with strong currents, **Tonel** (**IX**), has a sandy bottom but with rocky areas to watch out for. Works best with medium w-nw-n swell, small s-sw swell. Rarely surfable at low tide, best mid to high depending on sand levels. Experienced surfers: except for on the odd summer day, it's not really a beginner's wave. Even then we recommend taking advice from a reputable surf school. Parking gets busy but can park at Fortaleza and walk down/café in summer/surf rentals in summer.

Offering some shelter from n-nw-w wind, **Mareta**'s (**X**) a more gentle wave than those of its neighbouring breaks, until it gets above head high. Works beautifully with a decent south swell, very occasionally on a big w-nw swell. Sandy bottom with a couple of obvious low tide rocks. All levels. Parking difficult with traffic & parking controls/restaurants in summer.

Rocky-bottom **Ingrina** (**XI**) works with a medium to big n-nw-w swell or small to medium s-sw. A short wave that doesn't handle much size and hard to predict tides as sand shifts a lot from this spot with storms, changing shape and size regularly. Worth a drive-by if Zavial's too big or busy for you. Limited parking/restaurant in summer.

The classic wave when **Zavial** (**XII**) works at its best is very popular with the locals. Works with small to medium s-sw swell, medium n-nw-w. Slight shelter from west wind, but strong north can create quite a wind tunnel. Tide inconsistent with shifting sand, but usually low to mid with smaller size, mid to high with bigger swell. Beware of strong rips and fast wave. Beginners: take advice from surf school or life-guards (summer only). Difficult parking/restaurant in summer.

**Salema** (**XIII**) only works with a big nw-w swell or decent swell from s-sw, and not for long. Low tide can give a nice longboard wave but soon turns to shorebreak as the tide comes up. All levels. Limited parking/restaurants.

The sheltered cove of **Burgau** (**XIV**) offers good protection from n-nw-w wind and has a longer wave than most south coast spots. Works with big n-nw-w, or small to medium s-sw swell. Tides changeable depending on sand-banks and swell size, but a great spot to sit and warm up in the sun when the rest of the area's being windblasted! Gets crowded quickly when it's working. All levels. Parking can be difficult/restaurant.

The further east you go the less you notice the wind, and **Luz** (**XV**) can be a welcome respite from relentless northerly gusts. Plenty of space to spread out along the beach, gets busy on the reefbreak far off to the left. Works with big n-nw-w swell and with a good s-sw swell. Tides depend on sandbanks, usually low to mid is best, but can still work well at high. All levels. Great hike options up the cliffs all the way to the other side towards Lagos. Plenty of parking though busy in summer. Toilet/shower/restaurants.

Heading east from Lagos, **Meia Praia** (**XVI**) needs a big swell from the west coast or a good south swell. The wind's not so wild this side, so it can be a real haven during winter, or perfectly pond-like calm for a swim in the summer. Offshore with nw-w wind, all tides, all levels. Easy parking/restaurants.

Well-established (since 2003) family business, **Sagres Natura** (**112**), have a spacious surf camp with modern décor and a friendly home-from-home atmosphere. 5 minutes walk from the town centre, so an easy choice to go out, or chill out (in the jacuzzi? why ever not). Surf lessons are tailored to suit individual's level, using their thorough step-by-step method, which helps everyone progress in the way that suits them and makes sure they have fun at the same time! They also offer accommodation only, and separate surf lessons and rentals. You can find their well-equipped surf shop in town on Rua de São Vicente. Open March to October.

**a.** Rua Mestre António Galhardo, 8650-384 Sagres
**t.** 2 82 624 134
**w.** sagresnatura.com

**Wave Sensations** (**113**) surf school have knowledgeable local staff who take you wherever the surf's best for your level on the day – small group size and private lessons available. They also offer a Cave SUP Tour. Closed in January.

**a.** Casa Azul Sagres, Rua Dom Sebastião, 8650-341 Sagres
**t.** 2 82 624 856 / 911 580 520
**w.** wavesensations.com

Book your lessons and or rentals with **Freeride Surf School** (**114**) in advance, or drop into the wooden beach hut at Praia da Cordoama to find out more. Friendly local crew with knowledge of the area, individual lessons and packages to suit every surfer. Also optional 'surfcamp' 4* accommodation and yoga combinations, details on website.

**t.** 9 65 780 252 / 9 16 089 005
**w.** frsurf.com

# SCHOOL RENTAL REPAIR

**Chicks on Waves** (**115**) run surf and yoga weeks for small groups of ladies only. Shared twin rooms at the One Life Lodge in Salema, with outstanding views, beautiful healthy food and the perfect combination of relaxation and activity.

**t.** 9 67 580 530
**e.** info@chicksonwaves.com
**w.** chicksonwaves.com

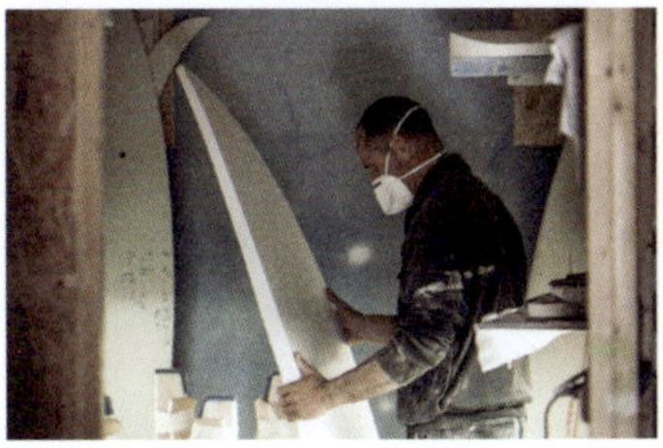

Uwe Kluba is the man behind **Kluba Surfboards** (**116**), which you'll see a lot of in this area, and further afield too. If you want a custom-made board or need a repair: call Uwe and he'll meet you at the parking of LIDL, his workshop's just behind. Using old-school traditional methods, he hand-shapes custom boards, putting effort into boards that work for normal people, rather than high performance models designed for professional surfers. Alongside traditional models, Uwe's experimental nature and desire to minimise environmental impact led to bamboo-laminated-epoxy boards – more durable and stronger; but he sought further improvement, which led to cork-sandwiches. Cork has a complicated shaping process, but is friendlier, stronger, and longer-lasting, with less glass - better for the environment, better for people working with the materials. And as Portugal's one of the largest cork producers in the world, Uwe uses locally sourced material that lasts. Uwe's advice on boards: "Surf everything. Experimenting with different shapes and sizes brings better understanding of what a surfboard can do, and how something might suit one person better than another. It's the same as life."

**t.** 9 15 434 240
**e.** klubasurfboard@hotmail.com
**w.** klubasurfboards.com

# SEASIDE LOCAL: NICOLAU DA COSTA

◆

**Surfer, fisherman, diver, perceves harvester - 'marisqueiro', sailor, traveller, speaker of 5+ languages, landscape architect, artist, writer, nature guide, forager, grower of food and incredible cook, environmental activist, natural bee-keeper and recently - shepherd: all these interests, occupations and pastimes combine to present a deeply thoughtful and knowledgeable man, with infinite respect for life in all its forms, who we like to think of as 'Nature's Guardian'.**

Nicolau grew up in the western Algarve, where his great grandfather once worked from Praia da Ingrina as a fisherman. He's lived in Turkey, England, France, Spain, the South Pacific... but it's here, in the wild landscape of the Costa Vicentina, that he's rooted. "This was my playground, and still is. I grew up and learned everything here; despite travelling, studying and working in other countries, I always knew that here were my origins and that this was my land."

His interest in and knowledge of the area encompass all: "Remembering our connection to the world, through plants, animals, and every living thing, brings with it more respect and compassion for each other and the world we live in. It helps us to value our relationship with our surroundings."

Nicolau is insatiably curious, observing, studying and learning from every experience and interaction he has with all that surrounds him. Dedicated to working alongside nature, and taking only what you need from land and sea, he's equally passionate about giving back what he can: and that's what brings us to the bees, the connection between everything.
Nicolau's strategically positioned hives provide the bees with the best chance of survival, with as little intervention as possible. "It's not about the honey," Nicolau says, "it's about allowing the bees to thrive naturally, allowing natural selection to do its work."

It's Nicolau's hope that as people begin to understand how disconnected they have become from nature, and how damaging the amount of control they exert over environmental factors has become, we may begin to reconnect and co-operate again, to work in harmony with the land and ocean, as nature intends.

*"Nature will put us back in our place, which is not one of mastery."*

◆

Learn much more and meet Nicolau in person by joining him for a walk: **w.** atalaia-walking.com
or find out more about his bee-keeping and his love for the great outdoors on: **w.** ilovetheseaside.com

◆

Photos: Vasco Celio

Photo: Melchior van Nigtevecht

# 9. POST SURF: ADHO MUKHA SVANASANA

*Downward Facing Dog Pose*

***This is a great post surf pose!***

*In Adho mukha svanasana, you get a bit of everything, working your legs and arms, creating extension for your spine, and you gain the benefit of being upside down. Moreover, it is extremely accessible and is also said to relieve fatigue, so may come in handy after a long surf session. This pose can be done right after your surf on the beach, still wearing your wetsuit and your nose dripping from the session.*

### *Benefits:*

*Lengthens the spine. Strengthens the muscles of the chest, increasing lung capacity. Stretches the shoulders, hamstrings, calves, arches, and hands. Facilitates muscle tone. Calms the mind and rejuvenates the body. Helps relieve back pain and fatigue.*

### *How:*

*Kneel on all fours. Separate your arms so that your palms are directly under and in line with your shoulders. Spread the palms and extend the fingers. Separate your legs to the same width as your arms, keeping the feet parallel. Lift your hips, stretch the thighs backwards and activate the kneecaps by pulling them up towards the thighs. Reach your heels towards the floor (but they don't need to touch the floor). Exhale, stretch the arms and the legs, and push the thighs back. Stay here for as long as comfortable, give your head a nice shake.*

### *Note:*

*If your back starts rounding while straightening the legs, you can start with bent legs instead, to really give length to the spine, then slowly begin to straighten.*

# THANK YOU!

This guide was made with love (and some sweat, tears, fears, and sleepless nights, but mostly love). And the help of many. We hope we've set things in motion; for travellers to get inspired, locals to share their stories, for entrepreneurs to run their businesses, and for us to create many more seaside guides. It's with your support, dear reader, supporter and partner, that we can all continue this seaside adventure. We hope to meet you in our next edition, on social media (#ilovetheseaside), or our website, but preferably in the ocean.

Let us know you're out there, sharing a story, photo or wave. It all starts from here!!

Big up, cheers and thank you to all supporters of our crowdfund campaign, friends and family for your faith. And of course Maaike, Kolja, Ravi, Bom, Sunny, Marinus, Melchior, Ananda, Jop, Shaini, Karo, Alrik, Frank, Mark, Jordi, Christiaan, Nout & Tim, Robin & Val, Sven & Elles, Camilla & Alessandro, Claudia & Brian. And Yves, Claudia and Norberto for your delicious recipes!

**SUNNY**

LEADER OF THE PACK, INSTIGATOR OF EXPLORING PATHS UNKNOWN

**I Love the Seaside**
Wassenaarsestraat 110
2586 AR Scheveningen – Holland

**t.** +31 6 53 178 129
**e.** info@ilovetheseaside.com
**w.** ilovetheseaside.com

**ISBN** 978 90 825 0790 4
**NUR** 512
**First edition** Summer 2016

Paper from responsible sources.
Printed in Holland by GrafiPlaza, **w.** grafiplaza.nl

**Concept & text:** zee-inkt.nl
**Art direction & graphic design:** re-act.nl
**Copyediting:** gailbennie.com
**Merchandise:** sourxing.com
**Photography:** northseajuice.eu, melchiorphotos.com
**Yoga:** yogaion.com (Photos by Edwin Grisinas)

**Cover photo:** Geert-Jan Middelkoop
**Inside photo:** Ananda van Welij



This guide has been compiled with the utmost care and attention to detail, however, details may change. Travellers should be aware that recommended providers and services may move, alter provisions or services, prices or opening times.

I Love the Seaside is not liable for any injury or inconvenience however caused, or any inaccuracies in the text.

To clarify, we would like to assure you that none of the recommendations listed in our guide have paid by any means for entry in this guide.

**Please note:** Maps are solely indicators of locations, they are not intended to be used as road maps. © OpenStreetMap.org

# ABOUT US

### ALEXANDRA GOSSINK

WRITER, EDITOR & CONCEPT

Between surf trips and travelling as a journalist, she teaches yoga and tries to maintain a healthy, happy lifestyle.

### GEERT-JAN MIDDELKOOP

PRODUCTION, SALES & DISTRIBUTION

Seaside explorer since childhood. Manages to do a lot of trade and business between sessions. When he's not on a surf trip in his campervan, he's planning one.

### DIM ROOKER

GRAPHIC DESIGNER & CONCEPT

Gets his inspiration from the ocean. Besides designing and working on concepts for brands, books and websites at his harbour office, he loves to take his family on van-adventures and his sons surfing.

### GAIL BENNIE

CO-WRITER, PROOFREADER & COPYEDITOR

Portugal-based surfer girl from Jersey, working on all sorts of writing projects. Easily distracted by the waves.

### MARINUS JORIS

PHOTOGRAPHER

Enjoys surf in and out of the water, camera in hand. Able to capture atmosphere and mood like no other.

### MELCHIOR VAN NIGTEVECHT

PHOTOGRAPHER

Waterperson. Loves to ride waves with anything from hand board to log. Shoots surf and lifestyle pictures for magazines and stock.

#ILOVETHESEASIDE
Share your I Love the Seaside stories!
facebook.com/ilovetheseaside
instagram.com/ilovetheseaside
ilovetheseaside.com